CLINICAL PSYCHOTHERAPY

A History of Theory and Practice

(from Sigmund Freud to Aaron Beck)

2nd Edition

By John H. Morgan

CLINICAL PSYCHOTHERAPY
A History of Theory and Practice

(from Sigmund Freud to Aaron Beck)

2nd Edition

By John H. Morgan, Ph.D., D.Sc., Psy.D.

978-155605-497-6 P
978-155605-498-2 E

Wyndham Hall Press
Levering, MI

Contents

INTRODUCTION

Believing that the use of primary sources is the best way of learning the thought system of a great thinker, I have decided to focus upon a single text of each of the psychotherapists considered in this book. Though the entire corpus of their work will be incorporated in this enquiry, our approach will be to critically consider a major text which established each one as a leading theorist in the field of psychotherapy. We will provide a biographical summary of each theorist followed by a textual analysis of a classic work in their *repertoire*. We will also include a comprehensive bibliography of each theorist relevant to each system of psychotherapy considered here. This work can be criticized for not incorporating all of each theorist's writings but for two reason, that will not be done. First, their literary output makes that impracticable, and, second, a carefully considered treatment of one classic text seems preferable to a cursory glance at their entire literary corpus. Finally, we will consider the fundamentals of their thought in relationship to the practice of psychotherapy. Following the biographical sketch there will be an in-depth consideration of a primary text in the published *repertoire* of the psychotherapists being considered here. This author is convinced that nothing can substitute for acquaintance with the primary source of a thinker no matter how good the secondary source is for the reading of the original thinker must always trump the reading of one who has thought about the original thinker! Then and finally, we will explicate a few key concepts and theories for closer examination.

This three-step process, i.e., biography, major text, key concepts and theories, I believe provides an easy to manage approach to both an introduction and a summary overview of each system of thought. By approaching the materials in this fashion, the uninitiated will have a quick and systematic exposure to the theorists and their theories and the already initiated veteran will enjoy an easy to use guide to that which they are already familiar. Thus, both the uninitiated and the veteran might benefit from our efforts here to present in a systematic fashion the life and work of these major psychotherapists in the 20th century.

Naturally and understandably, everyone will not be happy with the selection I have made here of the "classical" tradition. No one, I think, will fault the ones I have chosen but many will fault me for not having added more. And, indeed, I could have added more. I could have added more and still some would not have been completely happy with the roster of those treated in this little text. Yet, the ones chosen cannot be faulted for they have all earned their place in the history of behavioral science. The ones chosen are indisputably worthy of treatment and over the years I have taught a doctoral-level summer seminar at Oxford University dealing precisely with those considered here.

Let me simply say that I have chosen psychologists whose work has been particularly relevant to professional counselors as classical representatives of contemporary psychotherapy. From the birth of Freud in 1856 to the present has seen the rise and development of major theorists and major systems of psychotherapy which are to be discussed here. If we can learn anything from this summary text, then my work will have been justified. If we only have our memories jogged to recall the theories of these thinkers, I feel my time would not have been wasted. The worst that can happen, then, is that the reader will simply say, "I knew that already," to which I might reply, "Good, I thought you might." Not wishing to add anything "new" but simply to remind professionals of what we already know about the various schools of psychotherapy will do and my publisher seems to be happy with the agenda as well. As my grandmother used to say to me, "It doesn't hurt to be reminded of what you already know!" And, with that mandate, I have undertaken to remind my professional colleagues of what they already know.

Of course, before we can consider the concept of "psychotherapy" and its great theorists, we need at least to acknowledge the breadth and depth of "personality theory" as a major enterprise within the discipline of psychology. Not every theorist in the field of psychology is pleased to begin, or even end, their work with this concept but those theorists being considered in this enquiry have most certainly commenced their work here. Early in the last century, G. W. Allport of Harvard had already generated over fifty operational definitions of personality and in the subsequent generations, a plethora more have been generated. We need not review them all here! Rather, we will focus upon several "categories" of personality theories which more or less have relevance to our own specific agenda here. We will briefly summarize "Trait theories," "Psychodynamic and psychoanalytic theories," "behaviorism," "Social learning theories," "Situationism," and "Interactionism," and will draw particularly form Arthur S. Reber's thorough treatment in his now classic *Dictionary of Psychology* published by Penguin.

All theories of the "trait" variety operate from the assumption that one's personality is a compendium of "traits" or "characteristic ways of behaving, thinking, feeling, and reacting." The early trait theories were actually little more than lists of adjectives and personality was defined simply by enumeration. More recent approaches have used techniques of factor analysis in an attempt to isolate underlying dimensions of personality. Probably the most influence theory here is that of R. B. Cattell, which is based on a set of "source traits" that are assumed to exist in relative amounts in each individual and are the "real structural influences underlying personality." According to Cattell, the goal of personality theory is to have the individual trait matrix formulated so that behavioral predictions can be made. It should be noted that the "type" and "trait" approaches complement each other and, indeed, one could argue that they are two sides of the same coin. Type theories are primarily concerned with that which is common among individuals whereas trait theories focus on that which differentiates them. However, they certainly entail very different connotations of the base term "personality."

A multitude of approaches is clustered here as psychodynamic and psychoanalytic theories including the classic theories of Freud and Jung, the social psychological theories of Adler, Fromm, Sullivan and Horney, and the more recent approaches of Laing and Perls, to mention only a few key theorists. The distinctions between them are legion but all contain an important common core idea: namely, personality for all is characterized by the notion of "integration." Strong emphasis is generally placed upon developmental factors, with the implicit assumption that the adult personality evolves gradually over time, depending on the manner in which the integration of factors develops. Moreover, motivational concepts are of considerable importance, so that no account of personality is considered to be theoretically useful without an evaluation of the underlying motivational syndromes.

The focus in behaviorism has been on the extension of learning theory to the study of personality. Although there are no coherent, purely behaviorist theories of personality, the orientation has stimulated other theorists to look closely at an integral problem: how much of the behavioral consistency that most people display is due to underlying personality "types" or "traits" or "dynamics" and how much is due to consistencies in the environment and in the contingencies of reinforcement? Not surprisingly, the points of view below, all of which were influenced to some degree by behaviorism, look beyond the person for answers here and, to some degree or another, actually question the usefulness of the term "personality" altogether.

Much of the theorizing from the point of view of social learning theories derives from the problem just outlined. However, the notion of personality is treated here as those aspects of behavior that are acquired in a social context. The leading theorist here is Albert Bandura, whose position is based on the assumption that although learning is critical, factors other than simple stimulus-response associations and reinforcement contingencies are needed to explain the development of complex social behaviors (such as "roles") that essentially make up one's personality. In particular, cognitive factors such as memory, retention processes and self-regulatory processes are important and much research has focused on modeling and observational learning as mechanisms that can give a theoretically satisfying description of the regularities of behavior in social contexts.

The perspective of "situationism," championed by Walter Mischel, is derivative of the preceding two positions. It argues that whatever consistency of behavior is observable is largely determined by the characteristics of the "situation" rather than by any internal personality types or traits. Indeed, the very notion of a personality trait, from this point of view, is nothing more than a mental construction of an observer who is trying to make some sense of the behavior of others and exists only in the mind of the beholder. The regularity of behavior is attributed to similarities in the situations one tends to find oneself in rather than to internal regularities.

The position of "interactionism" is a kind of eclectic one. It admits of certain truths in all of the above, more single-minded theories, and maintains that personality emerges from interactions between particular qualities and predispositions and the manner in which the environment influences the ways in which these qualities and behavioral tendencies are displayed. It is far from clear that personality can be said to exist as a distinct "thing" from this perspective. Rather, it becomes a kind of cover term for the complex patterns of interaction.

It is interesting to note that the above theoretical approaches can be seen as representing two distinguishable generalizations concerning the very term "personality." For the categories of traits theory and psychodynamic and psychoanalytic theories, it represents a legitimate theoretical construct, a hypothetical, internal "entity" with a causal role in behavior and, from a theoretical point of view, with genuine explanatory power. For behaviorism, social learning theories, situationism, and interactionism, personality is seen as a secondary factor inferred on the basis of consistency of behavior -- while other operations and processes play the critical causal roles in dictating behavior -- and, hence, as a notion that has relatively little explanatory power.

What is Psychotherapy? The answer to this question is easy and it is not; it is simple and it is certainly complex. Before we can fairly commence a summary of the classical schools of psychotherapy, it might be fair to offer a working definition of this field of health care practice and to suggest the perimeters of its value and function. Beyond that, we will attempt here to offer a brief definition of the practice of psychotherapy which professional counselors can easily identify with for professional practice.

Thanks to the generosity of Arthur S. Reber and the publishers of the *Dictionary of Psychology*, by Penguin Books, we have ready access to "the" authoritative definition. Of course, we will not be hamstrung by this definition, we will simply commence here. Reber says, "In the most inclusive sense, the use of absolutely any technique or procedure that has palliative or curative effects upon any mental, emotional or behavioral disorder can be called psychotherapy." In this general sense the term is neutral with regard to the theory that may underlie it, the actual procedures and techniques entailed or the form and duration of the treatment. There may, however, be legal and professional issues involved in the actual practice of what is called psychotherapy, and in the technical literature the term is properly used only when it is carried out by someone with recognized training and using accepted techniques. The term "therapy" is often used in shortened form particularly when modifiers are appended to identify the form of therapy or the theoretical orientation of the therapist using it.

Psychotherapy is, as a professional practice, an interpersonal and relational "intervention" used by trained professionals in the treatment of clients who are experiencing difficulty in daily life. The focus is usually upon issues related to "well-being" and the attempt to reduce personal senses of dissatisfaction with one's life. Practitioners of psychotherapy use a wide variety of techniques devised by theorists in the field dealing with problematic issues of life's daily functions. Such simple things as improving dialogue skills, communication development, and behavioral modification are employed in such treatment. The goal is the improvement and enhancement of mental health on the part of the client/patient.

Though contemporary practices in psychotherapeutic counseling have reached far beyond its early modality of treatment which, by and large, was limited to a "conversational" style of patient/client/counselor relationship, to include today such modes of interaction as writing, artistic expression, drama, therapeutic touch and even aroma therapy. We will limit ourselves to the classic mode of encounter which is, of course, conversation. This structured and highly orchestrated therapeutic encounter between therapist and client/patient dates from the earliest beginnings of psychotherapy in the late 19th century. Whereas once psychotherapy was thought to be limited to behavioral crises and counseling to the more mundane behavioral adjustments needed for a well-directed life, that line of distinction has all but vanished these days with "psychotherapy" being used as both the term for and practice of intensive counseling encounters. Yet, whereas counseling has not frequently been thought of in terms of the medical model, interventionist psychotherapy is most commonly so characterized. Again, however, given the rise of clinical pastoral education which is most commonly practiced and taught in a medical setting, even that line of distinction has vanished more or less.

These variances in terminology and usage have created something of a problematic for pastors who both wish to be trained in and to offer psychotherapeutic counseling to their pastoral constituencies and yet wish to avoid any appearance of treading on the medical profession's rightful domain. The use of such terms as counselor, therapist, client, patient, clinical, etc. has often created ambiguities in the minds of both the practitioner and the recipient. There are no set rules though some have tried to establish them. There are, however, state laws affecting the use of such terms as counselor and psychologist which aspiring professionals would be wise to explore before launching out into this cauldron of psycho-medical and psycho-clinical practice. Let us agree here early on that we will use "psychotherapy" and its variants to apply to pastoral counseling and we will use the term "client" rather than "patient" to refer to the recipient of such psychotherapy. For pastoral counselors preferring to use the term "counselor" to describe what they do, we will honor that and, also, for psychotherapist who prefer to consider the recipients of their professional skills "patients" rather than clients, we will honor that position as well. For our purposes, however, we will say psychotherapist when referring to professional counselors and clients when referring to their patients.

Needless to say, since the time of Sigmund Freud, without doubt the father of modern psychoanalysis, there have emerged several rather distinctly identifiable systems or schools of psychotherapy. We will not consider any of these in detail except as relates to the "classical" traditions to be considered here later. As we know, Freud was a trained medical neurologist and was early on interested in the seemingly non-biogenic behavioral disorders and this interest led him to develop and utilize such analytical techniques as dream interpretation, free association, the concept of transference, and the tripartite id/ego/superego construct of the human psyche. Regardless of one's own ideological bias or professional training today, few would dispute the fact that Freud is the Father of the Movement known as psychoanalysis and its contingent, psychotherapy. Under the broader concept of "psychodynamics," many schools of thought were spawned by Freud's pioneering work with some staying close to his theoretical moorings as neo-Freudians while others moved far afield as post-Freudians. However, all schools of psychodynamics engaged in psychotherapeutic application addressed themselves necessarily and inevitably to the whole concept of the psyche.

Of course, not all psychologists and those engaged in the behavioral sciences chose to use Freud as a launching pad. The behaviorism of B. F. Skinner and others evolved a "behavioral therapy" which has become quite popular in certain circles which uses such concepts as operant conditioning, classical conditioning, and social learning theory. And, eventually, such ideological positions as existential philosophy came into play in the development of certain schools of psychotherapeutic treatment such as Viktor Frankl's logotherapy. Extending existentialism was the work of Carl Rogers and Abraham Maslow whom we will consider in detail later. Their work, of course, lead to the rather popular "person-centered" school of psychotherapy and from that came Fritz Perls' gestalt therapy and Eric Berne's Transactional Analysis, all falling into a rather lumpy collection of what is passionately labeled humanistic psychotherapy today. Other and diminishingly important schools of thought were spawned by this rash of post-Freudian and even post-Satrean existentialist thought into such things as cognitive therapy following Aaron Beck, and postmodernist trends know as narrative therapy, coherence therapy, transpersonal psychology, feminist therapy (as a separate school of its own!), somatic psychology, expressive therapy and, for want of a better descriptive term, brief therapy.

Most of these, of course, we will discard for our discussion of what I am insisting upon calling the "classical schools of psychotherapy," which, as we have already stated, will consist only of four members of the Viennese schools of psychoanalytic psychotherapy (including the Jungian variant) and the American schools of psychotherapy. The two schools, then are limited to, in the first instance, Freud, Adler, Jung, and Frankl and in the second instance, Maslow, Erikson, Rogers, and Sullivan.

For ease of cross referencing, I will refer to the first as the Viennese Schools and the later as the American Schools. I have already defended my right to include Carl Gustav Jung in the Viennese Schools even though he formally launched his analytical psychology school in Zurich after having left Freud and Adler in Vienna. Yet, without Freud and Vienna, there would arguably be no Jung. Whether I am right or wrong, I will stay with this operational perspective if, for no other reason, ease of reference.

Vienna is unquestionably the original city of psychotherapeutic psychology. The city produced Freud, Adler, and Frankl, founders of the three great school of Viennese psychotherapy. Jung, who fell under the sway of Freud and worked closely with Adler, hailed, however, from Zurich, but we consider him in this group owing to the influence upon his developing thought of those early Viennese years. Nevertheless, Vienna is the First City of depth psychology and it all began with Freud. Of course, before Freud there was psychology and before either there was Vienna. Vienna was, for centuries and without dispute, the center of European life and culture as the convergence point of East meeting West. Being located on the Danube river and just under the Austrian Alps, it was quite naturally a key trading center. For over five hundred years, the Hapsburgs had ruled there and under the care and nurture of the incomparable Maria Theresa and Joseph II in the late 1700s it gained an international reputation as the center of western music, producing such composers as Haydn, Mozart, Beethoven, and Schubert.

Jews and other religious and ethnic communities, however, found little to revel in under the Austro-Hungarian Empire, certainly until the revolution of 1848 when everything changed. Emperor Franz Joseph, for example in 1849, introduced a constitutional law mandating that "civil and political rights are not dependent on religion." Now, the Jews and other oppressed groups could breathe, for the moment, a breath of fresh air of freedom, including the opening of wider options in career choices and the ownership of real estate. By 1867 when a new constitution was adopted for the Austro-Hungarian people, Jews were even being elected to the Vienna City Council even while the Empire was constitutionally Christian. Because of this liberalism, the Jewish population of Vienna grew from 6,000 in 1860 to

150,000 in 1900 creating the largest Jewish population in Western Europe. Though racial and religious prejudices still thrived, to be sure, Vienna was a relative safe haven for aspiring Jews and it is at this point that we pick up our story of the development of psychoanalysis and the psychotherapeutic schools developed by the Jewish medical community under the separate but collaborative endeavors of Freud, Adler, and Frankl.

In the first eight chapters of this history, I considered in depth what are universally considered the classical theorists in psychotherapy. There I made a careful analysis of the life and work of Freud, Adler, Jung, Frankl, Erikson, Maslow, Rogers, and Sullivan. These theorists are considered the classical thinkers and practitioners in psychotherapy based on a national survey of the leading professors in the field at the top institutions in the U.S. These eight individuals' systems of psychotherapy were considered consistently as the classical schools.

However and nevertheless, there were critics who suggested and even insisted that other names should have been included. I held to the integrity of the individual scholars surveyed by staying with these eight theorists. I did so with reservations and with not a little regret. In the second eight chapters, I have attempted to address those concerns and correct any sins of omission by including eight of those who are without question considered to be the leading theorists today.

No individual knowledgeable in the field will argue with the dominance of those treated in the classical schools. Yet, these same professionals will agree with this author that those treated in the current book are equally justified in being considered as part of the "modern schools of psychotherapy." Though others arguably could be included, and maybe should have been, no professional in the field will dispute the legitimacy of these individuals as masters in contemporary psychotherapy. From the modified traditionalist perspective of Horney to the cognitive behavioral therapy of Aaron Beck, the following study will show both the developmental nature of psychotherapeutic theory and practice as well as the exponential growth of the profession of psychotherapy itself.

It has always been thought within the academy that to understand the *Sitz im Leben* of a theorist as well as the

Weltanschauung, i.e., its worldview and ethos, is crucial in order to contextualize the development of any thought system. No one will ever question the relevance of the life situation and the worldview of someone in the humanities -- an author, a poet, an artist -- but sometimes it is necessary to make a case for the relevant contextualizing of a theorist's life in the broad fields of science. Who would argue persuasively that such things are really important in the development of theories in nuclear physics or molecular biology. Was James Watson's personal domestic life with his wife and children really relevant to his work in DNA research? Was Einstein's difficulties in learning to read as a small boy really important in the discovery of relativity? However, when one thinks of the poetry of Frost, one cannot deny the crucial relevance of his relationship to the countryside of Vermont! Winston Churchill's history of the English people was most decidedly informed by his childhood and immersion within the British aristocracy. And so, when it comes to the psychological sciences, it is impossible to overlook the relevance of the life story in the theoretical development of psychoanalysis, logotherapy, humanistic psychology, etc. Could Erikson have written *Childhood and Society* without having had to struggle early with his own personal identity? Could Rogers have developed non-directive counseling and the concept of the "unconditional positive regard" had he not struggled himself with religious ethics? Can one imagine the emergence of logotherapy without Frankl having endured the concentration camps of Nazi Germany?

These things, of course, were explored in depth in our consideration of the classical schools and were predicated upon the premise that theories are connected to their creator and that to understand the former, one must understand the latter. But beyond the classical schools of psychotherapy, the western world has been inundated with a plethora of new schools of thought and practice. Psychotherapy as a perspective, a way of seeing, and a way of responding to mental illness has precipitated a wide range of theoretical interpretations and analytical modalities in the study and treatment of human relationships. However, it must be pointed out that psychotherapy has also be creatively responsible for providing interpretive grids for mental health and psychological healing as well.

Having written extensively of the classical schools, the time has come for me to speak of the modern schools of psychotherapy. In the study of the classical schools, I approached leading figures and leading institutions for assistance in determining who might be classified as representing the classical schools of psychotherapy. When a consensus was reached, I wrote the book addressing those eight individuals titled *Beginning With Freud: The Classical Schools of Psychotherapy* (2010). However, in the present study I have, either boldly or foolishly – only the reader must decide – chosen the representatives of the modern schools of psychotherapy without recourse to a consensus vote but merely and strictly my own assessment of what schools of thought should be considered. Of course, I can be and will be criticized for going it alone in this process but my nearly fifty years in the field must stand for something, and in this case I believe it stands for the right for me myself to decide who gets in and who is left out.

What I am considering the modern period begins with Karen Horney and the chapter on her life and work will vindicate the choice for beginning with her pioneering work. Practically, I chose to commence the modern schools following the death of Harry Stack Sullivan in 1949, that school of thought considered the last of the eight classical schools. His contribution to the post-Freudian world of psychoanalysis was demonstrated and lauded. Horney in many ways represents the turning of the page on the classical schools by introducing her own creative and dynamic corrective and advancement of psychotherapeutic theory and practice. Where to end this study and who to include (and exclude) represented a pragmatic but none-the-less demanding exercise of judgment on my part. I end the study with the outstandingly provocative and profoundly insightful work of Aaron Beck in the field of cognitive behavioral therapy. Will there be newer schools of psychotherapy coming upon the horizon? Indeed there will be and welcomed they will be as well. But for now, just at this juncture in the history of the care and treatment of mental illness and the exploration into the depths of what is meant by mental health, the schools considered here will serve our purpose very well.

CHAPTER ONE
Sigmund Freud and Psychoanalysis

BIOGRAPHICAL SKETCH

"Psychoanalysis is the sickness of which it claims to be the cure" say the critical pundits of Freudian psychoanalysis. Though he began in a cloud of professional suspicion, every professional today practicing in the cognate fields of counseling are beholden to Freud and his system of theory and analysis whether they will admit it or not. But to admit being beholden does not mean that one is bound to it. Gratitude has its place, however, and we will see in the following discussion the range of Freud's work as exemplified in his life, theoretical development, and analytical methodology. Whether one comes away from this discussion convinced or confused, for or against, it is our intention to make sure that upon leaving Freud and his system of psychoanalysis that the reader has a clearer idea of what there is to believe or disbelieve about it in its own terms. One can only be critical of that which one fully and clearly understands. We aim here, then, for clarity of vision and then, and only then, will we have a right to say "yeah" or "neigh" to Freud and his followers.

To be fair to the development of any theory, and some might suggest this is particularly true of psychological theory, there is the need to understand the theorist. By this we mean, know from whence he came, who he was, what he did, and, as best we can, grasp his own self-understanding of his life and work. So let's take a look or, if the case may be, another look at the life of Sigmund (Sigismund) Freud, a 19th century physician from Vienna. We will review his life, his theories, and then take a close look at his classic, *Civilization and Its Discontents*.

Freud's parents were practicing Jews and though he denied the existence of God, holding that such a belief was essentially a neurotic dependence as a substitute for emotional maturity, he did very much prize his Jewish tradition and culture. His father, Jakob Freud, was from a region in southeastern Europe called Galacia consisting of a large minority of Jews. He was a wool merchant and following the Emancipation of the Jews in the Austrian Empire and his marriage and the birth of their first son, Sigmund, the Freuds moved first to Leipzig and then to Vienna where Sigmund Freud would live the next eighty years. Jakob had done what many ambitious Jews were doing, namely, he embraced a reasonable compromise between his Jewish culture and the business and secular culture around him. Though it has been suggested that he was secretly a closet Hassid, i.e., Jews who embrace a kind of mystical tradition based on the sacred book called the *Kabbala*, he was able to effect an integration into Austrian secular culture without relinquishing his Jewish faith.

His mother, Amalia Nathanson, was from a well-to-do Jewish family of Galacia. She was Jakob's second wife for he already had two sons, approximately her own age, at the time of their marriage. Over the next ten years of marriage, Amalia gave birth to eight children, the first being Sigmund on May 6, 1856. She was acclaimed to have been very attractive, authoritarian, and a great admirer of her first born son, Sigmund. Though born in Freiburg, Moravia (now Pribor in the Czeck Republic), Freud at the age of four moved with his family to Vienna where he would live the rest of his 80 years except for the final 15 months of his life when he lived in London.

Without doubt, Freud was precocious, a mama's boy, and an excellent student in the schools of Vienna. It is said that his retentive visual memory and exceptional writing skills elevated him to the highest levels in school and, even though he was uncertain as to his career goals, he was early on predisposed to biology and was greatly influenced during his formative years by the evolutionary theory of Charles Darwin whose monumental work was published in 1859. In Vienna, Freud attended the Leopoldstadter Kommunal-Realgymnasium, a prominent high school, and Freud proved most outstanding, graduating the "Matura" in 1873 with honors. Eventually, Freud first considered studying law, which was now permitted to Jews, but finally entered medical school at the University of Vienna in 1873 which was under the direction of the famous Darwinist Professor Karl Claus. In no particular hurry, he completed his medical degree in eight years which allowed him an additional three years beyond the five year minimum for medical degrees to expand his interests in philosophy and literature. From research in zoology and comparative anatomy during his medical school years, Freud shifted his interests and activities to microanatomy, becoming the lab assistant to the distinguished Viennese Professor Ernst Brucke who, though a positivist, influenced Freud considerably in the areas of physics and chemistry. A German physiologist, Professor Ernst Wilhelm von Brucke, in collaboration with Professor Hermann von Helmholtz, were proponents of the use of the concept of "psychodynamics" in the study of living organisms. In 1874, this concept was radical and revolutionary and Brucke and Holmholtz explicated the theory in the publication of their studies entitled, *Lectures on Physiology*. Any living organism, of special interest being the human person, is a dynamic system to which the laws of chemistry and physics apply. This, it should be pointed out, is believed to be the beginning of Freud's dynamic psychology of the mind and his concept of the unconscious.

During these crucial formative years, Freud was greatly influenced by a postdoctoral fellow, Dr. Joseph Breuer, who worked in Brucke's laboratory and shared with Freud details of various cases of hysteria including the now famous case of Anna O. Following a mandatory year in the military in 1879, Freud returned to work in Brucke's lab after finishing his medical exams during which time he translated a book by John Stuart Mill dealing with empiricism. Though very much disinclined to practice medicine, Freud had fallen in love with Martha Bernays, an attractive and strong-willed Jewish girl from a very distinguished Viennese family including Martha's grandfather, Isaac Bernays, chief rabbi in Hamburg. The road to financial solvency was through the practice of medicine and that was a requirement to gain permission to marry. So, Freud resigned himself to practice medicine and the specialization he chose was clinical neurology and due to his having distinguished himself as a teaching assistant at the medical school, he was taken on staff at the highly prestigious Viennese General Hospital. Having tried hypnosis in his private practice, he was dissatisfied with the results and turned to what he eventually came to call simply the "talking cure" in the treatment of mental disorders.

During the following few years at the VGH, he engaged in various research projects including work on the use and effects of cocaine as a stimulant, an aphrodisiac, and a cure for morphine addiction which was quite common at the time due to medical practices in military hospitals. Unfortunately, he came under increasing scrutiny and criticism due to his work in the area of addiction and a major paper he wrote on the use of cocaine in opthamological surgery fell on deaf ears at the local medical association meetings. He subsequently passed in his examination to become a *privatdozent* (private lecturer) at the University of Vienna in the field of neuropathology and following his official appointment was given a traveling grant to study with the famous psychologist and neurologist of Paris, Jean Martin Charcot. Freud always attributed this experience to his turning from traditional neurophysiology and towards the practice of medical psychotherapy.

Two major experiences served Freud's long term interest in treating mental disorders. First, Charcot demonstrated how non-hysterical patients could be trained under hypnosis to exhibit hysterical symptoms such as paralysis and tremors, and second, Charcot demonstrated how physical symptoms of hysteria were derived from mental activity, thus, hysteria seemed clearly to be a "mental" disorder rather than merely a biogenic malfunction. Ironically, it was Charcot who first suggested to Freud the importance of sex by indicating that frequently sexual problems were related to mental disorder, particularly hysteria. Alas, whereas Freud went to Paris to become a neurologist, he returned as a fledgling psychiatrist!

Co-authoring with his old lab colleague, Dr. Josef Breuer, Freud drew more attention to himself with the publication of their 1895 highly acclaimed *Studies in Hysteria* which, according to historians of psychology, marks the actual beginning of psychoanalysis as a school of thought. Freud's chapter on psychotherapy established him as a major voice in this new field. Though deeply committed to his relationship with Breuer, Freud began a long and tedious journey away from his old colleague owing to Freud's heavy emphasis upon the essential role assigned to sex in the etiology of all neuroses. Breuer's tentative hesitation gave rise to a deepening gulf between them and finally resulted in a permanent break. This friendship was replaced by William Fliess, an ear, nose, and throat surgeon from Berlin who for the next several years proved to be Freud's closest confidant in the gradual development of the theories of psychoanalysis.

As is common knowledge, the fundamental bases of Freud's development of psychoanalytic theory grew out of his own self-analysis. Confidence in himself ebbed and flowed but overall Freud continued to believe in himself and his ability to development therapeutic modalities which would facilitate his capacity to plumb the depths of his own psyche, particularly his unconscious through, initially, the interpretation of dreams. On the strength of his insights into mental functions gained from his practice as a psychiatrist, he gradually and unequivocally developed a psychosexual theory of personality development that would dominate psychoanalytic theory for the next hundred years. His confidence is reflected in a statement made in correspondence to his friend and colleague, William Fliess, when he wrote: "I cannot give you an idea of the intellectual beauty of the work."

Freud became convinced over a period of years through intense self-analysis that dreams are essentially disguised forms of infantile wishes and thought processes and the meanings of them can be discovered by means of the analytical modalities developed in psychoanalysis, particularly dream analysis. In 1900, he published what has been recognized by most practitioners as his most distinguished book, *The Interpretation of Dreams*. The publication of this book marked the end of his emotionally wrenching self-analysis and the beginning of his drive to establish psychoanalysis as the dominant school of psychotherapy. He was now free to move beyond his old confidants of bygone days, namely, Charcot, Breuer, Brucke, and Fliess. He would no longer look to them for counsel nor seek from them advice in his future work. Psychoanalysis was his creation and it was his place to establish it throughout the western world as the undisputed leading school of psychotherapy.

Needless to say, Freud was neither revered nor loved by many of his professional colleagues. Freud was a Jew, a self-promoting Johnny come lately who proposed to plumb the depths of the human psyche using unorthodox methods and non-clinically tested techniques boarding on the scandalous. That a self-respecting physician and psychiatrist would propose to foist off on the unsuspecting public hocus-pocus spells designed to interpret mentally disturbed patients' dreams was more than many could take and they let it be known throughout Vienna that Freud was to be watched. The criticisms were in print and on the tongues of many respected physicians and psychiatrists of the day and, therefore, Freud had his work cut out for himself and his new school of psychotherapy which he labelled "psychoanalysis." His two books to-date didn't help much as they were hardly read until years after he had become a household name and respected internationally.

Yet, among the medical establishment there were brave and inquisitive physicians eager to learn more and to be engaged in this new adventure. Five key practitioners proved early on most helpful and though all but one eventually abandoned ship, while they were involved they proved most reassuring to Freud and his fledgling organization called the International Congress of Psychoanalysis held in Vienna for the first time in 1908. The next year saw the launching of the journal which proved pivotal in the stabilizing of the movement. The five key figures were Karl Abraham of Germany, Carl Jung of Switzerland, Ernest Jones of Great Britain, and Alfred Adler and Otto Rank of Austria.

Psychoanalysis was destined to become the American craze for the new and different. To facilitate that though unwittingly, the president of Clark University in Massachusetts, an ambitious new institution seeking to make a name for itself, invited Freud, among others, to come to America to participate in the celebration of the University's twentieth anniversary. G. Stanley Hall, the President of the University, was America's leading psychologist at the time, a position shared with William James of Harvard, and Hall had been known to say of Freud and psychoanalysis that it was "a series of fads or crazes." Yet, invite Freud he did and come Freud did, giving five outstanding, though essentially unpolished, lectures on psychoanalysis. Later, these essays were prepared for publication back in Vienna and went a long way in advancing the case for psychoanalysis in Europe and most especially in America.

However, as the professional organization of psychoanalysis began to grow by leaps and bounds, bringing on more and more young psychiatrists in Europe and especially in America, the seasoned veterans of the early formative years began to resist and counter theoretical developments within psychoanalysis which were approved by Freud but not by the old guard. Alfred Adler broke with the orthodox school over issues related to the dominance of sex-based theorizing, preferring to focus upon the human drive to mastery or "the will to power" whereas Carl Jung, who was designated the heir-apparent by Freud himself, moved with precision and strategy to establish his own school of thought, called "analytical psychology." These were major blows to the professional organization and only with sustained focus upon the orthodox theories did Freud and his followers weather the storm of dissent without permanent damage. These other schools of thought will be discussed later.

In the midst of it all, Freud never stopped treating patients. though a physician who early and publicly proclaimed a distaste for the profession, Freud, nevertheless, practiced nearly sixty years as a physician. During that time he concentrated upon fine tuning his theories, exploring new territory, and developing new insights in mental illness. He published extensively and prolifically, both in book form and periodicals. Three major works beyond those first two already mentioned were *The Psychopathology of Everyday Life* (1901), *Introductory Lectures on Psycho-Analysis* (1916-1917), and *New Introductory Lectures on Psycho-Analysis* (1933). One never to be accused of not continuing to press forward with investigations, analyses, and theoretical explorations, Freud moved beyond just an interest in the individual patient to broader social issues of the day. Both social psychology and social philosophy became a sustained interest of his during his waning years of productivity and his now highly acclaimed classic, *Civilization and Its Discontents,* represents him at his best. It is an application of psychoanalytic theory to the broad social issues of human behavior in society. This study of Freud's, written in his closing years of life, offers a pessimistic view of the human condition. The best life has to offer is merely a compromise between the inevitable and the irreconcilable demands that dominate our existence. The year he published this now famous work, 1930, was the year the German government awarded him the Goethe Prize in appreciation for his contribution to psychology and to German literary culture. It is this book we have chosen to study more systematically later in this chapter.

The very personal and tragic side to Freud's life has to do with both the necessity of his leaving his home in Vienna and the physical struggles with his health. When Freud turned sixty-six years old, he was diagnosed with mouth cancer brought on, it was believed, by his addiction to cigars. Over the next nearly twenty years he underwent thirty operations including the removal of the entire roof of his mouth which was replaced by a metal prosthesis which he called "the monster." Yet, he continued to write and see patients through it all. In 1938, Vienna saw the annexation of Austria to the German Reich by Adolph Hitler, bringing with it the oppression of the Jews without discrimination or regard for professional status in the community. With much insistence from his professional colleagues and friends who knew that both Einstein's physics and Freud's psychoanalysis were anathema to the Nazis, Freud with his wife and youngest daughter Anna fled to London where he died fifteen months later. Freud prevailed upon his personal physician and friend, Dr. Max Schur, to assist him in taking his own life. At this time, Freud wrote to Schur: "My dear Schur, you certainly remember our first talk. You promised me then not to forsake me when my time comes. Now it is nothing but torture and makes no sense any more." Schur administered three doses of morphine over many hours that resulted in Freud's death on September 23, 1939. The pain of the final stages of Freud's cancer led him to this decision. Freud's body was cremated in England with a service attended by many Austrian refugees and his ashes were placed in the columbarium there at Golders Green Crematorium where his wife, Martha, was likewise buried in 1951 and later his daughter Anna as well. His four younger sisters, in their old age, were murdered in the SS concentration camps of Germany. To those who rejected his theories, Freud is said to have responded to G. Stanley Hall: "They may abuse my doctrines by day, but I am sure they dream of them by night."

THE CLASSIC TEXT CONSIDERED

The primary text to be considered here was published by Freud in 1930 in Vienna under the title, *Das Unbehagen in der*

Kulture, and simultaneously in London in translation, *Civilization and Its Discontents.* All references here will be taken from the College Edition translated from the German and edited by James Strachey and published by W. W. Norton and Company of New York in 1962.

This little classic of Freud's will be reviewed for its address to and perspective upon the meaning of human life (a theme we will hold up throughout this study), especially as conceived in the context of human development which inevitably counter-poses the principle of pleasure with the principle of reality. Here, we will find Freud saying, "...the purpose of life is simply the programme of the pleasure principle," and since the human person is unable (for personal reasons) or not permitted (for social reasons) to gratify his desire for pleasure, he must learn that "satisfaction is obtained from illusions..." The tensions resulting from the desire for pleasurable gratification on the one hand and the encounter with social reality on the other hand make for a life-experience characterized by anxiety and neurosis which is most readily coped with through illusions. Therefore, in a real sense, says Freud, "Our civilization is largely responsible for our misery..." What then can the meaning of life be is a question Freud pursues here.

The impact that Freud's thought has had upon Western culture in the last century is profound. Since the publishing of his *Die Traumdentung, 1900 (The Interpretation of Dreams,* 1911), Freud's thought has gained such widespread usage that it would be difficult to imagine a modern world devoid of his contributions to the understanding of the individual in society. If his studies of the human psyche have revolutionized our thoughts about and attitudes toward the unconscious, his writings on religion, society, and culture have shaken older images of human experiences and ushered in a new era of religious and social theorizing.

Not unaware of the profound shock his thought would have on modern times, Freud saw himself in a select line of great minds who have shaken the Western World. There have been three narcissistic shocks to Western consciousness, thought Freud. First was the Copernican or Cosmological shock which shook Western culture loose from its anthropo-geocentric cosmology which located humanity and the earth at the center of the universe.

This rude awakening brought trauma to Western thinkers who then had to learn how to live in a world where neither the human person nor the earth could claim centrality, but rather had been pre-empted by a heliocentric cosmology. The sun, a gaseous ball devoid of life, became the center.

The second and equally traumatic shock to the Western mind was dealt by Charles Darwin – the Biological Shock – which demonstrated the biological relatedness of all living things, humanity included. If Copernicus had challenged the status of humankind in the universe, Darwin had surely succeeded in establishing the dependence of humanity upon the earth and our kinship with all earth's creatures. The fact that we had persisted even after Copernicus in an anthropocentrism which over-valued the differences between us and other animals as well as between various genetic groupings within the human family made even more difficult the acceptance of Darwin's revelation. To this very day, there are vocal if not large pockets of supposedly modern people who still decry the atheism assumed implicit in Darwin's biology which still lays claim to a primitive worldview nurtured by a creation-story literalism.

Last and most profound of the shocks to Western consciousness has been the Psychological Shock mercilessly dealt by Sigmund Freud. The shock was ushered in by a succession of scientific bomb-blasts: *The Interpretation of Dreams (1911), Totem and Taboo (1912), Beyond the Pleasure Principle (1920), The Future of an Illusion (1927), and Civilization and Its Discontents (1930).* By no means the whole bibliography of profound, challenging, and highly controversial studies, these works are, nevertheless, exemplary of the breadth of Freud's research and interests. His study of the origin and function of religion, published under the significantly descriptive title, *The Future of an Illusion*, is without question his most controversial and most widely read study outside the specific field of psychoanalysis. And yet, his *Civilization and Its Discontents*, which reviews the arguments in the religion book, represents his most mature thoughts on human society and the individual's relation to it. David Bakan, in his provocative and highly controversial study on Freud, entitled, *Sigmund Freud and the Jewish Mystical Tradition (1969)*, has cogently argued that Freud

John H. Morgan

was himself a most exemplary thinker in the Kabbalistic tradition of Jewish mysticism. Kabbalism was an esoteric tradition which chose for reasons of safety and privacy to speak of the human spiritual condition in terms of the dark mysteries and primitive symbolisms of sexuality. If Bakan is right in this bit of theorizing, then the following statement from Freud gains even more profound eminence in modern religious thought: "The tendency on the part of civilization to restrict sexual life is no less clear than its other tendency to expand the cultural unit." But let us look more closely at his work before we pass judgment on Freud's either apt or warped view of the human condition.

The opening remarks in this brief statement of Freud's under scrutiny here are in reference to a friend who, though he entirely agreed with Freud's analysis of religion in his 1927 study, was concerned to call himself religious on the basis of a "sensation of eternity" or "oceanic feeling." Not only was Freud disinclined to accept his friend's suggestion, but Freud also wished to demonstrate how his feeling of eternity corroborated the ego-development schema of psychoanalysis.

The emergence of the ego ("...there is nothing of which we are more certain than the feeling of our self, of our own ego (p. 12),") says Freud, is "through a process of development...(p. 13)." The ego is developmentally the inevitable result of a confronting of the pristine libidinal impulses of the undifferentiated id with the external world of sheer actuality. The id, having its motivational impetus centered in the *pleasure-principle*, confronts the *reality-principle* as the individual infant begins to discover the unpleasantness of the otherness, separateness, and outsideness of the real world. There is a strong motivation on the part of the id-driven child to "separate from the ego everything that can become a source of such unpleasure, to throw it outside and to create a pure pleasure-ego which is confronted by a strange and threatening 'outside' (p. 14)." The id begins necessarily to develop a negotiating capability – the ego as executor of libidinal powers — whereby the desires of the id are pacified with substitute gratifications which are physically accessible and socially acceptable. "In this way," says Freud, "one makes the first step towards the introduction of the reality principle which is to dominate future development (p. 14)."

28

Freud is here explaining a scenario of ego-development which will address the issue of the oceanic feeling, and thus the subject of religion. This executive function of the differentiated ego serves as the primary medium of negotiation between the pleasurable desires from within (the raw libido of the id) and the realities of the outside world (social restraints upon behavior). The more responsible the ego is to the reality-principle, the greater the experience of separateness from the external world – "Our present ego-feeling is, therefore, only a shrunken residue of a much more inclusive, indeed, an all-embracing feeling, which corresponded to a more intimate bond between the ego and the world about it (p. 15)." Freud concludes that to the extent that this earlier primary ego feeling of virtual undifferentiation of self and world in infancy has persisted alongside the narrower demarcated ego feeling of self-separation from the world in maturity, there is the likelihood that feelings of "limitlessness and of a bond with the universe," i.e., the oceanic feeling, will be present.

Freud contends that "...in mental life nothing which has once been formed can perish...(p. 16)," and, therefore, such feelings as these considered here are simply the residue of infantile experience. And, though Freud is reluctant to connect the feeling of "oneness with the universe" with the origins of religion, he is "perfectly willing to acknowledge that the 'oceanic' feeling exists in many people, and (is) inclined to trace it back to an early phase of ego-feeling." In conclusion to this topic of oceanic feelings, Freud is wont to trace the origins of the oceanic feeling to "a first attempt at a religious consolation," which is to say, a feeling resulting from the developing ego's growing awareness of the external world. Furthermore, he is anxious to rearticulate his 1927 theory of religious origins, which says that "The derivation of religious needs from the infant's helplessness and the longing for the father aroused by it...(is) incontrovertible, especially since the feeling is not simply prolonged from childhood days, but is permanently sustained by fear of the superior power of Fate (p. 16)." Though this point will be considered in a later context, it must be noted here that for Freud, the energy output demonstrated by the ego's undying efforts to responsibly direct the otherwise unbridled powers of the id is the result of a deep feeling whose function is the "expression of a strong need."

The religious feeling, says Freud, is a source of energy because it is expressive of a powerful need, viz., the helpless infant's longing for a powerful father. In considering religion, Freud consistently was "concerned much less with the deepest sources of the religious feeling than with what the common man understands by his religion...(p. 2).'" And yet, he was often so convincing in his critique of religion's object being nothing more than an "enormously exalted father" that it is difficult if not impossible to separate the "deepest" from the "common" in religion. Freud had no patience with the "great majority of mortals" who were, as infants, dependent on this projected father-image as a substitute for ego-development and personal maturity. "The whole thing is so patently infantile," complained Freud, a painful reality that most people, avoiding true maturity, opt for a "pitiful rearguard" attachment to childish fantasies of a loving Providence which, watching over us, will reward us eternally in heaven if we are good.

The question of "the purpose of human life," says Freud, bespeaks humanity's "presumptuousness." Religion alone can answer this question, for the whole "idea of life having a purpose stands and falls with the religious system (p. 23)." And though these metaphysical complexities lie outside Freud's investigation here, he chooses to get at the question by an inquiry into the nature of human behavior which demonstrates humanity's purpose and intention in life. And in answer to this question, "What do men show by their behavior to be the purpose and intention of life?," Freud answers simply, "They strive after happiness, they want to become happy and to remain so." That is, they seek the "absence of pain and unpleasure" while seeking the "experiencing of strong feelings of pleasure." Therefore, Freud concludes, the rhetoric of religion to the contrary notwithstanding, "what decides the purpose of life is simply the programme of the pleasure principle."

Happiness, i.e., the satisfaction of needs too seldom gratified, is difficult to realize and impossible to sustain. Society is ever ready to condemn violations of its laws, and unrestrained self-gratification, i.e., personal happiness, inevitably results in a clash of the individual's desires (pleasure principle) and society's rules (reality principle). Therefore, "unhappiness is much less difficult to experience" because the individual is threatened with suffering from three sides: from our own body due to its finitude, from the external world with all its rules, and from our relations with other people. Since happiness is hardly possible at all, and never for any significant duration, we have, necessarily, had to develop techniques for controlling the instincts which given free rein would inevitably bring catastrophe to the individual and to society.

Through the executive services of the ego, the libidinal forces are displaced (focused upon a secondary and socially acceptable object choice) and the instincts are systematically sublimated. In the movement from pleasure to reality, the individual adopts two kinds of "satisfaction...obtained from illusion...(which arise out of) the imagination (p. 27)." Both religion and the enjoyment of the arts are the result of sublimated instincts and displaced libido. Freud says: "A special importance attaches to the case in which this attempt to procure a certainty in happiness and a protection against suffering through a delusional remolding of reality is made by a considerable number of people in common. The religions of mankind must be classed among the mass-delusions of this kind. No one, needless to say, who shares a delusion ever recognized it as such" (p. 28). And, says Freud, those who define happiness in life as the pursuit and love of beauty fail to realize that the aesthetic impulse is simply the result of an ungratified primary sexual motivation. The tensions experienced in the perpetual struggle between the desire for happiness (pleasure principle) and avoidance of pain (reality principle) often lead to neurosis and even psychosis. "Any attempt at rebellion (against society, i.e., reality) is seen (either) as psychosis," or "as a last technique of living, which will at least bring him substitutive satisfaction, (i.e.)...that of a flight into neurotic illness." Freud's concluding remark regarding the function of religion in this context is worth quoting:

> Religion restricts this play of choice and adaptation, since it imposes equally on everyone its own path to the requisition of happiness and protection from suffering. Its technique consists in depressing the value of life and distorting the picture of the real world in a delusional manner which presupposes an intimidation of the

intelligence. At this price, by forcibly fixing them in a state of psychical infantilism and by drawing them into a mass-delusion, religion succeeds in sparing many people an individual neurosis. But hardly anything more (pp. 31-32).

Why has humankind singularly, collectively, and consistently failed in our quest for happiness and the prevention of suffering? In attempting to answer this question, Freud says that a kind of "suspicion dawns on us" which says that maybe the answer lies in "a piece of our own psychical constitution." That is, the contention which "holds that what we call our civilization is largely responsible for our misery...(for) it is a certain fact that all the things with which we seek to protect ourselves against the threats that emanate from the sources of suffering are part of that very civilization (p. 33)."

Can it be? Civilization serves both to protect us against nature and to adjust our mutual relations. Wherein lies the evil, then? Certainly our civilization bore the culture from which came technical skills, fire and tool usage, writing and dwelling houses. And also, we invented gods to whom were attributed our own cultural ideals. Furthermore, beauty, cleanliness and order became "requirements for civilization." Of all characteristics of civilization esteemed and encouraged most highly are our higher mental activities, i.e., intellectual, scientific and artistic achievements, and "foremost among those ideas are the religious systems." The "motive force of all human activities," argues Freud, "is a striving towards the two confluent goals of utility and a yield of pleasure...(p. 41)."

The last and significantly problematic characteristic of civilization is the manner in which relationships of individuals to one another are regulated, i.e., family and state. "Human life in common," contends Freud, "is only made possible when a majority comes together which is stronger than any separate individual and which remains united against all separate individuals." Thus, a concept of the right or social good develops in opposition to individual brute force. "This replacement of the power of the individual by the power of a community constitutes the decisive step in civilization (p. 42)." The first requirement of this newly formed community is, therefore, justice – the assurance that the good of the many expressed in law will be honored over the desires of any single individual. "The liberty of the individual is no gift of civilization." And in this connection, Freud would have us see that there is a great "similarity between the process of civilization and the libidinal development of the individual." As sublimation functions in the individual for the development of a strong ego and creative capacity to deal with the principle of reality, so likewise, "sublimation of instinct is an especially conspicuous feature of cultural development; it is what makes it possible for higher psychical activities, scientific, artistic or ideological, to play such an important part in civilized life (p. 44)."

As we move closer to Freud's perception of the nature of the individual in society – our stumbling futile attempts to construct a viable meaning to life – we are confronted by an indispensable dialectic between life and death, especially as Freud had earlier developed the idea in his book, *Beyond the Pleasure Principle (1920)*. He explains its development: "There still remained in me a kind of conviction...that the instincts could not all be of the same kind...Starting from speculations on the beginning of life and from biological parallels, I drew the conclusion that, besides the instinct to preserve living substance and to join it into ever larger units, there must exist another, contrary instinct seeking to dissolve those units and to bring them back to their primordial, inorganic state. That is to say, as well as Eros there was an instinct of death (p. 66)." Within every society, as within every individual, there are two conflicting instincts. The life instinct is at the service of society so long as society is devoid of aggression, for aggression is a stark manifestation of the Death instinct. Aggression, says Freud, "is an original, self-subsisting instinctual disposition of man...(and it) constitutes the greatest impediment to civilization." Eros and Death share "world-dominion" and explain the movement of civilization back and forth upon the scale of creativity and destruction. This eternal and unexplainable struggle is essentially what life is all about, and the evolution of civilization is simply described "as the struggle for life of the human species." There is only futility in attempting to explain the meaning of life beyond this simple reality – the meaning of life is the struggle of *life against death*. "And it is this battle of the giants," concludes Freud, "that our nurse-maids try to appease with their lullabies about Heaven (p. 69)."

It is the super-ego which constitutes the source of the human feelings of guilt. The super-ego evolves in consort with the development of the ego. As the ego gains relative control over the id, it does so by means of taking to itself the moral expectations of society, as society in turn, through the agency of parents, impresses its values upon the child. The super-ego is the projection of society's self-image into such an exalted state as to elicit devotion and adoration. But as the ego becomes educated to the reality principle, as a balancing source to the id's pleasure principle, the super-ego is being socially reinforced in the adoption of an ideal principle. As the ego's sense of reality confronts the super-ego's sense of the social ideal, tension results within the individual. The super-ego serves as the conscience which testifies against the ego's reluctance to support the ideals of society. "The tension between the harsh super-ego and the ego that is subjected to it," says Freud, "is called by us the sense of guilt; it expresses itself as a need for punishment (p. 70)." The stronger the ego, the weaker the super-ego, and vice versa. Society's moral expectations are mediated through the child's parents and give rise to a conscience educated to certain idealistic expectations. "Civilization, therefore," says Freud, "obtains mastery over the individual's dangerous desire for aggression by weakening and disarming it and by setting up an agency within him to watch over it..."

Guilt, which is really a social anxiety though frequently misnamed "bad conscience," often results from a "fear of loss of love" on the one hand and a "fear of punishment" on the other. But fundamentally, our sense of guilt springs from the Oedipus complex "which was acquired at the killing of the father by the brothers banded together" as classically illustrated in Freud's scenario of the development of primeval human community in his *Totem and Taboo* (1912). And thus, what began in relation to the father is completed in relation to the group. Freud reasons: "If civilization is a necessary course of development from the family to humanity as a whole, then – as a result of the inborn conflict arising from ambivalence, of the eternal struggle between the trends of love and death – there is inextricably bound up with it an increase of the sense of guilt, which will perhaps reach heights that the individual finds hard to tolerate (p. 80). It was Freud's intention from the beginning "to represent the sense of guilt as the most important problem in the development of civilization and to show that the price we pay for our advance in civilization is a loss of happiness through the heightening of the sense of guilt (p. 81)."

Quick to make a qualitative distinction between a "sense of guilt" and a "consciousness of guilt," Freud argues that guilt plays its greatest role in the human experience when operating in the unconscious. And when functioning here, "...the sense of guilt is at bottom nothing else but a topographical variety of anxiety; in its later phases it coincides completely with *fear of the super-ego* (p. 82)." To the extent that guilt remains unobserved in the dark chambers of the unconscious, we are condemned to writhe in our own dissatisfaction – a sort of *malaise* produced by civilization itself. "Religions," says Freud, "have never overlooked the part played in civilization by a sense of guilt." The sense of guilt, the harshness of the superego, the severity of the conscience – all are demonstrative of a need for punishment. This need, says Freud, "is an instinctive (manifestation on the part of the ego) which has become masochistic under the influence of a sadistic super-ego..." Religion, as an illusion produced out of the imaginations of sublimated instincts, functions as a social neurosis which protects us from the stark realities of life devoid of any ultimate transcendent meaning. Mature individuals must eventually rid themselves of illusion and imagination and learn to face squarely and without guilt the meaninglessness of life. Freud's attitude towards life's meaning is capsulated in a quotation from his study, *Civilization and Its Discontents*, with which we conclude our discussion:

> The fateful question for the human species seems to me to be whether and to what extent their cultural development will succeed in mastering the disturbance of their communal life by the human

instinct of aggression and self-destruction. One thing only do I know for certain and that is that man's judgments of value follow directly his wishes for happiness – that, accordingly, they are an attempt to support his illusions with arguments (p. 92).

THEORIES AND CONCEPTS

Unless we begin with Freud, we cannot proceed with any degree of insightfulness regarding the rise of modern day psychotherapeutic practice. That there are a myriad of psychotherapeutic modalities employed daily in hospitals, clinics, counseling centers, and residential treatment facilities goes without saying. But that the proliferation of these various and sometimes competing modalities of treatment is the outgrowth of Freud is indisputable. We have chosen in the first part of this study to focus upon the classical schools of thought and we have continued to insist that given their originality they all owe homage, even when ever so grudgingly given, to the birth of psychoanalysis.

Sigmund Freud has established himself as the instigator of one of the three Cosmic Shocks to western culture. As noted earlier, whereas Copernicus shocked the intellectual world by demolishing the notion that man is the center of the universe (the Cosmological Shock) and Darwin with his discovering of the emergent evolution of life on this plant (the Biological Shock), Freud presented to the modern world an insightful discovery of the nature and role of the unconscious in our daily lives (the Psychological Shock). Modern science and the understanding of humanity will never be the same due to these three great discoveries. And so, without dissent, we must begin with Freud who, during his many years of psychoanalytic practice, developed the first comprehensive theory of personality, developed a thoroughgoing method of treating mental illness, and produced an extensive body of clinical literature based upon his theories and methods of treatment.

In the following, we will look at four areas of Freud's work which have had the greatest impact upon counseling practice today, and they are (1) levels of consciousness -- conscious, preconscious, unconscious, (2) psychosexual development, (3) the structure of personality, and (4) psychoanalytic therapy. The intent is not to produce a comprehensive survey of Freud's work but to present the four major categories of his work which have an immediacy and relevance to the practice of counseling in the modern setting.

Freud's fascination with and desire to describe the functioning of the human mind, he set out to develop a map of how the human mind works. He was intrigued with the possibility, even the necessity, of delving into the inner workings of the human mind to understand the relationship between the function of the mind and human behavior and he came to believe that much of what goes on in human behavior is cued by the human mind in ways unknown to and not understood by the conscious person. He was, essentially, committed to a "psycho-cartography" of human behavior, a "mapping of mind function." In this process, he believed he had discovered that the human mind consists of three levels of function --the conscious, the preconscious, and the unconscious. To understand the nature of human behavior, the therapist must understand the interrelationship of these three levels, how they affect each other, and how to accept their content for closer scrutiny, for only by doing so can the therapist understand the "why" of behavior.

The conscious level of the human mind includes everything that the individual is aware of at any given moment. This, of course, includes thoughts, perceptions, feelings, memories, etc., but really constitutes only a small part of mental functioning. Freud believed that a "selective screening process" functioned to permit only certain information to be at any given moment immediately available to the mind and he was interested in why this screening process was necessary and what it excluded from immediate awareness of the conscious person.

The preconscious (or what is now more commonly called "subconscious") dimension of the human mind consists, said Freud, of all that which is available to memory but not to immediate awareness. It requires an intentional reflection but is free from the "screening" process of the unconscious. Freud believed that the subconscious functioning of the human mind constituted a sort of link between conscious and unconscious.

Most if not all of what is in the subconscious domain of mental function is available, upon demand, by the conscious functioning of the individual but, when that information is no longer needed in the immediacy of living, it falls back into the subconscious compartment of the human mind.

It is to the unconscious reservoir of the human mind that Freud was most attracted because it is here, he believed, that much of what affects human behavior resides yet subject to the screening function of the conscious mind. Though certainly not the first western thinker to ponder the unconscious mind, Freud was decidedly different in his queries from the 17th and 18th century philosophers who speculated about the complex functioning of the human mind because Freud brought both a medical and an empirical commitment and insight into his investigations. The unconscious was, for Freud, not merely a "hypothetical abstraction" to be pondered and wondered at, but rather was an empirically functioning part of the human mind. To understand the unconscious functioning of the human mind would provide real insight into human behavior, especially and particularly mental illness.

As a physician and psychiatrist, Freud was determined to plumb the depths of that compartment of the human mind which, while radically affecting human behavior, seemed ever to elude consciousness and the human will's capacity to control it. Because unconscious components of the human mind are inaccessible to the conscious mind, given the conscious mind's intent upon protecting itself from the materials found in its unconscious compartments, it was Freud's belief that a psychologically-driven archaeology of the mind would release this screened information which affects human behavior. By releasing or exposing this material, the patient suffering from mental illness caused by this protected material (later called "repressed" material) could commence a journey towards mental health. The screening and protecting mechanisms of the conscious mind for this unconscious material include dreams and fantasies and it was here that Freud set about to do his work and, eventually, to develop what he called "psychoanalysis."

Within the context of this psycho-cartography of the human mind, Freud believed that the human personality was comprised of three fundamental structures which worked in consort with the three levels of consciousness. These three personality constructs he called the "id," the "ego," and the "superego." Believing that these personality constructs were essentially "hypothetical" as are the three constructs of consciousness, due to the insufficiently of microanatomy to locate them within the central nervous system, he nevertheless insisted upon the reality of their primary functioning within the human mind and the human personality. Whereas the id functions within the domain of the unconscious, the ego is primarily located in the preconscious or subconscious and conscious portions of mental function. The superego is superimposed over the domain of the ego with capabilities of affecting the functions even of the unconscious domain of mental processes.

The id, Freud believed, was the repository of all instinctual functions of the human animal and is governed by the "pleasure principle" which we have discussed earlier. It is essentially uninhibited and irrational and functions strictly under the energy of animal drives, particularly sexuality and aggression, and is the cause of tension within the person owing to a confliction of instinct and control. To understand the relationship between the driving energy of the id and the mandated social comportment and propriety of the ego would go a long way in identifying the causes of human stress and resulting mental illness. The maturation process of the human animal, then, is directly related to the process of mediating between instinct and social order, between the demands of the id and behavior deemed appropriate by the ego.

The ego, then, is that part of the personality which seems to pacify the irrational desires of the instinctual id while guiding behavior to appropriately moderated forms of acceptable behavior. The stronger the ego, the more controlled the person is in terms of social expectations of propriety; the weaker the ego, the less control and, thus, the greater the danger of violating the rules of society. It is the ego which is responsible for the protection and survival of the individual for the id is only interested in immediate gratification without regard to safety or propriety. Whereas the id is governed by the pleasure principle, the ego is governed by the reality principle. Primary process governs the id because instincts are dominant; secondary process governs the ego because reason and logic take the upper hand. Finally, we can say that the ego is the "executive branch" of the human personality and the center of intellect and propriety.

The ego is the executive branch of the personality, moderating the demands of the id while honoring the propriety of the ego, it is to the superego that the personality must go for guidance regarding appropriate behavior. The ego is moderator but not the instigator of the individual's sense of values, norms, and attitudes. These fall to the domain of the superego. If the superego is extremely restrictive and controlling by providing only a short rope for existential decision-making, then the ego is repressed in its capacity to be creative. A repressed ego results in a warped and dysfunctional personality due to the lack of creative spontaneity for the ego to manage the id. The superego is an "outside" force, introduced in the maturation process of the human individual. It is the mother, the parents, the community, society at large and the world of religion which constitute the source of the superego. With the coming of issues related to good and bad, right and wrong, we see the emergence of the superego. Balancing the irrational demands of the id with the social demands of the superego is the responsibility of the ego and the ego develops in direct relationship to the capacity to manage the tensions produced by this balancing function. Herein lies the fertile ground for mental illness brought on by stress and anxiety.

The superego consists of two countervailing forces -- the conscience and the ego-ideal. The conscience is concerned with compliance to parental and social demands about right and wrong, good and bad, behavior. Whereas the conscience has to do with guilt-inducing non-compliance, the ego-ideal is derived from approved behavior of parents and society. The aim is for self-control to replace parental control, but whereas the id is controlled by instincts and is based on the pleasure principle, the superego is controlled by socially approved behavior and is based on the reality principle as negotiated by the ego. The trouble comes when the superego presses beyond the reality principle to perfectionist goals beyond the capacity of the ego to respond. Much psychiatric fall out from religious fanaticism is located in this complexity of interactive struggles between id, ego, and superego.

Complimenting Freud's concept of the three levels of mental functioning -- conscious, subconscious, unconscious -- is his notion of the four-stage sexual development of the human personality - oral, anal, phallic, and genital. It is quite evident that these stages are named for the specific regions of the body from which sexual energy is discharged. Each stage is identified, then, with what Freud called a "primary erogenous" zone. The term "psychosexual" emphasizes quite clearly his agenda in exploring these developmental stages and their functions in the development of human personality and, of course, their relationship to mental illness. Freud is emphatic about the nature and function of these development stages of human personality and paid a dear price throughout his career for his insistence upon their utility in analysis.

The *oral stage* characterizes the first year of life when the infant is fixated on oral gratification and its relationship to feeding. Though an important erogenous zone throughout life, the mouth is primary during the first year of life and sucking and tactile sensitivity around the lips is fundamental to the infant's development and ends at the time of weaning. Freud believed that in cases where either there was excessive or insufficient amounts of stimulation there is likely to emerge an oral-passive personality in adulthood. Such a personality is characterized by having an optimistic view of the world, having established trusting dependent relationship with others, and one who expects others to "mother" him. This person's psychological adjustment is characterized by gullibility, passivity, and immaturity.

The *anal stage* comes during the second and third year of life and involves a shifting of the child's attention from the mouth to the anal region of the body, particularly retention and expulsion of feces and urine. The bowels and bladder become a major focus of attention in children of this age and depending upon the parental guidance in this area, the child is destined to a sound personality development or one severely warped by mismanagement. Freud believed that many cases of mental illness derived specifically from this stage in personality development. He was convinced that the way in which parents carry out toilet training has specific effects on later personality development and claimed that all later forms of self-control and mastery issues have their origin in the anal stage of development.

The *phallic stage* comes during the fourth year of development when the libidinal interests of the child shifts erogenous zones from the anus to the sex organs. Psychosexual development during this stage includes genital manipulation for pleasure, masturbation, and a growing verbal interest in matters related to birth and babies and similar topics usually posed to the parent. It is during this stage that Freud's now famous concept of the Oedipus complex emerges. The classic concept in Freudian psychoanalysis is used to indicate the situation where the child of either sex develops feelings of love and/or hostility for the parent. In the simple male Oedipus complex, the boy has incestuous feelings of love for the mother and hostility toward the father. The simple female Oedipus complex exists when the girl feels hostility for the mother and sexual love for the father. Psychoanalysts generally agree that adult males who fixate at the phallic stage are usually brash, vain, boastful, and ambitious. Phallic types strive to be successful and attempt at all times to assert their masculinity and virility. In the case of women, Freud believed that the phallic fixation results in traits of flirtatiousness, seductiveness, and promiscuity even though the individual may appear naïve and innocent in sexual relationships. He further believed that the primary source of subsequent neurotic patterns of behavior related to impotency and frigidity derive from this stage of personality development.

The *genital stage* comes with the onset of adolescence and puberty. Following what Freud called the latency period of relative calm, the pubescent child experiences an increased awareness of and interest in the opposite sex. Due to biochemical and physiological changes in the body, the child is now subjected to an influx of drives and desires heretofore unknown or unacknowledged. Freud believed that most children at this point go through a homosexual stage during which time the child, girl or boy, fixates on a same-sex friend or acquaintance. Eventually, the shift to the opposite sex usually occurs with the onslaught of "crushes" and "puppy love." Freud believed that for an adult to attain the ideal genital development, that person must relinquish the passivity of early childhood days when love, security, physical comfort, etc., were freely available and must learn to work, postpone gratification, become responsible, and above all, assume a more active role in dealing with life's problems.

Though we have explored in detail Freud's personal life and his work, looked at a major text of his, and here have reviewed a few of his monumental contributions to psychoanalytic theory, we should not leave until we have explored briefly the therapeutic practice of psychoanalysis as employed by Freud. As with all of the schools of psychotherapy we are considering here, the theoretical foundations have been built for the purpose of psychotherapy rather than merely an exercise in theory building. Freud was intent upon constructing a psychodynamic psychotherapy utilizing his conceptual insights into the nature of the human mind as it relates to mental illness and mental health.

Psychoanalytic psychotherapy has been developed for the purpose of addressing virtually all forms of mental illness. Freud was not reluctant to draw from a variety of social and behavioral sciences such as sociology and anthropology as well as both philosophy and religion in the development of his system. It was Freud's clinical experience of working with neurotic patients which generated his fundamental insights into mental illness and which led to the development of this monumental school of thought. It was upon the clinical experience he had as a practicing psychiatrist that he relied in the testing of his hypotheses. "The teachings of psychoanalysis," Freud said, "are based on an incalculable number of observations and experiences, and no one who has not repeated those observations upon himself and upon others is in a position to arrive at an independent judgment of it."

The fundamental "tools" of the psychoanalytic practitioner include Freud's well-developed concepts of free association, interpretation of resistance, dream analysis, and analysis of transference to probe the patient's unconscious with the aim of making possible a deeper understanding of self. These newly acquired self-insights are then converted into the person's everyday life through the method of emotional re-education.

BIOGRAPHY

Freud: A Life for Our Time by Peter Gay. NY: W. W. Norton &

Company, 1988.

SIGMUND FREUD'S PRIMARY SOURCES

Studies on Hysteria (with Josef Breuer) (*Studien über Hysterie*, 1895)

With Robert Fliess: *The Complete Letters of Sigmund Freud to Wilhelm Fliess, 1887-1904*, Publisher: Belknap Press, 1986.

The Interpretation of Dreams (*Die Traumdeutung*, 1899 [1900])

The Psychopathology of Everyday Life (*Zur Psychopathologie des Alltagslebens*, 1901)

Three Essays on the Theory of Sexuality (*Drei Abhandlungen zur Sexualtheorie*, 1905)

Jokes and their Relation to the Unconscious (*Der Witz und seine Beziehung zum Unbewußten*, 1905)

Totem and Taboo (*Totem und Tabu*, 1913)

On Narcissism (*Zur Einführung des Narzißmus*, 1914)

Beyond the Pleasure Principle (*Jenseits des Lustprinzips*, 1920)

The Ego and the Id (*Das Ich und das Es*, 1923)

The Future of an Illusion (*Die Zukunft einer Illusion*, 1927)

Civilization and Its Discontents (*Das Unbehagen in der Kultur*, 1930)

Moses and Monotheism (*Der Mann Moses und die monotheistische Religion*, 1939)

An Outline of Psycho-Analysis (*Abriß der Psychoanalyse*, 1940)

A Phylogenetic Fantasy: Overview of the Transference Neuroses translated by Axel Hoffer by Peter Hoffer, Harvard University Press.

CHAPTER TWO
Alfred Adler and Individual Psychology

BIOGRAPHICAL SKETCH

What we have said about Freud's Vienna can likewise be said of Adler's Vienna as they were essentially contemporaries (Freud 1856-1939; Adler 1870-1937). And, they were both Jews and eventually physicians and psychotherapists. Adler's father, Leopold, was born in 1835 in the Burgenland but at the time Leopold married Adler's mother, Pauline Beer, in 1866, they became residence of Pauline's hometown. The Beers were Czechoslovakian Jews from Moravia, not unlike Freud's family, and were by the time of the marriage of Leopold and Pauline successful business people operating the firm of Hermann Beer and Sons, dealing in bran, oats, and wheat. The first child of this marriage of Leopold and Pauline was Sigmund (1868) followed two years later by Alfred, born February 7, 1870, in the village of Rudolfsheim, a near suburb of Vienna.

These were happy days for Adler as he says: "As far as I can look back, I was always surrounded by fiends and comrades, and for the most part, I was a well-loved playmate. This development began early and has never ceased. It is probably this feeling of solidarity with others that my understanding of the need for cooperation arose, a motive which has become the key to Individual Psychology." His outgoing and gregarious personality and the ease with which he made new friends he himself traced back to this blissful days of youth. Yet and alas, he failed to maintain such friendships into adulthood.

The preference shown Adler's older brother, Sigmund, and the unhappy death and circumstances of Adler's little brother Rudolf both conspired, in his mind, to rouse an interest in medicine. Never religious and no identifiable interest in the religious side of Judaism, the Adlers deemed Judaism an encumbrance to their progress in society. Yet, little Alfred did find the biblical stories a source of insight into human nature not unlike Freud's use of the *Kabbala*. Living in Leopoldstadt, the most Jewish district of Vienna, the Adlers were immersed in the Jewish culture from dawn to dusk throughout Alfred's childhood and adolescence. Being an eager assimilationist, Alfred Adler would eventually convert to Protestantism, with little regrets to hear him tell it.

Adler's pursuit of a medical career was indicative of the aspirations of many modern Jews of the time. Dominated by his older and more outstanding brother, Adler later would suggest that he was, to use a formalized term later in his theories, "compensating" for physical weakness by achieving success in the profession of medicine. In the spring of 1888, he graduated from the Hernals *Gymnasium* and, at the age of eighteen, he was accepted into the University of Vienna School of Medicine. He completed the entire course of study in seven years, average for the time, taking only the minimum courses and examinations and passing with the lowest possible grades from the medical school and, interestingly enough, received no training in psychiatry.

Because of Adler's parentage, he held Hungarian citizenship and, therefore, in Austria the only medical experience available to him was working as a volunteer medical worker in the Viennese Poliklinik, a free medical hospital for working-class families. During these years of service and growing out of the experience in the public hospital, Adler became an enthusiastic socialist and eventually became a member of the Social Democratic Party. Because of the financial success of his older brother, Sigmund, the entire Adler clan lived better than most during these economically and politically troubling years.

In 1897, everything changed for Alder because he fell in love for the first, and only, time in his life. She was Raissa Timofeivna Epstein. Alder never spoke nor wrote about how they met and the history of the relationship was forever veiled in mystery. She was born in Moscow in 1873 into an affluent Jewish family. Her mother died when Raissa was very young and her childhood was not happy. She attended the University of Zurich, rather than the University of Moscow which barred women from attending, studying biology, zoology, and aiming for a degree in the natural sciences.

At age twenty-seven and twenty-four respectively, Adler and Raissa were married on December 23, 1897, with a full complement of families on both sides in attendance in the city of Smolensk, Russia. Though she desperately missed her large family after the wedding when they returned to Vienna to Alder's medical practice, she gave birth the following year to their first child, Valentine Dina. In the meantime, Adler's medical practice and reputation was growing by leaps and bounds and he was already working on some theories of his own which included such formalized terms as "organ inferiority," "compensation," and "overcompensation" (about which more later).

At 28 years of age, Adler published his first of what would be a long series of scholarly articles. It was a short monograph entitled, *Health Book for the Tailor Trade*, and reflected his passion for working-class medical conditions, a concern which would characterize his entire professional career. During these years, domestic tranquility seemed to elude them as Adler had virtually no contact, by choice, with his two sisters and two brothers, and Raissa likewise had little family interaction. Yet, Adler's career continued to thrive and he continued to publish. Alder naturally came in contact with Freud as they both practiced medicine and psychiatry in Vienna and the history and complexity of that on-again off-again relationship we will only mention in passing later. Suffice it to say here that, at Freud's personal invitation, Adler was asked to join Freud's Wednesday Psychological Society as the youngest member of this small group of young psychiatrists and physicians.

In 1904, Adler published the most important article of his young career, an article that would set the stage for his climb to fame in Europe and America and a topic which would characterize the duration of his professional career. It appeared in *Aertzliche Standeszeitung*, entitled, "The Physician as Educator," with the overriding emphasis being upon the physician's role as "preventer" rather than "curer" of illness among children with special attention to their psychological health. That same year and without his wife, Alder and his daughters converted to Protestantism. Not an unusual occurrence at all among Jews of his status in Vienna, he was a nominal Christian at best but they all celebrated Christmas enthusiastically. Another bridged crossed and burned was the break with Freud, a long and tedious and never-to-be-clearly understood topic. Adler relied upon the "drive for assertion" rather than Freud's emphasis upon "sexual gratification" and, thus, since both were strong willed and strong minded, they broke at the same time Carl Jung was leaving as well (more on this later). To counter Freud's Vienna Psychoanalytic Society, Adler founded in Vienna his own independent Society for Free Psychoanalytic Study. The break was clean and final but happily issued in the most productive period of Adler's professional life.

His domestic life seems to have settled down quietly and the recollections of his adult children confirm that impression. Emphatically opposed to physical punishment, both Adlers chose to explore deprivation as a punishment rather than hitting. All the while, he worked on with his analytical psychology, the Society publishing a new monograph series and him publishing his most important book to-date, namely, *Ueber den nervosen Charakter*, in 1912 and simultaneously in the United States as *The Neurotic Constitution*. Two years later, his colleagues launched with him their own journal, the *Journal for Individual Psychology*, which set in motion the development of a whole school of psychotherapy called "Individual Psychology," all to the anger and hostility of Freud and his followers.

With the coming of World War I and the raging hostilities between Russia and the Austro-Hungarian Empire, the landscape seemed bleak in Europe and, naturally, individual psychology as a movement began to languish. In 1915 and after waiting for years for the appointment, Alder was finally being considered for an appointment as a Lecturer (without stipend) to the University of Vienna School of Medicine. But, where as Freud had enjoyed for years a professorial appointment there, Adler was finally rejected even for this lowly honor. Because Europe (and it seemed the entire world) was falling apart with strife and hostilities, Adler argued that what was needed was "not more individualism" but what he called more "social feeling" (*Gemeinschaftsgefuhl*), meaning more compassion, altruism, and selflessness. He argued that social feeling was the infrastructural support of his newly developed individual psychology. In this notion, he was strongly supported by the American William Alanson White who became a colleague of Harry Stack Sullivan (of whom more in a later chapter). What struck a common cord with White and later

Sullivan was Adler's contention that psychiatric disorders offered new evidence that "behind every neurosis is the existence of a weakling whose incapacity for adapting himself to the ideas of the majority calls forth an aggressive attitude taking on a neurotic form." This was particularly true of soldiers returning from the front lines of battle. At the war's end, some 15,000,000 soldiers and civilians had died in Europe and the face of western culture would forever be changed because of the carnage.

Following the war, there was a strong and growing movement towards Socialism and Adler found himself in the very midst of the activity. Arguing eloquently that "capitalism is inherently inequitable in the distribution of goods and services," he would eventually embrace a political position which suggests that socialism is the moral barometer of capitalism. However, Adler never embraced the use of violence by the Communists to gain their goals, saying, "Human nature generally answers external coercion with a counter-coercion. It seeks its satisfaction not in rewards for obedience and docility, but aims to prove that its own means of power are stronger ... When in the life of man or the history of mankind has such an attempt ever succeeded? ... No blessing comes from the use of power." Finally, in 1920, Adler published a major collection of essays designed to establish Individual Psychology as a school of thought within psychotherapy, entitled, *The Practice and Theory of Individual Psychology*. These twenty-eight essays did the job. Acclaimed throughout Europe and America, Individual Psychology came into its own, particularly in the field of child psychology.

Coming immediately on the heels of this major collection was the reestablishment, following the ravages of WWI, of the movement's periodical, called the *Journal for Individual Psychology*, in 1923 with an internationally distinguished board of editors including the renowned American psychologist G. Stanley Hall of Clark University. Yet and still, Individual Psychology as a school of thought, not unlike psychoanalysis of the Freudian camp, came under severe criticism from certain quarters. First, Adler and Adlerians were criticized for their casual if not indifferent attitude to statistics and their use in assessments and evaluations of treatment and counseling results, particularly as relates to children. Furthermore, this school of thought seldom if ever provided a systematic follow-up of their interventions when dealing with psychological problems of children and youth thereby leaving them open to criticism for failing to actually demonstrate effectiveness. Also, Adler's personal indifference to experimental work would eventually haunt him throughout the remaining years of his practice. Finally, Adler's inordinate emphasis upon environmental factors with a disregard to inherited behavior proved extremely problematic to establishing this school of thought as a major player in 20th psychotherapy. His naively employed motto when dealing with children of "Anyone can learn anything" made the movement seem thin and simplistic.

Yet, his involvement in child psychology and educational psychology did not go unnoticed in the wider profession. For example, in 1924, Adler was made professor of psychology with special interests in child developmental and educational psychology at the Pedagogical Institute's Division of Remedial Education. The Institute was a part of the University of Vienna and worked in consort with Karl and Charlotte Buhler's Institute of Psychology. But also in America, Adler and Individual Psychology were becoming a major point of interest within both the professional community and the general public at large. Emphasizing the two fundamental principles of his theory, Adler was always quick to point out that "two factors affect all human relations, namely, the inferiority complex and the striving for social feeling." The *New York Times* described this "new psychology" of Adler this way: "One of the most important schools of this new science of the soul is individual psychology, founded by the Viennese scholar and neurologist, Dr. Alfred Adler. Laymen sometimes make the mistake of regarding individual psychology as a mere subdivision of the psychoanalysis of Freud. It is no more that than is Protestantism a subdivision of Catholicism." Such praise went far to establishing Individual Psychology as a major player on the American stage.

In anticipation of and as a lead up to the publishing of his next major work translated into English in 1926 titled, *Understanding Human Nature,* Adler gave a cryptic summary for the press of what he meant by Individual Psychology. Individual Psychology regards the craving for power on the part of the individual and of nations as a reaction to deep feelings of inferiority. "Individual Psychology," he said, "could rally all the latent forces for good which are inherent in groups, just as it is already rallying such latent forces in individuals. Wars, national hatreds and class struggle -- these greatest enemies of humankind -- all root in the desire to escape, or compensate for, the crushing sense of their inferiority. Individual psychology, which can cure individuals of the evil effects of this sense of inferiority, might be developed into a powerful instrument for ridding nations and groups of the menace of their collective inferiority complex."

Adler's coming to America on the heels of this publication was fortuitously beneficial for his school of psychology. America was experiencing a major decline in religious attendance which was coupled with major upheavals in social values as regards marriage, romance, and sexuality. The popularity of the automobile was on the exponential rise as a portable living room for eating, drinking, smoking, gossiping, and sex. The liberation of American sexual mores centered in Hollywood and the coming of psychiatry and psychoanalysis as the new fads among the rich also served well the Adlerian agenda.

Freudian psychoanalysis, which was for a time the ruling school of thought among the top professionals and the wealthy in America, began to feel competition from Individual Psychology. Freud's anti-Americanism became increasingly known and unwelcome as the lead up to McCarthyism. The radically subjective nature of his therapeutic treatment, its unending demand for weekly visits over many years, the overall expense, etc., all conspired to create an atmosphere of welcome for Alderian psychology as a radically different approach to mental health. Freud's criticism, first, off the record, then in later years, on the record, of Americans as an uncouth, money-grubbing lot did not serve well his cause. Freud even went so far as to tell Ernest Jones, his famous biographer, that "America is a mistake; a gigantic mistake, it is true, but nonetheless a mistake." And, the fact that both Adler and Jung were experiencing a massive boost in their financial situations thanks to American interest grated hard on Freud and he didn't keep it to himself. A few clips from Freud's later statements about Americans and America will serve: "It often seems to me that analysis fits the American as a white shirt the raven." "What is the use of Americans if they bring no money?" "America is useful for nothing else but to supply money." "Is it not sad that we are materially dependent on these savages (Americans) who are not better-class human beings?"

America was ready for Adler thanks, ironically and in part, to the earlier arrival of Freud and psychoanalysis. Freud set the stage in America but Adler produced a more pragmatic approach to mental health. To professionals and the general public, Alder emphasized the concept of "inferiority" as a central theme in his understanding of human nature. "The behavior pattern of persons," he would say in all of his lectures, "can be studied from their relation to three things: to society, to work, to sex. The feeling of inferiority affects a man's relations to these." Again, he said: "The three great questions in life that require answers by each individual have to do with occupation, society, and love. ... (and the role of parents and teachers is to) help the child to create a style of life that is profitable for himself, for society, and for posterity." This was, indeed, well received in American audiences of professional counselors and teachers alike. His lecture series at the New School for Social Research in New York City in 1928 went a long way to furthering his reputation.

Adler never stopped emphasizing the need to stimulate in the child a sense of confidence, to evoke his cooperative dispositions, to socialize and humanize his ego, especially to teachers and parents. He was becoming the darling to the teaching profession and to educated parents concerned about the raising of their children in a "modern" world. In the *Saturday Review of Literature*, S. Daniel House of Columbia University wrote: "The Adlerian approach to the problems of disharmony and maladjustment resident in human nature constitute a new chapter in psychology and, what is more important, a fresh beginning in education.... We might refer to Adler's work as educational sociology and compare him in his general social philosophy and creative attitudes towards education with John Dewey. ... he might be referred to with considerable accuracy as the pioneer in the comparatively new field of educational psychiatry."

Benefiting from such praise and desiring more and more to distance himself from both Freud and psychoanalysis, Adler spoke specifically to the issue in his lecture series at the New School for Social Research. In speaking of the differences, he said that "Freud takes as premise the fact that man is so constructed by nature that he wishes only to satisfy his drives but that culture or civilization is antagonistic to such satisfaction. However, Individual Psychology claims that the development of the individual, because of his bodily inadequacy and his feeling of inferiority, is dependent on society. Hence, social feeling is inherent in man and bound up with his identity." This did it for the American audience. Leading up to the occasion of him receiving an honorary doctorate from Wittenberg College in America, Adler said: "the most important single factor in personality development is the relative presence of the inferiority complex ... This feeling of inferiority forms the background for all our studies. It ultimately becomes the stimulus among all individuals, whether children or adults, to establish their actions in such a way that they will arrive at a goal of superiority." He subsequently learned that the Soviet Union had elected him an honorary member of the Leningrad Scientific-Medical Child Study Society, an accolade he was not willing to refuse.

Returning to America for the third time in 1929 to promote his latest book, *The Technique of Individual Psychology,* he continued to lecture at the New School on optimism and human nature to the delight of the professionals and students who flocked to hear him. That year, he made the decision to relocate permanently to New York, but without Raissa who was most disinclined to leave her European home and roots partly because of her increasing involvement in Austrian Communist Party activities. Alder, nevertheless, settled into his new residence, a suite at the Windermere Hotel on Manhattan's West End Avenue and Ninety-Second Street. The New York years saw his national reputation grow even while he continued relationships, mixed as they were, with the New School and Columbia University, taking a visiting professorship in medical psychology at the Long Island College of Medicine.

As the war mongering continued to accelerate in Europe leading up to the inevitable World War II, Adler was very concerned about his European family, none of whom were willing to consider coming to America in spite of his pleadings. Adler never returned to Austria. At his leaving, he gave a book to a little boy who cared greatly for him. Adler later reported that as he left, the little boy ran down the road crying out to him: "Come back, and stay forever!" With this, Alder turned his back forever on Europe, save for a visit to England where he traveled with his wife, Raissa, for the last time. He returned to New York and continued to lecture, teach, and practice Individual Psychology until his death of a heart attack at the age of sixty-seven. Freud was reported to have rejoiced that he outlived Adler but many accolades from professional colleagues memorializing him were published from such giants as Maslow, Rogers, and Frankl.

THE CLASSIC TEXT CONSIDERED

As Adler began to feel the power and strength of his own theory-building enterprise, he began, at first quietly and subtly but gradually both aggressively and outspokenly, to move away from Freud's fundamental argument that sexual conflicts in early childhood caused mental illness. Adler gradually began to consign sexuality to a symbolic role in human strivings to overcome feelings of inadequacy, what he came to call the "inferiority complex." Adler was speaking out loudly and publicly against Freud's fundamentally erroneous mistake regarding the centrality of sexuality in child development. Adler and a group of colleagues eventually disassociated themselves from Freud and the classical psychoanalytic school's idea of sexual dominance in mental illness and began the eventual development of what has become known as Individual Psychology, best and most thoroughly developed in Adler's 1927 book, *Menschenkenntnis* (English translation, *Understanding Human Nature*). Without question, Adler's *Understanding Human Nature* (English translation by Walter Beran Wolfe) published and copyrighted in 1927 by the Greenburg Publishers of Garden City, NY, constitutes his most acclaimed work. We will review this book, commencing with excerpts from Adler's on Preface and followed by our review.

"This book is an attempt," wrote Adler, "to acquaint the general public with the fundamentals of Individual Psychology. At the same time it is a demonstration of the practical application of these principles to the conduct of one's everyday relationships, not only to the world, and to one's fellowmen, but also to the organization of one's personal life. ... The purpose of the book is to point out how the mistaken behavior of the individual affects the harmony of our social and communal life; further, to teach the individual to recognize his own mistakes, and finally, to show him how he may effect a harmonious adjustment to the communal life" (1927). Adler's book captures our attention here for it was this book, more than any other, which commended his optimistic worldview and hopeful approach to the study of human development, especially of children, to America and the world. We will take excerpts from this great classic and our comments upon them we will each citation.

"We have often drawn attention to the fact that before we can judge a human being we must know the situation in which he grew up." These are Adler's opening words when speaking of *"The Family Constellation."* He continues: "An important moment is the position which a child occupied in his family constellation. Frequently we can catalogue human beings according to this view point after we have gained sufficient expertness, and can recognize whether an individual is a first-born, an only child, the youngest child, or the life." Adler was the first to place a major emphasis upon what later became commonly called within psychotherapy "birth order" of the child. He was himself one of several children and always felt confident that the order in which a child is born into the family would/could/should have a major, and not always positive, impact upon his development. He spent a great deal of time researching and writing upon this factor even though, ironically enough, there is nothing anyone can do about the order of their birth in a family. His concern was for both parents to take full cognizance of the fact and to directly address that point in the childrearing practices employed in dealing with each child as well as the child, in adulthood, taking full cognizance of that reality as he reflects upon his childhood and how that reality may have affected his worldview.

"People seem to have known for a long time," explains Adler, "that the youngest child is usually a peculiar type. ... Not only is he the youngest, but also usually the smallest, and by consequence, the most in need of help. ... Hence there arise a number of characteristics which influence his attitude toward life in a remarkable way, and cause him to be a remarkable personality. ...One group of these youngest children excels every other member of the family ... But there is another more unfortunate group of these same youngest children ... which have a desire to excel, but lack the necessary activity and self-confidence, as a result of their relationships to their older brothers and sisters." Adler was keen to place a great deal of emphasis upon the first child, the youngest child, and the only child as being of particular types and quite susceptible to both analysis and study as well as themselves being personally susceptible to certain psychological dysfunctions. As an educator as well as psychotherapist, he was especially concerned that full awareness of these realities be integrated into the educational system of the day.

"We are really tired of having nothing but the first and best people," explains Adler. "History as well as experience demonstrates that happiness does not consist in being the first or best. To teach a child such a principle makes him one-sided; above all it robs him of his chance of being a good fellow man. The first consequence of such doctrines is that a child thinks only of himself and occupies himself in wondering whether someone will overtake him. Envy and hate of his fellows and anxiety for his own position, develop in his soul. His very place in life makes a speeder, trying to beat out all others, of the youngest. ... This type of the youngest child is occasionally to be found as a clear-cut type example, although variations are common. ... Another type, which grows secondarily from the first, is often found. When a youngest child of this type loses his courage he becomes the most arrant coward that we can well imagine. We find him far from the front, every labor seems too much for him, and he becomes a veritable "alibi artist" who attempts nothing useful, but spends his whole energy wasting time. ... He will always find excuses for his failures. He may contend that he was too weak or petted, or that his brothers and sisters did not allow him to develop."

Adler wishes to call attention to these two types of "youngest" personality options, the high achiever at any price and the low achiever at no price. Though parents could sense these characteristics in their children, Adler was the first to elevate the discussion to a clinical investigation, to an analytical study of data based upon observed behavior. He became recognized as the master in dealing with children in these situations and always with an eye towards their constructive education, thus becoming the darling of American educators.

"Both of these types are hardly ever good fellow human beings," Adler continues. "The first type (the strong youngest child) fares better in a world where competition is valued for itself. A man of this type will maintain his spiritual equilibrium only at the cost of others, whereas individuals of the second (the weak youngest child) remain under the oppressive feeling of their inferiority and suffer from their lack of reconciliation with life as long as they life. The oldest child also has well-defined characteristics. For one thing he has the advantage of an excellent position for the development of his psychic life. History recognizes that the oldest son has had a particularly favorable position. Even where this tradition has not actually become crystallized ... the oldest child is usually the one whom one accredits with enough power and common sense to be the helper or foreman of his parents. If his development in this direction goes on without disturbance then we shall find him with the traits of a guardian of law and order." Adler was especially sensitive, owing to his own personal life story, to the reality of this dominance of the first son as he was himself the subject of such an older brother. His further remarks regarding the "second-born child" are most insightful and led him to the development of one of his most important contributions to psychotherapeutic practice, namely, the concept of the inferiority complex. He says of the second born son: "The second born may place his goal so high that he suffers from it his whole life, annihilates his inner harmony in following, not the veritable facts of life, but an evanescent fiction and the valueless semblance of things."

"The only child, of course, finds himself in a very particular situation," reasons Adler. "He is at the utter mercy of the educational methods of his environment. ... Being constantly the center of attention he very easily acquires the feeling that he really counts for something of great value. ... Parents of "only" children are frequently exceptionally cautious, people who have themselves experienced life as a great danger, and therefore approach their child with an inordinate solicitude." Birth order, as we have said, played a major role in Adler's child psychiatry and whether dealing with the youngest or oldest child or the only child, he was most sensitive to the developmental personality issues which arise from the birth order phenomenon both as it relates to the individual child's self-understanding as well as that of the child's nurturing environment controlled by parents and teachers.

"We see, therefore," counsels Adler, "that the very position of the child in the family may lend shape and color to all the instincts, tropisms, faculties and the like, which he brings with him into the world. ... (therefore) it would seem to us that the theory of inheritance of acquired characteristics is based upon very weak evidence. ... From our previous descriptions we may assume that whatever the errors to which a child is exposed in his development, the most serious consequences arise from his desire to elevate himself over all his fellows, to seek more personal power which will give him advantages over his fellow man." Unlike Freud's rather positive emphasis upon the inevitability of the "will to pleasure" which he felt was the fundamental driving force in human life, Adler is keen both to point out that the "will to power" is, rather, the driving force but, rather than being merely positive about this drive, Adler believes that the social environment, particularly the parents and educators of small children, must assert themselves for the controlling and direction of this power-surge for superiority over the child's peers.

"In our culture," reasons Adler, "he is practically compelled to develop according to a fixed pattern. If we wish to prevent such a perilous development we must know the difficulties he has to meet and understand them. There is one single and essential point of view which helps us to overcome all these difficulties; it is the viewpoint of the development of the social feeling. If this development succeeds, obstacles are insignificant, but since the opportunities for this development are relatively rare in our culture, the difficulties which a child encounters play an important role." Adler is painfully aware of the developmental obstacles placed in the child's path by the child's social environment so Adler rails against parental practices of feeding the drive to dominant which our culture seems to cherish and

John H. Morgan

perpetrate. In *Understanding Human Nature*, Adler is eager for the informed parent and educational system to be aware of the drive or will to power which characterizes human nature and the absolute necessity of guiding and educating that drive for the welfare of human society. The notion of "social feeling," which Adler has so emphasized in his work, is central to this guidance.

THEORIES AND CONCEPTS

Individual Psychology, as we have seen, maintains that the overriding motivation in most individuals is a striving for what Adler early on called "superiority" but later modified to "compensational behavior" for feelings of inferiority. This human quest, commencing in early childhood, for self-realization, completeness, and perfection, is usually frustrated by feelings of inadequacy, or incompleteness arising from physical defects, low social status, pampering or neglect during childhood, and not infrequently birth-order. Compensational behavior relative to these feelings of inferiority can include the development of personal skills and abilities.

Here is the arena for the parent and the educator to take the initiative in nurturing positive responses to the child's need for a sense of fulfillment even in the face of stifling environmental and physical handicaps. Over-compensation for inferiority feelings can, says Adler, take the form of an egocentric striving for power and self-aggrandizing behavior at others' expense. This led Adler to propose an alternative to Freud's short-hand notion of the "will to pleasure" with his own idea of the "will to power." Simplistic and unfair to his own system of thought, this notion nevertheless emphasized the prominence in child development of feelings of inferiority and compensatory behavioral responses to assert jurisdiction over one's own life and destiny, namely, the will to power.

Adler was internationally recognized and acclaimed for his creative and innovative response to the need for the cultivation and monitoring of mental health among children. He established a series of child-guidance clinics in Vienna in 1921 for this purpose and international figures including Maria Montessori called attention to his outstanding efforts in this regard. Though the Nazi influence on the Austrian government forced the closing of these Adlerian child counseling centers in 1934, his reputation preceded him to New York in 1926, joining first the Columbia University faculty the next year and eventually the faculty of Long Island College of Medicine in 1932.

It is the contention within Individual Psychology that there is a direct relationship between the human person and the world around him as relates particularly to a few biological principles operative within human nature. Psychoneurosis, then, is seen as a disturbance in the relationship between the individual and his social environment. Therefore, therapeutics based on individual psychological data must be an etiological therapeutic in the proper sense of that word. Given the social etiology of mental disease, it is the intention of the psychotherapist in the modality of Individual Psychology to address the need for a readjustment of the interpersonal relationship between the patient and his social environment, the community and social circle within which he lives and works and loves.

The term "Individual Psychology" was chosen by Adler specifically to identify his system of theory and analysis because of his radical emphasis upon the essential subjective nature of the individual's striving, the innate creativity of human psychological adaptation, and the wholeness of the individual's unified personality. The drive for superiority in the face of compensatory behavioral response to personal feelings of inferiority constitutes the matrix of human development. "The goal of superiority, with each individual," says Adler, "is personal and unique. It depends upon the meaning he gives to life; and this meaning is not a matter of words. It is built up in his style of life and runs through it like a strange melody of his own creation." If individuals have developed a healthy social life through creative and responsible interests, their strivings for superiority will be shaped into a style of life that is warmly receptive of others and focused on friendship and interpersonal ties. If not, neuroses and psychoses will develop as the individual attempts to adjust his will to power, his personal agenda, to the conflicting demands and expectations of society.

Individual Psychology is built upon the notion of a fundamental unity of the human personality. All apparent dichotomies and duplicities of life are organized in one self-consistent totality. No definite division can be made between mind and body, consciousness and unconsciousness, or between reason and emotion. All behavior is seen in relation to the final goal of superiority or success, of the will to power. This goal gives direction to the individual within his social matrix. If he has developed strong "social feelings" for his social environment, he will thrive. If not, mental illness awaits him as he struggles unsuccessfully to assert his demand for superiority in the absence of a capacity to get along in his social environment due to the failure to have cultivated this strong social feeling.

In contrast to Freud and psychoanalysis, which places so much emphasis upon the assumption that man is motivated by instincts, and in contradistinction to Carl Jung's analytical psychology which emphasizes above all else man's dependence upon inborn archetypes, Adler believed that the human person is motivated by social urges. We are inherently social beings and our very nature is interpersonal, requiring cooperation in social activities. Whereas Freud relied upon sexuality and Jung upon primordial thought patterns, Adler stressed social interest or, what we have seen him call, "social feeling."

Furthermore, with respect to the emergence and development of personality, Adler placed emphasis upon the concept of the "creative self," the notion that the human is a highly personalized, subjective entity which interprets his social environment and tries to make sense out of it for his survival and betterment. Whereas Freud would have us believe that personality relies upon inborn instincts for self-aggrandizement, Adler believes that the human person seeks for experiences which will aid in fulfilling the individual's unique style of life. This concept of the "creative self" was new to psychoanalysis but over time has become a major conceptual framework in analyzing personality and behavioral disorders.

A primary distinction of Individual Psychology over against psychoanalysis was Adler's insistence upon the absolute "uniqueness" of each personality. Each person is a composite of his own personalized motivations, traits, interests, and values and each person, then, carries a distinctive style of life unique to his experiences and situation in the social environment. Adler minimizes Freud's emphasis upon sexual instinct as the dominant dynamic in human behavior, rather calling attention to man's social character, his experiences of inferiorities not sexually derived or driven. Adler's "dethronement" of Freudian sexuality was for many professionals and the laity a welcome relief from the monotonous pan-sexualism of the psychoanalysts in the Freudian camp.

It was personal consciousness as the center of human personality which Adler emphasized, studied, and with which he was fascinated. The human person is a conscious being, ordinarily aware of its reasons for his behavior. Fully cognizant of his inferiorities and well aware of his personal goals for which he strives in life, man is a being capable of planning and guiding his behavior, fully conscious of the meaning of such plans as relates to his self-realization as a person. Freud was completely at odds with this concept of personality and image of human nature for Freud and his school felt that human consciousness was a minimal component of human behavior with the individual primarily victimized by his unconscious.

Adlerian psychology is quite splendidly simple in terms of the minimal use of conceptual terms developed in his theory of personality. Six major concepts are operative within Individual Psychology and we will quickly review them here. They are (1) fictional finalism, (2) striving for superiority, (3) inferiority feelings and compensation, (4) social interests, (5) style of life, and (6) the creative self.

Once Adler and the Individual Psychology school of professionals distanced themselves from Freud and the psychoanalytic school of psychotherapy, they moved to adopt a rather well developed philosophical optimism, a kind of "idealistic positivism" over against Freud's rather dark notion of "historical determinism." Man, Adler argued, is motivated more by his hopes and aspirations about the future than he is by suppressed experiences of the past. The hopes and aspirations are not teleological, that is, they are not predestined or subject to fate, but rather are quite decidedly subjective, mental constructs of the hopeful personality. Adler called these "fictional goals," because they are subjective causations which may or may not be realized but are, nevertheless, ever present in the human heart. Rather than teleological in nature and, thus, the result of causation, the fictional nature of hopes and aspirations are based on the principle of finalism. Adler spoke to this issue decisively:

> Individual Psychology insists absolutely on the indispensability of finalism for the understanding of all psychological phenomena. Causes, powers, instincts, impulses, and the like cannot serve as explanatory principles. The final goal alone can explain man's behavior. Experiences, traumata, sexual development mechanisms cannot yield an explanation, but the perspective in which these are regarded, the individual way of seeing them, which subordinates all life to the final goal, can do it" (1927).

Adler was concerned primarily with the fundamental goal in an individual's life, that for which a person strives and results in a kind of consistency of personality, a unity of purpose and person. Even before he left Freud, he had come to the conclusion that "aggression" rather than "sexuality" was the driving force to the human person seeking fulfillment. These aggressive impulses of the human person result in what became known as the "will to power." A child of the time, Adler believed that masculinity was a sign of strength; femininity a sign of weakness. He developed a concept out of this called the "masculine protest" which simply meant that individuals develop a behavioral mode of response to life's situations called "overcompensation." This is the standard mode of operation when either a man or woman feels helpless or inferior or inadequate. This will to power notion was eventually given up in deference to a more sophisticated concept of the "striving for superiority." From aggression to power to superiority, Individual Psychology evolved into a more refined system of analysis. Not social distinction, leadership, or even a pre-eminent position in society, superiority for Adler in this analytical scheme simply means an endemic drive towards perfection, the "great upward drive" as he called it which characterizes every person, healthy or ill. "I began to see clearly in every psychological phenomenon the striving for superiority" Adler said. "It lies at the root of all solutions of life's problems and is manifested in the way in which we meet these problems."

The drive is innate to the human animal.

The etiology of this innate drive, Adler believed, was located in the feelings of inferiority which characterize every person in some form or another and in varying degrees of intensity. Early on in his medical training and beginning clinical work, he links the notion of what he called "organ inferiority" with "overcompensation." He later broadened the concept to include any feelings of inferiority which arose from subjectively felt psychological or social disabilities as well as from physical insufficiencies. Adler believed that feelings of inferiority are the basis for all human improvements and creativity in the world. When these feelings are exaggerated, mental illness is the results. When they are held at bay or educated into a viable self-understanding, they lead to success and leadership, superiority of deed and person. Though not inevitably or even commonly leading to pleasure, such development was designed to lead the individual toward perfection which, he believed, was the ultimate goal of life.

The idea of social interest, or social feeling as we discussed earlier in this chapter, came later to Adler and in response to pervasive criticism from the professionals in the field of counseling and therapy. The criticism was due to Adler's early emphasis upon aggression and the will to power at the expense, it was thought, of human cooperation. Because in his own life he was an outspoken proponent of social justice and social democracy, he worked tirelessly to broaden his understanding of human nature to include this sense of social interest and social feeling toward one's fellow man and fellow creatures. Cooperation, he began to say, is a fundamental characteristic of the human person. In this development, he moved further and further away from his earlier emphasis upon aggression and selfish interest, arguing, in his mature years for the centrality of social feeling as an indispensable component of personality.

"Style of life" became a slogan for Adlerians of the day. His whole theory of human personality was summed up in this one expression. Though every person has the goal of superiority (defined in the Adlerian sense of personal pursuit of perfection) as his foremost agenda, there are countless ways in which this superiority might be realized in one's life. The style of life one lives is early formed in childhood. Based upon social encounters with the outside world as well as birth order and family life, the style of life is constructed. His attitudes, feelings, apperceptions, and aspirations are set in motion. One's sense of inferiority in various aspects of life are contributing factors in the development of one's style of life always within the context of self-aware inferiorities and the self-administered pressure to seek perfection and personal fulfillment in one's life. It was the concept of the "creative self" which proved to be the crowning achievement of his theory of personality. All of his other concepts and notions about personality development fell into place when the idea of the creative self was discovered and expanded upon in his clinical work and theoretical writing. It is this creative self which gives a person meaning in life. It is the active principle of humanity. In essence, the doctrine of a creative self asserts that man makes his own personality. This was Adler's major contribution to personality theory and the one which assured the prominence of Individual Psychology.

Adler's humanistic theory of personality was in direct opposition to Freud's conception of human nature. Characteristics such as altruism, humanitarianism, cooperation, creativity, uniqueness, and awareness utilized by Adlerian psychology flew in the face of Freud's materialistic, instinctually driven, unconsciously motivated person. Whereas the Freudians were scandalized by the apparent naïve optimism about the human person, Adler's hopefulness toward the future rang clear in the public consciousness. Adler's system had arrived in America at a time when it was most welcome.

ALFRED ADLER'S BIOGRAPHY

The Drive for Self: Alfred Adler and the Founding of Individual Psychology by Edward Hoffman. NY: Addison-Wesley Publishing, 1994.

ALFRED ADLER'S PRIMARY SOURCES

The Practice and Theory of Individual Psychology (1927)

Understanding Human Nature (1927)

What Life Could Mean to You (1931)

In his lifetime, Adler published more than 300 books and articles. The Alfred Adler Institute of Northwestern Washington has recently published the first ten of the twelve-volume set of *The Collected Clinical Works of Alfred Adler*, covering his writings from 1898-1937. An entirely new translation of Adler's magnum opus, *The Neurotic Character*, is featured in Volume 1.
Volume 1 : The Neurotic Character — 1907
Volume 2 : Journal Articles 1898-1909
Volume 3 : Journal Articles 1910-1913
Volume 4 : Journal Articles 1914-1920
Volume 5 : Journal Articles 1921-1926
Volume 6 : Journal Articles 1927-1931
Volume 7 : Journal Articles 1931-1937
Volume 8 : *Lectures to Physicians & Medical Students*
Volume 9 : *Case Histories*
Volume 10 : *Case Readings & Demonstrations*
Volume 11 : *Education for Prevention*
Volume 12 : *The General System of Individual Psychology*

The Individual Psychology of Alfred Adler. H. L. Ansbacher and R. R. Ansbacher (Eds.). New York: Harper Torch books (1956)

CHAPTER THREE
Carl Gustav Jung and Analytical Psychology

BIOGRAPHICAL SKETCH

Carl Gustav Jung's contributions to personality theory were developed over an extended period of time covering more than fifty years and are fully displayed in his twenty-volume set of collected works edited by H. Read and others from 1953-1979, *The Collected Works of C. G. Jung* published by Princeton University Press. The founder of what is called Analytical Psychology, Jung has been praised and maligned by the intellectual and medical community for most of his productive life and certainly since his death. An early associate of Sigmund Freud, Jung would radically depart from psychoanalysis as he matured in his own thought. Without doubt, his original insights lay in a profound awareness of the powerful influence of myths and symbols on the human psyche. The reciprocity of symbol making and symbol using -- symbols make man and man makes symbols -- constitutes a significant starting point in the study of Jung.

We will here discuss Jung's life, a major text in his massive corpus of writings, and we will review some key concepts in his system of thought called Analytical Psychology. Let us begin with an extended quote from Jung to set the stage for our enquiry:

> *Anyone who wants to know the human psyche will learn next to nothing from experimental psychology. He would be better advised to abandon exact science, put away his scholar's gown, bid farewell to his study, and wonder with human heart through the world. There in the horrors of prisons, lunatic asylums and hospitals, in drab suburban pubs, in brothels and gambling-halls, in the salons of the elegant, the Stock Exchanges, socialist meetings, churches, revivalist gatherings and ecstatic sects, through love and hate, through the experience of passion in every*

form in his own body, he would reap richer stores of knowledge than textbooks a foot thick could give him, and he will know how to doctor the sick with a real knowledge of the human soul.

In a little town located on Lake Constance in the Canton of Thurgau in Switzerland named Kesswyl, Carl Gustav Jung was born on July 26, 1875. He was the fourth and only surviving child of Johann Paul Achilles Jung (1842-1896) and Emilie Preiswek Jung (1848-1923). Johann was a poor rural clergyman in the Swiss Reformed Church and Emilie was a member of a long-established Basel family of distinction and wealth. Taught Latin by his father and the teachings of exotic religions by his mother, Carl grew up in an atmosphere of learning and curiosity with deep sensitivities to mysticism and the occult.

From Carl's birthplace, the family moved when he was six months old to a better parish in Laufen in an effort to improve their living situation. Paul felt the pressure to please his wife of wealth and breeding and the tensions continued to mount between them. Emilie was not a well person and whether it was strictly emotional or had a biogenic origin, it was not certain, though she did spend some time hospitalized in Basel for several months after the move to Laufen. At home, she spent a great deal of time in her separate bedroom from Paul where she believed she was regularly visited by spirits which came to her at night. Maternal affection was rare and episodic and eventually Carl was taken by his father to live with Emilie's unmarried sister in Basel for a time but eventually returned to his father's home.

Eccentric and depressed, Emilie's bouts of depression and moodiness had a negative impact upon Jung's perception of womanhood which affected his entire life and work. Jung would later be heard to say that women were essentially "innately unreliable." His father, Paul, was eventually called to another parish in 1879 at Kleinhuningen which, happily, brought Emilie closer to her own family and proved most beneficial in lifting her spirits as the depression gradually dissipated.

Not surprisingly, given his birth and early life situation, Jung proved to be a solitary and very introverted child, believing, as he explained in his autobiographical reflections, that he actually had two distinct personalities. The first one, what he called "Personality Number One," was a modern Swiss citizen attuned to the 19th century, and was a typical schoolboy living in that time period. "Personality Number Two" was, however, a dignified authoritarian and an influential person from the past. Much of this early self-indulgence would revisit him in his mature years of theory building. At this time, Jung became painfully aware that he was somewhat disappointed in his father's lack of intellectual acumen in the assessment of the meaning and nature of religion and his approach to a faith-based life.

In his adolescent years, he attended the Humanistisches gymnasium in Basel. During his first year as a student there, age twelve, he was roughed up by another boy and a severe fall to the ground caused a momentary unconsciousness. This experience led him to believe that he would not now ever have to attend school again and when he was being told it was time to leave for school, he regularly fainted. Staying home, then, for six months, Jung at first enjoyed the power and the freedom of his situation. However, when he overheard his father explaining to a colleague that he feared Carl would never be able to support himself because of possible epilepsy, Carl was shocked back into facing reality and the inevitable need for academic achievement if true financial freedom was to ever be his. He rallied, commenced vigorously studying his father's Latin grammar text and, though he fainted three times in the process, he eventually overcame the urge and proved a distinguished student after all. In his adult reflections, he recounts this as the occasion when "I learned what a neurosis is." His studies, particularly of Krafft-Ebing's book entitled *Psychopathia Sexualis*, persuaded him to specialize in psychiatric medicine when he pursued his university education. He studied medicine at the Universities of Basel and Zurich with strong emphasis in biology, zoology, paleontology, and archaeology, all the while as a medical student working with patients in the training hospital. Studying psychiatric patients closely and employing what he would call word associations to which patients responded in what he called "complexes," he began his long journey towards his fundamental theories of Analytical Psychology. Interestingly enough, he combined a passion for psychiatry with an equal passion for the humanities, myths, symbols, esotericisms of all kinds (somewhat reflective of his own mother's preoccupations). As a young intern, he became a staff physician at Zurich's Burgolzli Psychiatric Hospital where he applied his method of free association which proved clinically helpful in his identifying of repressed complexes among the mentally ill in his care. He became acquainted with Freud's work upon reading *The Interpretation of Dreams*, while studying under the psychiatrist Eugen Bleuler who was a strong proponent of the new "psycho-analysis" just emerging out of Vienna.

In 1903, when he was finishing up his medical school training and looking to establish himself as a psychiatrist in Basel, he married Emma Rauschenbach, a young lady from one of the wealthiest families in all of Switzerland. Five children were born to Carl and Emma: Agathe, Gret, Franz, Marianne, and Helene. Though the marriage lasted fifty-two years, until Emma's death in 1955, it was not always calm and serene as Jung was very want to have many relationships outside of marriage with women who came and went in his life and practice. Two of the most renowned extramarital partners Jung had, going so far as having them in his own home on a regular basis, were Sabina Spielrein and Toni Wolff. These relationships were fully known by Emma and, owing to Jung's persuasive powers, agreed or at least tolerated them, Emma herself becoming a therapist in the process. Following Jung's publishing of his controversial book, *Answer to Job*, Jung established a life-long friendship with a Catholic priest from England named Father Victor White.

When Jung was thirty-one years old and in full service as a psychiatrist doing clinical work and research at the hospital, he published *Studies in Word Association* based upon his own analysis of mentally ill patients and the use of his developing method of word association as a key tool in the treatment plan. He sent a copy of this work to Sigmund Freud which resulted in the beginning of an acquaintance, not really a friendship, which would have important ramifications for psychoanalysis and psychotherapeutic history. Their relationship lasted six years during which time Freud became convinced that Jung was the heir apparent to lead psychoanalysis into the new century.

However, six years later in 1912, Jung published the book that would essentially bring their mutual respect and working relationship to a halt, namely, *Wandlungen und Symbole der Libido* (English translation in 1916, *The Psychology of the Unconscious*). They both contended their system of analysis was right and the other wrong and, as Freud had done earlier in his career, Jung went through a very severe psychological storm similar to Freud's which he called "neurasthenia and hysteria." For Jung, the break with Freud was further exacerbated with the coming First World War and the troubles in Europe which affected all medical, and especially psychiatric, practice in Austria, Switzerland, and Germany.

Within three years of making Freud's acquaintance, Jung was made editor of the newly founded publication of Freud's professional group called the *Yearbook for Psychoanalytical and Psychopathological Research.* Two years later Jung was also appointed by Freud and his colleagues chairman for life of the *International Psychoanalytical Association.* Troubles began to emerge as Freud and Jung came to challenge each other's views on religion and the libido.

Jung had become increasingly dissatisfied with Freud's heavy, even inordinate, emphasis upon sexual interpretations of the libido which, Freud argued, showed origins from infancy. Jung rather emphasized the close parallels between ancient myths and psychotic fantasies and by explaining human motivation in terms of a larger creative energy. Stepping down from the presidency of the International Psychoanalytic Society, Jung, like Adler before him, established his own professional body called Analytical Psychology. Jung moved his clinical practice to his home in the village of Kenssett on the shores of Lake Zurich where patients from all over the world were attracted to him by his increasingly voluminous publications. Abandoning Freud's famous "couch therapy," Jung chose to have his patients sit in a chair facing him for interactive dialogue. "I confront the patient as one human being to another," Jung explained, because "analysis is a dialogue demanding two partners; the doctor has something to say but so has the patient."

When Clark University invited Sigmund Freud to come to America to receive an honorary doctorate in 1909, Carl Jung was likewise invited to attend, though not to be so honored. Jung was only thirty years old when he published the book that gained him

Freud's attention, namely, *Studies in Word Association*. But at their first meeting, they talked thirteen hours straight according to Freud's wife and children. Freud was then fifty years old and this relationship, based on similar interests and a mutual desire to create something new, lasted six years, ending in May of 1910, the year after the visit to America. Their last face-to-face meeting was in 1913 in Munich where Jung gave a lecture on psychological types, the introverted and extraverted type, in Analytical Psychology. This constituted the introduction of some of the key concepts which came to distinguish Jung's work from Freud's for the next half century. The break was final but not clean. Jung suffered considerably over the next many years and his isolation from professional life outside his little world of patients and writing exacerbated his mental health considerably.

Their primary disagreement, at the end of the day and after all issues related to competing strong egos have subsided, has to do with the theory of the unconscious. Jung differed from Freud whose theory of the unconscious appeared to Jung to be incomplete and unnecessarily negative. Freud conceived the unconscious solely as a repository of repressed emotions and desires, or at least that is the way Jung says Freud's thought. Agreeing with Freud about the personal unconscious, Jung also believed in a collective unconscious where the archetypes of primordial experience reside. Freud would have none of it.

Unlike Freud, who preferred to stay and work strictly at home and, we should remember, suffered severely from cancer, Jung, on the other hand, became extremely active following World War I, not such publishing massive tomes of clinical and speculative studies, but traveling extensively, thanks to the wealth his wife inherited as well as his medical fees from rich patients and his publications.

Patients and the public were fascinated with his passion for analyzing the unconscious, not so much for the "dirt" which Freud believed to be the cause of mental illness, but for the mystery, awe, and excitement of delving into one's own inner self to discover who a person really is to himself. This was popularization of depth psychology at its most marketable best! After thirty books and hundreds of articles on the unconscious, Jung was the acclaimed master of the field. He believed in the power of dreams to interpret the workings of the unconscious. Dreams symbolize ignored or rejected aspects of our own personality, and we want to know what these are. "The dream," Jung wrote, "is the small hidden door in the deepest and most intimate sanctum of the world, which opens to that primeval cosmic night that was soul long before there was conscious ego and will be soul far beyond what a conscious ego could ever reach."

Jung's world travels allowed him to study a wide variety of religions, myths, and symbol systems. Likewise drawing from his patients' recounted dreams and their recurring symbols, Jung developed the concept of the "collective unconsciousness," later refining the concept to distinguish between the personal unconscious, or the repressed feelings and thought developed during an individual's life, and the collective unconscious, or those inherited feelings, thoughts, and memories shared by all humanity. "The unconscious is not just evil by nature, it is also the source of the highest good," Jung wrote, "not only dark but also light, not only bestial, semi human, and demonic but superhuman, spiritual, and, in the classical sense of the word, 'divine'." This "collective" is comprised, said Jung, of the "archetypes" of humanity, the primordial images, occurring time and time again in symbols of religion, myths, fairy tales, and fantasies.

Lecturing while visiting North Africa and the United States, among other places, he delivered the famous Terry Lectures at Yale University in 1938 which were published as *Psychology and Religion.* His visit to India, among all else, led him to become fascinated and deeply involved with Hindu philosophy, and in the process developing key concepts in his analytical psychology which integrated spirituality with studies of the unconscious. Jung believed, based upon his clinical studies and self-analysis, that life has a spiritual purpose beyond material goals. The human person's primary responsibility, then, is to discover and fulfill these innate potentials which must be identified and owned through the process of dream analysis. Furthermore, he believed that this spiritual journey of self-transformation is at the heart of the great world religions, particularly as articulated in their respective mystical traditions.

This "inward journey" was designed for the individual to meet the self while simultaneously and thereby meeting the Divine. Unlike Freud, Jung felt that spiritual experience was indispensable to the well-being of the person and the dream provided access to this inward journey

There are two kinds of dreams, according to Jung. There is the "Big" dream where the poetic force and beauty that occurs mostly during the critical stages of life such as puberty, onset of middle age and within sight of death. The "Little" dreams were those dealing with everyday occurrences. Jung placed great, even grave, importance upon dream content, particularly as he was able to connect the dream's symbols with the archetypal symbols of our primordial unconscious. The dream can be a major source of enlightenment and guidance to the listening, caring individual.

Jung was eighty-seven years old when he died on June 6, 1961, in his little village of Kensett. With thirty books and hundreds of articles published, he was world renowned and world acclaimed. He had traveled the world but towards the end wanted only to stay in a little stone tower he had built near his home in Switzerland. Widowed and with all his children gone away, he continued to see a few patients and continued to write. Though Freud had lived to rejoice at the death of Alfred Adler, Jung outlived Freud by six years and did not, like Freud, rejoice at the passing of his old friend and adversary.

THE CLASSIC TEXT CONSIDERED

Jung got busy and stayed busy, from the time he commenced his medical school training until his final demise, Jung was forever researching and writing, developing clinical modalities of treatment and producing conceptual frameworks for his analysis. It took thirty books and hundreds of articles for Jung to say it all. And, to be frank, he never suggested that he did say it all. Any one text of his published library could arguably be called a classic in its own right, but we have chosen his 1921 book, *Psychological Types*, for our attention here. At the time of its writing, Jung says he was working diligently upon the question, "What does one do with the unconscious?" His answer, he reported, was related to function of the ego and its role in balancing the personal unconscious and the collective unconscious.

He says in his autobiography that he was busy with preparatory work for *Psychological Types* as early as 1921. "This work," he wrote, "sprang originally from my need to define the ways in which my outlook differed from Freud's and Adler's." He came across the problem of "types" in addressing this fundamental distinction between Analytical Psychology and that of both Psychoanalysis and Personal Psychology. "It is one's psychological type," he suggests, "which from the outset determines and limit's a person's judgment. My book," he continues, "was an effort to deal with the relationship of the individual to the world, to people and things." This work yielded the insight that, says Jung, "every judgment made by an individual is conditioned by his personality type and that every point of view is necessarily relative."

Some have argued that these early musings about types derived from his Burgholzli experiences in dealing with differing patterns of hysterical and schizophrenic patients. Whereas hysterics find meaning in the outside world of objects (what Jung called a "centrifugal movement of libido"), schizophrenics, on the other hand, seek meaning within the inner world of their own making through dreams, fantasies, and archetypes (suggesting to Freud a "centripetal tendency of libido"). The former Jung came to label as a type called "extravert" and the later a type called "introvert." H. Crichton-Miller of the Institute of Medical Psychology in London chose rather, in his 1933 book *Psychoanalysis and Its Derivatives,* to trace Jung's interest in types to a 1896 book by Francis Jordan entitled, *Character as Seen in Body and Parentage.* Jung read this book in 1914 when it was brought to his attention by one of his first English disciples, Dr. Constance Long. Jung was at this time wrestling with the problem of inherited psychic traits and was baffled as to how to organize his thoughts on the subject.

Probably from both Burgholzli and Jordan, Jung began toying with the concept of psychological "type" and eventually evolved his now world famous schema of types and sub-types. The bipolar nature of extravert and introvert worked splendidly in his overall schematic. The extravert is primarily directed outwards; the introvert inwards. The extravert is self-expressive whereas the introvert has difficulty in articulation. The extravert is self-seeking in his liking of other people including being a propagandist if necessary; the introvert is detached and self-content to go it alone. The extravert prefers publicity and social interaction; the introvert prefers solitude. From all of this we gather that the extravert is gregarious whereas the introvert is a solitary figure.

From these two main types, now called "general attitude-types," Jung proceeds to a further subdivision of four primary functions, namely, thinking, feeling, intuition and sensation. Every person, Jung argued, possesses these four functions of the psyche, though everyone has a "dominant side" and a "subordinate side," or superior and inferior, when it comes to the functioning of introversion and extraversion. By pairing introversion with the four primary functions of thinking, feeling, intuition, and sensation, and pairing extraversion with thinking, feeling, intuition, and sensation, Jung came up with eight essential personality types. In order to fully appreciate the dynamic insight Jung brought to personality theory, we will spend a moment to characterize each of these eight personality types. Based upon the fundamental principles developed by Jung's concept of personality types, the Myers-Briggs and other personality tests have had a field day during the past fifty or so years. Let us consider each of the eight types briefly here by way of summary.

The *introverted thinker*, given the rationalistic externality of his subjective bias towards facts, Jung believed, is actually more taken with the idea of factual reality than with the facts themselves. Essentially theoretical, he is gifted with an attitude of aloofness and distance bordering on arrogance. Feelings being held at bay, intuition languishes and he struggles with maintaining any sustained friendships but rather embraces a defensive attitude akin to dogmatism and intellectual self-assertion. Commitment to the moral code is strong and a high level of rigidity and intolerance color his attitudes towards the rules of the game.

The *extraverted thinker* is, likewise, a rationalist and is intolerant and fanatical in his relentless pursuit of facts, the truth, what he considers the correct way of things. Discounting opposition, he is always in quest of a formula and promotes it when he finds it or creates it. Found prominently among professional politicians, his convictions are tied to his personal belief that he is right. He has found the answer for his way of logical analysis solves all problems. "Ought" and "must" are paramount in his assessment of duty. Not fearing criticism, he leans towards the sciences and the exactitude of objective analysis of data. Often numbered among the scientists, his method is to gather the facts as he understands and perceives them and then to produce a theory based upon his findings.

The *feeling introvert* is more often, says Jung, found among rationalistic women who appear to others as cold and distant from their feelings and the feelings of others. Appearing to disregard the feelings and opinions of others, there is a hint of superiority and critical neutrality in their social relations. Living by "affective valuation," their likes and dislikes are clearly identified and stated, they love and hate with equal passion and intensity but are deficient in expressing these feelings. More than other types of introverts, they fear and loath the thought of being dominated by outside forces. Though considered by others as cold and hard, they in reality are neither but fail to show their true selves for fear of domination by the outside world.

The *feeling extravert* is, says Jung, also more prevalent among women. These individuals are objective, conventional, and social. They enjoy and admire the common things of society. As an extreme counter to introverted personalities, they are extremely expressive of their feelings. Extremely suggestible by the social environment, their responses are often exaggerated in their attempt to reach a conformity to their social world. They make friends easily and are thereby greatly influenced by their friends' attitudes and values. Intense, effervescent, and sociable, these are the dominant characteristics of the feeling extravert.

The *sensorial introvert* "appreciates the good things of life" but is essentially irrational and is, therefore, often dominated by the changing flux of external events. Dominated by their susceptibility to objective reality, their personal feelings and responses are uppermost in their guiding responses to life. They assess the world, its demands, its ethical dilemmas, its surprises, with sensorial emotion, always personalizing the objective into something related and relevant only to themselves personally.

The *sensorial extravert* actively seeks out new and provocative experiences in the world for their life is entirely conditioned by their objective environment. They are the most easily bored of Jung's psychological types for their personal resources are minimal and undervalued by themselves. Constant external stimulus is their delight and demand, and they have no patience with any pursuit or theory that involves the abstract. A discriminating critic of sense impressions, they become connoisseurs of wine, art, poetry, and all things perceived as refined by the wider culture. Considered by all to be good company, they are realistic, sensual, jolly, and a social delight though devoid of personal intuition and objectivity.

The *intuitive introvert* is the exact opposite of the sensorial extravert and is singularly devoid of external facts. The world of the intuitive introvert is decidedly subjective and devoid of any concern for what others might call objective reality. Appearing to be aloof and unconcerned about the outside world of deeds and facts, they come across as slightly mad or debilitatingly artistic to their own detriment. Concentrating upon the creation of their own interior world, they often come across as a crank or oddball. Mystic, dreamer, and eccentric are characteristic terms for the intuitive introvert.

The *intuitive extravert* is pronouncedly unstable, always seeking change and something different. Constancy is taboo and their quest for the new, the different, the ever-changing world around them leaves the impression that they are optimists. Flighty is a common term for such individuals as they jump from one idea to another, one activity to another, never really finishing anything but ever questing for something new and different. Often and to no one's surprise, their decisions are frequently good ones even if they are unable to stay the course. They inspire people with their vision, their capacity to imagine a new and better world. Visionary, changeable, and creative are characteristic terms for the intuitive extravert.

His book on the subject, *Psychological Types,* catapulted him into world fame and the practical results of these ideas produced a plethora of personality tests, some based upon Jung's own eight types while other professionals in the field produced their own types and categories. The idea, however, of being able to divide and subdivide the human personality into identifiable and testable characteristics caught on and is still very much with us.

THEORIES AND CONCEPTS

The path to self-knowledge, the goal of all therapy, Jung believed, lies in expanding the perimeters of human consciousness. We are too narrow, too restricted, too self-protective in our thinking about life and our investigation of our inner selves. This quest for self-knowledge, Jung believed, was essentially the nature of human culture. "Attainment of consciousness is culture in the broadest sense, and self-knowledge is therefore the very essence of this process" (1921). The emphasis in Jung's work, writings, and therapy was all upon the need for "a personal, contemporary consciousness, but also a supra-personal consciousness with a sense of historical continuity." The psyche, according to Jung, "is a self-regulating system that maintains its equilibrium just as the body does. Every process," he explains, "that goes too far immediately and inevitably calls forth compensations, and without these there would be neither a normal metabolism nor a normal psyche." It is the psychic balance of conscious and unconscious materials which the ego seeks to monitor and nurture in the mentally healthy person.

Before we explore Jung's concept of consciousness, we are required to investigate the composites of the "psyche," which, says Jung, consists of three components, viz., the ego, the personal unconscious which includes its complexes, and the collective unconscious which includes its archetypes, the persona, the anima or animus, and the shadow. "A more or less superficial layer of the unconscious," wrote Jung in 1934, "is undoubtedly persona. I call it the 'personal unconscious.' But this personal layer rests upon a deeper layer, which does not derive from personal experience and is not a personal acquisition but is inborn. This deeper layer I call the 'collective unconscious.' I have chosen the term 'collective' because this part of the unconscious is not individual but universal; in contrast to the personal psyche, it has contents and modes of behavior that are more or less the same everywhere and in all individuals" (1934).

These three conceptual components of the human mind, viz., the ego, the personal unconscious, and the collective unconscious, also embody the characteristics of introversion and extraversion, the functions of thinking, feeling, sensing, and intuiting, and, finally, the self which is the fully developed and fully unified personality in search of self-actualization.

The ego, for Jung, is the conscious mind and is the center of personality and personality, says Jung, is essentially of two types driving the individual in either the direction of "extraversion" or "introversion" leading Jung to suggest that all people can be divided into these two groups. The ego, he argues, consists of conscious thinking, feeling, sensing, and intuiting. To these four psychological functions of personality must be added, then, the two orientations of extraversion and introversion, making it possible for eight personality types as we have discussed: thinking introvert, thinking extravert, feeling introvert, feeling extravert, and so on.

The ego, unlike Freud's mere executive arbitrator between the id and the superego, is responsible for the individual's feelings of identity and continuity, and is essentially at the center of personality. The personal unconscious is a component of the human mind adjacent but not contiguous with the ego. Its content is comprised of past experiences now forgotten, or ignored, and which failed to make a lasting impression upon the conscious mind. This data is all accessible to human consciousness by using the right means of retrieval and there is a great deal of mutual interaction between the personal unconscious and the ego. A grouping of this data in the personal unconscious Jung calls a "complex." A complex is a constellation of feelings, thoughts, perceptions, and memories grouped and sorted in the personal unconscious and may, with proper guidance and effort, be retrieved for analysis, utility, and therapeutic benefit to the individual. The "mother complex" is an example of this grouped constellation of experiences spanning an individual's infancy, childhood, adolescence, and adulthood, all of which are accessible to the ego but deposited in the personal unconscious.

The concept of a collective unconscious, a sort of

transpersonal unconscious, is unique to Jung's Analytical Psychology, at least in the fashion in which he has chosen to define and use it. Both original and highly controversial, this concept in Jungian psychology, particularly his personality theory, has caused a great deal of stir among clinical psychotherapist and theorists. It is the core and power source of the human psyche and when mental illness appears it dominates both the ego and the personal unconscious. Jung believed the collective unconscious to be the repository of latent memory traces inherited from man's ancestral past, a past that included racial history as an animal species. He called it the storehouse of "psychic residue" of man's evolutionary development and it is almost completely detached from anything personal in the life of an individual and it is present in all human beings at all times and in all places. It is the foundation, Jung argued, of the whole structure of human personality. Jung says that "the unconscious holds possibilities which are locked away from the conscious mind, for it has at its disposal all subliminal contents, all those things which have been forgotten or overlooked, as well as the wisdom and experience of uncounted centuries, which are laid down in its archetypal organs."

The fundamental foundation of Jung's whole argument for a collective unconscious (that concept which got him into trouble and kept him in trouble throughout his professional life) was, as we have been saying, the notion of "archetype." The human mind sorts our experiences in the ego into clusters based upon the grand categories of primordial archetypes. There are many of these and their origins are from the ancient past of human evolution carried forward from generation to generation, by means of the collective unconscious. Freud's use of the concept of the collective unconscious, he called "phylogenetic endowment" and placed little importance on it for therapeutic purposes. For Jung, it constituted the core of analysis and treatment. In his 1934 book, *The Archetypes and the Collective Unconscious,* Jung attempted to address skeptics and critics of his notion of the archetype particularly as relates to empirical proof of their reality. We must now turn to the question of how the existence of archetypes can be proven.

Since archetypes are supposed to produce certain psychic

forms, we must discuss how and where one can get hold of the material demonstrating these forms. The main source, then, is dreams, which have the advantage of being involuntary, spontaneous products of nature not falsified by any conscious purpose. "By questioning the individual one can ascertain which of the motifs appearing in the dream are known to him. ... consequently, we must look for motifs which could not possibly be known to the dreamer and yet behavior functionally of the archetype known from historical sources." Jung, then, in his clinical practice became the great interpreter based upon his incomparable knowledge of the mythic literature and religious symbols of the world.

The ARCHETYPE functions, for Jung, as a center of energy which moves from generation to generation, carried by repetition and continual elaboration in the complex of human experiences. The nucleus of a complex is usually an archetype and the archetype can enter into the personal consciousness of an individual by way of certain types of associated experiences, revealed in the dream or word associations. There are countless archetypes accumulated over the centuries of human development and some of these have such identifiable characteristics as to constitute entities identifiable through analysis, such as in particular the persona, the anima and animus, and the shadow.

The PERSONA is a mask which is put on by an individual in response to demands required of the social environment and tradition and in consort with his own archetypal needs. It constitutes the role society expects him to play and which he, in turn, is willing to play, within reason. When conflict arises, mental illness appears. To the extent that the individual is living in consort with his archetypal inner needs reflected in the persona he has been given and has chosen to adopt, he will remain healthy. The "nucleus" from which the persona develops, then, is one's own archetype.

The ANIMA and the ANIMUS are generally recognized in all branches of the psychological sciences as indicative of the bisexual nature of the human animal. Physiologically, the human animal secretes both male and female sex hormones, and on the psychological level, masculine and feminine characteristics are found in both sexes as well. Man, says Jung, apprehends the nature of woman by virtue of his anima, and woman apprehends the nature of man by virtue of her animus. Mental illness results when there is an imbalance or a disconnection between an individual's "idealized" (archetypal) image of the opposite sex and the reality of that person.

The SHADOW is possibly the most ancient of archetypes and originates from the lowest forms of evolutionary life which we have inherited and, therefore, the Shadow typifies the animal nature of man more than any other and expresses itself in images and ideas of evil, the devil, wickedness and the enemy. It constitutes the content base of feelings of evil thoughts and desires within the human person. It is the dark side of a controlled ego and personality must have the energy which derives from the Shadow just as it must have the energy derived from the images of other archetypes such as mother and wise old man.

The SELF is the center of personality and all other components of the human mind form a circling constellation around it. It holds the mental structure in place, providing unity, equilibrium, and stability to the individual's state of mind. The self functions as an archetype and constitutes the goal of every person striving for a sense of wholeness and completeness in their lives. Jung believed that true religious experiences are as close as most people get to a fully realized sense of self. Before the fully actualized self can emerge, says Jung, it is necessary for the various components of the personality which we have discussed to become fully developed and individuated. Jung believed that this realization is not possible until at least middle age and more probably old age is the most likely time for the true self to emerge.

SELF-ACTUALIZATION is, says Jung, the fundamental goal of personality development. This occurs only when the person has developed the capacity to differentiate the various systems operative within his psyche, called "individuation," and has realized a harmony of all component parts, called the "transcendent function." When the self has attained to its rightful place as the center of the personality, self-actualization is realized. It is more a process than a point at which to arrive. This process takes years of intentional effort and usually can occur, if ever, during old age when ego-affirmation behavior has taken a back seat to the quest for self and personal individuation leading to self-actualization of the individual. Jung's therapeutic treatment aimed at reconciling the diversity of personality components, of integrating the points of opposition between extroversion and introversion, between feeling and thinking, sensing and intuiting. The achievement of this integrality of the self leads to an intentioned state of individuality which gives rise to wholeness of self or what Jung called "self-actualization."

Not known for his humility, Jung nevertheless in 1933 wrote in his book, *Modern Man in Search of a Soul,* this: "It is in applied psychology, if anywhere, that today we should be modest and grant validity to a number of apparently contradictory opinions; for we are still far from having anything like a thorough knowledge of the human psyche, that most challenging field of scientific enquiry. For the present, we have merely more or less plausible opinions that defy reconciliation" (1933).

With modern molecular biology, there has been no evidence of such archetypal primordial residue found in human DNA and, thus, much of Jung's system is called into scientific question.

CARK GUSTAV JUNG'S BIOGRAPHY

Carl Gustav Jung by Frank McLynn. NY: St. Martin's Griffin, 1996.

CARL GUSTAV JUNG'S PRIMARY SOURCES

Works arranged by original publication date if known:

Psychiatric Studies. The Collected Works of C. G. Jung Vol. 1. 1953, ed. Michael Fordham, London: Routledge & Kegan Paul, and Princeton, N.J.: Bollingen. (This was the first of 18 volumes plus separate bibliography and index. Not including revisions the set was completed in 1967.)

Jung, C. G. (1904–1907) *Studies in Word Association*. London: Routledge & K. Paul. (contained in *Experimental Researches*, Collected Works Vol. 2)

The Psychology of Dementia Praecox. (1907; 2nd ed. 1936) New York: Nervous and Mental Disease Publ. Co. (Contained in *The Psychogenesis of Mental Disease*, Collected Works Vol. 3. This is the disease now known as schizophrenia).

The Psychogenesis of Mental Disease. 1991 ed. London: Routledge. (Collected Works Vol. 3) (1907)

Psychology of the Unconscious : a study of the transformations and symbolisms of the libido, a contribution to the history of the evolution of thought. London: Kegan Paul Trench Trubner. (revised in 1952 as *Symbols of Transformation*, Collected Works Vol 15, (1912)

Collected Papers on Analytical Psychology (2nd ed.). London: Balliere Tindall & Cox. (contained in *Freud and Psychoanalysis*, Collected Works Vol. 4) (1917)

Two Essays on Analytical Psychology (1966 revised 2nd ed. Collected Works Vol. 7). London: Routledge, (1917, 1928).

Psychological Types, or, *The Psychology of Individuation*. London: Kegan Paul Trench Trubner. (Collected Works Vol.6, (1921).

Contributions to Analytical Psychology. London: Routledge & Kegan Paul, (1928).

The Psychology of Kundalini Yoga: notes of a seminar by C.G. Jung. 1996 ed. Princeton, N.J.: Princeton University Press, (1932).

Modern Man in Search of a Soul. London: Kegan Paul Trench Trubner, (1955 ed. Harvest Books, (1933).

The Archetypes and the Collective Unconscious. (1981 2nd ed.

Collected Works Vol.9 Part 1), Princeton, N.J.: Bolingen, (1934–1954).

Psychology and Religion The Terry Lectures. New Haven: Yale University Press. (contained in *Psychology and Religion: West and East* Collected Works Vol. 11, (1938).

The Integration of the Personality. London: Routledge and Kegan Paul, (1940).

Psychology and Alchemy (2nd ed. 1968 Collected Works Vol. 12). London: Routledge, (1944).

Essays on Contemporary Events. London: Kegan Paul, (1947). *On the Nature of the Psyche*. 1988 ed. London: Ark Paperbacks. (contained in Collected Works Vol. 8), (1947, revised 1954).

Foreword, pp. xxi-xxxix (19 pages), to Wilhelm/Baynes translation of *The I Ching or Book of Changes*. Bollingen Edition XIX, Princeton University Press.(contained in Collected Works Vol. 11), (1949).

Aion: Researches into the Phenomenology of the Self (Collected Works Vol. 9 Part 2). Princeton, N.J.: Bollingen, (1951).

Synchronicity: An Acausal Connecting Principle. 1973 2nd ed. Princeton, N.J.: Princeton University Press, (contained in Collected Works Vol. 8), (1952).

Mysterium Coniunctionis: An Inquiry into the Separation and Synthesis of Psychic Opposites in Alchemy. London: Routledge. (2nd ed. 1970 Collected Works Vol. 14), (1965). This was Jung's last book length work, completed when he was eighty.

The Undiscovered Self (Present and Future). 1959 ed. New York: American Library. 1990 ed. Bollingen, (50 p. essay, also contained in collected Works Vol. 10), (1957).

Psyche and Symbol: A Selection from the Writings of C.G. Jung.

Garden City, N.Y.: Doubleday, (1958).

Basic Writings. New York: Modern Library, (1959).

Memories, Dreams, Reflections. London: Collins. This is Jung's autobiography, recorded and edited by Aniela Jaffe, (1962).

Conversations with Carl Jung and Reactions from Ernest Jones. New York: Van Nostrand, (1964).

Man and His Symbols. Garden City, N.Y.: Doubleday, (1964).

The Practice of Psychotherapy: Essays on the Psychology of the Transference and other Subjects (Collected Works Vol. 16). Princeton, N.J.: Princeton University Press, (1966).

The Development of Personality. 1991 ed. London: Routledge. Collected Works Vol. 17, (1967).

Four Archetypes; Mother, Rebirth, Spirit, Trickster. Princeton, N.J.: Princeton University Press. (contained in Collected Works Vol. 9 part 1), (1970).

Dreams. Princeton, N.J.: Princeton University Press (compilation from Collected Works Vols. 4, 8, 12, 16), (1974).

The Portable Jung. a compilation, New York: Penguin Books, (1976).

(1978). *Abstracts of the Collected Works of C.G. Jung*. Washington, D.C.: U.S. Govt. Printing Office, (1978).

The Essential Jung. a compilation, Princeton, N.J.: Princeton University Press, Jung, (1983)

Psychology and the East. London: Ark. (contained in Collected Works Vol. 11), (1986).

Dictionary of Analytical Psychology. London: Ark Paperbacks,

(1987).

Psychology and Western Religion. London: Ark Paperbacks. (contained in Collected Works Vol. 11), (1988).

The World Within C.G. Jung in his own words [videorecording]. New York, NY: Kino International : Dist. by Insight Media, (1990).

Psychological Types (a revised ed.). London: Routlege, (1991).

Jung on Active Imagination. Princeton, N.J.: Princeton University Press, (1997).

Jung's *Seminar on Nietzsche's Zarathustra* (Abridged ed.). Princeton, N.J.: Princeton University Press, (1998).

Atom and Archetype : The Pauli/Jung Letters, 1932-1958, Princeton, N.J.: Princeton University Press, (2001).

CHAPTER FOUR
Viktor Frankl and Logotherapy

BIOGRAPHICAL SUMMARY

The Third School of Viennese Psychotherapy was established by Viktor Emil Frankl. As with Freud, the founder of the school of Psychoanalysis and with Adler, the founder of the school of Individual Psychology, Frankl was a Jew, a physician, a neurologist and a native of Vienna. These points of continuity with Freud and Adler are not inconsequential and will appear again and again in the discussion of his life's work more so than in the work of either Freud or Adler. The reasons for this are complex and numerous and we will point them out as we explore the world in which logotherapy appeared.

His father and previous ancestors were civil servants (*Beamtenfamilie*), were moderately practicing Jews and were citizens of Vienna through the good times and bad. Viktor was the middle of three children and, reportedly, knew he wanted to be a physician by the time he was four years old. He became interested in psychology early in his life and at the time of his graduating from the Gymnasium, his leaving paper dealt with the psychology of philosophical thinking. In 1923, he entered the University of Vienna's school of medicine, later choosing to specialize in neurology and psychiatry with depression and suicide his primary fields of concentration. During these years he had personal contact with both Freud and Adler. He went so far as to publish an article in Adler's journal on a topic of mutual interest to Frankl and to psychoanalysis.

He was dedicated to his studies and respected by his peers and professional colleagues alike. In 1924, while still a student, he was elected President of the *Skozialistische Mittelschuler Osterreich* which provided the arena in which he and his assistants counseled students during their examination trials, a difficult time for many students when not infrequently students took their life due to failure. On his watch, there was not a single instance of student suicide and this would set the stage for his life's work following his own severe trials in the concentration camps of Hitler's Third Reich.

The immediate result of this great success was his being appointed, following medical school, to head the *Selbstmorderpavillon* (the so-called "suicide pavilion") at the General Hospital in Vienna. During his tenure from 1933-1937 and under his clinical supervision, he and his colleagues treated over 30,000 women prone to suicide. However and commencing in 1938 with the rise of anti-Semitism in Austria, he was prohibited from treating the so-called Aryan patients because he was a Jew. Feeling compelled to move into private practice during these troubled times, he did so but in 1940 he was called to head the neurological department of the Rothschild Hospital where, among other things, he practiced as a neurosurgeon in keeping with his medical training. Jews were allowed, indeed, welcomed to practice medicine in this Vienna hospital and it is reported that on countless occasions his medical opinion was crucial in the saving of patients' lives who were otherwise earmarked for euthanasia under the Nazi euthanasia program.

In 1941, he married Tilly Grosser and the very next year, on the 25th of September, he and Tilly, with his parents, were deported to the concentration camp of Theresienstadt where his father died the next year of enforced starvation. While being forced to do day labor, Frankl, along with two distinguished colleagues, Drs. Leo Baeck and Regina Jonas, continued to practice medicine as best they could, concentrating primarily upon psychiatric practice as relates to depression and suicide. Psychiatry happily did not require much medical paraphernalia and their practice thrived in this inhuman situation.

At Theresienstadt, he was initially assigned to serve as a general practitioner in the clinic for inmates but his psychiatric skills being observed and his training coming to light, he was asked by the camp directors to establish a special unit to help newcomers to the camp overcome shock and grief. From this, he eventually created a suicide watch unit. It is said that during these dark days, he was known to have regularly, upon finishing his day's labor in the suicide unit, stood outside in the cold, lonely darkness giving lectures on various aspects of psychiatric health as a means of maintaining his own sanity and, as he reflected later in life, attempting against all odds to objectify his experience for purposes of scientific analysis and pragmatic assessment of its relevance to the meaning of life.

Frankl was fortunate enough to have been assigned to the psychiatric care ward and was made head of the neurological clinic in Block B IV which had been established and was being maintained as a camp service for psychic hygiene and the mental care of the sick and weary who were suffering primarily from acute depression. Camp rules precluded, under pain of punishment, any attempt to intervene in a suicide of an inmate at the camp. Interestingly enough and not without its own irony, Frankl was granted permission to host a series of lectures at Theresienstadt on such topics as "Sleep and Its Disturbances," "Body and Soul," "Medical Care of Soul," "Psychology of Mountaineering," "Rax and Schneeberg," "How I Keep My Nerves Healthy," "Existential Problems in Psychotherapy," and "Social Psychotherapy." None of his lectures survived the camp!

During the summer of 1943, Frankl organized a closed-session meeting of the Scientific Society in which he lectured on the topic, "Life-Exhaustion and Life-Courage in Terezin." Such a meeting of the camp physicians and scientists being held was extremely dangerous but the hunger for professional conversation overrode any impeding fears they harbored while living and surviving in the death camps. These enduring interests of his in psychotherapy, depression, and life-based issues telegraph his great contribution to mental health research which would eventuate in the development of his system of psychotherapy, first called "existential analysis," and finally "logotherapy."

In October of 1944, Frank was transported to Auschwitz. Shortly thereafter, his mother and his brother died in Turkheim, a concentration camp not far from Dachau where Frankl was subsequently transported that same month. Simultaneously, Frankl's wife had been shipped to the Bergen-Belsen concentration camp where she soon died of labor exhaustion and forced starvation as well. Amidst the suffering, humiliation, and diminishment of the value of human life on all fronts, Frankl managed to write a book in manuscript form reflecting upon his experiences as a Jew and a psychiatrist in these unbelievable circumstances. The manuscript, alas, was taken from him by the guards even though he attempted to hide it in his clothing. Subsequently, he commenced the rewrite of the document on bits of paper, sequestering it in the lining of his coat. After the Liberation, it was eventually published and became an internationally acclaimed best seller, namely, *The Doctor and the Soul.*

In the spring of 1945 with the invasion of the Allied Forces into Germany, Frankl was liberated. Of all of his many relatives from Vienna and the rural countryside of Austria, only his sister survived the camps. All others perished before the Liberation. Through it all, Frankl continued to believe that even in the midst of the most absurd, painful and dehumanizing situations, life has potential meaning and that even in the midst of such suffering, meaning can be found with proper guidance. This belief was the basis upon which he launched his psychotherapeutic methodology called logotherapy. In his now famous, *Man's Search for Meaning,* Frankl wrote: "If a prisoner felt that he could no longer endure the realities of camp life, he found a way out in his mental life -- an invaluable opportunity to dwell in the spiritual domain, the one that the SS were unable to destroy. Spiritual life strengthened the prisoner, helped him adapt, and thereby improved his chances of survival."

Following his three awful years of concentration camp life, Frankl chose to return to Vienna in 1945 during which time he wrote the now famous book, in English titled *Man's Search for Meaning,* but in its original German title was "*trotzdem ja zum Leben sagen*": *Ein Psychologe erlebt das Konzentrationslager* (translated literally, "...saying yes to life regardless: a Psychologist Experiences the Concentration Camp."). Astoundingly and amazingly, this book is a recounting of his concentration experiences from the perspective of a psychiatrist, an objective observer as medical professional and neurologist. It captured the imagination of all who read it, whether layman or professional.

The next year, 1946, he was appointed director of the Vienna Poliklinik of Neurology and he remained in that position until 1971. The year following his appointment there, he married his second wife, Eleonore Katharina Schwindt, whom, says he, he fell in love with the "first time I saw her" even though he was twice her age. Nine years following his appointment to the Poliklinik, he was made professor of neurology and psychiatry at the University of Vienna, where he had taken his medical training as a youngster, and was also made a visiting professor while he resided at Harvard University. He won, among many other honors, the Oskar Pfister Prize from the American Society of Psychiatry. He continued to teach until the age of eighty-five and in 1995 completed his autobiography and his final book was published in 1997. Of his thirty-two published books, many have appeared in numerous translations. He is acclaimed, most conspicuously, as the founder (and creator) of logotherapy and he lectured and taught all over the world, receiving twenty-nine honorary doctorates in recognition of his great contribution to psychotherapy and the philosophy of the meaning of life. Frankl died quietly on September 2, 1997, in Vienna, at the age of ninety-two.

From Freud's "will to pleasure" to Adler's "will to power," Frankl believed that logotherapy lead people to an understanding of the "will to meaning," and to this understanding he gave his life's work. Frankl said,

> We need to stop asking about the meaning of life, and instead, to think of ourselves as those who were being questioned by life ... Our answer must consist, not in talk and meditation, but in right action and in right conduct. Life ultimately means taking the responsibility to find the right answer to its problems and to fulfill the tasks which it constantly sets for each individual ...It does not really matter what we expect from life; rather, what matters is what life expects from us (1959).

THE CLASSICAL TEXT CONSIDERED

No psychotherapist considered in this study will have published just one book. Some have published many and each has published a few which have gained international acclaim. Certainly this is true of Viktor Frankl, for his two major books, namely, *The Doctor and the Soul: From Psychotherapy to logotherapy,* and *Man's Search for Meaning,* have established Viktor Frankl as an undisputed authority on psychotherapy in the modern world. So, in all fairness, we will look at both these works as relates to Frankl's Third School of Viennese Psychotherapy.

In introducing his work, Frankl reports the following:

> I remember my dilemma in a concentration camp when faced with a man and a woman who were close to suicide; both had told me that they expected nothing more from life. I asked both my fellow prisoners whether the question was really what we expected from life. Was it not, rather, what life was expecting from us? (1959).

The humility of Frankl was often extremely disarming. For example, he once said that "the aim of logotherapy is not to take the place of existing psychotherapy, but only to complement it, thus forming a picture of man in his wholeness -- which includes the spiritual dimension." "Spiritual distress" was a concern of his. Not particularly religious himself, he was concerned, however, about the inner person. In this sense, he says, "the sense of despair over the meaning of life may be called an *existential neurosis* as opposed to clinical neurosis." Furthermore, he explains, it is conceivable that frustration of the will-to-meaning may also lead to neurosis, what "I have chosen to call *existential frustration.*" And, explains Frankl, because neuroses are commonly noogenic in nature and origin, logotherapy is a specific therapeutic treatment.

Frankl believed that "life has a meaning to the last breath" and even in the midst of the inhumanity of his concentration experience, where, says he, consuming one's own mucus from a cold meant salvaging a few extra calories or peeing on oneself to experience momentarily the pleasure of warmth against one's body or the warmth which came by developing a fever in the work camps, all spoke of our quest for meaning in our lives. The right kind of suffering, he explains, "facing your fate without flinching--is the highest achievement that has been granted to man." Always the clinician, he chose to illustrate this point with a clinical case study and I quote it in its entirety:

A nurse in my department suffered from a tumor which proved to be inoperable. In her despair the nurse asked me to visit her. Our conversation revealed that the cause of her despair was not so much her illness in itself as he incapacity to work. She had loved her profession above all else, and now she could no longer follow it. What should I say? Her situation was really hopeless; nevertheless, I tried to explain to her that to work eight or ten hours per day is no great thing -- many people can do that. But to be as eager to work as she was, and so incapable of work, and yet not to despair -- that would be an achievement few could attain. And then I asked her: "Are you not being unfair to all those thousands of sick people to whom you have dedicated your life; are you not being unfair to act now as if the life of an incurable invalid were without meaning? If you behave as if the meaning of our life consisted in being able to work so many hours a day, you take away from all sick people the right to live and the justification for their existence.

Herein lies the essence of the "will-to-meaning" in Frankl's thought. The pragmatic realism of Frankl's insight into the meaning of life was one of his most profoundly disarming qualities. He wasn't a romantic nor was he an idealist. He was bluntly realistic about life and the suffering and pain, as well as the joys, which come every individual's way sooner or later. "It goes without saying," he wrote, "that the realization of attitudinal values, the achievement of meaning through suffering, can take place only when the suffering is unavoidable and inescapable." Suffering and pain are not to be sought; but when encountered, the human person has choices as to how they are to be met. "I have said," says Frankl, "that man should not ask what he may expect from life, but should rather understand that life expects something from him." Herein lies the essence and genius of logotherapy. The logotherapeutic process, Frankl has argued, is itself educational, educating the individual not simply to look for personal meaning but to explore the meaning which he himself brings to the life situation. "Logotherapy is ultimately education towards responsibility," Frankl wrote, "the patient must push forward independently toward the concrete meaning of his own existence."

In the treatment of the individual, Frankl believed therein was the broader treatment for society at large. No individual is alone in the world and the embracing of one's collectivity with the world, with the social environment of his life situation, is the beginning of mental health. Frankl's concern over the existence of what he called a "collective neurosis" gave way to his belief that the individual's own neurosis, what he called an "existential neurosis," constituted the cure for society at large. Cure the individual's existential neurosis and society's collective neurosis doesn't have a chance. This collective neurosis, which so fascinated Frankl, consisted of four symptoms. First, there is the "planless, day-to-day attitude toward life" which simply indicates that each individual wonders mindlessly through life without direction, hope, or strategy. The dread of war, the overarching fear of global destruction, fosters a kind of do-nothing attitude in the face of this debilitating fear, a gripping kind of anticipatory anxiety which creates helplessness and indolence on the part of a whole society.

Furthermore, beside this absence of motivation and in the wake of no planning, there is the onset of a "fatalistic attitude" toward life. Life has no plan and we are the pawns of fate, helpless to help ourselves. Outside circumstances control the individual and society and there is nothing that can be done to change that. The triumph of a fatalistic worldview, then, gives rise to the third symptom of the collective neurosis, which is "collective thinking" rather than individuated, self-motivated thought. The numbing attraction of the "mindless masses" is strong for those in the grip of the collective neurosis. Man abandons any thought of personal freedom, gives up individual responsibility, and submerges himself into the collective thoughts of the mindless masses. Finally, the collective neurosis produces fanaticism. "While the collectivist ignores his own personality," explains Frankl, "the fanatic ignores that of the other man, the man who thinks differently." The individual and the group alike are possessed by their mindless opinions rather than having and controlling opinions and insights of their own. Group think produces fanaticism and the collective neurosis, then, is in full sway.

It is the "moral conflict," explains Frankl, which produces the cure for the collective neurosis and that cure is what he has chosen to call "existential neurosis." This existential neurosis, an individual rather than collective neurosis, is the product of a moral conflict, a "conflict of conscience." It is the moral conflict itself which serves as a protection for the individual from the symptoms of the collective neurosis, symptoms such as the life without plan or direction, the life of fatalism, of the group think, and fanaticism. "A man who suffers from collective neurosis will overcome it," says Frankl, "if he is enabled once more to hear the voice of conscience and to suffer from it. Existential neurosis will then cure the collective neurosis!"

Within this context, we are reminded of one of Frankl's favorite philosophical statements about the meaning of life, adopted and adapted, ironically, from Frederick Nietzsche. "He who has a WHY to live can put up with almost any HOW." Throughout his writing and lecturing career, he used this statement over and over again. From his autobiography, he relates a story which captures the essence of his fascination with this statement. Here is a paraphrase of his story as told by Edward Kim.

> One night when his fellow prisoners of a concentration camp had received word that they would all be gassed the next day, the people looked to the Viennese psychiatrist for solace. He in turn was able to help each person discover personal reasons to endure which carried them through that dark night with hope and dignity. For example, Frankl helped one person overcome despair by reaffirming the man's fleeting hope that his suffering and death would somehow mean that his wife and family would be saved from such a fate. Instead of perceiving his situation as mere waste and tragedy, this man was enabled to convert his inescapable plight into a noble, heroic deed (2001).

Elaborating upon the modified quote from Neitzsche, Frankl says: "a man who becomes conscious of the responsibility

98

he bears toward a human being who affectionately waits for him, or to an unfinished work, will never be able to throw away his life. He knows the 'why' for his existence, and will be able to bear almost any 'how'."

Logotherapy, according to Frankl, "considers man as a being whose main concern consists in fulfilling a meaning and in actualizing values, rather than in the mere gratification and satisfaction of drives and instincts." The nature of being human requires the individual, at all times, to be aware of one's own personal responsibility. The humanizing component of an inhuman experience is the individual's willingness and determination to salvage from the situation an opportunity to serve. "It is life itself that asks questions of man," says Frankl, "It is not up to man to question; rather, he should recognize that he is questioned, questioned by life." Two guiding principles, according to Frankl, direct us to answering the questions of life, namely, conscience and regret. "Live as you were living for the second time and had acted as wrongly the first time as you are about to act now. ... Once an individual really puts himself into this imagined situation, he will instantaneously become conscious of the full gravity of the responsibility that every man bears throughout every moment of his life: the responsibility for what he will make of the next hour, for how he will shape the next day" (1965).

THEORIES AND CONCEPTS

According to Frankl, life has meaning under all circumstances, even in the most dire situations. "What matters is not the meaning of life in general," Frankl wrote, "but rather the specific meaning of a person's life at a given moment." Meaning is not "invented" but rather "detected," he points out. We can discover meaning in life, he suggests, in three different ways: (1) by doing a deed; (2) by experience a value -- nature, a work of art, another person, love, etc., and (3) by suffering. In his autobiography, Frankl relates a story relative to this third way of finding meaning in life, the way he spent so much time analyzing:

Once, an elderly general practitioner consulted me because of his severe depression. He could not overcome the loss of his wife who had died two years before and whom he had loved above all else. Now how could I help him? What should I tell him? I refrained from telling him anything, but instead confronted him with a question, 'What would have happened, Doctor, if you had died first, and your wife would have had to survive you?' 'Oh,' he said, 'for her this would have been terrible; how she would have suffered!' Whereupon I replied, 'You see, Doctor, such a suffering has been spared her, and it is you who have spared her this suffering; but now, you have to pay for it by surviving and mourning her.' He said no word but shook my hand and calmly left the office (1959).

A concept of humanity is held, consciously or not, by every school of psychotherapy. We have seen it in Freud, Adler, and Jung, and so likewise here with Frankl. That "concept of man," says Frankl, affects everything, all conceptual development, all theories of treatment, all clinical perceptions. We must raise this concept of man into the light of day for critical analysis if we ever hope to understand the differences in psychotherapeutic modalities of treatment. "For," says Frankl, "a psychotherapist's concept of man ... can reinforce the patient's neurosis, can be wholly nihilistic." For Frankl, there are three fundamental characteristics of human existence which converge to define the human person, namely, spirituality, freedom, and responsibility. We will here take a closer look at these fundamental characteristics for, according to Frankl, they affect every attempt to understand who we are and what we are to do.

Neither a proponent of religion and religious institutions nor an opponent, Frankl simply intends for spirituality not to be tied up with a specific notion of religion. Where religion helps a person through the day, Frankl has no objection to it. Where religious worldview and ethos stifle, cripple, or delude an individual, Frankl is opposed to it. What Frankl means by "spirituality" as a fundamental component of human nature is man's capacity for a sense of awe, wonder, and mystery, even reverence, in one's assessing the experience of life. The connectedness of all things as experienced in moments of high sensitivity or even ecstasy is the role spirituality plays in the human character. A deeply felt sense of beauty and power and wonder in the universe, a heightened experience of integrality, what I have in another place chosen to call "systemic integrality," constitutes what spirituality means in logotherapy. Whether one is a theist, an atheist, or an agnostic, Frankl contends that the dynamics of spirituality can be equally and meaningfully operative within a person's life.

Complimenting spirituality, Frankl suggests, is the characteristic of "freedom." "Freedom means," he explains, "freedom in the face of three things: (1) the instincts; (2) inherited disposition; and (3) environment." Frankl engages in a long and definitive discussion of freedom in his little classic, *The Doctor and the Soul*, owing no doubt to his own personal experience with its presence and absence in his trying experiences in captivity. The converging of these three components of instincts, heredity, and environment constitutes the matrix out of which the human experience of freedom can grow and thrive in a person's life. To rise above one's instincts, says Frankl, is a distinctively human possibility and, unlike Freud's obsession with the power of instincts in governing human behavior, Frankl specifically calls upon the responsible person to take his instincts in hand, use them but control them, for service to others. Likewise with heritage, one cannot deny one's own genetic composition but in the acknowledging of it one asserts power over its domination. A determinist, Frankl was most certainly not. He believed in the human person's ability to respond responsibility to self-knowledge. Knowing one's instincts and one's genetic heritage comes with a source of strength and power to control, direct, and utilize the primordial nature of these characteristics for the good of self and humanity. Finally, Frankl was not a member of the "nurture" crowd of behavioral psychologists who would attribute, even blame, one's social and physical environment for the way individuals turn out in their maturity. These three components of freedom, namely, instincts, heritage, and environment, may be used by man to realize freedom if he becomes aware of them, embraces them, and directs them towards a meaningful purpose in life.

Besides spirituality and freedom, however, there is responsibility. Having been greatly influenced in his formative years with the writings of the existentialists, not least being Kierkegaard, Sartre, and Heidegger, Frankl was most insistent that in order for man to be fully human, he must exercise responsibility. Man is responsible to his own conscience first and foremost, says Frankl. Conscience, says he, is a "thing in itself," it is *sui generis*. It is so fundamental to the human person that humanity cannot exist without it nor the human person remain human without it. Conscience has to do with the drive to do the right thing because it is the right thing to do. This is so fundamental to the human experience that without it humanity and civilization itself could not exist. In his arguments against Freud, Frankl has said. "If we present a man with a concept of man which is not true, we may well corrupt him."

"When we present man as an automaton of reflexes, as a mind-machine, as a bundle of instincts, as a pawn of drives and reactions, as a mere product of instinct, heredity, and environment," elaborates Frankl, "we feed the nihilism to which modern man is, in any case, prone." He believed earnestly that the "ultimate consequences of the theory that man is nothing but the product of heredity and environment" were the gas chambers of Auschwitz. And in speaking of the meaning and function of conscience in the lives of every individual, he wrote: "I am absolutely convinced that the gas chambers of Auschwitz, Treblinka, and Maidanek were ultimately prepared not in some Ministry or other in Berlin, but rather at the desks and the in the lecture halls of nihilistic scientists and philosophers." Frankl summed up his assessment of man's capacity for evil this way: "Since Auschwitz we know what man is capable of. And, since Hiroshima, we know what is at stake."

Of the many conceptual contributions Frankl and logotherapy have made to modern psychotherapy, three stand out most conspicuously, namely, tragic triad, existential vacuum, and paradoxical intention. Let us consider each here briefly in concluding our discussion of Frankl and logotherapy as a classic school of thought.

The *tragic triad* of human existence is made up of pain, guilt, and death. These are universal human experiences and no one can escape them. An address by logotherapy to the tragic triad should not be perceived as indicative of a pessimistic therapy but rather logotherapy specifically addresses these human experiences to demonstrate how even the most acutely emotional experience of negativity can be transmogrified into a cause for optimism and hope. Because a fundamental feature of the human spirit is the capacity to change, to redirect oneself, to take on a new outlook on life, the individual can address the realities of pain and guilt and the eventuality of death with a personal sense of empowerment, of responsibility, of courage to face and change the future. We cannot, of course, undo the past but we can, with courage and responsibility, address the present and anticipate the future with hope. We cannot forgo pain but we can address its reality with a sense of fulfilling our life with meaning and purpose in the face of it. Logotherapy says that out purpose in life is not merely to seek pleasure, as with Freud and the psychoanalysts, but to embrace life with courage and responsibility, to convert meaningless pain and suffering into a purposeful direction by identifying the perimeters of its meaning. Because life is not forever, the human person is under an imperative to utilize the time and talent he has to make a difference in the world. If life were eternal, then we would never have to do anything! Because of the inevitability of our demise, with the clock ticking, with time running out for each individual, we have the responsibility and, indeed, the privilege of finding the meaning of life by addressing the demands of life in service to others. Through the exercise of the will to meaning, meaning is found and life is fulfilled.

The *existential vacuum* in Frankl's thought is considered by him to be rampant in the modern age. This existential vacuum has emerged due to two fundamental causes. First, we lost a sense of animal security through the evolution of our species from merely animal instinct to human behavior. Instincts provide a kind of security because behavior is more or less determined. With the coming of reflective self-awareness, that is, consciousness, the human animal shed such instinctual dominance and took on the responsibility of controlling and directing his behavior. With the loss of instincts to guide our behavior, a certain sense of security was lost as well and we became responsible for our own behavior, its consequences and its ramifications. But furthermore, we also through time lost the security which traditions have offered us as mechanisms of security, pointing the way, establishing and maintaining acceptable behavior, and providing perimeters of human social interaction. With the loss of instincts, we must discover or explore and establish modes of conduct, patterns of acceptable behavior, and consequences for failing to conform to the will of the people. When we desire to do what other people do, we call this "conformism." When we do what other people wish us to do, we call this "totalitarianism." And, finally, when we refuse to follow anyone's direction or guidance in our behavior, we call this "rebellion." The existential vacuum caused by these two losses, instinct and tradition, leads to a neurosis characterized by the four symptoms which we have discussed earlier, namely, (1) a life without direction, (2) a fatalistic view of life, (3) group think, and (4) fanaticism.

Finally, the third major conceptual development in logotherapeutic theory gave rise to the *paradoxical intention*. As is common knowledge in clinical studies of anxiety, the very thing one fears is often the very thing that is produced by that fear. This Frankl has chosen to call "anticipatory anxiety." An example he commonly used to explain this phenomenon is that of insomnia. In such a case, the patient reports that he has trouble getting to sleep. The very fear of not sleeping brings on the thing feared. The same is true of sexual problems such as impotence, the more one thinks about it the more that fear makes it a reality. From this commonly observed clinical situation, logotherapists have developed paradoxical intention as a treatment modality. Frankl tells the story of a young physician who sweated excessively when in the presence of his chief. At other times, he was not bothered by this problem. The patient/physician was advised to resolve deliberately to show the chief just how much he really could sweat. Through this paradoxical intention, he was able to free himself of his problem. The treatment consists not only in a reversal of the patient's attitude towards his problem, whatever it might be, but also that it introduces a level of humor in the process. The logic is simple. Phobias and obsessive-compulsive neuroses are partially due to the increases of anxieties and compulsions caused by the endeavor to avoid or fight them. The subconscious, Frankl points out, cannot tell the difference between a fear and a wish and so attempts to bring either into reality. A phobic person usually tries to avoid the situation in which his anxieties arise, while the obsessive-compulsive tries to suppress and fight his problem. In either case, the result is a strengthening of the symptoms.

More so with Frankl than with any other psychotherapist considered in this book, personal life story proved to be a major factor in the development of a therapeutic system of theory and practice. Freud's life, Adler's life, and Jung's life have all proven interesting and have in their own way showed how their life and work were integrated. But with Frankl, it is inconceivable to imagine logotherapy as a school of thought being produced in the absence of his concentration camp experience. The viability of his theory and the utility of his clinical practice both rely upon the life history of its creator. Frankl's relevance to contemporary treatment in therapeutic settings is becoming increasingly recognized and appreciated within a broad spectrum of clinical practice. The impact of his therapeutic system of theory and treatment has yet to reach its maximum level of influence in contemporary counseling circles.

VIKTOR FRANKL'S BIOGRAPHY

When Life Calls Out to Us: The Love and Lifework Of Viktor and Elly Frankl by Haddon Klingberg, Jr.
NY: Doubleday, 2001.

VIKTOR FRANKL'S PRIMARY SOURCES

Man's Search for Meaning. An Introduction to Logotherapy,
Boston: Beacon and Random House / Rider, London 2004, also Washington Square Press; (Softcover, December 1997)

On the Theory and Therapy of Mental Disorders. An Introduction to Logotherapy and Existential Analysis, Translated by James M.

DuBois. Brunner-Routledge, London-New York 2004

Psychotherapy and Existentialism. Selected Papers on Logotherapy, New York: Simon & Schuster

The Will to Meaning. Foundations and Applications of Logotherapy, New York: New American Library

Man's Search for Ultimate Meaning. (A revised and extended edition of The Unconscious God; with a Foreword by Swanee Hunt). Perseus Book Publishing, New York, 1997; Paperback edition: Perseus Book Group; New York, July 2000

CHAPTER FIVE
Abraham Maslow and Humanistic Psychology

BIOGRAPHICAL SKETCH

Abraham Harold Maslow was born in Brooklyn, New York, on the first of April, 1908, the first of seven children to parents who were uneducated Jews from Russia. Pushed hard to succeed by ambitious but misguided parents, he took solace in books from his loneliness and shyness perpetrated somewhat by an extremely aggressive and, as he later said, a schizophrenic mother. Maslow wrote late in life: "With my childhood, it's a wonder I'm not psychotic. I was a little Jewish boy in the non-Jewish neighborhood. It was a little like being the first Negro enrolled in the al-white school. I was isolated and unhappy. I grew up in libraries and among books, without friends." During the summers, he worked for his family's barrel manufacturing company with his three brothers who still own the company. Because he was intellectually gifted, he did find some happiness and a sense of fulfillment during his four years at the Brooklyn Borough High School where he distinguished himself academically.

The study of law, his father's ambition for him, lasted only a few weeks at the City College of New York and he then transferred to Cornell for a few courses but returned to CCNY yet failed to complete his degree course. Later in life, he explained that he felt that law dealt too much with evil people and was not sufficiently concerned with the good, and it was the good, the wholesome, the fulfilling experience of a meaningful life that captured his imagination. At the time, Maslow married his high school sweetheart who was also his first cousin and, as he put it, his first and last love, Bertha Goodman, a local girl from a good Jewish family and they eventually had two daughters, the experience of which Maslow said changed the direction of his life forever. "Life didn't really start for me," he says, "until I got married and went to Wisconsin." They were married on Christmas Day, 1928, when Maslow was 20 and his bride 19.

Fascinated with the prospects of studying with some of the greatest scholars of the day, Maslow applied to and was accepted at the University of Wisconsin where he earned his B.A. in 1930, his M.A. in 1931, and his Ph.D. in 1934, all in psychology, enjoying the privilege of working with the then famous Professor Harry Harlow. It was his early involvement in the study of behaviorism, from which he later departed with a loud flourish of protestation, and the opportunity of working with Harlow, that he considered the two driving forces in his academic pursuit of a life's goal as research scholar and teacher. A whirlwind of study, research, writing, and teaching, he had taken Wisconsin by storm and after completing his studies, though somewhat disappointed that he wasn't able, after all, to study with the renowned scholars he went to Wisconsin with whom to study. "I was off to Wisconsin to change the world. But off to Wisconsin because of a lying catalog. I went there to study with Koffka, the psychologist; Dreisch, the biologist; and Mieklejohn, the philosopher. When I showed upon campus, they weren't there. They had just been visiting professors, but the school put them in the catalog anyway!" (1988).

After serving on the Wisconsin faculty as Assistant Instructor in Psychology (1930-1934) and Teaching Fellow in Psychology (1934-1935), Maslow was back to New York in a flash upon graduating with his doctorate specifically to work with E. L. Thorndike as his research assistant at Teacher's College, Columbia University, where he became interested specifically in research on human sexuality. At Columbia, he served as a Carnegie Fellow from 1935-1937. His Ph.D. dissertation was an observational study of sexual and dominance characteristics of monkeys! But this study introduced him to a whole new world of research. A full time teaching post was offered him at Brooklyn College and it was during these years, he reflected in older life, that provided him the unparalleled opportunity to meet and work with such people as Adler, Fromm, Horney, and several distinguished Gestalt and Freudian psychologists. Adler, at this time, was holding seminars in his home in New York on Friday nights and Maslow was invited to participate. He always expressed his gratitude for the invitation and the experience. Not inconsequently, he also went through psychoanalysis during this time in Brooklyn. Also, and a world expanding experience it was for him, he served as plant manager of the Maslow Cooperage Corporation, the family factory owned and operated by his three brothers.

He was particularly influenced by two mentors of his during these years, the anthropologist Ruth Benedict and the Freudian psychologist Max Wertheimer. Unlike Freud, Jung, and Adler, Maslow was disinclined to focus his attention and research upon the mentally ill, preferring to study why and how people are mentally healthy, happy, and fulfilled. Eventually, he would develop a whole psychodynamic schema of theoretical constructs and conceptual framework called the hierarchy of needs. Maslow saw needs arranged in a sort of ladder, leading from basic to more advanced levels in the maturation of human fulfillment. It was becoming a father that seems to have transformed him into a real force in humanistic psychology. "Our first baby changed me as a psychologist," he wrote, "It made the behaviorism I had been so enthusiastic about look so foolish I could not stomach it anymore … I'd say that anyone who had a baby couldn't be a behaviorist." His two baby daughters made a profound effect upon him for two reasons. First, because they had such different temperaments, he was forced to assume that many basic personality characteristics were inherited. Second, the birth of his first daughter influenced him to relinquish his belief in behaviorism. He later wrote: "I looked at this tiny, mysterious thing (his first child), and felt so stupid. I was stunned by the mystery and sense of not really being in control. I felt small and weak and feeble before all of this."

Without doubt, it was World War II and the aftermath that changed Maslow forever. It was the defining moment in a research psychologist's life when he turned from behaviorism to humanism and launched a whole new way of thinking about human personality. For him, war epitomized the prejudice, hatred, and baseness of humankind. The experience of witnessing a Victory Day parade, he explains, changed him for good. "As I watched," he recorded years later, "the tears began to run down my face. I felt we didn't understand -- not Hitler, nor the Germans, nor Stalin, nor the communists. We didn't understand any of them. I felt that if we could understand, then we could make progress. I had a vision of a peace table, with people sitting around it, talking about human nature and hatred and war and peace and brotherhood ... that moment changed my whole life and determined what I have done since. Since that moment in 1941, I've devoted myself to developing a theory of human nature that could be tested by experiment and research."

From 1951 to 1969, he enjoyed the privilege of teaching at Brandeis University near Boston and for several of those years was department chairman and it was during these fruitful years that he met Kurt Goldstein who planted the seed of an idea in Maslow which gave rise to his now internationally acclaimed concept of "self-actualization." Maslow eventually became the head of what was known as the Third Force in psychology, the humanistic school *vis a vis* Freudian psychology and behaviorism. He ended his teaching carrier by moving to California to become the first Resident Fellow of the W. P. Laughlin Charitable Foundation in Menlo Park. Here he had complete freedom to pursue his interests in the philosophy of democratic politics and ethics but it was here he died on the 8th of June, 1970, at the age of sixty-two.

Maslow was affiliated, albeit tangentially more often than not, with many professional societies. He served on the Society for the Psychological Study of Social Issues Council and was elected president of the Massachusetts State Psychological Association. He presided over the Division of Personality and Social Psychology of the American Psychological Association and was elected president of the APA in 1967. He was the founding editor of both the *Journal of Humanistic Psychology* and the *Journal of Transpersonal Psychology.*

THE CLASSIC TEXT CONSIDERED

Not a prolific writer but one who was able to put his major contributions into a coherent presentation, Maslow established himself as a major figure in American psychology and personality theory with his book, *Towards a Psychology of Being.* "If we wish to help humans to become more fully human," Maslow wrote, "we must realize not only that they try to realize themselves, but that they are also reluctant or afraid or unable to do so. Only by fully appreciating this dialectic between sickness and health can we help to tip the balance in favor of health." In his book, there is a constant optimistic thrust toward a future based on the intrinsic values of humanity. Maslow states that "This inner nature, as much as we know of it so far, seems not to be intrinsically evil, but rather either neutral or positively 'good.' What we call evil behavior appears most often to be a secondary reaction to frustration of that intrinsic nature." He demonstrates that human beings can be loving, noble, and creative, and are capable of pursuing the highest values and aspirations.

Maslow had become disenchanted with classical psychoanalysis and contemporary behaviorism alike for some of the same reasons, primarily because of their intrinsic negativity about the human person and his potential. The first chapter in Maslow's classic is characteristically entitled, "Toward a Psychology of Health." Throughout his career, it was mental health, not illness, which fascinated him, that stirred within him the desire to know more and more about what it means to be human and to grasp the potential of humanity. From within the matrix of this optimism about humanity and our desire to realize our potential grew Maslow's now highly acclaimed fundamental contributions to humanistic psychology, namely, the "hierarchy of human needs" and "self-actualization." Then, as we shall see later, his third insight had to do with the emergence of humanistic psychology and what he chose to call the "Third Force."

"There is now emerging over the horizon," he wrote as his opening remarks in this classic text, "a new conception of human sickness and of human health, a psychology that I find so thrilling and so full of wonderful possibilities that I yield to the temptation to present it publicly even before it is checked and confirmed, and before it can be called reliable scientific knowledge." He would not be stopped. The basic assumptions implicit in this new way of thinking about mental health were these: (1) every person has an essential biologically based inner nature, (2) each person's inner nature is in part unique to himself and in part species-linked, (3) this inner nature can be scientifically studied, (4) this inner nature is not intrinsically evil but rather neutral or good, (5) because of this the inner nature should be nurtured and brought out into the light of day, (6) and if this inner core of our fundamental human nature is suppressed or stifled, we get ill, (7) this inner human nature, not like instincts, is frail and in need of much care and attention, (8) and even when suppressed, it endures within the core of human personality, and (9) the nurturing, the fostering, the supporting of these inner drives and characteristics inevitably bring mental health.

Toward a Psychology of Being is built upon the humanistic psychology of Maslow's Third Force and constitutes the cornerstone of his work. To read this book is to learn of the breadth and depth of the Third Force and to know Maslow at the very core of his professional enthusiasm. Its influence continues even today to spread not just throughout the psychotherapeutic community but through the general public, through the humanities, social theory, and pastoral counseling. Its enduring popularity rests with its address to the important questions of the day regarding mental health and the nurture of human potential. Its address to human nature and psychological well-being is a breath of fresh air after the depressing, if not oppressive, nature of classical psychoanalysis and individual psychology which are both built upon the presumption of a "dark closet" needing a good cleaning. Not so with Maslow for his aim is to promote, maintain, and restore mental and emotional health. "Capacities clamor to be used," he wrote, and "cease their clamor only when they are well used … Not only is it fun to use our capacities, but it is necessary for growth. The unused skill or capacity or organ can become a disease center or else atrophy or disappear, thus diminishing the person."

In this classic, Maslow has put forth a great deal of thought and effort into producing a needs-based framework of human motivation based upon his clinical experiences with humans rather than on the behaviorism of Skinner and followers which was fundamentally based upon animal behavior. He was, of course, at odds with Adler, Jung, and Freud as relates to their pessimistic assessment of the human situation for he was both optimistic about human nature and enthusiastic about the development of ways and means of nurturing and fostering human potential and the fulfillment of human aspirations. Form his theory of motivation, many in the fields of management and leadership find Maslow's theory of motivation provocative and stimulating.

The basis of Maslow's theory is that human beings are motivated by unsatisfied needs, and that certain lower factors need to be satisfied before higher needs can be met. We will discuss these in more detail in the "concepts and theories" section but for now let it be said that according to Maslow, there are "general types of needs" such as physiological, survival, safety, love, and esteem, which must be satisfied before an individual can act unselfishly. These he called "deficiency needs" and as long as the human person is being motivated by these drives, we are moving towards growth, toward what he came to call "self-actualization." Satisfying needs, then, according to Maslow, is healthy, necessary, beneficial to the individual, whereas the stifling of this drive to satisfy the fundamental needs leads to mental illness.

Maslow understood human needs to be hierarchical in the sense that one builds upon another like the steps of a ladder or like a staircase. The most basic and almost primordial or instinctual needs, he suggests, are air, water, food, and sex. Above those, which must be met in order to progress up the hierarchy, are safety needs such as security and stability and those are followed by more psychologically charged social needs including the need to belong, for love and acceptance. At the upper echelons of the needs ladder are the self-actualizing needs by which Maslow meant the need to fulfill oneself, to realize one's own potential. In order to progress up these stair steps to fulfillment, each level must be realized. There is no "skipping" of the various needs recited here, says Maslow, otherwise, the stifling at one level precludes full realization at the next level. Not everyone is destined to progress; some never do and thus mental illness is forever a reality. Few reach the highest echelon of self-actualization and Maslow would have us understand that these are not static levels but fluid and fluctuating with time and life circumstances.

The goal, of course, is to reach the highest realms of human potential and that, Maslow calls "self-actualization." The fundamental features of this level of personal growth includes such things as focusing upon the problems outside oneself, others' problems and issues rather than one's own. Also, having a genuine sense of what is true versus the false and phony are features of this level. Being spontaneous and creative while honoring, not mindlessly conforming to social conventions, all bespeak the self-actualized person. Maslow enjoyed identifying such individuals within society, particularly within his own social circles. He often used Ruth Benedict as the quintessential example of the truly self-actualized person.

In *Toward a Psychology of Being*, Maslow ventured into the swift and changing waters of "peak experience" as a way of addressing those moments in some people's lives, though not everyone, when the most provocative and stimulating experiences of inner ecstasy occur. These "peak experiences" are, according to Maslow, those profound moments of love, understanding, happiness, rapture, or insight, when a person feels "more whole, alive, self-sufficient and yet a part of the world, more aware of truth, justice, harmony, goodness, and so on." These peak experiences are reserved for the few self-actualized people in society.

Few psychologists of his day questioned but what Maslow was creative and astoundingly original in his thoughts, insights, and manner of presentation. Before Maslow, psychology and psychotherapy seemed to be dominated by the mentally ill and all theorizing focused upon the "cure" for those individuals. Not discounting the need to address the complex issues of mental illness, Maslow and the humanistic orientation of the Third Force movement turned its attention to human potential, to mental health and its nurture and development. Humanistic psychology gave rise to several different therapies, all guided by the idea that people possess the inner resources for growth and health and that the point of therapy is to help remove obstacles to individual's achieving this. Erik Erikson and Carl Rogers become major bearers of this new way of thinking about psychotherapy.

CONCEPTS AND THEORIES

Few would argue that Maslow's lasting contribution to psychotherapy and personality theory are his three fundamental concepts of (1) the Third Force, (2) the hierarchy of needs, and (3) self-actualization. All of his other contributions are subsumed within these three insights. Let us look at each of these more closely in our discussion of the fundamental contributions Maslow has made to psychotherapy.

Maslow's theory of personality represents an alternative to the two major shaping forces of contemporary psychology evidenced in both behaviorism and in Freudian psychoanalysis. This alternative personality theory construct and treatment modality led Maslow and his compatriots to think of what they were developing as a third way of treating mental health and mental illness. Thus, it became known and first called "The Third Force" by Maslow himself. This humanistic psychology was decidedly developed intentionally as a third and alternative way from behaviorism and psychoanalysis, both perceived to be pessimistic about human nature and rather inclined to think of the human personality as in some way fundamentally flawed by instinctual motivations at the expense of personal health and wholeness.

Maslow's emphasis and that of the Third Force movement was on mental health and ways of fostering that process of fulfillment evidently desired by all human beings. Toward the end of his life, Maslow pointed out that he did not intend to distance himself and his movement from behaviorism and psychoanalysis for each of those schools of thought had a contribution to make in the understanding of mental illness. He felt, rather, that he had embodied the best of both of these viewpoints and had gone beyond them to a psychology of transcendence. Near the end of his life, Maslow became increasing hopeful about fostering this commitment of the profession to a focus upon mental health and wholeness. He envisioned a psychological Utopia in which healthy, self-actualized people would live and work in harmony.

"Humanistic psychology" was a term coined by a group of psychologists in the 1960s who joined Maslow's movement towards an alternative psychotherapeutic orientation to that of Skinner and the behaviorists and Freud and the psychoanalysts. It was a movement, not a school of thought. Calling themselves the Third Force, humanistic psychologists shared a wide range of views and certain fundamental conceptions about the nature of the human person and personality development. Embracing the existential philosophy of "life is what you make it" found in Kierkegaard and Sartre, these psychologists found the fundamental tenants of existentialism to be at the core of their own thought and work, particularly the concept of "becoming." A person is never static; he or she is always in the process of becoming something different. Thus, it is the individual's personal responsibility as a free being to realize his own potentialities. Only by actualizing these potentials intrinsic to the human person can a truly authentic life emerge. Requiring more than biological needs and sexual and aggressive instincts, the human person must build upon these needs towards a higher self-understanding. The process of becoming, of self-actualization, is, they contended, inherent to human nature itself and to stifle that or demean that character is to diminish humanity itself thereby destroying the person.

The Third Force held certain insights to be endemic to the movement and to their understanding of human potentiality. (1) The individual is an integrated whole and must not be chopped up into component parts but studied, nurtured, and guided as a single entity. (2) They held to the belief that animal research was essentially a waste of time for human psychologists. Self-reflective awareness and a sense of hope towards the future make the human person unique in the animal kingdom and must be studied in terms of these realities. (3) Man's inner nature is essentially good, not evil, and, therefore, the psychotherapeutic agenda is to nurture the inner self of every individual. (4) The human person's own unique potential is to be cherished above all else. This is often perceived to be the most significant concept in humanistic psychology. (5) The emphasis upon psychological health was the reigning principle guiding the development of humanistic psychology and was the guiding principle of the Third Force. Maslow ranted against the notion that the human person is fundamentally demented by instinctual drives. He said that the two other schools of psychological thought did an injustice to the healthy human being's functioning, modes of living, and life's goals. Freud's obsession with the study of neurotic and psychotic individuals came under particular criticism from the Third Force.

Now let us turn again and more closely look at the nature of Maslow's "Hierarchy of Needs." The fundamental idea behind Maslow's hierarchy of needs is that our lowest level of needs must be satisfied or relatively so prior to moving higher up the scale. We are motivated proportionate to the level of needs we have fulfilled and our motivation comes from their fulfillment. Each level has its own integrity and no movement upwards can occur until there is a reasonable satisfaction of the lower level needs. Those who fail to satisfy the lower level needs are doomed to failure in their aspirations for better things and, says Maslow, mental illness awaits those who try it.

We will here explore the major needs categories developed by Maslow when proposing the "hierarchy." They are (1) Physiological Needs, (2) Safety Needs, (3) Love and Belongingness Needs, (4) Esteem Needs, and (5) Self-Actualization Needs. Later in their development and with insights gained from the Third Force, Maslow added Aesthetic Needs, Cognitive Needs, and Neurotic Needs to fulfill his attempt at comprehensiveness.

The most fundamental of human needs are the physiological needs without which there is no life. They include food, water, oxygen, maintenance of body temperature, etc. They are essentially the basic needs of all living things. These physiological needs differ from the higher human needs in two important ways. First, they are the only needs that can be completely satisfied or even overly satisfied. Too much food, for example, is always a possibility. A second characteristic peculiar to these physiological needs is their recurring nature. One is recurrently hungry regardless of how satisfied one is at any given moment of eating. Hunger reoccurs.

When once these most basically fundamental needs are being met, one then is motivated to seek safety and its cognates, such as physical security, stability, dependency, protection, and freedom from such threatening forces as illness, fear, anxiety, danger, and chaos. The need for law, order, and structure are also safety needs, explains Maslow. Though these are likewise on the lower end of the spectrum with physiological needs, they are indispensable for the further development of the human person. In modern societies, these are routinely met but for children, who are more often than adults conspicuously motivated by these needs, protection from the threats of darkness, animals, strangers, and punishments are most common and motivate the child to seek their removal from their daily lives. Neurotic adults, also, feel relatively unsafe most of the time. These individuals spend much more time and energy than do healthy individuals in seeking to satisfy their needs for safety and reassurance about the world. These individuals, says Maslow, suffer from what he calls "basic anxiety" which comes with the failure to meet the safety needs of the individual.

If physiological and safety needs are commonly and regularly met in modern society, the need for love and belonging has a somewhat different story to tell. Here we notice that most of us find ourselves spending a disproportionate amount of time addressing this need for love and belonging. Within the needs complex is the need for friendship, the wish for a mate and family, the need to belong to a group, a neighborhood, a political body, or even a nationality. Sexual relations, human contact, and social interaction are all components of this driving need for love. Without love, Maslow explains, a child cannot grow to psychological health. Adults, however, sometimes become proficient at disguising their need for love just as they may also be adept at hiding the fact that their safety is threatened. Adults who have failed to receive love or have failed to develop the capacity to give love often find themselves engaging in self-defeating behavior. They frequently take own such characteristics as cynicism, coldness, aloofness, calloused disregard for interpersonal interaction, all as a protective mechanism, denying themselves the opportunities for securing love thereby. Others go to the opposite extreme and become so outspokenly needy and solicitous as to drive others away, losing the very thing they seek and need.

Contrary to the Beatles' song, "Love is all we need," Maslow says not so. Beyond love and belonging and when those needs are being effectively met, the human person reaches higher up the ladder to what is called the "esteem needs" of human experience. With the strength and assurance of the basic needs having been met and with love and belonging well in hand, the human person seeks more, seeks the respect of others as well as self-respect, confidence, competence, and the esteem of others. The esteem needs function, says Maslow, on two levels. The first is reputation, which is the person's perception of the prestige, recognition, or fame he has achieved in the eyes of other people, and second is self-esteem, defined as the person's own feeling of worth and confidence. Esteem needs, then, are bidirectional. One needs the esteem of others and one needs to have esteem for oneself. You really can't have one without the other and maintain mental health. Self-worth must, however, precede esteem of others. When one has self-confidence, self-esteem, and self-worth, one can then begin to develop a sense of reciprocal esteem from the social environment. It cannot, however, work the other way around. Without self-esteem, one cannot experience the esteem of others. When this void does occur, mental illness is most commonly the result.

The final and highest level of the hierarchy of needs is that of self-actualization. But it doesn't automatically follow for most people in the world. To have reached the level of esteem needs, most people have arrived at their functional level of behavior and do quite well at it throughout their lives. Only a few can even aspire to another higher, but, for those who do, there is a great sense of personal fulfillment, what Maslow calls "self-actualization" which occurs. Only those who embrace what Maslow has called the "B-Values" can make the final step to self-actualization. Those who hold in high respect, says Maslow, such values as truth, beauty, and justice are potentially likely to reach the fullest level of human personal development. We will consider this final step separately and more fully below.

Maslow went on to suggest that there are three more levels of needs beyond self-actualization! As surprising as that might appear, he felt that the aesthetic needs of individuals come after, not before, self-actualization. Not every person and not every culture is particularly susceptible to the aesthetic needs of human development. But, there are individuals who are themselves fulfilled by this need, namely, the need for beauty an aesthetically pleasing experiences. From the artistic displays of Paleolithic man, the human person and the human community has been aware of and appreciative of this need for beauty. Preferences for beauty over ugliness, order or chaos, structure over disarray has characterized the human community from earliest times.

A complimenting balance to the aesthetic needs beyond self-actualization are the cognitive needs. There is that intrinsic curiosity of the human animal, the human person has a desire to know, to understand, to grasp the meaning and purpose and direction of things. This is a fundamental human drive and has characterized the human animal from Paleolithic times. When these needs, the cognitive needs, are stifled, all other needs are potentially threatened because without knowledge, with information, without understanding life becomes problematic! Self-actualization, says Maslow, depends on utilizing fully one's cognitive potentials, though self-actualizing people need not have outstanding inherent intellectual powers. They do, however, need to know and understand what is going on in the world around them. Knowledge brings with it the desire to know more, to theorize, to test hypotheses, or to find out how something works just for the satisfaction of knowing. This is a human compulsion.

Maslow was no superficial optimist and was fully cognizant of the potential for mental illness within any person. When needs are not met, psychological stagnation and pathology often are the result. Maslow introduced the concept of "neurotic needs" to refer to behavior which is not productive, nurturing, or beneficial to human personality. These neurotic needs perpetuate an unhealthy style of life and have no value in the striving for self-actualization. Usually reactive rather than active, they serve as compensation for unsatisfied basic needs. In the absence of safety, for example, a person may have a strong desire to hoard money or property and this motivator is worthless and even destructive to mental health. This, says Maslow, is the indicator of a neurotic need, namely, it fails to contribute to mental health. "Giving a neurotic power seeker all the power he wants does not make him less neurotic, nor is it possible to satiate his neurotic need for power. However much he is fed he still remains hungry (because he's really looking for something else). It makes little difference for ultimate health whether a neurotic needs to be gratified or frustrated." In therapy, the counselor will seek to determine what need is not being met and assist the client in addressing that issue, thereby reducing or displacing the neurotic need caused by the unfulfilled legitimate need of self-actualization.

Finally and in concluding our discussion of Maslow, we must address his major contribution to personality theory called "self-actualization." The development of this concept came about due to Maslow's concentration on mental health rather than mental illness. Adopting the term "self-actualization" from Kurt Goldstein at Columbia University, Maslow went on to develop it into a fully operational concept and focal point of his personality theory. Self-actualization is the highest level of human motivation characterized by full development of all one's capacities.

It is the rare individual, says Maslow, who reaches this level of needs fulfillment in their personality development. First, the individual seeking self-actualization must not be neurotic nor have any psychopathic personality disorders. Furthermore, the individual must have the "full use and exploitation of talents, capacities, potentialities, etc." These individuals, rare though they be, are the embodiment of all needs fulfillment. They have the capacity to deal with delayed or denied needs for they have a full understanding of themselves, their capacity to abstain, to do without, to postpone needs gratification without panic or feelings of deprivation. Maslow summed up a thoroughgoing description of just who these individuals really are.

> They listen to their own voices; they take responsibility; they are honest, and they work hard. They find out who they are and what they are, not only in terms of their mission in life, but also in terms of the way their feet hurt when they wear such and such a pair of shoes and whether they do or do not like eggplant or stay up all night if they drink too much beer. All this is what the real self means. They find their own biological natures, their congenital natures, which are irreversible or difficult to change (1966).

In another major work, *Motivation and Personality,* in 1970 and in response to a continual plea for a recitation of the scope of characteristics of the self-actualized person, Maslow listed fifteen quality which characterize this category of person. Let us list them here and in most instances they appear self-explanatory. (1) More efficient perception of reality (they really see things as they are and not as one would like them to be), (2) Acceptance of self, others, and nature (they are realistic in their assessment of themselves, those around them, and the world outside themselves), (3) Spontaneity, simplicity, and naturalness (they are not phonies in their life and work and are eager to respond to situations as they arise), (4) problem-centered (they are quick to recognize problems outside themselves and equally ready to address them), (5) The need for privacy (they are pleased to have social interaction but equally happy to be alone within themselves without having the experience of loneliness), (6) autonomy (they are not demanding of others or the environment around themselves but enjoy the freedom of personal self-satisfaction), (7) Continued freshness of appreciation (they are those people who are forever able to see the new and different with appreciation and a valuing of each moment and each experience for its own merits), (8) The peak experience (These are the ones who have both the capacity and the reality of entering into a fundamentally ecstatic experience of life through love, art, music, beauty, the challenge of living, etc., with a sense of purpose. Transcendent experiences are not alien to them nor are they frightened by them but rather enjoy the opportunity of living through them to their fruition.), (9) Gemeinschaftsgefuhl or social feeling and interest (An Adlerian term which characterizes the self-actualized person in his capacity to commit to the whole community with passion and care and selflessness), (10) Interpersonal relations (they have the gift of focusing upon relationships which nurture and enrich each participant), (11) The democratic character structure (they embody the sense of fair play, what is right for each and every one, how to make it happen, and how to foster it in others), (12) Creativeness (they experience the joy of creating things, not just writing poetry or music nor simply doing crafts but a thoroughgoing sense of happiness with their own ability to create something new and different which reflects their own interests and values and passion without the need of praise from others for having created it). (13) Philosophical sense of humor (the thoroughgoing capacity to see the humor in life and in interpersonal relationships without cynicism or rancor). (14) Discrimination between means and ends (they have a healthy capacity to determine what is important to be done and how best it might be accomplished without there being the gross contradictions of means and ends issues about what is of value and worthy of effort). (15) Resistance to enculturation (these are the people who can rise above an existential situation and thereby gain a broader, more complete picture of life's situations and, therefore, are not victimized by their own cultural or situational myopia).

A word about the actual psychotherapeutic approach of Maslow seems to be a fitting closing statement for all of his work grew out of clinical practice and was designed to serve clinical training to those who joined the Third Force in psychology. Maslow realized that those who need psychotherapy are normally those least likely to seek it out for they have not met their own needs for fulfillment and, thus, seeking help is not in their purview of options to solve their life's problems. Most individuals who come to therapy have difficulty satisfying love and belongingness needs, says Maslow, and therefore psychotherapy is largely an interpersonal process for these individuals, when and if they choose to seek help. Through a nurturing experience with the therapist, the client may gain satisfaction of their need for love and a sense of belonging and thereby gain confidence and a sense of self-worth. This experience gives the client the capacity to establish healthy relationships outside the clinical environment. To bring this about, the therapist himself must be mentally healthy, a situation which does not always exist and, in fact, many times individuals are attracted to clinical psychotherapeutic practice owing to their own mental instability. "The aim of Maslovian therapy," explains Jess Feist, "is to free the person from dependency on others so that the natural impulse toward growth and self-actualization ca become active." He goes on to point out that psychotherapists, because they are just people, do not have the capacity to operate in a value-free clinical environment. Yet, their mission is to foster the sense within each client of their own quest for wholeness by pointing out ways and nurturing efforts on the part of the client to reach a sense of needs satisfaction, of fulfillment, of eventual self-actualization.

ABRAHAM MASLOW'S BIOGRAPHY

The Right to be Human: A Biography of Abraham Maslow by Edward Hoffman. Los Angeles: Jeremy
P. Tarcher, Inc., 1988.

ABRAHAM MASLOW'S PRIMARY SOURCES

A Theory of Human Motivation (originally published in *Psychological Review*, 1943, Vol. 50 #4, pp. 370-396).

Motivation and Personality (1st edition: 1954)

Religions, Values and Peak-experiences, Columbus, Ohio: Ohio State University Press, 1964.

Eupsychian Management, 1965; republished as *Maslow on Management*, 1998

The Psychology of Science: A Reconnaissance, New York: Harper & Row, 1966; Chapel Hill: Maurice Bassett, 2002.

Toward a Psychology of Being, (2nd edition, 1968)

The Farther Reaches of Human Nature, 1971

CHAPTER SIX
Erik Erikson and Development Psychology

BIOGRAPHICAL SKETCH

Erik Homburger (Erikson) was born on the 25th of June, 1902, in Frankfurt-am-Main in Germany and died in Harwick, Massachusetts, on May 12, 1994. His mother was a young woman named Karla Abrahamsen FROM A PROMINENT Jewish family in Copenhagen and his natural father, a Dane named Erik Salomonsen, deserted his mother before Erik was born. At the time of his birth, his mother was "officially" married to a Jewish stockbroker and at his birth, he was registered as Erik Salomonsen. She later trained as a nurse in Karlsruhe and in 1904 married a Jewish physician named Dr. Theodor Homburger who was, at the time, serving as Erik's own pediatrician. IN 1909, Erik Salomonsen became Erik Homburger and in 1911 he was officially adopted by his stepfather. Personal identity was an obsession with Erik throughout his childhood and adolescence for at the temple school the children teased him for being "Nordic," owing to his blonde hair and blue eyes, and at public school he was teased for being a Jew.

Upon Erik's eventual arrival in America as his adopted homeland, having fled Germany with the rise of Nazi proliferation, he changed his surname to Erikson when he took U.S. citizenship. Personal, racial, and religious identify seemed to have plagued Erickson from his earliest memories and haunted him throughout his childhood, adolescent, and adult life. It has been suggested that possibly this life experience itself was a significant ingredient in leading him to the development of his now famous eight stages of development.

Following public school in Germany where his first love was quite clearly art, Erikson studied at a variety of places in Munich and Florence and eventually arrived at the door of what was then still a newly emerging discipline in psychology, namely, psychoanalysis. It should be pointed out here that Erikson did not ever pursue formalized educational training beyond the high school diploma, relying rather upon his own confidence and insights into the field of which he was most interested. He did attend a "humanistic gymnasium" in Karlsruhe, Germany, where he was not a particularly good student while, nevertheless, doing quite good work in ancient history and art as his records show. Refusing to heed his step-father's urgings to pursue medicine, Erikson left home to travel across central Europe and within the next year enrolled in an art school and, for a brief time, accepted the fact that even an aspiring artist could learn something in an educational setting.

Becoming restless yet again, he left that school and set out for Munich to study at the famous art school, the Dunst-Akademia. Two years there, he then moved to Florence while generally wandering aimlessly around Italy "soaking up sunshine and visiting art galleries." He later would write that he finally came to realize that "such narcissism obviously could be a young person's downfall unless he found an overweening idea and the stamina to work for it."

In 1927 at the age of twenty-five, Erikson took up a teaching post at an experimental school for wealthy American children living with their parents in Vienna. This school, called the Kinderseminar, was founded to serve the needs of American professionals studying in Vienna to become psychoanalysts and was under the directorship of a psychoanalyst, Dorothy Burlingham, who was the daughter of the internationally acclaimed New York jeweler, Charles Tiffany. She was herself a professionally trained psychoanalyst and not reluctant to promote this school of thought to all with whom she came in contact. Needless to say, the young Erikson fell under her spell from whom not only did he study and learn as well as undergo psychoanalysis but also was introduced to the Montessori education method and to Anna Freud herself, a lifelong collaborative friend of Dorothy Burlingham. Erikson also and quite naturally was introduced to and welcomed into the Vienna Psychoanalytic Society which was Sigmund Freud's center of teaching and training psychoanalysis to medical professionals and selected layman alike. Besides undergoing psychoanalysis at the hands of Anna Freud herself, Erikson also took the Certificate from the Maria Montessori Teachers Association in Vienna, his only academic credential throughout his whole professional life.

Naturally, young man Erikson was greatly influenced by these heady relationships and professional experiences which, undoubtedly, were instrumental in fostering his passion for analytical studies of childhood maturation. From a modest teaching appointment, Erikson managed to squeeze out an incredibly provocative life experience which led to his now famous ideas and theories about human personality development. In 1929, he married Joan Serson, an American teacher and dancer who was at the time a member of Anna Freud's and Dorothy Burlingham's experimental school in Vienna where Erikson himself taught. By 1933, they had two sons and the whole Erikson family then attempted to emmigrate to Copenhagen where he had hoped to secure citizenship based upon his natural father's nationality. He had hoped to establish a psychoanalytic practice there, little known in Denmark at the time, but the effort failed and they were forced to look elsewhere to begin again, having feared Hitler's rise to power. That same year he completed a course of study at the Vienna Psychoanalytic Institute.

His enthusiasm for this general field of work and study eventually led him to emmigrate to the U.S. in 1933 where he was, quite fortuitously, provided study and teaching opportunities at some of America's most distinguished centers of learning including Harvard, Yale, and the University of California at Berkeley. Upon his arrival in Boston in 1933, he set up as one of the very few child psychoanalysts in the country and carried out research on children at the prestigious Harvard Psychological Clinic where he enjoyed a close friendship and working relationship with both Henry Murray and Kurt Lewin. From 1933 to 1935, he enjoyed an appointment as a clinical and academic Research Fellow in Psychology in the Department of Neuropsychiatry at Harvard Medical School. He momentarily enrolled in a Ph.D. in psychology at Harvard but quickly, within months, withdrew never again to make such an attempt. From 1936 to 1939, he served under an appointment in the Department of Psychiatry in the Institute of Human Relations at the Yale University Medical School where he thoroughly enjoyed continuing his work and interest in personality development and cross-cultural studies.

Erikson's early work concentrated primarily upon psychological testing with special attention to the ways and means of extending Freudian psychoanalytic theories in relation to the effect of social and cultural factors upon human development and personality. He was particularly fascinated with the impact of these insights upon how society affects childhood and development. Because of his driving interest in multi-cultural studies of childhood and society, he became a great student of cultural anthropology, especially as relates to the study of children and personality development cross-culturally. As with Maslow, the works of Margaret Mead and Ruth Benedict proved pivotal to his own conceptual framework and subsequent theoretical development in this area. To further deepen his understanding of cross-culturalism and child development, he journeyed to the Native American communities of the Oglala Lakota (Sioux) and the Yurok peoples where he stayed for an extended time of observation, interviews, etc. The richness of these experiences fed his ambitions in theory and conceptual development while also demonstrating to him some of the apparent deficiencies of Freudian theory as relates to personality development. This encounter with psychoanalytic shortcomings coupled with the richness of his cross-cultural experiences eventually led to his development of what came to be called the "biopsychosocial" perspective on childhood and society.

Eventually migrating with his family to the University of California at Berkeley in 1939, he continued his concentrated efforts in the study of child welfare and personality development and practiced as a clinical psychologist at the San Francisco Veterans Hospital where he treated trauma and mental illness. By 1942, Erikson had risen to the position of professor of psychology at the University of California at Berkeley where he enjoyed assisting Jean MacFarlane in the Child Guidance Study. During the McCarthy era, he moved back to Massachusetts from whence he had come owing to his refusal to sign a loyalty oath which was now being required of all teachers in the State of California. In 1951, he joined a group of mental health professionals at the Austen Riggs Center in Stockbridge, Massachusetts, which was a private residential treatment center for mentally ill young people. He also, and amazingly, continued to maintain a part-time teaching appointment at the Western Psychiatric Institute in Pittsburgh, Pennsylvania while also teaching at the University of Pittsburgh and the Massachusetts Institute of Technology.

From 1951-1960, he taught and worked in New England, but in the summer of 1960, he spent a year at the Center for Advanced Studies of the Behavioral Sciences at Palo Alto, California, and was the next year rewarded by being invited to teach at Harvard University from which he retired in 1970 from his clinical practice but not from his busy schedule of research and writing. He died in Harwick, Massachusetts, on May 12, 1994 and was followed three years later by his Canadian wife, Joan, whom he had met and married while still living and teaching in Vienna. She was herself an academic and particularly fascinated with the study of childhood development and became a major collaborated with Erikson in his research and publications. They had three sons, one of whom was institutionalized as an infant with Down Syndrome, and a daughter. The experience of having a Down Syndrome child almost wrecked their marriage and the pain and suffering, denial and prevarications, to say nothing of the physical and psychological distancing of themselves from this child, Neil, scared the parents and quite decidedly the other children as well.

Most biographers do the disservice of failing to mention

Neil Erikson in their biographical sketches of Erikson to the detriment of both Down Syndrome research and the Eriksons alike. Neil was institutionalized from the hospital as a newborn and his siblings were simply told that he died at birth. Later on, the older son was told of Neil's birth and that he was still alive living in an institution but the other children remained in the dark until Neil's death. Joan visited him infrequently and later he was permanently institutionalized in a prestigious public hospital for mentally retarded children. No photos of Neil were ever taken. At forty-one years of age at the time of Neil's birth, Joan blamed herself and was eaten up by the guilt. The marriage suffered severely as Erik continually attempted to close out the reality of Neil's life. When the Eriksons were moving back to New England, they told their other children of their seven year old brother, Neil, and that he was to be left behind in California. None of the children had ever seen him. The experience of leaving a little brother behind as they moved away frightened the daughter profoundly and parental trust suffered severely as a result. Neil lived to be twenty-two years old and died in 1965 while Erik and Joan were in Europe. They called their oldest son and daughter who were now living back in California and asked them to arrange for the burial of Neil. Neither parent returned for the funeral or internment of his ashes.

A prolific writer, it has been suggested that all research and publication subsequent to his first and indisputably his most famous book in 1950, *Childhood and Society*, was merely a continuing commentary on that book. He continued to push his interest in the life cycle (eight stages of development) during which time he introduced the concept of the "identity crisis" within adolescence. A gradual movement away from psychoanalytic theory and practice was seen as he moved closer to the Third Force and humanistic interests within psychological research and writing. This shift was reflected in his subsequent books such as *Young Man Luther* (1958), *Identity and the Life Cycle* (1959), *Insight and Responsibility* (1964), *Identity: Youth and Crisis* (1968), and *Gandhi's Truth* (1970) which won for him the Pulitzer Prize. In 1974, he published *Dimensions of a New Identity*, and with the editorial revisions made by Joan Erikson, his 1982 book, *The Life Cycle Completed: A Review*, was republished in 1996 which happily extended the stages of old age within the life cycle model, thus completing Erikson's contribution to developmental psychology.

CLASSICAL TEXT CONSIDERED

Many distinguished scholars have established themselves on the strength of one great book such as Frankl and Adler and Rogers, while others wrote and wrote and wrote, leaving behind a library of research and scholarship such as Freud and Jung and Maslow. It can be argued that Erikson's name and reputation was established and secured with the publication of his first book in 1950, *Childhood and Society*. Erikson's fascination with the study of children, their personality development and their maturation, resulted in the writing of his opus text. Here, he elaborated his approach of "triple bookkeeping," as he called it, namely, that understanding a person or behavior involves taking into account somatic factors, social context, and ego development, each in relation to the other. To unpack the somatic aspect of child development, Erikson developed and helpfully expanded Freud's theory of psychosexual development. Erikson chose to explore the power of social context in relation to child-rearing practices and their effects on later personality through some fascinating anthropological and psychoanalytical analysis of the Native Americans, particularly the Sioux and the Yurok cultures.

Though trained by Anna Freud and within the psychoanalytic tradition of Freudian analysis, Erikson was not disinclined to move in his own sphere of thought just as he had chosen not to pursue a traditional university education. Erikson looked at ego development in particular through an analysis of the significance and role of "play," for it was in child's play that he was able to emphasize the need for integration. These three processes, somatic, social, and ego development, are interdependent and that each is both relevant and relative to the other two. This was quite decidedly an advance over traditional Freudian concepts of personality development and child sexuality.

Before we go further in our appreciative assessment of this classic text, let us simply here recite the primary contributions to the understanding of child development which Erikson has brought to the table of psychological insight. First, he elaborated and modified the theory of psychosexual development as produced by Freud; second, he drew from his own clinical experience in working with ego development among children for his theory construction; and third, he employed anthropological data to emphasize the significance of the social context for child rearing and cultural process for personality development.

A fundamental component of Erikson's theory of ego development is the assumption that the development of the person is marked by a series of stages that are universal to humanity. This was, of course, a very bold claim. The process whereby these stages evolve, he explains, is governed by the "epigenetic principle" of maturation. By this Erikson is asked to explain: "(1) that the human personality in principle develops according to steps predetermined in the growing person's readiness to be driven toward, to be aware of, and to interact with, a widening social radius; and (2) that society, in principle, tends to be so constituted as to meet and invite this succession of potentialities for interaction and attempts to safeguard and to encourage the proper rate and the proper sequence of their enfolding."

In his great classic, Erikson outlines a sequence of eight separate stages of psychosocial ego development, commonly called "the eight stages of man." Far from the speculative mysticism of Jung and his genetically inherited "archetypes," Erikson is keen to postulate that these stages are the result of the epigenetic unfolding of a "ground plan" of personality that is genetically transmitted, and this is a "universal phenomenon." By epigenetic (*epi* means "upon" and *genetic* means "emergence"), Erikson has proposed a concept of development which mirrors the notion that each stage in the life cycle has an optimal time, I.e., "critical period," in which it is dominant and hence emerges, and that when all of the stages have matured according to plan, a fully functioning personality comes into existence.

Going further, Erikson is eager to emphasize that each psychosocial stage is accompanied by a "crisis," that is, a critical turning point in the individual's life that arises from physiological maturation and social demands made upon the person at that stage. The various components of personality are, in his theory, determined by the manner in which each of these crises is resolved. Conflict is a vital and integral part of Erikson's theory, because growth and expanding interpersonal radius are associated with increased vulnerability of the ego functions at each stage. However, it is important to keep in mind that, according to Erikson, each crisis connotes "not a threat of catastrophe but a turning point and, therefore, the ontogenetic source of generational strength and maladjustment."

In a review of Erikson's *Childhood and Society* over fifty years ago, the now famous Dr. Eric Berne wrote a critically appreciative assessment of Erkson's book for the *New York Times*. We will quote extensively from that review to give an idea of the impact Erikson was having on the psychological professional at the time. Berne himself at the time was being established as a major force for what he called "transactional analysis." He was extremely complimentary of Erikson's pioneer spirit in the study and treatment of children as relates to psychoanalytic understanding of ego development. Erikson, Berne points out, early emphasized the importance of early frustrations and leniencies on the development of adult anxieties and actions, believing that while sexual conflict was at the basis of most neuroticism in Freud, the main reason for emotional disturbances in America today lies in the lack of "an emotional integration." This harps back to emotional immaturity caused by a prolonged period of childhood and to certain unique characteristics of American culture and family training. Erikson, of course, and due to his study of cross-cultural childrearing practices, was very cognizant of the fact that personality development is deeply imbedded in the social mores of the child's own culture. This constituted the fundamental starting point of Erikson's monumental work, *Childhood and Society*. In the next section, we will consider some of the major conceptual frameworks and theoretical constructs which were presented in Erikson's entire corpus of research on personality development.

CONCEPTS AND THEORIES

Without doubt, Erikson was one of the leading 20th

century psychologists working in the area of personality development, what he called the psychosocial growth of the ego. Interestingly and not particularly to his credit nor benefit, Erikson always insisted that he was not a creative thinker but rather a commentator and, possibly, an elaborator of the psychoanalytic theories of personality development introduced by Freud. He claimed simply to have complimented Freud's work with further investigations of sociological, anthropological, and biological data relevant to personality. In spite of his protestations to the contrary, there are four distinct areas in which Erikson moved away from and beyond Freudian psychoanalytic theory of personality.

First, Erikson shifted the emphasis from the prominence of the id in Freudian theory to the ego which Erikson believed to be the center and basis of human behavior. Called "ego psychology," this shift proposed an understanding of the ego as an "autonomous structure of personality" which follows a course of social-adaptive development that is distinct from but parallels the id and the instincts. Second, Erikson distinguished himself with his emphasis upon the child's relationship to parents and the socio-historical matrix within family life in which each child's ego develops, for good or ill. Third, Erikson's ego development theory covers the entire span of psychological growth and development throughout the individual's life. Freud's theory was woefully brief after adolescence. Finally, there was a great divide between Freud and Erikson when it comes to the nature and resolution of psychosexual conflicts within an individual's life. Whereas Freud wished to resolve these issues by delving into the unconscious reservoirs of the adult through dream analysis and word association, Erikson wished to focus upon the adult's capacity to move forward by assessing life's situations and embracing a mode of operation designed to foster healthy living.

The fundamental ingredient in Erikson's theory of ego development is the assumption that the development of the individual is marked by a series of "stages" that are universal to every person throughout the world. The process whereby these stages evolve is governed by the fundamental principle of maturation, what he called the "epigenetic" principle. Hear him: This concept means "(1) that the human personality in principle develops according to steps predetermined in the growing person's readiness to be driven toward, to be aware of, and to interact with, a widening social radius; and (2) that society, in principle, tends to be so constituted as to meet and invite this succession of potentialities for interaction and attempts to safeguard and to encourage the proper rate and the proper sequence of their enfolding."

In his highly acclaimed, *Childhood and Society,* Erikson identified and extensively elaborated upon a sequence of eight separate stages of psychosocial ego development, what was usually in shorthand fashion referred to as the "eight stages of man." These eight stages he carefully identified, in his clinical practice and in his laboratory research, as the epigenetic unfolding of a "ground plan" of personality that is genetically transmitted. Whereas Jung would have us believe that archetypes are genetically transmitted, Erikson is keen for us to see that the stages of life are genetically transmitted throughout the human species. The fully matured human person arrives on the scene when each of these eight stages have been allowed to mature and function in their own time within the personality of each individual. However, it must be pointed out that Erikson was also eager for us to understand that each stage of development carries with it a "crisis," that is, a critical turning point in the individual's life that arises from physiological maturation and social demands made upon the person at that stage. Each component of the individual's personality develops in relationship to the method in which and the success with which each crisis is met and handled. Conflict, in Erikson's psychosocial theory of development, is crucial and indispensable for healthy development of the ego in each person.

For Erikson, the psychosocial stages of ego development were chronologically sequenced and each was companioned with a "crisis" component which could work either positively or negatively. Though accused of being "too mechanistic" in his developmental stages, he was insistent throughout his career that these stages were, indeed, sequential, and most definitely universal to the human animal. We will discuss briefly each stage of psychosocial development and its corollary crisis.

Corresponding only somewhat to Freud's "oral stage" of infant development, Erikson's first stage (Infancy) placed "trust" and "mistrust" in juxtaposition to each other with the psychosocial strength gained by the individual to be that of "hope." He believed that a sense of trust was essentially the cornerstone of a healthy personality. This sense is sometimes thought of as "confidence," and it grows out of an infant's "inner certainty" about the world as a safe, stable place and people as nurturing and reliable. It all stems from the infant's earliest experiences with mother and feeding rituals. Erikson explains:

> Mothers, I think, create a sense of trust in their children by that kind of administration which in its quality combines sensitive care of the baby's individual needs and a firm sense of personal trustworthiness within the trusted framework of their culture's life style. This forms the basis in the child for a sense of being 'all right,' of being oneself, and of becoming what other people trust one will become (1950).

The first major psychological crisis for the child wherein mistrust emerges is related to the quality of maternal care which is unreliable, inadequate, and rejecting, thus fostering a psychosocial attitude of fear, suspicion, and apprehension in the infant. Erikson believes that the development of a healthy personality is not just based on the rise of trust versus mistrust in the infant's earliest maternal experiences but rather of the dominance of trust over mistrust. The psychosocial strength gained from this successful management of trust over mistrust, says he, is the emergence of "hope" in the child's attitudes towards the future and his social relations with others.

By a year and a half, the child is ready to move to the stage of "autonomy versus shame and doubt" and the personality skill to be learned here is that of "will power." As the child gains in neuromuscular maturation, verbalization, and social discrimination, he begins to explore and interact with his environment more independently and the parents are, therefore, confronted with decisions regarding balancing "holding on" with "letting go." The meeting and handling of this psychosocial crisis, both for the child who wants to "let me do it" and the parent who wants to "let me help you," will set in motion wheels of positive or negative development which not only will encourage or stifle autonomy and shame but will both inculcate a sense of "will power" while affecting the earliest stage of life's sense of trust and mistrust. Each stage of ego development is linked to the previous one and a kind of building block phenomenon occurs such that strong ego boosters grow while weak ego boosters stifle personal development. Failure to inculcate and nurture a sense of autonomy in the child, Erikson believes, will instill in the child a sense of shame, something Erikison believes to be akin to "rage turned upon himself" because he has not been allowed to exercise his personal freedom. Shame grows in the personality traits as autonomy is stifled and, thereby, the curtailment of a responsive feeding of the child's "will power." Erikson goes on to say: "Will power is the unbroken determination to exercise free choice as well as self-restraint in spite of the unavoidable experience of shame, doubt, and a certain rage over being controlled by others. Good will is rooted in the judiciousness of parents guided by their respect for the spirit of the law." Parental guidance at this stage must be firm, Erikson says, but protective of that sense of trust achieved during the previous oral stage. He continues, "Firmness must protect him against the potential anarchy of his as yet untrained sense of discrimination, his inability to hold on and to let go with discretion. As his environment encourages him to 'stand on his own feet,' it must protect him against meaningless and arbitrary experiences of shame and of early doubt."

From trust to autonomy to a sense of "initiative" is the developmental process of the four to five year old child. The resolution of the conflict between initiative and guilt is the final psychosocial experience in the preschool child's personality development, during what Erikson calls the "play age" of childhood from about four years old to the beginning of formal schooling. This resolution of conflict versus guilt produces in the child a deep sense of purpose or, if negatively resolved, the loss of direction and purpose towards the future. "Initiative," explains Erikson, "adds to autonomy the quality of undertaking, planning, and 'attacking' a task for the sake of being on the move, where before self-will, more often than not, inspired acts of defiance or, at any rate, protested independence."

At this time, a child begins to experience the feeling of

being a person who actually counts, one who thinks for himself, "I am what I will be." The balancing of this sense of initiative with the experience of guilt is very much dependent upon how parents handle this last pre-school developmental stage in the child's life. Successful development of this sense of initiative produces what Erikson calls a "goal-directedness" in the child. "The child begins to envisage goals for which his locomotion and cognition have prepared him. The child also begins to think of being big and to identify with people whose work or whose personality he can understand and appreciate. 'Purpose' involves this whole complex of elements." A sense of guilt, on the other hand, is fostered by parents who employ excessive amounts of punishment (verbal or physical) in response to the child's urge to love and be loved. The child's future potential to work productively and achieve self-sufficiency within the context of his or her society's economic system depends markedly upon the ability to master this psychosocial crisis of "purpose" produced by the initiative versus guilt dialectic.

At stage four, the school age years, the child moved to another major level of ego development and personality. This "school age" period covers the years between about six and eleven and in classical psychoanalysis is referred to as the "latency period." Here, industry versus inferiority appear and the crisis produced by this tension is that of a sense of competency. We have now moved, in the positively developed personality, from trust to autonomy and initiative to industry or, contrariwise, for the negatively developing personality of the child from mistrust, shame, and guilt to a sense of inferiority. Hope, will power, and purpose as character traits developed in response to the psychosocial crises of each developmental stage now give rise to what Erikson calls a sense of competency on the part of the healthy child. Erikson has summarized these developmental stages as a movement from "*I am what I am given*" to "*I am what I will*" to "*I am what I can imagine I will be*" to, now at the fourth stage, "*I am what I learn.*" "In school," Erikson explains, "with varying abruptness, play is transformed into work, game into competition and cooperation, and the freedom of imagination into the duty to perform with full attention to the techniques which make imagination communicable, accountable, and applicable to defined tasks." Learning, demonstrating, moving forward in one's capacity to perform, to compete, and to demonstrate ability is now in full sway. The danger at this stage, of course, lies in the potential of failure which will inculcate a sense of inferiority or incompetence. The child's sense of competency and industry is, in modern society, primarily affected by and determined by his educational successes. Yet, cautions Erikson, a genuine sense of industry involves more than simply one's educational achievements and occupational aspirations for it also includes a feeling of being interpersonally competent, the confidence, if you will, that one can exert positive influence on the social world in quest of meaningful individual and social goals. This fundamental strength, namely, competency, is the basis for participation in the social, economic, and political order of one's culture and society.

The fifth stage of ego development falls between childhood and adulthood and is a pivotal period in the development of the individual. Adolescence is that period in a person's development where "ego identity" and "role confusion" come face to face with the resulting psychosocial crisis of "fidelity." This stage in Erikson's developmental scenario is the most well developed in his overall schema. He elaborates on the nature of "ego identity." "The growing and developing youths, faced with this physiological revolution within them, are now primarily concerned with attempts at consolidating their social roles. They are sometimes morbidly, often curiously, preoccupied with what they appear to be in the eyes of others as compared with what they feel they are and with the question of how to connect the earlier cultivated roles and skills with the ideal prototypes of the day ... The sense of ego identity, then, is the accrued confidence that one's ability to maintain inner sameness and continuity (one's ego in the psychological sense) is matched by the sameness and continuity of one's meaning for others." Three fundamental elements characterize ego identity. First, individuals must perceive themselves as having inner sameness and continuity. They are the same person over all. Second, the individual's social *milieu* must also perceive a sameness and continuity in the individual, so group affirmation is crucial. Third, the adolescent must have gathered confidence in the relationship between his world and that of his social group by having a sense of who he is and having that affirmed by others. However, when this mutuality of ego identity affirmation is absent, adolescents will encounter what Erikson calls "role confusion." In the absence of a personal identity which is strong enough to see a youngster through these developmental years, an identity crisis is inevitable. This crisis is most often characterized by an inability to select a career or pursue further education with the added deficit of a deep sense of futility, personal disorganization, and aimlessness. The feeling of inadequacy, depersonalization, alienation, and even a negative identity may result. When the adolescents has confronted the challenge and ego identity has finally emerged sound and operational, "fidelity" emerges and this, says Erikson, refers to the individual's "ability to sustain loyalties freely pledged in spite of the inevitable contradictions of value systems." Being true to one's own ego identity while remaining loyal to the social matrix within which that ego identity has developed and emerged is a characteristic of fidelity and prepares the adolescent for the next stage of development.

By virtue of a well-established ego identity characterized by fidelity or loyalty to oneself and one's social *milieu*, the individual, says Erikson, is now "ready for intimacy, that is, the capacity to commit himself to concrete affiliations and partnerships and to develop ethical strength to abide by such commitments, even though they may call for significant sacrifices and compromises." This is the stage in which courtship, marriage, and early family life come on the scene. By "intimacy," Erikson has in mind the sense of intimacy most of us share with a spouse, friends, brothers and sisters, and parents or other relatives. He also, however, speaks of intimacy with oneself, that is, the ability to "fuse your identity with somebody else's without fear that you're going to lose something yourself." This two pronged sense of intimacy is crucial in a well-developed relationship -- intimacy with others within the framework of intimacy with oneself. The inevitable danger in this developing sense of intimacy is, of course, a sense of isolation where neither intimacy nor social involvement are possible or productive.

The inability to enter into positive and intimate personal relationships leads the individual to feelings of social emptiness and isolation. Merely formalized and superficial social relationships are inadequate to meet the developmental needs of these individuals, however, and given the fact that they may be suffering from an over dependence upon self-absorbing behavior to relieve their sense of loneliness, they drift further and further away from realistic opportunities to experience and nurture feelings of intimacy. Their behavior, then, becomes inevitably counterproductive. The psychosocial strength being sought here and the one which is realized in the healthy development of a sense of intimacy is that of love. In addition to its romantic and erotic qualities, Erikson regards love as the ability to commit oneself to others and to abide by such commitments, even though they may require self-denial and compromise. "Love," explains Erikson, "is mutuality of devotion forever subduing the antagonisms inherent in divided function."

The "middle years" of an individual's stages of life are fraught with prospects of creative activity or degenerative stifling. What is not possible is for nothing to happen to the individual's ego development and psychosocial maturation. This process continues throughout life, it does not stop for age and only ends with death. The countervailing options for the middle age adult is either what Erikson calls "generativity" or "stagnation" and the psychosocial crisis produced is that of "care."

"Generativity" occurs, says Erikson, when an individual begins to show concern not only for the welfare of the next generation but also for the nature of the society in which that generation will live and work. This developmental stage in life has to do with the willingness, or not, of the individual to meet the challenge of assuming responsibility for the continuation and betterment of whatever is instrumental to the maintenance and enhancement of the society in which the individual lives. It represents the older generation's concern in establishing and guiding those who will replace them. Failure to assume this responsibility, to assert oneself into the mainstream of social betterment and improvement leads to individual and societal stagnation. The sense that one does not wish to be involved, not participate in teaching the next generation the values necessary for successful and fulfilled living, all lead to a failure of courage and a diminishment of one's social worth and the worth of society at large. Those in their middle years who embrace and nurture generativity will produce a sense of "care" needed for the ongoing contribution to the improving quality of life for the next generation. Individuals lacking generativity cease to function as productive members of society, live only to satisfy their needs, and are interpersonally impoverished. This is often called the "crisis of middle age" where the person has a sense of hopelessness and tends to feel that life is meaningless. Caring for oneself, for others, for society at large is the benefit and reward to those who develop and nurture a sense of contribution to the wider society.

The "mature years" constitutes the last stage in life's journey. Every culture has this stage well developed according to its own social values, history, and composition. It is a time when the individual's ego is confronted with the option of "integrity" or "despair" and the crisis which comes with this confrontation can lead to a general sense of "wisdom" about life and how to live it. "Only in him who in some way has taken care of things and people," says Erikson, "and who has adapted himself to the triumphs and disappointments adherent to being, the originator of others or the generator of products and ideas -- only in him may gradually ripen the fruit of these seven stages -- I know no better word for it than ego integrity." With the inevitable demands brought on by these declining years of the need to adjust to deterioration of physical strength and health, to retirement and reduced income, to the death of a spouse and close friends, and the need to establish new affiliations with one's age group, there is a marked demand for shifting one's attention from a focus upon future life to that of one's past life.

The sharing of past experiences, of days gone by, with those who are younger characterize this stage in life and often, depending on the culture, is perceived by the listeners and observers of these older persons as a sense of "wisdom," a kind of helpful knowledge about what is important and how to live a meaningful and fulfilled life. "The wisdom of old age," explains Erikson, "involves an awareness of the relativity of all knowledge acquired in one lifetime in one historical period. Wisdom is a detached and yet active concern with life in the face of death." On the other hand, the lack or loss of ego integration in older individuals is earmarked by a hidden dread of death, a feeling of irrevocable failure, and an incessant preoccupation with what might have been." "Fate," he explains, "is not accepted as the frame of life, death not as its finite boundary. Despair indicates that time is too short for alternate roads to integrity: this is why the old try to doctor their memories." Ego integration leads to a sense of real and practical wisdom worthy to be shared with the young and in that process the individual comes to a deeper sense of self-fulfillment and contentment with life as he has lived it with hope for the future.

Though a trained and never rebellious psychoanalyst in the true Freudian school of thought, Erikson, nevertheless, never ceased to claim allegiance to Freud while boldly asserting the further development and contribution of his thought to the Freudian school of psychotherapy. His psychosocial theory of personality development relied upon a strong argument for the centrality of ego psychology, developmental changes throughout the life cycle, and an understanding of personality against the background of social and historical forces. Contrary to Freud, Erikson held that the ego was an autonomous personality structure and he concentrated his efforts, therefore, upon ego qualities that emerge during the fundamental stages of maturation.

Erikson argued that the ego continued its development throughout life and identified eight stages in which that development occurs. These psychosocial stages characterize the human life cycle, as he called it, and he contended that the individual's personality is determined by the resolutions of the conflicts which emerge in each of these developmental stages. His theory is, of course, rooted in his basic assumptions concerning human nature itself, namely, (1) a strong commitment to the assumptions of holism and environmentalism, and (2) a moderate commitment to the assumptions of determinism, rationality, objectivity, pro-activity, heterostasis, and knowability.

Though some have registered concern over the relationship between the personal life of Erikson, his family life and his failure to come to both an emotional and professional embracing of the life of his mentally retarded child, and the profundity of his thought, most psychotherapists today are, however, indebted to Erikson for calling attention to the eight stages of the life cycle. Granted, they are mechanistic, sometimes even antiseptic, they have, nevertheless, spawned a whole new way of viewing human maturation and have nurtured a deeper appreciation for what a modified psychoanalytic theory of personality can still offer to the modern practice of psychotherapy.

ERIK ERIKSON'S BIOGRAPHY

Identity's Architect: A Biography of Erik H. Erikson By Lawrence J. Friedman. Cambridge, MA: Harvard University Press, 1999.

ERIK ERIKSON'S PRIMARY SOURCES

Childhood and Society (1950)

Young Man Luther. A Study in Psychoanalysis and History (1958)

Identity: Youth and Crisis (1968)

Gandhi's Truth: On the Origin of Militant Nonviolence (1969)

Adulthood (edited book, 1978)

Vital Involvement in Old Age (with J.M. Erikson and H. Kivnick, 1986)

The Life Cycle Completed (with J.M. Erikson, 1987)

Identity and the Life Cycle. Selected Papers (1959)

A Way of Looking at Things: Selected Papers 1930-1980 (Editor: S.P. Schlien, 1915)

The Erik Erikson Reader (Editor: Robert Coles, 2001)

Erikson on Development in Adulthood: New Insights from the Unpublished Papers (Carol Hren Hoare, 2002)

Erik Erikson Worked For His Life, Work, and Significance (Kit

Welchman, 2000)

Identity's Architect: A Biography of Erik H. Erikson (Lawrence J. Friedman, 1999)

Erik H. Erikson: The Power and Limits of a Vision, N.Y., The Free Press (Paul Roazen, 1976)

"Everybody Rides the Carousel" (documentary film) (Hubley, 1976)

Erik H. Erikson: the Growth of His Work (Robert Coles, 1970)

Ideas and Identities: The Life and Work of Erik Erikson (Robert S. Wallerstein & Leo Goldberger, eds., [IUP, 1998])

CHAPTER SEVEN
Carl Rogers and Person-Centered Psychotherapy

BIOGRAPHICAL SKETCH

The fourth of six children, Carl Ransom Rogers was born on the 8th of January, 1902, in Oak Park, Illinois. His father, Walter Alexander Rogers, was a civil engineer and his mother, Julia Cushing Rogers, a devout Christian woman and traditional housewife. His father held both a degree in engineering and some advanced graduate training as well, all from the University of Wisconsin, and his mother had completed two years of college before she married Walter. In his closing years of life, Carl described his parents as "down to earth individuals" but "rather anti-intellectual, with some of the contempt of the practical person toward the long-haired egg-head." Carl was the fourth child and third son but nearly six years later he had two more brothers, Walter and John, who were born in 1907 and 1908 respectively. His oldest brother Lester and his sister Margaret were nearly nine and seven years his senior and he found himself closest emotionally to his younger two brothers. Because Carl was both obviously a gifted child and could read before entering public school, he began in the second grade, and one of his classmates was Ernest Hemingway as well as the children of Frank Lloyd Wright. At the age of twelve years old and owing to the financial success of his father's career, the family relocated to a farm about an hour west of Chicago and for the remainder of Carl's adolescent years, they lived there.

Life was hard for a city boy moved abruptly to the country where farm chores were difficult and demanding, carried out within the strict spirit of an aggressive Protestant ethos and worldview. He believed that his parents were masters of the art of subtle control for he wrote, "I do not remember ever being given a direct command on an important subject, yet such was the unity of our family that it was understood by all that we did not dance, play

145

cards, attend movies, smoke, drink, or show any sexual interest."
Little encouragement was given for free time, day dreaming, and
child's play and, in the face of such a restricted life, Carl became
somewhat introverted, isolated from his fantasy world,
independent of spirit, however, and quite decidedly self-
disciplined.

Rogers often spoke of his boyhood in less than glowing
terms for, says he, they were years of structured, strict, and
uncompromising religious and ethical standards dominated by
devotion to a fundamentalist kind of faith. "I think the attitudes
toward persons outside our large family," he wrote, "can be
summed up schematically in this way: Other persons behave in
dubious ways which we do not approve in our family. Many of
them play cards, go to movies, smoke, drink, and engage in other
activities -- some unmentionable. So the best thing to do is to be
tolerant of them, since they may not know better, and to keep
away from any close communication with them and live your life
within the family" (1961). This uppity condescension
characterized the family and, unfortunately, too often
characterized his own behavior. In speaking of his high school
years, he wrote: "I made no lasting associations or friendships. I
was a good student and never had any difficulty with the work.
Neither did I have problems in getting along with the other
students so far as I can recall. It is simply that I knew them only
in a very surface fashion and felt decidedly different and alone, but
this was compensated for by the fact that my brother and I went
together much of this time and there was always the family at
home" (1961).

It was to the University of Wisconsin, in 1924, that Carl
was sent to pursue a mixed bag of interests. Both his parents and
three of his siblings had attended the University of Wisconsin and
an alternative school was never seriously contemplated.
Beginning, typically, as an agriculture major with youthful plans
of becoming a successful farmer, he drifted towards history, then
religion for what he thought would be the ministry, and then,
eventually and finally, he took up a serious and sustained interest
in clinical psychology. Of course, the University of Wisconsin was
just the right place to study clinical psychology for it was
becoming rather quickly the leading center in the mid-west for that

discipline. He always professed to believing that the discovery of psychology constituted the fundamental turning point in his life.

This turning point came during his third year at the University when he was chosen to go to Peking for the "World Student Christian Federation Conference" for the purpose of "evangelizing the world for Christ in this generation!" He wrote later, "I consider this a time when I achieved my psychological independence. In major ways I for the first time emancipated myself from the religious thinking of my parents, and realized that I could not go along with them." He recounts a particularly insightful moment while on board ship returning from the Peking evangelism trip.   One evening, aboard ship, a traveling companion, Dr. Henry Sharman, a student of the sayings of Jesus, made some provocative remarks. "It struck me in my cabin," Rogers later wrote, "that Jesus was a man like other men -- not divine! As this idea formed and took root, it became obvious to me that I could never in any emotional sense return home." The major result of this trip to Peking and this new insight into his own faith-based self-understanding was that he developed a duodenal ulcer. "Something of the gently suppressive family atmosphere," he mused, "is perhaps indicated by the fact that three of six children in our family developed ulcers at some period in their lives.   I had the dubious distinction of acquiring mine at the earliest age" (1961).

He earned his B.A. in history from the University of Wisconsin in 1924 having taken only one course in psychology and that by correspondence. In 1924, he married Helen Elliot, a childhood sweetheart, and they soon thereafter moved to New York City where he pursued a master's degree from Columbia University while simultaneously attending the Union Theological Seminary, a bastion of liberalism in the 1920s and 1930s. He and Helen eventually had two children, a boy and a girl. At the seminary, he took a course on the pursuit of the ministry, the nature of the career, its demands and expectations, and during this time he decided, against his parents' wishes and expectations, to transfer to psychology at the Teachers College of Columbia University in 1926 and where, in 1927, he won a fellowship to work in the Institute of Child Guidance. At the Institute he gained an elementary knowledge of Freudian psychoanalysis, but was not much influenced by it as his later theoretical work demonstrated. At the Institute he also attended a lecture by Alfred Adler who shocked Rogers and the other staff members with his contention that an elaborate case history was unnecessary for psychotherapy.

Rogers subsequently took from there a masters in psychology in 1928 and a doctorate in psychotherapy in 1931. He was enthralled with clinical work and had already commenced his lifelong career in this field at the Rochester Society for the Prevention of Cruelty to Children. There, he studied Otto Rank's theory and therapy techniques and that experience drove him to believe that he himself could develop operational theories and techniques unique to his own insights and experience. For the next ten years, Rogers applied himself to psychological services for delinquent and underprivileged children.

At the age of thirty-eight, Rogers received an appointment as "full professor of psychology" at Ohio State University. Despite his fondness for teaching he might have turned down the offer if his wife, Helen, had not urged him to accept and if the University had not agreed to start him at the top, with the academic rank of full professor. He often told his younger students and colleagues that the only way to enter the academy was to do so as full professor. Anything less was not acceptable as it required too much work in areas of no particular interest to the young professor but necessary in order for him to prove himself worthy of the appointment. A major breakthrough in his own self-understanding occurred quite surprisingly in response to a lecture he was invited to give to the Psi Chi chapter at the University of Minnesota. The lecture, entitled, "Newer Concepts in Psychotherapy," raised such furor and controversy that it occurred to him that he was saying something quite new and provocative. This lecture became the backbone of the second chapter in his new blockbuster book, *Client-Centered Therapy,* published in 1942.

From 1940 to 1945, he taught psychology and, in 1942, he published his first of several major books. This one, entitled, *Counseling and Psychotherapy: Newer Concepts in Practice,* was the first of its kind in the profession of psychological counseling where the psychologist's clinical results based upon the recording and transcript of the client's therapy sessions were used for analysis in print. He set a precedent and the profession burst upon the scene with therapy-session based clinical reports and analyses like it had never done before. His publishing became prolific in the journals as a result of this new method of presenting psychological data.

After five years of teaching at Ohio State, Rogers took a one year appointment in 1944 in New York as Director of counseling services for the United Service Organization. Rogers was subsequently offered a post at the Counseling Centre of the University of Chicago where he served from 1945 to 1957 and where he wrote, in 1951, the most important book of his career, entitled, *Client-Centered Therapy: Its Current Practice, Implications, and Theory.* The groundbreaking nature of this book's fundamental theories about counseling would change the face of that profession forever and would catapult Rogers into international acclaim. That same year and thanks to the notoriety of the book, he was appointed head of the Counseling Center at the University of Chicago. At the time, the famous Dr. C. George Boeree made this following assessment: "Rogers' theory is particularly simple -- elegant even! The entire theory is built on a single 'force of life' he calls the actualizing tendency. It can be defined as the built-in motivation present in every life-form to develop its potentials to the fullest extent possible. We're not just talking about survival: Rogers believes that all creatures strive to make the very best of their existence. If they fail to do so, it is not for a lack of desire."

Though his six years at the University were outstandingly successful, he left in 1957 to take up a joint post at the University of Wisconsin as both Professor of Psychology and Professor of Psychiatry. He stayed, however, only two years for he found that he was becoming disillusioned with the therapeutic and diagnostic techniques of the establishment at the time particularly in the psychopharmacologically-driven department of psychiatry as well as with the overall pedagogical philosophy of the graduate program generally. So, in 1959, he joined the Western Behavioral Sciences Institute in La Jolla, California. In 1961, he wrote what has become his most internationally recognized publication, *On Becoming a Person.* During the years 1962-1963, he was a Fellow at the Center for Advanced Study n the Behavioral Sciences at Stanford University. He concentration was on group social relations, and by 1968, he had a handful of colleagues who chose to separate from the Institute and found their own, known as the Center for the Studies of the Person, based in La Jolla as well. A summary report indicated that, "...subsequently, throughout the 1960s and 1970s, Rogers spearheaded the development of personal-growth groups, and his influence spread to working with couples and families; and his idea were also applied to administration, minority groups, interracial and intercultural groups, and international relationships." At the Center, he continued to provide therapy for select individuals and couples, and was prolific in his research and writing. In 1987, having broken his hip, he died in surgery on the 4th of February, at the age of 85.

Rogers early on avoided the development of a formal theory of personality but eventually, from peer pressure, he worked on his concept of personality which became a core of all of his writings. First expressed in sketchy form in his 147 Presidential address at the American Psychological Association, he further developed it in his great classic, *Client-Center Therapy* in 1951 and eventually fully developed it in his greatest work of all, *On Becoming a Person.* Nevertheless, he was always insistent that the theory should remain tentative. It is with this thought that one must approach any discussion of Rogerian personality theory.

Carl Rogers was honored the world over and towards the end of his life was nominated for the Nobel Peace Prize for his work with national inter-group conflict in South Africa and Northern Ireland. He had received countless honorary degrees from distinguished institutions such as the University of Santa Clara, Gonzaga University, the University of Cincinnati, and Northwestern University as well as a D.Ph. From the University of Hamburg in Germany and the Doctor of Science degree from the University of Leiden. As early as 1944, he was president of the American Association for Applied Psychology and two years later assumed the presidency of the American Psychological Association. In 1956, he became the first president of the American Academy of Psychotherapists and in 1964 was selected Humanist of the Year by the American Humanist Association. We can close this biographical sketch with the citation given to Rogers by the American Psychological Association when, in 1972, they awarded him the coveted Distinguished Professional Contribution Award. It reads:

"His commitment to the whole person has been an example which has guided and challenged the practice of psychology in the schools, in industry, and throughout the community. By devising, practicing, evaluating, and teaching a method of psychotherapy and counseling which reaches to the very roots of human potentiality and individuality, he has caused all psychotherapists to re-examine their procedures in a new light. Innovator in personality research, pioneer in the encounter movement, and a respected gadfly of organized psychology, he has made a lasting impression on the profession of psychology."

CLASSIC TEXT CONSIDERED

Some psychotherapists we have considered in this study established their reputation on one major book. Others wrote numerous books to establish themselves. Rogers, though he wrote much and often, established himself on the basis of two major works, namely, *Client-Centered Therapy* (1950) and *On Becoming a Person* (1961). Roger's first and overriding characteristic in the writing of his first major book was to emphasize the warmth and acceptance of the counseling relationship between the counselor and the client. His first major book was meant to emphasize the new rationale of his approach, namely, "The client, as the term has acquired its meaning, is one who comes actively and voluntarily to gain help on a problem, but without any notion of surrendering his own responsibility for the situation."

From non-directive counseling to client-centered counseling to, finally, person-to-person therapy, Rogers' thought continued to grow and expand. Yet, his initial entry into the cauldron of psychotherapeutic theorizing in his first book (1950) to his major opus of 1961 finally culminating in his latest works all bespeak a capacity to grow through learning in the clinical environment. He gradually came to realize that the relationship between therapist and client is the most important aspect underlying personality change. Herein lay his interest and this is where he concentrated the bulk of his entire career.

Rogers brought to the psychotherapeutic table a new way

of seeing the counselor's role in relationship to the client. He suggested that the emphasis shift should be from an objectified standoffish posture to rather an "empathic" approach in understanding the client's world, and then to seek to "communicate" that understanding directly to the client. In mirroring back to the client the feelings the counselor picked up on in the interview encounter, the counselor simultaneously transmitted the desire to perceive the world as the client perceived it, thus, the role of "non-directivity" in the dyadic relationship. Rogers insisted that the counselor's role was to achieve an "internal frame-of-reference" with the client. "It is the counselor's aim," says Rogers, "to perceive as sensitively and accurately as possible all of the perceptual field as it is being experienced by the client ... and having thus perceived this internal frame of reference of the other as completely as possible, to indicate to the client the extent to which he is seeming through the client's eyes."

In the "new" psychotherapy, Rogers emphasized four important principles. First, the new therapy "relies much more heavily on the individual drive toward growth, health, and adjustment. Therapy is not a matter of doing something to the individual, or of inducing him to do something about himself. It is instead a matter of freeing him for normal growth and development." Second, "this new therapy places greater stress upon the emotional elements, the feelings aspects of the situation, than upon the intellectual aspects." Third, "this new therapy places grater stress upon the immediate situation than upon the individual's past." And, fourth, this new approach "lays great stress upon the therapeutic relationship itself as a growth experience."

Here the individual learns to understand himself to make significant independent choices, to relate himself successfully to another person in a more adult fashion. Rogers firmly believed that individuals by and large had it within themselves to solve their own problems. The task, then, of the therapist in Rogers' view was to establish the conditions which would allow individuals to attain this insight for themselves. "Attainment of insight" was, therefore, one of the key goals of nondirective therapy. On the other hand, the counselor's chief task was to reach the "clarification of feelings" through rephrasing the emotional content of the client's statements such that the client gained a new insight into his own stated condition. "Effective counseling," says Rogers, "consists of a definitively structured, permissive relationship which allows the client to gain an understanding of himself to a degree which enables him to take positive steps in the light of his new orientation."

The three major elements characterizing Rogers' theory of personality were (1) the necessity for the counselor to provide a warm and permissive relationship for the client, (2) the necessity for the counselor to assume the internal frame of reference of the client and to communicate empathic understanding of the client's world, and (3) finally, to reach a mutual expression of feelings between the client and the counselor thereby realizing the full potential of the client-centered theory of personality and psychotherapeutic treatment.

Rogers identified six conditions of client-counselor relationships which, if met, would constitute the basis for a successful therapy. He believed he had already proven clinically that a theoretical rationale for personality change in therapy was possible which implied that constructive alterations in personality could occur regardless of the specific verbal techniques employed by the counselor. He recited these six conditions to reinforce his theory. First, two persons are in psychological contact such that each of them is fully aware that the other's presence makes a difference. Second, the client is in a state of incongruence in relationship with the counselor due to a "discrepancy" between the client's self-image and his existential experience in the counseling environment. Third, the therapist is, on the other hand, congruent (which means integrated) in the relationship due to the pre-set definition of his role in the situation. Fourth, the therapist experiences unconditional positive regard for the client as this is crucial in order to establish a connectedness to the client in the counseling *milieu*. Fifth, the therapist experiences an empathic understanding of the client's internal frame of reference and endeavors to communicate this experience to the client such that the encounter proves therapeutically successful in direct correlation to the therapist's capacity to emote empathy. And, sixth and finally, the communication to the client of the therapist's empathic understanding and unconditional positive regard must be minimally achieved or, otherwise, no helpful therapeutic result will occur.

CONCEPTS AND THEORIES

Rogers was a conspicuous member of the Third Force, the humanistic psychological school which set itself alongside but *vis a vis* both psychoanalysis and behaviorism. His understanding of human nature was, of course, central to his position as a leader in the Third Force movement. He speaks of the driving force in his work which is "the continuing clinical experience with individuals who perceive themselves, or are perceived by others to be, in need of personal help." Since 1928, for a period now approaching thirty years (he wrote in 1958), "I have spent probably an average of 15 to 20 hours per week, except during vacation periods, in endeavoring to understand and be of therapeutic help to these individuals. From these hours, and from my relationships with these people, I have drawn most of whatever insight I possess into the meaning of therapy, the dynamics of interpersonal relationships, and the structure and function of personality." Rogers firmly believed that at the core, every human being is fundamentally good, being essentially purposive, forward-moving, constructive, realistic, and trustworthy. Because of this essential goodness of the human person, every individual given the right opportunity for growth, love, and affirmation will blossom forth in his own innate potential, optimum personal development and effectiveness.

Christianity, he argued, has nurtured a core belief in the innate evil of the human person, an inclination to evil and sin. Furthermore, he is unabashed in arguing that this demented notion of human nature has been influenced, even trumped, by Freud and the psychoanalytic school of psychotherapy. If permitted to run free from the scrutiny and domination of the ego and the superego, the human personality's id and unconscious would manifest itself, according to Freud and Christians, in incest, homicide, thievery, rape, and other horrendous acts of self-destructive behavior. People do engage in such behavior and this occurs when they have been stifled, been misdirected, or their personality development has been suppressed from its natural inclinations. When, however, people are able to function as "fully human beings," when they are free to experience and express themselves, they show a positive and rational approach to life which elicits trust and nurtures harmony in interpersonal relationships.

Rogers protested against those cynical and jaded psychotherapists who thought of him as naïve and simplistic: "I do not have a Pollyanna view of human nature," he argued. "I am quite aware that out of defensiveness and inner fear individuals can and do behave in ways which are incredibly cruel, horribly destructive, immature, regressive, anti-social, and harmful. Yet, one of the most refreshing and invigorating parts of my experience is to work with such individuals and to discover the strongly positive directional tendencies which exist in them, as in all of us, at the deepest levels." This driving force in human nature towards the good and self-fulfillment he calls the "actualizing tendency," and he believes it is latent in every human being. He defines it as "the inherent tendency of the organism (the personality) to develop all its capacities in ways which serve to maintain or enhance the person." Therefore, says he, the fundamental principle guiding every person's life is the drive to actualize, maintain, or enhance themselves, indeed, to become the best that their inherited natures will permit them to be. This is, essentially, the sole motivating principle in Roger's theory of personality.

To be sure, there are certain definitive characteristics which establish this actualizing tendency. Let us explore them momentarily here. Of course and to begin with, says Rogers, there is a "biological factor" which is operative here, namely, this tendency is an inborn characteristic necessary to maintain the individual but also for the enhancement of the individual by providing a mechanism for the development and differentiation of the body's functions, growth, and development. But, of more importance than even this is the motivating force which the actualizing tendency provides for in increased autonomy and self-reliance in pursuit of the individual's full potential in life. Furthermore, the actualizing tendency is not merely for the reduction of tension in the stresses of one's physical or biological life, contrary to Freud's insistence on the prominence of instincts. Rather, the individual is motivated, says Rogers, by a growth process in which potentialities and capacities are brought to realization. This actualizing tendency, then, says he, "is the essence of life itself."

The actualizing tendency, explains Rogers, serves as a criterion against which all of one's life experiences are evaluated and, particularly, when individuals engage in what he calls the "organism-valuing process." This process involves the individual's overt effort in maintaining and enhancing the sought after and valued positive behaviors and experiences in life for they produce within the individual a strong feeling of satisfaction in the realization of one's full potential. This "process" is a mechanism for the evaluation, the weighing, the determining whether or not an experience is affirmative or negative to self-fulfillment. And, the most critical aspect of this actualizing tendency, says Rogers, is the individual's drive toward self-actualization, what he has called the "self-actualizing tendency." This particular tendency, then, is what gives a forward thrust to life, to the individual who must encounter and incorporate life's complexities, self-sufficiency, and maturity. "Self-actualization," then, is the process of becoming a more adequate person.

Rogers counted himself among the phenomenologists of the day who were practicing humanistic psychology as members of the Third Force. The Third Force was never a formal body but consisted of humanistic psychologists who pushed their worldview as a viable alternative to Freud and Skinner, or psychoanalysis and behaviorism, in both theory and practice. Phenomenological psychology contends that the "psychological reality" of the individual's world is exclusively a function of the way in which the world is perceived by that individual. The truth doesn't really matter because it can never really be identified. What really matters to the individual is what that person thinks is true, sees to be true, acts in relationship to what he sees and thinks to be the truth. Phenomenological psychology argues that what is real to an individual, that is, what reality is thought, understood, or felt to be, is that which exists within that person's "internal frame of reference." It is this frame of reference which is important in the psychotherapeutic relationship. Rogers was insistent upon this point, namely, that every individual interprets his world and that interpretation is what the therapist must come to grips with. The only way to "understand" an individual's behavior and attitude is to come to an understanding of this internal frame of reference. It is the "subjective reality" of the client's perceived world which is important, not the objective truth.

Needless to say, Rogers' identification with the phenomenological approach to personality theory is based upon his strong conviction that the complexity of human behavior can only be understood within the context of the "whole person." His emphasis upon the "holistic view of personality," namely, that the person reacts as an integrated organism and that his unity cannot be derived from mere behaviorism, is at the core of his therapy. It is the "self" which constitutes the focus of his analysis for it is the fundamental center of human personality. His theory of personality development is based upon this conviction. "The self, or self-concept," says Rogers, "is defined as an organized, consistent, conceptual gestalt composed of perceptions of the characteristics of the 'I' or 'me' to others and to various aspects of life, together with the values attached to these perceptions. It is a gestalt which is available to awareness though not necessarily in awareness." The "self-concept" is comprised of (1) what the individual thinks he is, (2) what he thinks he ought to be, and (3) and the "ideal self" or what he thinks he would like to be. This tripartite composition of the self constitutes the core of Rogers' personality theory.

Rogers does not believe that the "self" *per se* manages and monitors the individual's behavior but rather it "symbolizes" the individual's conscious experiences of the world -- who he thinks he is, who he thinks he ought to be, and who he thinks he wants to be. He discounts, not possibly the reality of unconscious data, but its irrelevance to the individual's self-concept and its viability in the therapeutic situation for it is the individual's own self-understanding, as he explains it, describes it, characterizes it, that is important therapeutically. Phenomenology trumps unconscious data as the basis for psychological therapy, says Rogers, for the structure of the self is formed through the individual's interaction with the familial, social, and cultural environment. The "content of one's self-concept," argued Rogers, is fundamentally a social product and not the result of the bombardment of the psyche with unconscious and repressed data.

Therefore, there are identifiable components needed for

the development of a healthy self-concept and when they are absent or twisted from experience, the individual suffers. First, Rogers suggests that every person has a basic desire for warmth, respect, admiration, love, and acceptance from people important in his life. He calls this the "need for positive regard." Whether innate or socially learned, this drive is strong from the earliest days of childhood. A person as infant, child, adolescent, or adult, he believes, will do almost anything to meet this innate need for "positive regard." There is a reciprocal component to this drive as well, namely, in the giving of this positive regard, one receives it in turn. The reciprocity of positive regard is a strong re-enforcer of social relationships. The self, says Rogers, is profoundly influenced by this need and rather than suggest that individuals are driven to satisfy the demands and expectations of their "self-concept," he argues that people are driven to satisfy their need for positive regard, both to give it and to receive it. Where there is a conflict between what the individual wants in service to his "self" and what he recognizes as in service to his "need" for regard, Rogers call this "incongruence." "This, as we see it, is the basic estrangement in man. He has not been true to himself, to his own natural organism valuing of experience, but for the sake of preserving the positive regard of others has now come to falsify some of the values he experiences and to perceive them only in terms based upon their value to others." The conflict internally, that is, "incongruency," is the result of the individual choosing to service his need for positive regard at the expense of serving his own self's perceived personal needs. The conflict often leads to psychological stress, tension, and mental illness. "Yet," Rogers continues, "this has not been a conscious choice, but a natural -- and tragic -- development in infancy. The path of development toward psychological maturity is the undoing of this estrangement in man's functioning. The achievement of a self which is congruent with experience, and the restoration of a unified organism valuing process as the regulator of behavior." Too often, it is the "people pleaser" who emerges from this incongruity, the individual who is so driven to please the other person that he forgets to please himself in the process.

Within the context of self-concept development in every individual from childhood is the presence of "conditional positive regard," namely, that situation in the family and society in which the individual is the recipient of positive regard only so long as that individual conforms to the expectations of the positive regard provider. In other words, positive regard is contingent upon compliance with outside expectations of family and society members. "I will love you so long as," or "only if" situations constitute conditional positive regard. This situation, Rogers believes, are detrimental to the child becoming a fully functioning and self-actualized individual. The child, and eventually the adult, "relinquishes" ownership of his own needs and desires in order to conform to the "conditions" laid out by the parent, the family, and society for the giving of positive regard. The individual runs the serious risk of "losing himself" to himself in the process of conforming to the conditions established by others for the giving of positive regard. The "condition of worth" is compliance with the expectations of others, regardless of one's own sense of what is valued. This was painfully true in Rogers' own personal life as a child raised in an extremely restrictive religious home environment.

To counter act the mental health dangers of "conditional positive regard," Rogers developed the concept of "unconditional positive regard" and this concept characterizes all of his psychotherapeutic practice and theorizing. In light of his own childhood experience, Rogers developed this concept as a counterpoise to the detrimental character of the conditions of worth operative in conditional positive regard. He believed strongly that it is possible to give and receive positive regard without attaching it to behavioral compliance. Positive regard can be given to individuals in situations where the behavior of the other individual is not necessarily to the liking of the positive-regard-giving individual. This requires every individual to be accepted and respected for who and what they are, without conditions of ifs, ands, or buts. Such unconditional positive regard is most evident in a mother's love of a misbehaving child. Parental love is not, then, given to the child when and only when the child "conforms" to the parents' behavioral expectations but love, positive regard, is given "unconditionally." Rogers was quick to criticize the Christian saying from Jesus, "You are my friends if you do what so ever I tell you." This is conditional worth and not love Rogers contends.

Rogers believes that children raised in the unconditional positive regard family environment, "then no conditions of worth would develop, self-regard would be unconditional, the needs for positive regard and self-regard would never be at variance with organism evaluation, and the individual would continue to be psychological adjusted, and would be fully functioning. This chain of events is hypothetically possible, and hence important theoretically, though it does not appear to occur in actuality" (1961). Discipline is not absent from the family environment, but the circumstances under which it is used and understood by child and parent are radically different when disassociated from self-worth. The creation of an unconditional love "atmosphere" provides the mechanism for a positive use of discipline wherein the child can grow into a fully functioning and potentially self-actualized person with a deep and unchallenged sense of self-worth.

Growing out of Rogers' understanding of the nature of the experience of "incongruity" were the experiences of "threat," "anxiety," and "defense." These three very common experiences are all interrelated and are manifested in the presence of the individual's awareness or lack of awareness of an incongruous situation. Every individual strives for what Rogers' calls "consistency" in behavior, attempting at all times to keep an even keel in interpersonal relationships based upon the individual's self-concept. Where there is incongruity between the individual's self-concept and the social situation making demands upon him inconsistent with his idea of himself, that individual feels a "threat." The threat in Rogers' theory occurs when a person recognizes an incongruity between his self-concept and its condition of worth corollary and the experience which precipitates the incongruity. This "threatening" situation is not always self-evidently conscious but the individual feels "anxious" by the encounter. Whenever this experience of incongruity exists in the individual's encounter where self-concept and outside experience are at odds, the individual feels a sense of vulnerability and often personality disorganization. Anxiety is, then, an emotional response to a threat to the individual's self-concept such that there is real danger of a debilitating discrepancy between the person and the situation.

When this situation arises, namely, a perceived conflict between self-concept and objective situation, the individual attempts to protect himself by the use of a defense mechanism. The process of defense, explains Rogers, is the behavioral response of the individual to the threat. The goal is for the reestablishment and maintenance of the self-concept. "This goal," Rogers continues, "is achieved by the perceptual distortion of the experience in awareness, in such a way as to reduce the incongruity between the experience and the structure of the self, or by the denial of any experience, thus denying any threat to the self." The production of defenses, then, is the individual's primary method of protecting himself, his self-concept, and his self-worth.

These defense mechanisms are of two kinds, says Rogers. There is the "perceptual distortion" and the "denial." The first occurs when an incongruent experience is allowed into an individual's perception but only in a form that makes it consistent with that individual's self-image and not something alien to his own experience. Thus, when an experience occurs challenging the individual but not outside the sphere of possibility, that individual employs a defense mechanism to explain the "distortion" in the experience rather than denying its reality. This occurs when someone is caught in theft when that individual is awareness that even though he is not habitually a thief it can, does, and might happen that he takes something that is really not his. This often occurs with employees of a company who help themselves to various items, aware that it is theft, but explaining to their own satisfaction that it is acceptable behavior. This, Rogers calls, "rationalization." Perceptual distortion produces rationalization thereby allowing an individual to maintain his self-concept without any or much jeopardy. However, in the case of "denial" as a defense mechanism, the individual attempts to protect his self-concept by simply denying that the situation of incongruity has occurred. When this defense mechanism, much more so than the previous one, is permitted to reign in a person's life, there is grave potential for the development of mental illness.

Throughout his writing career, Rogers made much of what he called the "good life" in which he used a term for that experience, namely, the "fully functioning person." The good life, for Rogers, is not a static state of experience, but a process, a direction, a way of living and comporting oneself through all of life's trials and tribulations. The good life "is a process of movement in a direction which the human organism selects when it is inwardly free to move in any direction. The general qualities of this selected direction appear to have a certain universality," Rogers contends, and "the person who is psychologically free moves in the direction of becoming a more fully functioning person." There are five major personality traits of such individuals and we will recite them briefly here. (1) Openness to experience (wherein the individual is not temperamentally closed to new situations, encounters, opportunities, challenges), (2) Existential living (wherein the individual is ready and willing to face whatever may come his way with hope, courage, and fortitude), (3) Organismic trusting (wherein the individual has confidence in his ability to make sound decisions and to act upon them with assurance of their wisdom), (4) Experiential freedom (wherein the individual embraces the possibilities of life without false or shallow constraints superimposed by family and society but with a willingness to explore possibilities for living), and (5) Creativity (wherein the individual is fully at liberty to venture into new realms of experiential living and expressiveness of life's possibilities). "The good life," Rogers expounds, "involves a wider range, a greater richness, than the constricted living in which most of us find ourselves. To be a part of this process means that one is involved in the frequently frightening and frequently satisfying experience of a more sensitive living, with greater range, greater variety, greater richness."

The juxtaposition of Rogerian psychology and that of Freud and Skinner is most profoundly realized in their differences over the nature of the human person. The Third Force of humanistic psychology was intentionally launched to counter the negativity and pessimism of both Freud's determinism and Skinner's behaviorism. Eight distinguishing ideologies are counterpoised in these schools of thought with Rogers and the phenomenological humanists on the one hand and the psychoanalysts and behaviorists on the other. First is that of freedom versus determinism, with Rogers strongly for the former and Freud and Skinner quite conspicuously on the side of the latter. Freedom, for Rogers, is an indispensable characteristics of human nature and without it the fully functioning individual has no chance of self-actualization. Again, rationality versus irrationality characterizes the radical distinction between these schools of thought. For Rogers, the human person is essentially a rational being, controlling and directing his own life when given the opportunity and, with help, can correct misdirection in one's life in a way that Freud and Skinner could never conceive nor would they allow. Holism, for Rogers, is the contra to behaviorism's "elementalism," by which is meant the behaviorist's happy dissecting of the human personality into elemental parts for analysis whereas with the humanists the person is treated and respected as an entity in its entirety.

A further distinction has to do with the difference between "constitutionalism" and "environmentalism," with the former on the side of the humanists who know that individuals are constituted with an innate tendency to self-actualization whereas the behaviorists would have us rely upon the organic and instinctual situation of the individual as determinate in behavior. Whereas Skinner and Freud would emphasize the "objectivity" of the human person's behavioral modalities of being without reference to the individual's own self-understanding, Rogers would have us know that the human person is essentially a "subjective" being with thought processes and behavioral modalities employed at his own initiative and to his own desired ends. Again, Rogers would have us know that the human person is "proactive" rather than "reactive" to life's situations and that the positive view of the human person is one in which every individual has the ability and is encouraged to assume responsibility for his actions rather than rely helplessly upon his instinctual urges and unconscious prodding for behavioral responses.

We are a proactive being rather than a mere reactive animal say the humanists of the Third Force. Because human beings are predisposed towards self-actualization, every individual is "heterostatic" rather than "homeostatic," that is to say, every person is in a mode of action, moving towards greater fulfillment, greater self-actualization, rather than bound and gagged by the instinctual and unconscious variables operative in his life but outside his control. Man is moving forward, not staked to his mere animal confines. And, finally, Roger would emphasize "knowability" whereas the behaviorists would claim "unknowability" as our life situation and destiny. Because of his embracing of the phenomenological school of psychology, Roger believed that man cannot use scientific knowledge to better understand who and what we are without a much greater reliance upon our own capacity at self-understanding. We are not merely the objective subject of scientific enquiry, but we are the subjective focus of interpersonal self-understanding. Science can help, but it must serve rather than dominate our enquiry.

Early on in our discussion, we called attention to the "evolution" of Rogerian psychotherapeutic methods of treatment, moving from a non-directive to client-centered to finally person-to-person centered focus. In this context, Rogers has identified six conditions necessary for the therapeutic relationship to be beneficial. In closing, we will itemize these and comment briefly.

(1) Two persons are in psychological contact (wherein two individuals, one self-defined as therapist and the other as client, meet together to address a personal issue of the client); (2) The client is in a state of incongruence, being vulnerable or anxious (wherein the situation presumes an interactive relationship of the two individuals addressing the incongruent feelings of the client), (3) The therapist is congruent or integrated in the relationship (by which is meant that this individual is aware of his role, his situation, and his responsibility in relationship to the client), (4) The therapist experiences unconditional positive regard for the client (such that the client does not raise defenses and is rather openly convergent with the therapist about his situation of anxiety), (5) The therapist experiences an empathic understanding of the client's internal frame of reference and endeavors to communicate this experience to the client (such that the client is enabled to better see and assess the situation which has arisen in his life which has produced the incongruence), and (6) The communication to the client of the therapist's empathic understanding and unconditional positive regard is to a minimal degree achieved (thereby setting the client on the road to recovering or discovering a sense of self-worth and fulfillment).

Roger's person-to-person therapeutic method is a reflection of his whole image of man in general and more specifically of the therapist as a facilitator of personal growth of the client towards self-actualization. Believing individuals are innately inclined to personal fulfillment, Rogers is ever optimistic about the healing process. His phenomenological theory has produced a great deal of research dealing with self-concept and his methodology has been widely adopted by various schools of psychotherapy, and not least with the ranks of pastoral counselors who have benefited the most and utilized his method extensively in their training and practice. Without question, Rogers and his followers have set a high standard of excellence in theory and practice.

CARL ROGERS' BIOGRAPHY

On Becoming Carl Rogers by Howard Kirschenbaum. NY: Delacorte Press, 1979.

CARL ROGERS' PRIMARY SOURCES

Clinical Treatment of the Problem Child, (1939).

Counseling and Psychotherapy: Newer Concepts in Practice, (1942).

Client-centered Therapy: Its Current Practice, Implications and Theory. London: Constable, (1951).

"A Theory of Therapy, Personality and Interpersonal Relationships as Developed in the Client-centered Framework." In (ed.) S. Koch, *Psychology: A Study of a Science. Vol. 3: Formulations of the Person and the Social Context.* New York: McGraw Hill, (1959).

On Becoming a Person: A Therapist's View of Psychotherapy. London: Constable, (1961).

Freedom to Learn: A View of What Education Might Become. (1st ed.) Columbus, Ohio: Charles Merill, (1969).

On Encounter Groups. New York: Harper and Row, (1970).

On Personal Power: Inner Strength and Its Revolutionary Impact, (1977).

A Way of Being. Boston: Houghton Mifflin, (1980).

CHAPTER EIGHT
Harry Stack Sullivan and Interpersonal Psychoanalysis

BIOGRAPHICAL SKETCH

Herbert "Harry" Stack Sullivan was born on the 21st of February, 1892, in a small farming village called Norwick in New York State. The only surviving child of a poor Irish family, his childhood was lonely and uneventful exacerbated by the fact that his family were the only Catholics in an all Protestant town. His father, Timothy Sullivan, was quiet and distant and his mother, Ella Stack Sullivan, with whom he was close, was sickly and of a complaining nature. Two sons died in infancy before Harry's birth and, needless to say, this bore heavily upon his mother. She was unhappy in marriage, having chosen a mate well below her family's station in life, as she thought of it romantically back in Ireland, and she was not disinclined to verbalize her disappointment in marriage and with her life to her only son and companion. When Harry was three, his mother disappeared for about eighteen months, probably for a mental hospital stay, during which time he was cared for by his maternal grandmother whose Gaelic accent was often indecipherable to the child. When his grandmother died in 1903, a maiden aunt came to share the duties of motherhood so, in a sense, he had three mothers to raise him. As a child with only one friend, a little boy named Clarence Bellinger up the road who, interestingly enough, also became a psychiatrist, Harry invented several imaginary playmates but remained essentially an outsider during his school years. It is said that his Irish brogue was strong and his high marks set him apart from his peers at school. Brilliant and taciturn, "Harry" was an outstanding student and was groomed, not for farm work, but for university. He graduated, at the top of his high school class, earlier than most of his peers.

At sixteen, he was off to Cornell University to which he had won a scholarship from the State of New York, but, for various speculative reasons offered up by friends and relations in his home town, Harry did not graduate with a major in physics as he had planned but failed out his second semester. For two years, he disappeared and often referred to his hospitalization during this time for a mental breakdown. However, in 1911, he entered medical school and completed his studies in 1915 but did not receive his diploma until he was able to pay his outstanding tuition debt in 1917. He graduated without a sterling academic record from the Chicago College of Medicine and Surgery, a legitimate but somewhat disreputable institution not unlike many at the time in all large cities. He always spoke disparagingly of the quality of medical education he received. Because of his poor training and virtually nothing in psychiatry, he was not exposed to the major theoretical systems in psychiatry and psychology of the day. This later proved to be an advantage in the development of his own school of thought.

During these trying years of effort to establish himself, he worked with schizophrenic patients at various hospitals, demonstrating a notable capacity to bring some success in dealing with schizophrenics using what he was already calling "interpersonal therapy." This approach he was developing involved the training of staff to enact safe, corrective interpersonal interactions with the patients, arguing as he did that the institutional environment was artificial and counterproductive to personality development. He subsequently served as a staff physician in the U.S. Army but two years later, during which time his fortunes were neither sterling nor well documented, he landed a position at the St. Elizabeth's Hospital in Washington, D.C, where, without any previous training in psychiatry what so ever, he was most fortunate in working with the notable Dr. William Alanson White, an early and successful psychiatrist trained in the Freudian school of psychoanalysis. Additionally, clinical research at Sheppard and Enoch Pratt Hospital consumed a portion of his life and passion from 1923 to 1930 as did a brief appointment in the University of Maryland's School of Medicine. He quickly established a reputation for successfully treating patients with schizophrenia and began to write and publish his research findings.

During what he called his "Baltimore period" of

theoretical development, he was engaged in extensive clinical experience and reach with schizophrenics. It was here that he began to think about interpersonal relations as a key ingredient in the therapeutic treatment of the mentally ill. In attempting to decipher the non-sensical speech of the schizophrenic, he realized that their illness was a means of coping with anxiety generated from a social or interpersonal environment rather than of biogenic origins. (Since his death, DNA research has shown that Chromosome 11 is absent in 89% of the cases of schizophrenia.)

By 1931, he was sufficient well-known and established to be asked to participate, indeed, even head up an initiative which led to the creation of the Washington School of Psychiatry. At this time he moved to New York where he developed a large and lucrative private psychotherapeutic practice and, interestingly enough, underwent 300 hours of pscyhoanalysis from Dr. Clara Thompson, a well-established Freudian therapist. In later years, he was both a professor and head of the department of psychiatry at the Georgetown University Medical School and subsequently served as the president of the William Alanson White Psychiatric Foundation. Part of his role was to serve as editor of a newly created and soon to be considered internationally distinguished journal, *Psychiatry*, commenced in 1938, while simultaneously serving as chairman of the council of Fellows of the Washington School of Psychiatry. During these very productive years, he became a colleague and friend of Edward Sapir, a cultural anthropologist, and Harold Lasswell, a political scientist, both from the University of Chicago. Of special relevance to his theory-building enterprise of international relations was his friendship with George Herbert Mead, Robert Ezra Park, and W. I. Thomas, all international distinguished sociologists at the University of Chicago. Other major figures with whom he came in contact and with whom he established personal friendships included such professionally distinguished persons as Karen Horney, Erich Fromm, Frieda Fromm-Reichmann, and of special mention is Adolf Meyer. These experiences greatly broadened Sullivan's grasp of the behavioral and social sciences which eventually had a profound effect upon his theory of personality.

On the 14th of January, 1949, at age 57, he died of a persistent cardiovascular disease while visiting Paris, having been attending an international conference, the World Federation for Mental Health which he helped found, in Amsterdam where his life's work was being discussed in some depth, both positively and negatively. He was buried in Arlington National Cemetery, having had a well-respected term of service in the U.S. Army as a practicing psychiatrist during and following the 2nd World War.

Sullivan never married though he did adopt a young man who was considered by all his friends as his "son," and, though considered anti-Catholic and non-religious by his friends and colleagues, his will called for a Catholic burial which he received. One distinguishing characteristic of his interpersonal psychotherapy was his desire, not always realized, to stay away from professional nomenclature when speaking of human relations. "I think," he wrote, "we should try to pick a word in common usage in talking about living and clarify just what we mean by that word, rather than to set about diligently creating new words by carpentry of Greek and Sanskrit roots." In spite of his desire and intent, his system itself produced a plethora of neologisms which require a glossary to wade through them.

CLASSIC TEXT CONSIDERED

In 1939, the William Alanson White Foundation decided that a series of lectures should be given to honor the memory of White, a colleague of Sullivan's, who had died in 1937, and, of course, Sullivan was chosen to give the first series. He actually gave five lectures to small groups in an auditorium in a building owned by the Department of the Interior in Washington, DC. In these lectures, Sullivan made his first public attempt to present both a comprehensive and well-thought-out explanation of his concept of personality development including psychiatric disorders and treatment. In February of 1940, they were all published in the journal, *Psychiatry*, at the insistence of Sullivan's friends and colleagues, but against his best judgment. He was not pleased with his performance but finally consented and they appeared. Not surprisingly, they attracted much attention within the psychiatric and social science communities and in the following years many mental health and social science professional workers wrote to secure copies of this issue of the periodical.

Finally, in 1947, much to the chagrin of Sullivan who believed his presentation of his thoughts was "grossly inadequate," a new printing of these lectures came out again in *Psychiatry*. This issue was in hardback and carried the somewhat dubious title of *Conceptions of Modern Psychiatry*. This was actually his only book, at least in his lifetime, to see the light of day though several subsequent volumes of his lectures and essays, all touted to be Sullivan's books, finally appeared. This one, however, sold 13,000 copies over the next several years and the William Alanson White Foundation gained considerable attention because of them. Under the same title, this book was published four years after the death of Sullivan and it still sells well. Sullivan, however, denounced many of the premature conceptual developments in the work and discounted its value.

Nevertheless, it is a pivotal work for our consideration and a few remarks are justified before we move to the driving concepts and theories of Sullivan's notions of personality. "Psychiatry," he wrote, "is the study of processes that involve or go on between people. The field of psychiatry is the field of interpersonal relations, under any and all circumstances in which these relations exist." This is the thesis set forth by Sullivan in this book. It is the first place where he expressed the central ideas of his theory of personality. Through his development of the theory, he made not only a vital contribution in the treatment of mental disorder -- in particular, schizophrenia -- but he opened an entirely new approach to the study of human personality. In the view of many analysts, he made the most original contribution to psychiatry since Freud. Rollo May has gone on record as saying, "As Freud was the prophet for the Victorian age of sexual suppression, Sullivan is the prophet for our schizoid age -- our age of unrelated ness, in which, beneath all the chatter of radio and newspapers and all the multitudes of 'contact,' people are often strangers to each other." Sullivan's book, *Conceptions of Modern Psychiatry* consists of reprints of the first William Alanson White Memorial Lectures, delivered by Sullivan in 1939, as has already been mentioned. They are profound and open a whole new world of interpretation of the nature of personality and the practice of psychiatry as an interpersonal relations science.

In this work, he created a new viewpoint which is known today as the "interpersonal theory of psychiatry." Sullivan's fundamental emphasis related to a theory of personality which is a "relatively enduring pattern of recurrent interpersonal situations which characterize a human life." Radically shifting from the psychoanalytic focus on the unconscious, Sullivan brought to his clinical research and practice a behavioral and social science perspective which had not been considered a significant component of personality theory until he did it himself. He argued that the concept of "personality" is itself a hypothetical entity which cannot be isolated from interpersonal situations and, indeed, interpersonal behavior is all that is observable about personality. The rest, he suggests, is strictly metaphorical speculation and creative imagery. It is futile and fruitless to speak of a person's personality outside the social interactive matrix of the living person. Not discounting the significance of heredity and the maturation process affected by the physical environment, the real thing that determines the nature of a human person is social interaction with others. Of this, Sullivan was very insistent and unrelenting.

Never before had such an attempt been made to merge psychiatry and social psychology. His theory of personality is the product of such a merger and it is greatly enriched by his acquaintance with and utilization of the social sciences. He writes: "The general science of psychiatry seems to me to cover much the same field as that which is studied by social psychology, because scientific psychiatry has to be defined as the study of interpersonal relations, and this in the end calls for the use of the kind of conceptual framework that we now call *field theory*. From such a standpoint, personality is taken to be hypothetical. That which can be studied is the pattern of processes which characterize the interaction of personalities in particular recurrent situations or fields which include the observer." This attitude about the place and relevance of the "observer" in the clinical situation became a benchmark of Sullivan's innovative approach to the therapeutic encounter. He was, of course, influenced by the science philosopher, Heisenberg, on this point particularly.

Modern psychiatry as defined and practiced by Sullivan

consists of a study of personality characteristics which can be directly observed in the context of interpersonal relationships. Systems of psychiatry based on statements about what is going on in the patient's mind are therefore similar to a system of thought which is built on axioms such as "All events are controlled by Divine Providence." The truth or falseness of this statement cannot be established by things that reasonably well educated people can see, hear, and feel. Much human experience can be cited to support such a statement, and much human experience can be cited to nullify it, but it is so set up that it must always remain a matter of faith. For Sullivan, a "personality characteristic" is defined as a thing which people can see, hear, and feel in their relationships with other individuals. This is the most fundamental working hypothesis in his personality theory.

Though Sullivan is only willing to allow personality to be purely hypothetical apart from the actually observable reality of social interaction, he does assert that it is a dynamic center of various processes which occur in a series of interpersonal fields. This "dynamism" is a key concept in his overall personality theory. He give significant place to these processes by identifying and naming them as he constructs a platform of their characteristics. These processes, then, are *dynamisms*, *personifications*, the *self-system*, and *cognitive processes*. Let's explore each briefly here as they constitute the backbone of his major work, *Conceptions of Modern Psychiatry*.

The smallest unit of study in interpersonal relationships is what he calls "dynamism." It constituted an energy transference which meant any unit of behavior, either actual act or mental experience. They become habitual ways of acting which involve the physical body of the person, such as the mouth, hands, arms, legs, etc. These dynamisms can then be broken down into a plethora of subsets, such as the fear dynamism, intimate dynamism, etc. The dynamisms which are distinctively human in character are those which characterize one's interpersonal relations and function primarily to satisfy some basic needs of the individual. Three major dynamisms are malevolence, lust, and intimacy. Malevolence is the driving dynamism that one is living among one's own personal enemies and, if this negative dynamism emerges early in a child's life, he may find it difficult ever in adulthood to reach a fully trusting relationship with another person. Sullivan expressed it poignantly: "Once upon a time everything was love, but that was before I had to deal with people." Lust is another driving dynamism of the individual. Lust for Sullivan consists of the complex urges, feelings, and interpersonal actions which have genital sexual activity as their distant or immediate goal. Lust begins in early adolescence.

Sullivan rejected the Freudian concept of sexuality and suggested that it was more or less inconsequential in childhood and early adolescence, but lust constitutes a major driving force in later adolescence. Intimacy for Sullivan is potentially a profoundly positive dynamism. It occurs when the well-being of another person is as important to an individual as his own well-being. It does not occur in parent-child relationships and does not involve lust or sexual behavior and, says he, occurs only between members of the same sex. Lust becomes, then, a contaminant of intimacy for lust seeks to serve itself rather than the other person.

Personifications consist of an image that an individual has of himself or of some other person. It is a complex of feelings, attitudes, and conceptions that grows out of experience with need-satisfaction and anxiety. Sullivan speaks often of the "good-mother," "bad-mother," and "overprotective mother" as examples. When these personifications are shared by a large social grouping, they become stereotypes such as "all Irishman are drunks," "all Catholics lie," etc., and these stereotypes are held by social groups without experience of their reality but of a shared personification of imagined peoples' behavior.

The self-system is another dynamism which is crucial to personality structure. It functions as a security measure to protect the individual from anxiety. In order to avoid or minimize actual or potential anxiety, the person adopts various types of protective measures and supervisory controls over his behavior. These security measures form the self-system which sanctions certain forms of behavior, such as the "good-me" self, and forbids other forms of behavior, such as the "bad-me" self.

Sullivan's unique contribution to the role of cognition in personality theory has to do with his development of a threefold classification of experiences, for, says he, experiences occur in three different modes -- *protaxic, parataxic, and syntaxic.* These experiential modes merit a brief description of each in order to appreciate their relevance to Sullivan's interpersonal relations description of psychiatry. Sometimes called "types of experience" and sometimes called "types of cognition," this tripartite foundation of personality is worthy of close attention.

The simplest and most fundamental mode of experiencing reality at the beginning of life is what Sullivan chose to call the *prototaxic* mode. It consists of essentially a flowing of sensations, feelings, and images without any necessary connection between them, a kind of "stream of consciousness," if you will. Sullivan himself describes it this way: "It may be regarded as the discrete series of momentary states of the sensitive organism" (1953). It occurs, of course, during the earliest months of infancy and must precede the others as a preparation for them. The *parataxic* mode of thinking, Sullivan explains, consists of seeing causal relationships between events that occur at about the same time but which are not logically related. Getting the connection wrong is what this mode of experience is all about. It is magical thinking, says he, for there is no logical connection between two events experienced by the child in which the child assumes there is. It is essentially the "elementary externalization of causality." In childhood it occurs regularly when the child assumes that something he has done is the cause of something that is quite decidedly unrelated but he thinks it is. In adulthood, the residuals of parataxis modes of experiencing occur in such things as the presumed relationship between "praying hard" and "getting well."

Finally, the third and most advanced mode of experience is called *syntaxic* and it corresponds to logical, analytical thought. *Syntaxic* experience of reality thus presupposes the ability to understand physical and spatial causality, and the ability to predict causes from knowledge of their effects. The meaning of words and the use of numbers constitutes the most poignant examples of the function of *syntaxic* experience and when the child learns the meaning of specific words and their uses and the nature of numbers and how they work, the child has reached this level of experiential sophistication needed in the development of interpersonal relationships.

CONCEPTS AND THEORIES

Harry Stack Sullivan's distinguishing contribution to contemporary psychiatry was his heavy emphasis upon the social factors which contribute to the development of human personality. Though schooled in Freudian psychoanalysis, he was not a Freudian in the sense that he differed from Freud in viewing the significance of the parent-child relationship as being an early quest for security rather than, as in Freudian psychoanalysis, primarily sexual in origin and nature.

Drawing from his own personal life's story, Sullivan saw this child-mother relationship as central, not the sexual drive of libidinal instincts. Sullivan, on the other hand, was intent upon integrating the multiple disciplines of the behavioral and social sciences into the work of psychiatry such that sociology and social psychology in the tradition of George Herbert Mead and Charles Horton Cooley proved most helpful in Sullivan's eventual development of what became known as interpersonal psychiatry, later interpersonal psychotherapy. He was not averse to reaching across disciplinary lines for theory and method, from evolution to communications, from learning theory to social organization. It was "interpersonal relations" which, he believed, constituted the fundamental ingredient in the personality structure.

Sullivan was averse to that form of psychiatry and clinical psychotherapy which dealt with mental illness through the study of institutionally-isolated patients. He had extensive experience in working with the mentally ill, particularly with schizophrenics, and he felt that persons institutionally committed constituted a weak source of clinical insight. Personality characteristics, for instance, he felt were determined by the interpersonal relationships between therapists and patients and that the institutional environment was artificial and counterproductive. Sullivan contended that personality develops according to people's perception of how others view them. "Others," in Sullivan thought, included personifications, like the government, as well as imaginary and idealized figures like Jesus or Moses or even movie stars. He believed, based upon his own clinical encounters with severely mentally ill patients, that cultural forces were largely responsible for their psychological condition. He contended that a healthy personality is the result of healthy relationships and that most of what goes in our society as mental illness is neither biogenic nor psychogenic but rather "sociogenic." Sullivan refused to employ the concept of "personality" as a unique, individual, and unchanging entity as so often was the case with traditionalists. He much preferred to define personality as a manifestation of the interaction between individuals, namely, interpersonal relations.

Sullivan's clinical work in a variety of settings over several years of medical assignments led him to firmly believe in the impact interpersonal relationships have upon personality development. He noted that individuals tend to carry distorted views and unrealistic expectations of others into their relationships. His solution was to become, as a clinical psychotherapist, a "participant observer" in dealing with his clients, taking a more active therapeutic stance than the traditional psychoanalytic "blank screen" approach popular at the time and particularly with the Freudian school of psychoanalysis. By focusing upon what he called "interpersonal behavior," he would observe the client's reaction to the therapist and the therapeutic environment. He believe that emotional well-being could be achieved by making an individual "aware" of their dysfunctional interpersonal patterns of interaction and thereby grow into a healthy self-awareness of their interactive behavior.

Before we consider Sullivan's now paradigmatic stages of personality development, we should say something about his concept of human nature and, it has been suggested by him many times, it can be summed up in the expression, "everyone is much more simply human than otherwise." Having made this his standard operational modality, he utilized it throughout his career and summed up its meaning this way: "In other words, the differences between any two instances of human personality from the lowest grade imbecile to the highest-grade genius -- are much less striking than the difference between the least-gifted human being and a member of the nearest other biological genus." Sullivan was outspoken on this point.

Denying that there were any really operative instincts left in the human person, and thus separating himself profoundly from Freud and the classical school of psychoanalysis, Sullivan contended that it is the social environment in which we mature that determines the effectiveness of our maturation. Interpersonal relationships are the essence of human development. We are only human in so far as we develop within the context of other people. We need to learn to compete, cooperate, and compromise with other children as we mature in order to maintain mental health. "Personal individuality is an illusion." We exist only in relationship to other people. When we mature within a healthy social environment, this positive progression of interpersonal events leads to an integrated personality, an adult who is capable of establishing satisfying interpersonal relations and who is able to both give and receive love. This is the essence of the human personality.

Sullivan's elaborate and well-developed description of the stages of human development were reminiscent of Freud's elaborate system. But, whereas Freud built his developmental scheme around the central core of childhood sexuality, Sullivan built his around the fundamental core of interpersonal relationships. There are seven developmental stages in his schema and we will just mention them briefly here before concluding with remarks about his therapeutic method. Infancy is from the beginning to about eighteen months and the first expressions of the "self system" appear when the infant encounters and relates to the "good me", "bad me" feeding experience in relationship to his mother. Childhood commences with the acquisition of language and goes through the preschool years. *Syntaxic* experience develops and the child encounters and deals with the reality and necessity of living with others as peers and authority figures. The juvenile person corresponds to the grade school years to about age eleven and here interpersonal relations included competition, cooperation, and comprise as developmental necessities. Preadolescence is short, eleven to thirteen more or less, and here intimacy emerges in relationship to same-sex peers and chums and marks the first real instance of what Sullivan calls "genuine human relations." Early adolescence commences the heterosexual years of stress and physical development and the intimacy dynamic is matched with lust and lasts through the beginning of the high school years when late adolescence produces the profound demands of complex interpersonal relationships and particularly heterosexual ones which are inevitably fraught with anxiety.

Adulthood is arrived at with the composite of strengths and weaknesses in the personality which have developed through the interpersonal experiences of the maturing process.

Sullivan's psychotherapeutic methodology was quite unique to his own understanding of the function and nature of interpersonal relationships. Sullivan firmly believed, based upon his extensive clinical experience, that mental disorders derive from interpersonal failures and, therefore, therapeutic procedures must be based upon a genuine effort to improve the patient's relationship skills in dealing with others. In keeping with his overall worldview, interpersonal relationships constitute the core of psychotherapeutic treatment. In this situation, it is imperative that the therapist understand that his role is primarily that of a "participant observer," for, despite all protestations to the contrary from traditionalists, the therapist becomes necessarily part of an interpersonal, face-to-face relationship with the patient. This process actually creates the opportunity for the patient to establish a syntaxic communication with another person, namely, the therapist himself.

Because of the emphasis upon the therapeutic role being that of an "observer," the therapist is exempt from becoming "involved" with the patient but, as with the Freudian tradition, the therapist must establish a relationship based upon his role as an expert in relationships, instead of as a friend, chum, or colleague. Unlike the work of Carl Rogers, Sullivan is insistent that the therapist "not" become a friend of the patient, thereby destroying the "observational" character of the therapist's relationship to the patient. Sullivan had three primary objectives in the therapeutic situation. First, he intends to help the patient improve foresight, discover difficulties in interpersonal relations, and restore the ability to participate in consensually validated experiences. This occurs when three questions are addressed: "(1) How can I best put into words what I wish to say to the patient?, (2) What is the general pattern of communication between us?, and (3) What precisely is the patient saying to me?" Are these simplistic? Certainly not!

The therapeutic interview is divided into four stages: (1) formal inception, (2) reconnaissance, (3) detailed inquiry, and (4) termination. Let's explicate just briefly the character of each stage. At the first meeting, the psychiatrist promotes confidence in the patient by demonstrating interpersonal skills and permits the patient to express the reasons for seeking therapy in the first place. The therapist, then, formulates tentative hypotheses regarding the declared cause for seeking treatment, and then decides on a possible course of action.

During reconnaissance, there is a general personal and social history established between the patient and the therapist who attempts to determine how the patient came to develop a particular personality type. Here, the therapist asks specific questions about the patient's age, birth order, mother, father, education, occupational history, marriage, children, etc. Open ended questions are asked to invite the patient to feel free to express his emotional state at the time. Then, the therapist's detailed inquiry attempts to improve upon his understanding of the patient and the patient's understanding of his own situation, particularly articulating why he has sought therapy. The fourth and final stage of the interview is termination, or, in some cases, interruption. Of course, this means that the interview has come to an end. Quite commonly, the therapist gives the client "homework," something to do or some memory to recall for the next session. After each such session, the therapist makes copious notes about the session, what progress has been made and what issues have arisen that need addressing in the next session. For Sullivan, the therapeutic ingredient in this process is the face-to-face relationship between psychiatrist and patient, which permit's the patient to reduce anxiety and to communicate with others on the syntaxic level.

In some circles, Harry Stack Sullivan is considered the "father of modern psychiatry," but, of course, this is prior to the emergence of the psychiatrist as "meds monitor"! Today, unlike in his day, psychiatry has been disastrously reduced to monitoring medication without the slightest effort to offer therapeutic counseling which has, by and large, been left to either the social worker or the pastoral counselor. Psychiatry can no longer function as the therapeutic dispenser it was from Freud to Sullivan because the insurance companies and the HMOs have precluded the affordability of such functions. Psychiatrist must dispense and monitor the psychopharmacological industry's involvement with clients and patients, leaving what counseling even occurs to other professionals, namely, social workers and pastoral counselors. Of course, it is the patient and client who suffer, but such is the fee-driven market system operative in American society today.

HARRY STACK SULLIVAN'S BIOGRAPHY

Psychiatrist of America: The Life of Harry Stack Sullivan BY Helen Swick Perry. Cambridge, MA: The Belknap Press of Harvard University Press, 1982.

HARRY STACK SULLIVAN'S PRIMARY SOURCES

Conceptions of Modern Psychiatry: The First William Alanson White Memorial Lectures, NY: W. W. Norton & Co., 1953.

Personal Psychopathology, NY: W. W. Norton & Co., 1972.

The Interpersonal Theory of Psychiatry, NY: W. W. Norton & Co., 1953.

The Psychiatric Interview, NY: W. W. Norton & Co., 1954.

Clinical Studies in Psychiatry, NY: W. W. Norton & Co., 1956.

Schizophrenia as a Human Process, NY: W. W. Norton & Co., 1962.

The Fusion of Psychiatry and Social Science, NY: W. W. Norton & Co., 1964.

CHAPTER NINE
Karen Horney and Psychoanalytic Social Psychotherapy

INTRODUCTION

The contributions made by Karen Horney to contemporary psychology generally and psychotherapy specifically are still being counted, labeled, and evaluated. That she has been one of the most prolific theorists in 20th century psychoanalytic theory is indisputable, whether one is insistent upon calling her an adulterated Freudian, a neo-Freudian, or a psychoanalytic innovator. Both her creative genius in appropriating psychoanalytic theory to new realms of application as well as her ingenuity in creating a whole new world of theory development in relationship to Freudian criticism and Feminist psychology have contributed profoundly to her reputation, both among her many antagonists and her countless protagonists. That she questioned, even occasionally challenged, traditional Freudian theories and practices is well known, especially as relates to psychoanalysis' early emphasis on infantile sexuality and this, as we shall see, led to her establishing what eventually became commonly known as Feminist Psychology. Freud was wrong, she believed, in his over emphasis upon the differences between men and women preferring *vis a vis* Freud to trace such differences to social and cultural bias rather than to a biological determinism. In the following essay, we will attempt to identify and delineate the scope of her creativity and the depths of her contribution to a therapeutic theory and practice best known as psychoanalytic social psychotherapy.

BIOGRAPHY

We call Karen Horney a modern psychologist because she lived more than have a century as an adult in the 20th century. Born Karen Danielsen in Blankenese, Germany, on the 16th of September, 1885, the daughter of a noted sea captain, Berndt Wackels Danielsen, known by his children as "the Bible-thrower" owing to his traditional patriarchal ideas and ways of living. Her mother Clotilde of the van Ronzelen family was called "Sonni" and, unlike her husband, was an open-minded woman of the time. Karen's own elder brother Berndt was a favorite of hers but she also cared deeply for her four step-siblings from her father's first marriage. Her recollections of childhood as regarding the memory of her father were not good as she characterized him in the diary of youth as "a cruel disciplinary figure." He was, she recalls, particularly inclined to favor her brother over herself all the while her father chose rather to disregard such feelings as she reported, even going so far as to favor her with special gifts brought back from his business travels. Nevertheless, her clear and public preference was for her mother.

Even in pre-adolescence, Karen made a conscious determination to cultivate her intellect rather than her beauty which was, as all agreed, rather inconsequential. Her ambition was fed by this realization of not being beautiful but quite possibly intelligent. Though not everyone discounted her being pretty, she was affirmed in her intellectual ambitions. Whether the precipitating cause or not (this she pondered throughout her life), depression appeared not infrequently during early adolescence and plagued her throughout her life, the origin of which, she believed, was the rejection of her older brother's puppy love crush she had for him. He pushed her away owing to understandable embarrassment and consequently the first early appearance of life-long depression.

When she was nineteen years of age, her mother separated from her father and while never divorcing, her mother took all of the children, her own two and her husband's four by the previous marriage. While only a mild and intermittent factor in the family's life, the father opposed Karen's entering medical school though she enjoyed the support of her mother in this venture. The German universities precluded women from entering medical studies until 1900, but by 1906 she was able to enter the medical school of the University of Freiburg which had pioneered the way for women early on in the century. At the time, this now famous university was small with only 2,400 students of which only 58 were women. Within two years of commencing her studies, she transferred to the University of Gottingen and subsequently to the University of Berlin, finally graduating in 1913. Attending multiple universities in Germany before taking one's degree was and somewhat still is a common occurrence, students following individual scholars in their field of study from one university to another to broaden their exposure to a variety of ideologies.

During these medical school years, Karen Horney met and married Oscar Horney in 1909, the following year giving birth to the first of eventually three daughters. Brigitte was her firstborn in 1910 followed by Marianne and Renate in 1913 and 1916, respectively. She actually relied upon her Freudian studies of psychoanalysis to work through her own personal problems, thereby learning with a passion the efficacy of this method of psychotherapy. Besides marriage and motherhood, Horney had become fascinated with the newly emerging and soon to be burgeoning field of psychoanalysis, thanks to Freud and his professional society of psychoanalysts. Losing her mother two years after her marriage, she found that her husband Oscar was a duplicate of her own father but chose not to challenge his heavy-handed authoritarianism as she was consumed with both the task of mothering three daughters while completing her medical degree. Later, she would look back with regret for having permitted these paternalistic child rearing practices and would write extensively upon the topic.

Within seven years of graduating from medical school, Horney was offered a position in the Institute for Psychoanalysis in Berlin, a prestigious institution where she was able to cultivate her knowledge of the field lecturing extensively for several years. She also had the opportunity of teaching at the New School for Social Research in New York City during this time. One of many notable colleagues of Horney's was Karl Abraham who was himself a friend of Freud's. Abraham kept it no secret that Horney was a gifted and talented psychoanalyst as well as a scholar in the field of psychoanalysis. To both practice as well as teach psychoanalysis provided a unique opportunity for Horney to cultivate her skills as well as her international reputation.

In 1923, just three years after Horney took the teaching position in Berlin, Oscar's business failed during which time he had developed meningitis. Becoming depressed, bitter, and irascible, Oscar became increasingly problematic to the serenity of family life with his interventionist posture towards Horney and their children. Concurrently, Horney's brother died during this same year of pulmonary infection, precipitating a severe strain on Horney's mental health. Another near debilitating bout of depression overtook her approaching near suicide. Struggling through these dark years of depression while maintaining her role as both mother and researcher/teacher at the Institute, she eventually made the decision to make a new start in life in a new place with her daughters.

Though early on and still loyal to the fundamentals of Freudian psychoanalytical theories and practice, true to her nature Horney began to venture out, challenging and questioning the domain assumptions of the orthodox practitioners particularly as related to the Freudian view of women and the implicit bias against female psychology which, according to Freud, was merely and solely a by-product of male psychology. "Penis envy" was the simple justification for such prejudice. Horney was solid and relentless in her criticism of such unquestioned assumptions about female psychology. Mental disturbances among women, she argued vociferously, was located within the matrix of male-dominated cultural prejudices which both fed and was fed upon by Freudian theory of sexuality. Countering Freudian bias, Horney proposed "womb envy" as the nexus of male envy towards pregnancy, nursing, and motherhood, i.e., the female capacity for creating and sustaining life, and this feeling of male inferiority spawned male superficial superiority in culture, society, and family relations.

Moving to the United States in 1930 at the age of forty-five, she had great fortune in having as her first American job that of Associate Director of the Chicago Institute for Psychoanalysis, a position she held for two years. Subsequently, she and her daughters moved to Brooklyn where she found a lively intellectual and professional community of Jewish refugees primarily from Germany. Here to her great joy and personal professional development and success, she became friends with both Erich Fromm and Harry Stack Sullivan. Though the intimate relationship which developed with Fromm ended in great bitterness, the friendships she cultivated within the professional psychotherapeutic community of New York at the time served her career splendidly. Sullivan was particularly credited with introducing her to the value and place of the behavioral sciences in psychotherapy and their relevance to the understanding of the etiology of mental illness traced to a failure of social interactional skills development during childhood.

Horney's drift away from orthodox psychoanalysis and Freudian theory of sexuality came early in her career as she explored more substantively her fascination with what she thought of as lifelong growth and development. Though she continued for a while both practicing and teaching in the Berlin Psychoanalytic Society (at least until 1932), Freud had become increasingly distant towards her believing, as he did and rightly so, that Horney was moving away from his school of theory and practice towards a more female-expansive view of psychotherapeutic practice. Owing to her increasing fears of Nazi expansionism in Germany, she accepted an invitation from Franz Alexander to join the Chicago Institute of Psychoanalysis. Her marriage having come undone prior to this invitation and upon her immediate acceptance, she took her daughters to Chicago where she became increasingly convinced of the central importance of socio-cultural factors in psychological development. Besides Erich Fromm and Harry Stack Sullivan, she was befriended by such scholarly giants of the time as Margaret Mead, Paul Tillich, and Ruth Benedict, all representing the behavioral and social sciences as well as philosophy.

Unstoppable in her quest for a deepening and broadening of psychoanalytic theory and practice outside the pale of Freudian orthodoxy, Horney based her emerging theories upon her own clinical practice wherein the experience of working with patients allowed her the opportunity of exploring new methods, new insights, new approaches to previously established practices. Her confidence, as was true of Harry Stack Sullivan, in her patients' own ability to work out their neurotic causalities with an assisting practitioner was anathema to accepted practice but she found this approach rewarding to her patients.

Inevitably, her resistance to adherence to Freudian received practice, to the orthodox interpretation of psychoanalytic theory, resulted in her being dismissed from membership in the New York Psychoanalytic Institute in 1941 following years of successful practice and a broadly established reputation as a scholar and therapist. The result of this dismissal was that she predictably created her own professional body, viz., the Association for the Advancement of Psychoanalysis.

Eager to advance herself, she set about researching, writing and teaching upon a topic of genuine interest to her professionally, viz., a composite theory of neurosis and personality based on her own clinical experience in psychotherapy within the context of psychoanalytic theory. As noted above, while her first major career appointment was as the Associate Director of the Chicago Institute for Psychoanalysis for a two-year commitment, in 1937 she made a major advancement in her American reputation, just seven years after coming to America, by publishing a major book titled, *The Neurotic Personality of Our Time,* which gained her a foothold in the field given its popularity as a readable book within psychotherapy. This book was followed two years later by another extremely popular work titled *New Ways in Psychoanalysis.* Here she explicated her argument that environmental and social conditions, not just instinctual or biological determinism as argued by Freud, constituted the basis for personal development. These socio-cultural factors must be taken full account of in both the development of human personality and in the etiology of mental illness. One of her major disputes with orthodox psychoanalysis was over the inordinate use of the concept of libido as well as the death instinct and the whole matrix embodied in Freudian Oedipus complex theories. Drawing from the insights learned from her behavioral science colleagues, particularly Fromm and Sullivan, she was convinced that the socio-cultural matrix of personality growth and development had been underplayed by psychoanalytic theory and must be corrected.

Agreeing with Harry Stack Sullivan, Horney was convinced that the etiology of neurosis could be traced to the infantile experience of anxiety in which the child experiences acute isolation and helplessness in a hostile world. Coping strategies can and do become the basis for the emergence of neurotic behavior and personality disorders. Within four years of these books' publication, she had become the Dean of the American Institute of Psychoanalysis, a major training institute in the U.S. During this time, Horney also established her own organization, the Association for the Advancement of

Psychoanalysis, owing to her growing dissatisfaction with the restrictive and overly orthodox practice of psychoanalysis within the established medical community of committed Freudian psychoanalysts. Again, in 1945 she published a major work on interpersonal relationships titled *Our Inner Conflicts* and within five years followed it with *Neurosis and Human Growth*. Much later, her ideas regarding female psychoanalytic theories regarding sexual development were expounded extensively in her now classic in the field titled *Feminine Psychology* released in 1967. As she was influenced by Fromm and Sullivan, so those who followed after Horney who became the founders of the Third Force of Humanistic Psychology, namely, Abraham Maslow and Carl Rogers, were always quick to credit the influence of Horney in the development of their own work.

As we have said, this breach between her innovative approach and that of the orthodox practitioners eventually led to her resignation as the Dean of the AIP. Taking a teaching post at the New York Medical College, she ventured out into the scholarly world of publishing by launching her own professional journal, *The American Journal of Psychoanalysis*. She continued in this professional matrix of teacher/scholar/practitioner until her death on December 4, 1952, in New York City at the age of 67. In 1952, the year of her death, colleagues and friends proposed the establishing of a clinic in her name and dedicated to the practice of her expanded type of psychotherapy. She died of cancer that year, but The Karen Horney Clinic opened as a research, training, and low-cost treatment center three years later on May 6, 1955. This Clinic was dedicated to research and the training of medical professionals with special emphasis upon psychiatric practice as well as providing an inexpensive treatment facility for the City of New York. Patients were treated with psychotherapeutic modalities such as supportive psychotherapy and psychoanalytic social psychotherapy based upon the fundamental teachings and principles of Horney's system of analysis and patient care.

The contributions of Karen Horney to psychology are well known and greatly valued. Her particular insights regarding the psychology of women and the adjustments made to the practice of psychoanalysis have withstood the test of time. Still and unquestionably considered one of the most important and first psychologist to establish the general field of feminine psychology, her adjustments made to Freudian psychotherapeutic theory based on her own clinical practice and critique of that school of thoughts' inordinate emphasis upon the masculine nature of the psyche has endured and thrived. Drawing from her exposure to behavioral and social sciences in the U.S., Horney has demonstrated the centrality of socio-cultural factors in personality development and their relationship to the etiology of mental health and mental illness. Counter balancing the so-called penis envy of Freudianism with her concept of womb envy, she argued persuasively with clinically empirical evidence for the uniqueness of feminine psychology and its necessary and equal status within the broad field of clinical psychology and psychotherapy. The culturally mandated dependence of women upon men for love, money, security, and protection has driven the female population in western society to the over emphasis upon personal beauty thereby elevating the male population to an inordinate and superficial level of power and authority over society generally and women specifically. Her contributions to both the Third Force of humanistic psychology, particularly as credited by Maslow and Rogers, and to Gestalt psychology are well known. But also, her work in the field of what is now respectfully labeled self-psychology as well as neo-Freudian psychoanalytic social psychotherapy must be acknowledged. The rational emotive therapy of Albert Ellis, feminism generally, existentialist thought in a post-Sartrean world, and the clinic named for her all bespeak her enduring legacy.

THOUGHT
THEORY OF NEUROSIS

Horney's theory of neurosis is based upon her own personal life experience and situation and draws from her own knowledge of how she navigated through her childhood and adolescence where interpersonal relationship dysfunctions were common and pervasive. That which distinguishes her theory of neurosis and psychoanalytic practice involves her awareness of inner conflicts occurring within the social matrix of family and society. Neurosis, she contended, is the mechanism whereby individuals are able to cope with interpersonal relationship dysfunctions, events which occur in everyday life for children and adults alike. And many professionals in the field today would argue that Horney's theory of neurosis is still the most insightful and productive theory available for psychotherapists in practice. As with Harry Stack Sullivan, she contended that neurosis was much more contiguous with normal daily life than practitioners of the past were willing to admit or acknowledge. Neurosis itself, she suggested, was a survival mechanism, an attempt to make an otherwise unbearable life livable. It essentially constitutes a coping technique for survival.

Differing from Freud and the psychoanalytic contention that mental illness generally and neurosis specifically was a result of childhood abuse or neglect, Horney contended with Sullivan that it was parental indifference wherein interpersonal relationship skills were neglected or denied the child during personality development as the etiology of mental illness. The key to understanding this perspective, she explained, was to grasp deeply the fundamental characteristic of the child's own perception of his life situation rather than that of the parent's presumed intentions in child care. What a child feels is what is important for it is the determining variable in accounting for the child's sense of a lack of warmth and affection, for instance, from a parent who too frequently is suffering from neurosis. Such failure in parenting results in broken promises and insensitivity to the child's purported sense of abandonment.

Understandably, given her personal life story, Horney was particularly interested as both a researcher and therapist in the meaning and nature of neurosis and though trained in psychoanalysis, her inclinations reached far beyond the orthodox approach to analysis and treatment. Her extensive clinical records based on patient reports constituted the basis for her innovative approach to neurosis, treating it not as a biogenic dysfunction of mental processes but rather tracing its etiology to environmental conditions particularly in childhood and adolescence. Agreeing with Harry Stack Sullivan that mental health and mental illness are more commonly traceable to social environmental events, situations, and interactional relationships between children, parents, siblings, and playmates, Horney placed much more emphasis upon the child's perception and interpretation of events and relationships, whether those perceptions and interpretations were correct or not. It is the child's feelings about these events which matter in personality development and, naturally, in the emergence of mental illness if there is a negative assessment of these relationships on the part of the child.

In her book on the neurotic personality, Horney suggested that neurosis consists of a psychic disturbance which is brought on by fears and defenses against these fears and by the inevitable attempts on the part of the neurotic to identify a compromise solution between conflicting inclinations. A neurotic individual struggles with mechanism for coping and managing psycho-social environmental stressors which occur commonly in everyday life. These individuals, as neurotics, cannot, however, have been diagnosed and treated in the absence of a thorough assessment of their socio-cultural behavioral matrix, i.e., their social environment involving interpersonal relationships. Neurosis emerges out of the dysfunction of interpersonal relationships and, whereas Freud believed that instinctual drives and biologically determined behavior constitutes the generative *milieu* for mental illness, Horney, on the contrary, agreed with Harry Stack Sullivan and others that the socio-cultural matrix of interpersonal relationships constituted the fundamental arena for the etiology of both mental health and mental illness.

According to Horney, the neurotic has come by his fears through the medium of the culture and social environment. In orthodox Freudian psychoanalysis, the neurotic person's real self is determined by the individual's concept of the ego, an ego without initiative or power. Horney, on the other hand, argues that the neurotic person is driven by emotional forces generated by the social life of the individual, the social and cultural as well as interpersonal environment. Rather than agreeing with Freud that neurotic behavior is essentially instinctual and, thus, biogenic, Horney argues to the contrary that neurotic behavior is generated psychogenically through the influence of the social environment and interpersonal relations. Neurotic behavior, then, constitutes a matrix of compensation and coping mechanism to permit life to continue in the face of fears and anxieties, stress and self-doubt.

Not out of character with most theory-builders in psychotherapy, Horney, like Adler, Erikson and Maslow, believed in itemizing components of a system of theory. So, her "ten patterns of neurotic needs" were based on her psychiatric and psychotherapeutic experience in clinical practice. Successful living, she believed, required these basic ingredients, adjusting them according to individual idiosyncrasies and, though theoretically possible that a single individual might manifest all of these needs, it was her clinical experience which led her to suggest that only a few of these were necessary in an individual to manifest neurosis. Classified as "coping strategies" in her nomenclature, they are as follows:

Moving Toward People

1. The need for affection and approval; pleasing others and being liked by them.

2. The need for a partner; one whom they can love and who will solve all problems.

Moving Against People

3. The need for power; the ability to bend wills and achieve control over others—while most persons seek strength, the neurotic may be desperate for it.

4. The need to exploit others; to get the better of them. To become manipulative, fostering the belief that people are there simply to be used.

5. The need for social recognition; prestige and limelight.

6. The need for personal admiration; for both inner and outer qualities—to be valued.

7. The need for personal achievement; though virtually all persons wish to make achievements, as with No. 3, the neurotic may be desperate for achievement.

Moving Away from People

8. The need for self-sufficiency and independence; while most desire some autonomy, the neurotic may simply wish to discard other individuals entirely.

9. The need for perfection; while many are driven to perfect their lives in the form of well being, the neurotic may display a fear of being slightly flawed.

10. Lastly, the need to restrict life practices to within narrow borders; to live as inconspicuous a life as possible.

Horney found that this listing provided a quick and meaningful reference point in her therapeutic practice. And, with further use, she realized that by combining these into three more broadly conceived classifications, the analysis and treatment plan could more readily be employed. Compliance Needs, Aggression Needs, and Detachment Needs became her three categories for classifying neurotic behavior. "Moving towards people" constituted her description of compliance needs, a behavior pattern characterized by self-effacement where, for example, children confronted with difficulties in interacting with parents. In such situations, the fear of abandonment or general helplessness she lumped into a sense of basic anxiety. Such children often demonstrate a conspicuous need for affection and approval from parents, siblings, and/or peers and identifying a friend or confidant in whom reliance fosters a false sense of enduring security. These individuals, both children and adults suffering from this basic anxiety, usually fail to place demands on others in their relationships, often denigrating themselves to a self-state of inconsequentiality.

The second classification of coping strategies Horney labelled "Aggression Needs," or more commonly characterized as aggressive behavior "moving against people." Somewhat more elaborate and expansive than the first category of compliance needs, the neurotic individual, child or adult, commonly manifests anger and hostility towards his social environment. The sense of a need for power, control and even exploitation is conspicuous and there is a recognizable veneer of omnipotence in social situations. Within this behavioral matrix, Horney is quick to suggest that social recognition, if not outright social approval, is very much sought by such an individual. Popularity seems not to be the driving force but rather acknowledgment and possibly being feared as the desired effect. This aggressive neurotic type produces an avoidance behavior of others within his social arena for this type of individual is perceived by the social group as willing to do whatever it takes for personal happiness even at the cost of hurting or alienating members of the social peer group.

Horney was particularly keen on exploring what she chose to call *Detachment Needs* for it was within this matrix of behavior that she found an opportunity to explore child/parent relationships in a detailed fashion. She called this category "moving-away-from" and sometimes "resignation solutions" which characterized the detached personality of the abandoned or overlooked child. There are those children for whom the social environment has fostered a sense of self-sufficiency which distinguishes them from both the aggressive as well as the compliant behavioral categories. This withdrawal characteristic is more non-aggressive in nature, seeking rather solitude and personal independence as the preferred behavioral posture towards the social group. The driving desire, however, for perfection can become an inordinately motivating behavioral pattern such that a high level of intolerance for others and for oneself in the face of behavior assessed as less than perfect. Because of this driving force towards perfection, tolerance of others is often a low priority and the suppression of such feelings as love and hate become paramount in this type of personality.

Never willing to stand still when work in theory development was needed, she continued to refine these categories of assessment throughout her professional career. Just two years before her death in 1952, she published what became the most commonly quoted summary of her latest theories regarding personality development in a book titled *Neurosis and Human Growth: The Struggle Toward Self-Realization* (1950). More than merely a summary of her ideas regarding neurosis and neurotic needs, she further clarified and extended her concepts of the three neurotic solutions to the stress and anxiety of living. Herein she proposed a tripartite combination of narcissistic, perfectionistic, and arrogant-vindictive approaches to life which essentially constituted a rethink of these concepts which had first appeared in print in her 1939 book *New Ways in Psychoanalysis*. Using clinical case studies from her own practice, she developed a concept called "morbid dependency" which addressed those individuals suffering from the neurotic characteristics of narcissism and resignation. In a concluding statement, she emphasizes that where non-neurotic individuals may act out components of these three needs categories, the truly neurotic person will inevitably display deeper, stronger, more willful drives to fulfill these needs. This last book was acclaimed by both her protagonists and antagonists as her finest work.

NARCISSISM AND INNER CONFLICTS

Whereas Freud and the orthodox school of psychoanalysis placed a great deal of emphasis upon the central function of narcissism within the context of psychoanalytic theory, Horney preferred, and said so emphatically, to view the narcissistic personality as having been produced by social environmental situations and circumstances rather than biogenically. Whereas her concept of self-idealization was thought of as compensatory in the behavioral matrix of the developing personality (as are all defense strategies), she argued that the narcissistic personality is inclined to self-indulgence even and essentially in the absence of a genuinely merited self-esteem. Therefore, she contended that weak self-image produces narcissistic behavior. Furthermore, whereas Freud was not indifferent to the reality of inner conflicts within the neurotic or narcissistic patient, he merely saw them as illustrative of repressed anxiety. He regarded the individual's inner self with a sort of disbelief in the essential goodness of the human person and in personality growth and development.

With Jean-Paul Sartre, Freud was content with the idea that individuals are condemned to destroy themselves through self-induced suffering brought on by unrealistic desires and ambitions. Horney was not satisfied with this pessimistic view of the human condition but strove for a reason to hope for a better world in the nurture of the human spirit's drive for self-fulfillment. The conflict in life between contradictory neurotic tendencies, Horney suggested, and the attitudes embodied in the individual who is suffering from neurosis towards the self, personal qualities, and social values, constituted a life situation which could, with effort and intentionality, be directed towards personal fulfillment and self-actualization. The prospects for such a corrective in behavior for the neurotic narcissist suffering from inner conflicts is to be found within the individual himself, confident that the human person embodies the very source of his own mental health. This comes, of course, from the cultivation of meaningful and enriching interpersonal relationships wherein lies the prospects for a deepening of a sense of self-esteem and self-worth and a divestiture of narcissistic self-indulgence and inner conflict.

PSYCHOANALSIS

For Horney, psychoanalysis consisted of a theory of assessment and description as well as a modality of treatment based upon the centrality not in the Freudian psychoanalytical tradition of the biogenic etiology of mental illness but on the meaning and relevance of interpersonal relationship skills development beginning in early childhood and progressing throughout adolescence. The socializing factors of the individual child in relationship to the parent proves crucial in the development of mental health or the appearance of mental illnesses such as narcissism and personality dysfunction. Self-image as well as self-esteem and self-worth all constitute the challenge to the healthy maturation process of children into adolescence. Childhood neurosis finds its origin precisely here in the early skills development of interpersonal relationships, says Horney. As in childhood, so in adulthood, neurotic individuals are those persons who have struggled against the odds of a poor social environment to gain a sense of self-worth, rather losing their capacity to make good decisions, gripped by fear of relationships and the unknown as well as obsessive-compulsive behaviors, anxiety, and depression. The goal of psychoanalysis, according to Karen Horney, is to facilitate a systemic change in the individual's personal assessment of his life situation, changing opinions and perceptions of and about life by assisting the individual in reaching deep within his own sense of self-worth towards a looming potential found in self-realization and self-actualization.

Horney's work led her to believe that neurotic behavior is spawned by social environmental conditions and provides the foil for understanding the etiology of mental illness itself. Individuals, at whatever level of self-actualization, have the capacity, opportunity, and responsibility of seeking to realize their full potential through personal relationships and self-understanding. Psychoanalysis in the form of Horney's understanding cannot, she explains, solve the world's problems, such as they are. However, self-analysis can lend itself to a deepening of one's own sense of self, the real self, a self which has the capacity of seeking greater fulfillment. Psychoanalytic therapy, Horney contended throughout her professional life, lends itself to the development of a deeper sense of self and a greater capacity for self-fulfillment. Transference or love for the therapist by the patient Horney downplayed *vis a vis* the orthodox Freudian notion of transference and counter-transference being the glue that binds the patient to the therapist and vice versa. Rather, says Horney, the patient's fear of others, the unknown, the outside world of conflict, constitutes the drive towards the therapist rather than a Freudian notion of "love for the therapist." Facilitating the patient who suffers from feelings of helplessness and naturally a sense of dependence upon the therapist, psychoanalysis in the Horney tradition, is designed specifically to foster a sense of self-confidence and self-reliance within the framework of a clinical relationship built upon trust.

NEO-FREUDIANS

Though initially a cause of anxiety and stress, eventually Horney came to view her departure from the orthodox Freudian psychoanalytic school of analysis and therapy as a good thing, joining Alfred Adler and many others later in the formation of what became known, ironically, as the Neo-Freudian school of psychoanalysis. While Adler despised the use of Freud's name and his school of thought and avoided it with a passion, the emergence of the Neo-Freudian school by name, theory, and practice could not finally be avoided. With less rancor and more critical acumen than Adler seemed capable of, Horney was able to delineate the points of subtle as well as significant variances in theory and practice between the orthodox Freudians and the neo-Freudians without rancor.

Carl Jung would eventually join the ranks of Horney in her aggressive disputing with Freud over the centrality of sex and aggression as the primary determiners of personality. Furthermore, Freud's inordinate emphasis upon the nature and function of "penis envy" proved to be a significant point of departure in these two competing schools of psychoanalysis. Freud's naïve assessment of female jealousy of what he thought of as the male's natural power and dominance was, according to Horney, indicative of an overly inflated masculinity rather than a truly natural assessment of the male-female relational matrix. Whereas a neurotic woman may be susceptible to penis envy, Horney believed that "womb envy" occurs just as frequently among insecure men owing to a natural male tendency to resent woman's ability in child birth, mothering, and nurturing of the young. The male drive to success, Horney contended, may actually be a reflection of the substitutionary character of the absent womb in men. She further extended this, at the time, controversial assessment of male vulnerability by suggesting that men have a tendency to envy women, unconsciously, for their capacity for simply "being" in society rather than, as with men, having to prove themselves worthy of their elevated place in society.

Horney was somewhat baffled by the Freudians' inordinate emphasis on the centrality of the male sex organ and found it necessary to reformulate the psychoanalytic concept of the Oedipal complex by suggesting, based on her own personal experience as a child and her clinical experience as a therapist, that the child grasping and holding tight to one parent over the other and jealousy towards one in favor of another was merely the inevitable result of anxiety produced in a dysfunctional interpersonal relationship with one or the other parent. Socio-cultural etiology rather than a biogenic etiology constituted the best explanation for such behavior according to Horney. Not early willing to separate herself professionally or ideologically from the Freudian school of psychoanalysis, Horney struggled admirably in an attempt to reformulate concepts, theories, and modalities of treatment which had been produced by Freud and his psychoanalytic group of practitioners, seeking all the while for a more comprehensive, socio-culturally sensitive and informed theoretical matrix based on a behavioral science awareness of personality development.

THEORY OF THE SELF

The humanistic school of psychology called the Third Force by Maslow and Rogers, the First Force being Skinner's Behaviorism and the Second Force being Freud's psychoanalysis, was very attractive to Horney and the relationship was mutually complimentary of both theory and practice within her own school of psychoanalytic social psychotherapy. With Maslow, she believed that all people fundamentally seek "self-actualization" in which she defined the self as an individual's own personal being and potentiality. The individual who has a comprehensive grasp of his own self, that individual is thereby at liberty to seek his full potential in the achievement of reasonable goals. The healthy person realizes self-actualization through this process of quest and achievement rather than, in a Freudian sense, a neurotic individual's inevitable search for self-interest and pleasure based on a set of key needs.

Individuals essentially have two separate views of themselves, according to Horney, viz., the "real self" and the "ideal self." The former is the actual person as he really is and the latter is that type of person each individual feels they should be or desires to be. The former has the capacity for growth, development, and maturity towards a self-fulfilling happiness through the employment of will power and the utilization of personal gifts. The ideal self, however, is used as a "model" in guiding the real self towards self-actualization. Knowledge of the difference is a sign of personal maturity and a healthy self-image. Horney was convinced that the neurotic person's self was divided between an idealized self and a real self. However, the neurotic person finds himself being self-critical for having not been able to live up to the standards of the ideal self. Anxiety rises in these persons in relationship to the rising awareness of a "flawed nature," having failed themselves by not meeting their ideal standards. Unfortunately, the goals for self-actualization set by the neurotic person are unrealistic, not attainable, and therefore the individual is set up for failure by producing a diminished self-esteem boarding on self-contempt. Furthermore, this diminished self-image becomes, then, in the mind of the neurotic person the true self thus creating an oscillation between the ideal perfect person and the diminished flawed person. Fluctuating between narcissism and self-contempt, the neurotic person continues to fall deeper and deeper into neurotic behavior. Horney chose to call this "the tyranny of the shoulds" in which the neurotic person's quest for perfection leads to a demented self-image. Unless this "cycle of neurosis" can be broken, the individual is doomed to a perpetual state of neurosis.

FEMININE PSYCHOLOGY

A pioneer in more ways than one, that one which has so characterized her reputation and scholarship was that of being one of the first female psychiatrists and the credited founder of what has become established as feminine psychology. Between 1922 and 1937, she wrote fourteen papers on various aspects of the topic which were published in a single volume titled *Feminine Psychology*. With so very few women recognized or even accepted into the psychoanalytic society of medical practitioners, Horney was determined both to call attention to that void in the profession and to offer a substantive contribution as a psychoanalyst to the professional practice. In an essay entitled, "The Problem of Feminine Masochism," for example, she set out to demonstrate that cultures and societies globally encourage women to be dependent on men for love, wealth, and protection. Concomitantly, these societies have balanced this directive to women towards masculine dependency by emphasizing male dominance in power and authority. This diminution of the role of women as creators, nurturers, and bearers of the species to satisfaction for men as merely the embodiment of beauty and self-absorption has reduced both the role of men as well as women. Women as objects of grace and beauty with men as objects of power and authority serve neither the potential of women nor men in their quest for self-actualization.

Within this same collection of essays, Horney's paper titled "The Distrust between the Sexes" scoped out the complexities of the conflict. Women have historically been valued based on child birth and the mother/wife figure in the family. The husband-wife relationship too often and historically compares to the parent-child relationship, i.e., the conflict of authority and power, miscommunication and misunderstanding, all of which have fostered a debilitating neurosis of family members – for all involved including husband, wife, mother, father, and children. And finally, her essay on monogamy became her most notable essay in the collection titled "The Problem of the Monogamous Ideal." Here she explicated the complex and unbalanced relationship between husband and wife, men and women as perpetuated by the male-dominated society in western culture.

Horney contended that both men and women are possessed of a drive to be productive with women satisfying this need normally yet interiorly through pregnancy and childbirth while men through externality such as work and constructive creativity. Horney, to the disbelief of male psychoanalytic practitioners, contended that this externality of male ingenuity was motivated by the male's attempt to compensate for not being able to give birth, namely, womb envy! Such a notion, not well received by the established professional community, nevertheless launched Horney into the public eye resulting in a practical publication of a "self-help" book in 1946 with the title *Are You Considering Psychoanalysis?* Extremely controversial within the orthodox profession of psychoanalysis specifically and psychotherapy and psychiatry generally, she suggested that for the normally healthy man or woman there is the possibility of them being their own personal psychotherapist! Self-treatment for the self-helper was the theme with heavy emphasis upon the notion that an awareness of the self can and should foster self-esteem producing stronger, more confident, and more fulfilling lives for both men and women. This drift towards the popularization of psychotherapy was, in the minds of many professionals, a downward trajectory of her otherwise distinguished career as teacher, researcher, and clinician. Later, we will see other modern schools of psychotherapy pick up on the "self-help" theme in which Horney excelled including particularly Berne and Ellis.

PERSONALITY DEVELOPMENT

Throughout her professional career, Horney was keen to emphasize the central role of parenting in personality development. She believed that the etiology of mental illness could be traced, as did Freud and the whole school of psychoanalysis, back to childhood. However, rather than child sexual abuse or physical neglect as the cause of neurosis, she believed, based on her own personal experience and her clinical practice, that the fundamental root cause of mental illness could be traced to parental indifference during a child's early formative years. This notion was so very central to her theory of personality development and the etiology of neurosis that she labelled it the "basic evil," namely, parental indifference wherein there is a lack of parental warmth and affection towards the child. In the absence of warmth and expressive love, children develop a plethora of neuroses which can plague them throughout their adult lives.

Understanding this "basic evil" of parental indifference was key to Horney's psychotherapeutic assessment and treatment of mental illness, particularly neurosis. This understanding is based upon the child's perception of the meaning and nature of the parental relationship and with emphasis upon perception rather than what objectively may be thought of as the real situation. A well-intentioned parent who thinks of themselves as trying their best to be a good mother (or father) may very well fail in the effort by presenting a style of parenting which is perceived by the child to exemplify indifference. Gifts and favors, for example which Horney experienced from her father, do not substitute for warmth and nurture regardless of the intention of the parent. Again, as in her case, preferential treatment of one child over another or falsely blaming one child for another child's misdemeanors can constitute the basis for a perception of indifference. Furthermore, such things as on-again off-again favors and affirmations, warm one moment, cold another, failed promises, inordinate teasing about a child's appearance or ideas or attitudes all can converge into a matrix of neurosis-producing parental behavior. Whether exemplified by a neurotic parent or merely a parent periodically (and understandably) distracted by the demands of life, the results can be disastrous for the child.

The self-survival instincts of children Horney was quick to identify and applaud. Again, as in her own life, there are response mechanisms endemic to child maturation which can work for their benefit in a survival mode of interpersonal relationships. Often and to their credit, a child's response to the "basic evil" of parental indifference is anger giving rise to a persistent hostility which manifests itself most commonly as protesting against the injustices characterizing the indifferent parent's parenting behavior. The effectiveness of this hostility can, if it proves beneficial to the child's coping with the family situation, becomes an habitual response to many of life's difficulties which, Horney explains, can and does often become an aggressive coping strategy throughout adulthood. However and Horney is quick to make this point, many children rather find themselves overwhelmed by the experience resulting in an often debilitating anxiety about life and relationships. Such anxiety produces a persistent experience and fear of helplessness and even abandonment in the face of parental indifference. Horney notes that an alternative to anger and hostility is the realization by the child that if stability is to be maintained in the relationship with parents, then anger and hostility must be replaced by a copying mechanism she has called compliance. In the absence of love, at least the child can avoid in his own perception parental hatred. When neither aggressive nor compliant behavior can produce the desired relationship between child and parent, then the only apparent solution is withdrawal from family interaction and activity. This Horney called the third coping strategy.

CONCLUDING REMARKS

That Karen Horney was a pioneering psychoanalytic social psychotherapist has been shown without question. The first woman psychiatrist to venture into the troubled waters of Freudian psychoanalytic theory, Horney's courage both as a professional in the field and a woman in a man's world cannot but be admired and applauded. And, to put a fine point on it, the correctives as well as elaborate improvements to many of the orthodox theories and concepts within psychoanalysis which she developed have stood the test of time. Combining a thorough training in traditional Freudian psychoanalysis with her not reluctant readiness to spot a weakness and address it with creative improvements, Horney demonstrated the unique insights which a woman psychiatrist could and did make to the male dominated professional practice of psychotherapy at the time. Her critique of Freud's overly enthusiastic fascination with the sexual origins of mental illness and her dismissive posture relative to female penis envy and the introduction of the profoundly important concept of male womb envy all converged to make her insights both attractive and viable. Furthermore and to her profound credit, she joined Adler and Sullivan in their embrace of the behavioral sciences and the application of the insights of social psychology to psychotherapeutic theory and practice. Moving the argument for the etiology of mental illness away from deterministic biogenics to the psychogenics of socio-cultural environmental circumstances and situations as the origin of most mental illness proved both liberating and empowering to the therapist who was not solely dependent upon either pharmacology or psychoanalytic probings of the unconscious through dream analysis and free association.

Horney's approach has been subsumed within the broader school of humanistic psychology called the Third Force but her unique composition of a school of thought best labeled psychoanalytic social psychotherapy encompasses both the best of Freudian theory and the best of the humanistic school of psychology in emphasizing the centrality of interpersonal relationship skills development as the source of both mental illness and mental health. She has become a giant in her own field and an admired practitioner and theorist in the broad field of psychotherapy.

KAREN HORNEY'S PRIMARY SOURCES (still in print)

Neurosis and Human Growth, Norton, New York, 1950.

Are You Considering Psychoanalysis? Norton, 1946.

Our Inner Conflicts, Norton, 1945.

Self-analysis, Norton, 1942.

New Ways in Psychoanalysis, Norton, 1939.

The Neurotic Personality of our Time, Norton, 1937.

Feminine Psychology (reprints), Norton, 1922–37 1967. *The Collected Works of Karen Horney* (2 vols.), Norton, 1950. *The Adolescent Diaries of Karen Horney*, Basic Books, New York, 1980.

The Therapeutic Process: Essays and Lectures, ed. Bernard J. Paris, Yale University Press, New Haven, 1999.

The Unknown Karen Horney: Essays on Gender, Culture, and Psychoanalysis, ed. Bernard J. Paris, Yale University Press, New Haven, 2000.

Final Lectures, ed. Douglas H. Ingram, Norton, 1991.

SECONDARY SOURCES

Hitchcock, S. T. (2004). *Karen Horney: Pioneer of feminist psychology*. New York: Chelsea House Publishers.

O'Connell, A. N. (1980). Karen Horney: Theorist in psychoanalysis and feminine psychology. *Psychology of Women Quarterly, 5*(1), 81-93.

O'Connell, A. N. (1990). Karen Horney (1885-1952). *Women in psychology: A bio-bibliographic sourcebook*, (pp. 184-190). Westport, CT: Greenwood Press.

Paris, B. (1994). *Karen Horney: A psychoanalyst's search for self-understanding*. New Haven, CT: Yale University Press.

Paul, Henry (1991). "A report on the Karen Horney Clinic," *The American Journal of Psychoanalysis*, September, 51(3):341-2.

Quinn, S. (1987). *A mind of her own: the life of Karen Horney*. New York: Summit Books.

Rubins, J. L. (1978). *Karen Horney: Gentle rebel of psychoanalysis*. New York: The Dial Press.

Sayers, J. (1991). *Mothers of Psychoanalysis: Helene Deutsch, Karen Horney, Anna Freud, Melanie Klein*. New York: W. W. Norton and Company.

Westkott, Marcia. *The Feminist Legacy of Karen Horney*, Yale University Press, New Haven, 1986.

CHAPTER TEN
Melanie Klein and Psychoanalytic Child Psychotherapy

INTRODUCTION

The brilliance and wide spread pervasiveness of object relations theory in the modern practice of child psychology and psychotherapy in western countries and particularly the United States is counter balanced by the common absence of knowledge within the general population of the creator of that theory. Ironic it is that Melanie Klein has been one of the most important theoreticians in modern psychotherapy while either name recognition or credit for her pioneering work in the field is singularly absent. With Karen Horney and Anna Freud, Klein is considered within the hallowed halls of the academy and in the clinical setting of therapeutic practice one of the most important psychologists of the 20th century. While Anna Freud and Karen Horney are universally heralded as key figures in modern psychology owing particularly to their profoundly important contributions to female psychology and feminine psychotherapy, Klein is held up within the professional community as a brilliant theoretician and clinician owing to her development of object relations theory and its expansive application and relevance to child psychotherapy. She is recognized not only as a major female psychologist but as a major psychologist in the field of a modified application of neo-Freudian psychoanalysis. Credited rightfully as the major force in the development of a new school of psychoanalysis known by its governing theory of object relations, she demonstrated the effectiveness of this system of thought in her work with mother-infant-child relationships as related particularly to personality development. The influence of this profoundly insightful modality of analysis and treatment has been felt and reflected by and in the work of John Bowlby and Donald Winnicott to name only two of a plethora of psychotherapists. Though indirectly through her psychoanalytic psychotherapy, she

207

has made and her work continues to make major contributions to the general fields of social psychology and developmental psychology, especially in the sub-fields of parent-child relations and personality development theory.

As with Anna Freud and Karen Horney, Klein's brand of psychoanalytic theory and practice represents one of the major schools in the broad field of psychotherapy. Followers of her system of theory and practice referred to as Kleinian psychoanalysts are recognized members of the International Psychoanalytical Association which has a distinguished following in the United Kingdom, Latin America, and throughout Western Europe. However, within the United States, the Psychoanalytic Center of California is presently the only major center for training in Kleinian psychoanalytic practice owing, possibly, to the fact that the Kleinian practice of psychoanalysis still follows the traditional orthodox Freudian system of the proverbial couch and four to five sessions a week. Rather than focusing upon the patient's ego development, Klein's approach is to focus on the deeper and more primordial emotions and fantasies of the patient. While questioning some of the fundamental components of traditional Freudian psychoanalysis, as did Karen Horney, she with Erikson and Horney and somewhat with Sullivan still very much considered herself a psychoanalyst in the Freudian tradition. Emphasizing that allegiance, Klein was recognized as the first orthodox psychoanalyst to employ Freudian theory and practice in the treatment of children. Modifying and patenting her methodology in the treatment of children, such as play therapy and the use of toys and childhood props, she cultivated a whole system of treatment and theory relative to infant personality development and, most decidedly like Freud himself, she was extremely demanding of her understudy students requiring loyalty to her theory and modality of treatment out of which grew a highly refined and respected training program in psychoanalysis. Its distinguishing feature centered around the development and use of object relations theory about which we will have much more to say later in this chapter.

BIOGRAPHY

Born in Vienna on March 30, 1882, into a middle-class Jewish family, Melanie was the youngest of four children. Her father, Moriz Reizes, was a general practitioner of medicine in Galicia. Her mother, with whom she had a troubled and complicated relationship, Libussa Deutsch Reizes, was never a real source of nurture or encouragement. Melanie's closest family tie was with her only brother, Emanue,l who died at an early age in 1902 when Melanie was just twenty years old. Melanie Reizes took her education in the local city gymnasium, but her childhood dreams of pursuing the study of medicine were not realizable at the time owing to a serious decline in the family fortune. The alternative was marriage and so she married Arthur Klein, an industrial chemist, and, thus, they began their family life together eventuating in the birth of three children. Understandably, she suffered early on in her marriage from depression and a nervous disorder resulting from, as she explained it many years later, a difficult relationship with her overly dominating mother. First living with him in Rosenheim, in 1910, she moved with her husband and children to Budapest and there she was fortunate to have the opportunity of entering psychoanalysis with the famous Sandor Ferenczi. This analysis and relationship proved of monumental importance in her future development professionally as well as personally. Her therapist, Ferenczi, recognized her intellectual acumen and was fully cognizant of her passion for psychoanalytic theory, so he encouraged her to employ her growing understanding of psychoanalysis in the care and treatment of her own children. Extremely unorthodox, if not unprofessional, this trajectory of psychoanalysis applied to children was the first instance of such practice to occur and, fully aware of the originality of this approach, Klein began to develop a schema of techniques in child analysis which has endured the test of time and is still employed today virtually unchanged. In what she early on chose to call her "play technique," Klein would note the child's play activities and interpret them as symbolic of unconscious data within the child's psyche, interpreting this data in the same orthodox and traditional way as was applied in adult analysis. Eventually, she became the first practicing psychoanalyst to approach children's play as providing meaningful data in their analysis and treatment. This concept of play technique naturally contributed to a more formalized development in America of what we commonly think of today as play therapy in child counseling.

Klein's own personal life was full of tragedy and the scars of such were seen and carried throughout her professional and personal life. She learned even as a child that she was an unwanted birth to her parents who showed her little affection. This experience, of course, resonates closely with Karen Horney's notion of the emergence of anxiety, fear, and anger within the child who has experienced parental indifference as a developmental phenomenon. Klein had an older sister whom she dearly loved but who died when Klein was only four years old. The result was that she was felt to feel responsible for the death of both of her siblings.

Klein attended the International Psycho-Analytic Congress in Budapest in 1918 at age 36 and there for the first time had an opportunity to meet Freud himself. "I remember vividly how impressed I was and how the wish to devote myself to psychoanalysis was strengthened by this impression" (quoted in Grosskurth, 1986, p.71). She was very eager to become a member of that professional body of psychoanalysts in Hungary based on the scholarly strength of a paper she presented before that professional assembly dealing with the application of psychoanalytic practice to the treatment of children. She eventually, and to her great professional advantage, became a member of the Hungarian Psycho-Analytic Society. However, her marriage to Arthur Klein was rapidly declining and as a result she left him, taking the children with her to Berlin where fortunately she was welcomed into the Berlin Psycho-Analytic Society. At age 38, the separation for Klein was wrenching and the move to Berlin was seen as a real opportunity to immerse herself into the most exciting center at the time for psychoanalytic study. Little money and few friends did not deter her as she believed deeply that her future lay within the practice of child psychoanalysis. As we will see later, she pleaded with Karl Abraham to take her on as a trainee analyst. One of the leading voices in Berlin in the field of psychoanalysis, he was not afraid to challenge some of the theories and practices of Freud himself. They were of kindred spirits for it is reported that Abraham himself once said that "the future of psychoanalysis rests with child analysis."

It was in Berlin that Klein began to blossom both as a student and theorist. While studying with Abraham, she began to study and analyze children's behavior which was to become the basis of her own developing theory of object relations. The approach, i.e., the studying of children as young as two years old, was too radical for the orthodox establishment of psychoanalytic practitioners in Berlin and she understandably met with great hostility. Being both a divorced woman in conservative Berlin and without even a college degree to show for credentials to practice psychoanalysis, she found the environment stifling and counter-productive to her professional desires as a woman in a male dominated medical community. She would later find quite the opposite reaction when she made her move to London. When Abraham died suddenly in 1925, she was essentially cut off from professional access to the practice of psychoanalysis and her theory-development enterprise suffered severely. The end of the following year saw her determined to immigrate to England and establish herself (and her young family) in London where she would spend the rest of her life.

Without question, her arrival in London as a practitioner of psychoanalysis and a theory builder related to the treatment of children met with much interest. Personally very beautiful, according to all reports, and rather young to be a practicing therapist, Klein became quietly referred to as "the black beauty" and being Jewish simply added to her mystique. The professional community, primarily made up of older men, became intrigued with her. Klein was unquestionably committed to her work and set about to further, through clinical experience, her deeper understanding of the nature of child development from a psychoanalytic perspective. Besides the standard texts in psychology and Freudian analysis, she was an enthusiastic reader of the classics in Russian, French and English. The theatre and classical music were high on her list of interests and, of course, given her middle-class Viennese childhood education, she played the piano and was an inveterate concert patron and, indicative of her cultural refinements, even won a wine tasting competition in the South of France, she was purported to hold her own with the highest level of professional practitioners in London in terms of both intellect and class.

But, alas, the picture was not all roses and wine. Klein experienced a great deal of sadness in her life, as a youngster, an adult, a professional, and as a mother. Owing to the early death of her older sister whom her mother made no secret of her being the favorite, Klein developed a periodic and near debilitating depression which persisted throughout her adult life. Subsequently when she was in her 20's, Klein's bother died which proved a real shock owing to their closeness as siblings in a troubled household. The death of Karl Abraham soon after she had begun her analysis with him and from whom she was receiving great encouragement in her theories of child development proved both personally and professionally devastating as well. Later losing a son to apparent suicide and with her daughter turning against her both personally and professionally during the highlight of her rising reputation in London stifled her otherwise gregarious public pursuit of an ever enlarging forum for her lectures on child neurosis and personality development.

As we have noted above, during her time in Berlin, she felt she needed to enter further psychoanalysis and she did so under the care of Karl Abraham, a noted and well-respected psychoanalyst in Berlin admired by Freud himself. Abraham was at the time working on the Freudian concept of the death instinct, developing his own understanding of this concept with ideas related to oral and anal sadistic tendencies he had identified in his treatment of children. We now see that Klein was early influenced by this insight and she soon and aggressively adopted and adapted these ideas into her own understanding and interpretation of children's play activities. Not all practicing psychoanalysts in Berlin either agreed with Abraham or approved of Klein's approach and when Abraham died in 1926, she chose to move with her children to England. There, she set up house-keeping in London, joining the British Psycho-Analytical Society at the personal urgings of Ernst Jones, the colleague and official biography of Freud.

Unlike her cool reception in Berlin excepting for Abraham, Klein found the British psychoanalysts enthusiastically welcoming both of her involvement in the Society and her energetic development of the treatment of children using her ideas of play therapy. For the duration of her professional life, Klein concentrated her efforts in this regard, eventually producing a system of child development theory within the psychoanalytic school of psychotherapy. This approach became so internationally recognized and endorsed that the emergence of a whole school of Kleinian psychoanalysis was the result. The training of these professionals who were attracted to whole developmental theories constituted a major part of her work and these innovative insights employing play activities as the basis for analysis and treatment proved to be valued within the professional community as a unique and extremely valuable contribution. Drawing from her early work with Abraham, she developed an interpretive approach to the death instinct Abraham had identified in early childhood conjoined with the emergence of an early superego construct within the maturing child which offers a corrective to Freud's notion of the Oedipus complex.

Naturally, this reinterpretation of Freudian theory of ego development combined with Klein's notion of play therapy as an analytical technique produced an international incident of controversy between the English therapists and the Viennese Society which at the time was headed by Anna Freud who was herself developing a whole construct of analytical theory of child therapy not in consort or agreement with Klein. Nevertheless, the 1927 Symposium on Child Analysis launched a periodical titled the *International Journal of Psychoanalysis* wherein both Anna Freud and Melanie Klein produced some of their most important work in the broad field of child psychology and psychotherapy. However and it cannot be overlooked, Anna Freud, who had fled the Nazi persecution in 1938, and the Viennese Group consisting also of Edward Glover and particularly Melani Klein's own daughter, the distinguished and highly respected psychoanalyst Melitta Schmideberg, were outspokenly critical of Klein's work. From 1927, she and Anna Freud had disagreed as to the proper interpretation and application of psychoanalytic theory to child therapy. This disagreement first became public in the 1927 London Symposium on Child Analysis wherein Anna Freud particularly challenged some of the key theories of Klein in Anna Freud's book titled *Einfuhrung in die Technik der Kinderanalyse* (English translation *An Introduction to the Technique of Child*

Analysis). The disagreement centered especially upon the origin of the super-ego within the child for both Anna Freud and her father argued that the super-ego superseded the Oedipus complex whereas Klein argued that the early primordial and harshly emergent super-ego occurred as a result of early experiences within the child's life and evolved out of the child's sadistic impulses, not, according to the Freuds, in the identification with the parents.

Consistent with her whole system of child-world construction, Klein described the inner world of early childhood primarily as independent of and free from the influence and experience of the outer world. This inner world, as Klein saw and constructed it from within the perspective and interpretation of the child, was comprised of phantasies of good and bad objects which had their origin from instinctual conflicts growing out of the parent-child relationship. Drawing from Sigmund Freud's theory of the death instinct, Klein argued that these internal objects were essentially manifestations of the inevitable, natural, and fundamentally innate conflicts which emerge between parent and child as the child encounters the outer world from within the inner world construct of the psyche. The driving force for Klein in this matrix of child behavior was that of fear, fear which was an instinctual and naturally destructive impulse originating in the death instinct itself.

In 1932, she took the opportunity to demonstrate the analytical effectiveness of this theory and application in her book titled *The Psycho-Analysis of Children.* She further explicated this theory and delineated its clinical effectiveness in a series of collected essays published in 1935 titled *A Contribution to the Psychogenesis of Manic-Depressive States,* in 1940 titled *Mourning and Its Relation to Manic-Depressive States,* and again in 1946 titled *Notes on Some Schizoid Mechanism.* She eventually finalized her overall theory of object relations therapy with the defining concept of the paranoid-schizoid and the depressive position which included a serious accounting of the counter-balancing feelings within the child of love and hate. This refinement gained her much international attention and respect but the seriousness of the conflict with the Sigmund and Anna Freud and the entire Freudian school, a debate subsequently referred to in the journals as the Controversial Discussions, occurring in the heat of the Second World War, led to the establishment of a competing school of thought within the British Psycho-Analytic Society. Some have suggested two while others have identified three separate schools of thought and practice – Klein, Freud, and the Independents.

The first major appearance of what would become the defining characteristic of Kleinian psychoanalysis, namely the term and concept "object relations therapy," was in her 1932 book titled *The Psychoanalysis of Children.* In this now classic text based on her own clinical work as a therapist, she suggested that every infant has a primary object relationship to its mother and in this relationship the infant experiences a psychic life which is essentially dominated by what she chose to call "sadistic phantasies" (*NOTE: Klein preferred the "ph" spelling of fantasies and with only a few exceptions we will honor this idiosyncrasy in her thought system.*) which originate from what most psychoanalysts, including Karen Horney, then and now recognize as an innate aggressive drive. Extending this what at the time was considered an extremely controversial proposal, she published a major paper dealing with the explication of this object relations theory titled "A Contribution to the Psychogenesis of Manic Depressive States" in 1935. The timing was suggestive of a personal passion and obsession as her son Hans had just recently died prior to the paper's appearance in the journal. Herein she explored and explicated the components of parental mourning and the sense of primitive defense mechanisms in the Freudian orthodox sense in which she introduced her fundamental idea of two phases of personality development. The first phase of her system she called the paranoid-schizoid position and the second phase the depressive position. Her idea of the first phase centered round the concept of defense mechanisms within the child. However, this specific idea precipitated heated debate within the British Psycho-Analytic Society itself, resulting in a series of discussions fraught with controversy occurring during the second World War years around the question as to whether or not what was now being called everywhere "Kleinianism," really constituted an operationally accepted use of the term psychoanalysis or whether, indeed, it was too far removed from orthodox Freudian theory as to preclude its acceptance as a theory and a practice within the British Society. Amazingly British in the resolution of the controversy was the decision to actually teach and practice two different schools of thought, viz., both the Kleinian school and the Freudian school. By doing so, Klein's system of psychoanalysis was the first nationally and eventually internationally recognized challenge to orthodox Freudian definitions of psychoanalysis while still remaining within the tradition of psychoanalysis. Clearly Freud would not agree, but the British sense of compromise facilitated this historic divergence in theory and practice without an actual brake within the professional community of practicing psychoanalysts!

"The book," as her friends and colleagues commonly referred to her 1932 opus of creative, provocative, and quite controversial essays, was very early on recognized and promoted as one of the most original pieces of clinical and theoretical work in the general field of psychoanalysis to date. Whereas Freud, the father of the movement, had proposed a construct of the human psyche which differentiated structures and developmental stages over time from infancy to adulthood, Klein proposed and illustrated a much more dynamic portrayal of psychic development. She contended, for example, that there were a set of processes operative within the human psyche which constituted a complex of emotions built upon a developmental operation concomitantly emerging with profound intensity within the developing child, an explosion of trajectory of consciousness she chose to call "a mosaic of turbulence." It was within this matrix of developmental coalescence within the child psyche that led her to experiment with play through the use of children's toys as a hermeneutical tool for probing the child psyche. This, she argued, was not dissimilar to the function of free association analysis with adults used by Freud.

Interestingly, Klein began to report in her clinical studies that children's play often was characterized by violent phantasies which were acted out within the context of severe and acute anxiety and fear. No clinician had yet engaged in the systematic and laboratory study of child behavior from the psychoanalytic perspective and orientation and her work quickly became both the topic of conversation within the profession and also the basis for ground wars among professionals, those both for and against this approach and interpretation. This psychoanalytic approach to probing the child psyche became the basis upon which subsequent child studies were conducted for she showed her colleagues how to open up the child's interior world for scrutiny and analysis. Child psychoanalysis thereby became a real and viable agenda for the professional practitioner who was willing to employ the Kleinian modality of analysis and therapy. Klein's emphasis was upon "listening to the child" as the child reported on the interior world of their daily experience, a world that for the child is as real as the external world of interactional encounter and personal experience for adults. Through these clinical encounters with the child's psyche produced by play therapy, Klein was able to probe more deeply and substantively the childhood experience of ambivalence, conflicted experiences of love and hate felt towards the mother. These insights led her to a more expansive grasp of the development of human consciousness and the mind itself in relationship to the mother/infant/child matrix of interactional relationships.

Not one to shy away from the problematic or disturbing complexes within human behavior and the psyche, Klein was eager to decipher the tendency, for example, within the human person to destructiveness and the resultant demand for coping with destructive behavior as a complex within social relationships and personality development. Furthermore and not unrelated to this destructive tendency within the human psyche is the ever-present reality of pervasive envy in human relationships. Her developmental theory of adulthood required a kind of "depressive position" in which the individual is challenged to confront and manage polarization and discrimination. This depressive position or phase as she portrayed it emergences from within the individual's encounter with pain caused by or administered by the other, the "not me" in Sullivan's system. From infantile dependency emerges the individual, a trajectory of development from anxiety towards self-awareness and self-competency.

Needless to say but worthy here of emphasizing, Klein had become a very powerfully influential professional within the British Psycho-Analytic Society for she was made a member of the prestigious Training Committee, made a training analyst herself, and became the designated and indisputable leader of what was now being called the Kleinian group which, incidentally, included such notable figures as John Bowlby and Donald Winnicott. Nevertheless, such powerbase building was not without its drawbacks as the price paid for the development and exercise of such power within the Society came dearly. Her daughter, the well-known and highly regarded psychoanalyst Melitta Schmideberg, had openly opposed her during these controversial years of struggle and fighting within the British Psychoanalytic Society. She became and remained estranged from her mother until the end of Klein's life. Having immigrated to America, Melitta was never reconciled with her mother and failed even to attend her mother's funeral.

Having lost two of her children already, Klein drove herself more deeply into her professional writing, research, and counseling. Her ideas regarding the early controversial theory of schizoid defense mechanisms she continued to pursue including the nuanced concept of "splitting" and the central role of play in what she began to call "borderline conditions" in mental illness. A major contribution to her psychoanalytic theories centered round the concepts of envy, gratitude, and reparation as exist within the mother-infant relationship matrix. Clearly, these were intimate themes to herself personally as she was both a daughter and a mother. The 1961 book *Narrative of a Child* was her last major work and it consisted of detailed case study of an analysis of a young boy during the war years and appeared the year following her death. She died on 22 September 1960, at the age of 78.

Not surprisingly and without doubt, Klein's modifications and adjustments in orthodox psychoanalytic theory and practice have merited her many followers and not a few detractors. She never stopped working and even towards the end of her life she remained aggressively enthusiastic about clinical research. Always attractive and never failing to dress with aplomb, she lived with a maid and always had a contract secretary to assist in her writing. Living in Hampstead in a spacious flat overlooking the rolling hills and meadows of the countryside, she continued to entertain, research, and write all with vigor and enthusiasm. Delighting in her grandchildren, the children of her son Erich, ironically her last paper addressed specifically the difficulties of old age and the loneliness it brings.

THOUGHT

As with Adler, Jung, Erikson, Horney and so many other psychotherapists in the psychoanalytic school of Freud, Klein was not able and did not herself choose to completely separate herself from the work of Freud in the creating of her brand of psychoanalysis. She, like other practitioners, did, however, wish to extend and expand Freud's original work and this, too often, led to both a misperception of her intentions and a misplaced hostility to her work. Her passion for psychoanalysis and particularly its potential application to the therapeutic treatment of children drove her to extend Freud's work even when Freud and his daughter as well as their immediate cohort of followers wished her not to do so. Freud's emphasis upon the meaninglessness of life and, therefore, the need for an existential embrace of the moment constituted for the lay person a sense of life's anomaly, a sense of life with neither purpose nor direction. Yet, in Freudian terms, there was an inevitable call towards what he thought of and developed as the concept of the instinct to die, the death wish, of every person. That sustaining principle, what he called "Eros," which causes us to seek life is counterbalanced by an instinct towards death, what he called "Thanatos." This counterbalancing of life and death, an instinct to live and an instinct to die, Klein became fascinated with and wished to extend its application to the treatment of children in whom she, more than others, had found this counterbalancing phenomenon of life and death.

Klein was quick to point out that Freud's relative indifference to child psychoanalysis was the natural result of his having spent all of his professional career working with adult patients (and Horney would remind us that most of those patents were upper middle-class Jewish women in Vienna). Klein, on the other hand, was driven with a passion for the care and treatment of children rather than adults. She developed remarkable techniques for eliciting insights into the psyche of the child through the use of play wherein a child could feel free in emotional expressive behavior without fear of censorship from watchful adults. Today we would think of phenomenology as this method of allowing the individual to express their emotional feelings without censorship or judgment. This play therapy, as it would eventually be called, encouraged the child to communicate deep feelings of fear and anxiety, hatred and compassion, in a way that the talking therapy of traditional psychoanalysis could not do. Through the use of this posture towards child play Klein applied herself to the development of interpretive techniques of therapeutic intervention without stifling the child's exploration of his inner world. Observing closely but non-intrusively the play behavior of troubled children in a play environment including dolls, animals, pencil and paper, etc., she sought out effective methods of interpreting such behavior and its relative meaning in relationship to their personality disorders.

A failure in interpersonal relationships, as Horney and Sullivan have said earlier, constitutes the basis for the emergence of mental illness and Klein was keen to demonstrate the effective use of psychoanalysis in interpreting such disturbed behavior on the part of troubled children. This had not been done so far with the consistency of analysis and the drive towards operational theory which Klein brought to the subject. Just for example, Klein was able to demonstrate in her analysis how parental figures constituted a central role in childhood fantasies whereas Freud's Oedipus complex method proved consistently ineffective as an analytical tool. Klein was able, to the horror of the orthodox psychoanalyst, to identify evidence of the early emergence in the child psyche of the superego long before the appearance of the Oedipal phase of personality development. This proved to be a "deal breaker" in terms of her collegial relationship with orthodox psychoanalysis for it cut at the very heart of much of Freud's notion of personality development and the interplay between ego and superego.

In every school of psychotherapy, there must be a theory of the unconscious. Freud and psychoanalysis constituted the first serious attempt to explicate the nature and function of the unconscious through clinical research and counseling data. Klein proved to be one of the most important clinicians of the time engaged concurrently in theory-building, particularly the development of object relations theory as well as clinical practice.

Klein's theory of the unconscious was informed by Freudian orthodoxy but she proposed to deepen and expand its applicability in the treatment of mental illness particularly among children. She was keen to point out that in object relations theory, the fundamental concern of the therapist is with how an individual experience of other people from their past affects their present and future relationship with other people. Those early and initial experiences, in infancy and early childhood according to Klein, become a part of the individual's own self-image and are then projected onto future relationships. Object relations theory, then, suggests that an infant's primordially instinctual drives are inevitably directed towards particular objects of experience informed by their phantasies. Therefore, for example, an infant's orientation towards and relationship to an object such as the mother's breast is limited in its totality owing to the infant's present inability to distinguish the breast from the mother. Klein calls this a "partial relationship" and its significance, for the maturation of the infant, has to do with the fact that this relationship, limited and constricted as it necessarily is, functions as a prototype for future relationships with the totality of an object, such as the mother in her complete self.

Owing to this process of gradual development from partial objectivity to total objectivity, the initial experience of the infant is essentially unrealistic owing to its limitations. The phantasy does not completely convey the reality – mother is more than her breast. When this process is nurtured responsibly, the child gradually differentiates the phantasy from the reality and this capacity to differentiation leads to healthy relationships with others in the future. Where there is a failure in this maturation process, the infant as an adult is destined to suffer from a deficient capacity to cultivate meaningful and rewarding interpersonal relationships. This internalization of object relationships, from partial to completion, plays a key role in the nature of an adult's capacity to interact with others. These object relations in infancy, says Klein, are inevitably and necessarily internalized and subsequently unconsciously projected onto others in adult interaction. If the early experiences were positive and the movement from partial to complete recognition of object differentiation meaningful, then the establishment of mental images of personal interrelationships will prove mature and nurturing. Where the experience has been negative and characterized by a failure to consistently move from partial to complete objectivity, then the individual is destined to suffer from the anxieties and fears of infancy and childhood, not having cultivated a differentiation capacity towards reality of object-phantasy coalescence.

Owing to her dauntless courage, Klein was able to press on with this trajectory of theory and analysis even in the face of professional criticism and attempted censorship. For example, she applied herself to the study of ultra-aggressive fantasies of such behavior as hate, envy, and greed within the very young troubled child wherein she proposed an interpretation based on her modified and expanded theory of the human psyche suggesting that in this complex behavioral matrix there is a constant oscillation between Eros and Thanatos, between life and death, love and hate. This became a very sophisticated and central theme in much of her therapeutic practice in the treatment of troubled children. The state of the child's psyche when being sustained by the will to live, when this feeling is dominant, she called it the "depressive position," but when the emotional state is preoccupied with the destructive tendency towards death and disintegration of life, she called it "paranoid-schizoid position." This duality of concepts became a hermeneutical tool for analytical interpretation of disturbed child behavior. This approach was quickly adopted by her followers who consistently indicated its effectiveness in treatment. She always insisted on viewing aggression within the life of the child as a central factor when analyzing the troubled child and this posture towards aggression within child behavior precipitated a direct conflict with Anna Freud who, at the time, was considered the major voice in child psychology in the England of that day and, needless to say, this conflict constituted a pervasively hostile atmosphere in their continuing professional lives.

The "death instinct" as a central component of her approach to the psychoanalysis of troubled children was not a passing fancy and would not go away as a point of controversy with non-subscribers within the psychiatric profession. Klein believed firmly that she was incorporating the Freudian concept of what Freud had first called the "death instinct," which, as he carefully explained it early in his system's development, was an endemic component of all living things. All life had a tendency towards non-life, towards an "inorganic state" and, therefore by extension, there endures an inclination towards death. According to psychoanalytic theory, the "life instinct" called Eros constituted the contra tendency towards life rather than death and aimed at the embodiment of a unifying principle implicit in life itself. Eros, then as the life instinct, was counterbalanced by Thanatos, the death instinct with the former nurturing life, the later seeking its destruction. Klein agreed with Freud that this bio-mental force of counterbalancing tendencies to life and death constituted the fundamental and foundational nature of the human psyche. These tendencies were human drives and were not reducible to animal instincts for they are primarily unconscious drives made up of the tripartite matrix of id, ego, and superego. These truncated terms – id, ego, superego – constituted a very sophisticated understanding and delineation of the complex nature of the human psyche. Freud's essential *psychocartography* of the human psyche was never abandoned by either Freud or Klein as they found this schematic design of the components of the human psyche useable and manageable as well as efficiently applicable in therapeutic analysis.

As the early psychoanalysts trained by Freud understood the concept of object relations, it was used to describe the bodily drives which serve to satisfy the infant's instinctual needs through the use of an object or focal point of attention and solicitation. Rather simplistic and narrowly applied was this concept in early psychoanalytic theory. However, when Klein came along seeking to extend and expand the concept in her work with mentally disturbed children, she saw the concept of object relations playing a much more central and decisive role in the development of personality in early childhood. She began to differentiate, on the basis of her clinical experience with children, what she saw as either "part-objects" or "whole-objects," that is to say, the difference between a single organ such as the mother's breast and the whole organ such as the mother in her entirety. Either object, partial or entire, can for the infant be the source of satisfaction depending on the drive being served. Two types of drives are operative within the infant at this stage, namely, the libido (recognized as Eros) and the death instinct (recognized as Thanatos). Therefore, argues Klein in her quest to expand the limited Freudian notion of the death instinct in object relations, the object being fixated on by the infant may receive both love and hate with the drive and situation dictating which emotion is being served at what time and under what circumstances.

Never content with the status quo, however, and to the disgruntlement of many of Freud's followers as well as himself particularly, Klein moved ahead in her further explication and application of the principle understanding in psychoanalysis of the unconscious particularly as relates to her work with children. Demonstrating how the analysis of children's play was not unlike Freud's analysis of adult dreams, Klein continued her adventurous exploration of the mind of the infant and early childhood during which time, to the great horror and chagrin of Freud and his orthodox followers, she claimed as we noted earlier to have discovered the roots of the superego prior to the emergence of the Oedipus Complex, the darling concept of the orthodox practitioners. By plumbing the child's deepest fears and anxieties through careful observation and analysis of the child's play, she was able to identify the mechanism employed by the troubled child to defend himself against such fears and anxieties and this became the great contribution she and her followers believed she had made to the refinement and extension of psychoanalytic practice in the care and treatment of the troubled child. These very insights constituted a means whereby through child therapy the origins of mental illness within the adult were identified. The etiology of adult mental illness, therefore, could be traced to the troubled mind of the child suffering from incomprehensible fears and anxieties too often perpetrated, sometimes unwittingly, by the indifferent parent.

The origin of what eventually became the signature characteristic of Kleinian psychoanalysis, namely object relations theory, had to do with a revisionist approach to the traditionally used concept by Freud and his followers of what was called "splitting," namely, that procedure whereby the child was able to distinguished between love and hate, anger and compassion, particularly as applied to the parental relationship. The good mother/bad mother, good me/bad me binary self-understanding which had its origins in early personality development constituted a sore point of divergence between Klein and the Freudians. The splitting, it was argued, which produced in fairy tales the good mother and wicked mother or the good fairy and the evil witch constituted a mechanism where the child could separate out his feelings of anger and compassion, love and hate felt intermittently towards one parent or the other. The maturation process in personality development necessarily required the ability to distinguish, that is, to separate out, these conflicting feelings held by the child in an oscillating sway of emotional responses to divergent experiences and encounters with a parent. It is generally agreed among professionals in the field that Melanie Klein's major contribution in respect to this concept had to do with her use of the term good/bad objects and the splitting of the objects of encounter such that the child became able to distinguish between the good parent and the bad parent, the right object and the wrong object. In object relations theory, according to Klein, the early infant experiences call for a distinguishing between good objects and bad objects, "splitting" the whole experience of interpersonal encounter using this simple differentiation. This occurs acutely to the child attempting to make functionally viable the struggle between love and hate, creation and destruction, the good and the bad, the right and the wrong. The maturation process centered upon the child's increasing ability to relate these binary experiences, breaking down the false and dysfunctional distinction between each by "depolarization" of these two instinctual drives of life and death, love and hate. Where there is failure to make such distinctions without bifurcation, there is the matrix for the emergence of mental illness and the rise of anxiety and fear leading to neurosis and, when untreated, psychosis.

Ever eager to deepen and extend the relevance of psychoanalytic theory to her practice particularly with troubled children, Klein frequently introduced new terms and concepts or modified and altered older ones to mean more than originally intended. We have seen this with object theory and the death instinct, concepts developed by Freudians but extended by Klein and her school of psychoanalysis. The concept of "projective identification" was introduced by Klein as relates to children and their capacity or lack of ability to handle anxiety and fear.

Projection, explains Klein, functions to facilitate the ego's ability to overcome anxiety by dislodging the ego from feelings of danger and evil. The inculcation of the good object, what she called "introjection," is employed by the young child's developing ego as a defense mechanism against this feared anxiety. Expanding Freud's notion, Klein believed that the process of "splitting off" parts of the self-image of the child and then projecting those split-off characteristics into external objects is a process and function profoundly important for the natural development of the child's sense of self. The fundamental effect of this process of introjection in object relations theory is the introduction or inculcation of the good object, whatever that might be. For example, the mother's breast, is, she argues, a precondition for normal personality development. This process nurtures the child's ego-development by focusing upon the good object characteristic of nurture which is anxiety free. This process Klein chose to call "projective identification."

The development of this capacity for self-defense, the creation of a functional defense mechanism, Klein believed was indispensable for the development of a normal ego within the infant including, she suggested, both ego structure and object relations capacity for integration of reality informed by infantile phantasy. The introjection of, for example, the good breast creates an environment wherein the infant can seek protection and hide from danger which, she suggested, constitutes an early step in the child's development of the capacity for self-soothing which is key to emotional stability within the infant and early nursing child.

The stages in personality development, what Klein called interestingly enough "positions" rather than stages, are a central component as we have been emphasizing in her theory of maturation from infancy through childhood. With the unconscious phantasies as an infrastructural foundation upon which the reality principle of Freud must be encountered, Klein explored the relationship between ego structure, formation and development in terms of object relationships. As we have seen, these relationships carry within them their own set or matrix of defense mechanisms and organizational structures. The two positions which occur in Klein's analysis, contrary to the orthodox Freudian perspective, in the pre-Oedipal oral phase of personality development are the paranoid-schizoid position and the depressive position. As we have discussed earlier, Klein felt that the "introjection" (her word) or the inculcation of the sense of both good and bad as relates to object relations was natural to the infant and the development and internalization of good object experience was crucial for the development of a healthy ego.

The depressive position, she contended, constituted the most mature posture relative to ego formation and this orientation can and should continue throughout life. This depressive position orientation occurs, Klein argued from clinical experience, during the second quarter of the first year of a child's life. The paranoid-schizoid position precedes the depressive as the most primordial experience and orientation of the new-born infant. Persecutory anxieties and the splitting mechanisms of project, introjection, and omnipotence all characterize this stage of development and it includes such protective features as idealization and denial used to stave off anxieties and fears of the young infant. The stage called paranoid-schizoid is characterized by what Klein called the "part object relationship," namely, the part object function as a splitting mechanism which occurs in the infant's phantasy where experience can only be either all good or all bad as there is no room here for tolerance. The function of a part object is identified by the experienced self of the infant as the whole object. For example, the hungry infant is eager for the good breast to appear and feed it. In the absence of the good breast the frustrated angry infant experiences distress and anxiety precipitating destructive phantasies manifested in oral aggression towards the absent bad breast.

Splitting the object into good and bad objects is paralleled by the concomitant splitting of the ego. So, the infant who phantasizes (Klein's spelling emphasizing its distinction from "fantasy") the destruction of the bad breast is not distinct from the infant who is presented with the good breast owing to an inability to modulate the presence and absence of the desired object. When it is present, the infant is good; when it is absent, the infant is gripped by frustration, anxiety, and manifest anger. The development of the depressive positon, however, brings with it tolerance allowing for the interplay between good and bad with the inculcation of both the capacity for remorse and reparations in interpersonal relationships which occur, for example, between mother and infant. Klein has emphasized that the anxiety precipitated during the paranoid schizoid period is essentially fear of the ego's destruction. Splitting, as Klein has redefined Freud's notion, provides a false sense to the infant and young child of allowing for the good to remain separate from the bad, a static bifurcation of the positive and the negative experience of the mother's breast, for example. The employment of projection is the use of a mechanism which attempts to repel the bad and embrace the good by assuming a mastery over one's social environment. Splitting, Klein counseled, is never completely or fully effective for the infant because the ego's agenda in the maturation of personality development is towards integration, not separation. The inculcation of tolerance and a ready willingness to live with the balancing act of good and bad constitutes a sign of the progress of maturation.

Whereas the paranoid-schizoid stage embodied splitting and the part object relations without the capacity to differentiate good mother/bad mother clearly and functionally, the depressive position (or stage) constituted an important further maturational development consisting of the operative capacity to perceive the real world of dual presentations, namely, the one who frustrates is also the one who satisfies. The good mother is also the bad mother and feelings of guilt, anger, grief and the desire to make amends in relationships begin to take precedence over the paranoid-schizoid stage. Unlike in the earlier stage where differentiation was not possible, in the depressive position the infant gains in the ability to actually encounter others as whole objects rather than part objects and this differentiation capability radically transforms the infant and early child's interpersonal relationships. The level of maturity in the depressive position is seen, Klein says, when it becomes evident that the early child is able to realize that the polar qualities of good and bad are integrated into the same object, not distinct and separate objects so that the good mother is the bad mother or the good breast is the bad breast, depending on the perceived situation and circumstance of need and response. The increasing awareness of the nearness of both good and bad fosters a resulting integration of the ego. Maturity is the result of the depressive position realizing that the polarization of characteristics are actually integrated into one reality.

One of the key results of this emerging integrated ego is the shifting on the part of the child from a fear of being destroyed to a fear of destroying the other. The realization that the ability to harm or repel the other, particularly in this case the mother who feeds and scolds, carries with it the price of repelling the one who is loved. Defenses cultivated by the child in confronting anxieties resulting from this maturation process include both repression and reparation, called by Klein the "manic defenses." Though having first become evident in the first position of infancy, these same defenses have now become activated so as to protect the child psyche from a debilitating anxiety. As the ego becomes increasingly integrated, the defense mechanisms become less intense and foster a deepening sense of the awareness of the psyche and the real world of encounter.

Klein's clinical experience lead her to realize that as the infant works through this depressive anxiety it begins to reduce dependence upon projections and greater maturational characteristics begin emerging such as autonomy, awareness of the real rather than the imaginary world, and a sense of separateness from others. Whereas the young infant's destructive phantasies were directed towards the bad mother/bad breast which caused anxiety and frustration (even anger), this emerging sense of self with an integrated ego begins to realize that both bad and good, frustration and satiation, are always within the same mother. Klien agrees with Freud here in pointing out that unconscious guilt produced by the destructive phantasies swell up with the child in proportion to the love and nurture provided by the mother. Evolving out of this sense of guilt owing to a false sense of having hated the mother, there is a rising fear of losing the loved mother and this fear emerging from this sense of unfairness in judging the mother becomes a major step in child maturation. These feelings of guilt and distress now constitute significant components of a deepening capacity for love, becoming an indispensable part of love. Here both Freud and Klein have conjoined the experience of guilt and love as a major maturation step in the development of the personality and self-consciousness.

The amazing thing about this progression towards an interfacing of the child with the real world, explained Klein, is that the individual's capacity for such emotions as sympathy and a sense of responsibility towards others as well as an increasing ability to actually identify with the subjective experiences of other people for whom the child cares accelerates proportionately to this deepening sense of self. When the destructive projections of which Klein has spoken extensively began to recede there is a concomitant capacity and inclination to repress aggressive impulses which were so commonly employed in an earlier phase of development. Control over the child's reactions becomes a positively repressive preference to anxiety and anger towards the loved parent. Klein is keen to point out that in this process the child is much more willing to acknowledge the separateness of the other, whether parent or sibling or cohort, which then serves the on-going development of a functional capacity to distinguish and differentiate the inner self from the outer reality of the world of others. The sense, Klein explained, of the infant's omnipotence towards his emotional environment begins to lessen resulting in a decrease in his feelings of guilt and the fear of loss. The desired result is eventually realized through this maturation process when the child begins to understsand that external others are actually free and separate people, autonomous of the child's governance, for the others have their own needs and wishes, their own subjectivity and their rightful place in the matrix of a social environment. This is, Klein reasoned, the desired result of a positive maturation process.

To elaborate further, what Klein called the "paranoid-schizoid position," as has already pointed out, constituted a radical distinction in the child's mind between those things that are loved – the good parent, the gratifying objects of childhood -- and those things which the child hates – the bad parent, the frustrating and problematic objects of childhood. This polarization of extremes – everything, every object is perceived to be either good or bad, one way or the other, without the rational capacity to depolarize these objects thereby making them more compatible to the personality – constitutes the origin and basis of mental illness or mental health. Klein's favorite example of this conflicting object orientation, which we have discussed earlier, is that of what she called the "good breast" and the "bad breast," a split which occurs in the infant's mind but in reality are the same breast. However, and this was the driving interpretation of Klein's object relations theory, as the child grows and develops to the realization that things can be simultaneously good and bad, loved and hated, desired and despised, depending on the situation, the circumstances, and the interpersonal relationship matrix at any given moment, then maturation occurs. At this level of maturing, the child moves to the next phase called the "depressive position," which, as understood and explained by Klein, results in a gradually emerging sense of personal reality of oneself and of others. It is a painful, troubling, aggravating processual movement towards maturity but is inevitable if the child is to move beyond the mechanistically simplistic notion of everything being always strictly good or strictly bad, completely right or completely wrong. The mature person is more fully aware of the integration and connectedness of right and wrong, good and bad, than the infantile personality has the capacity to imagine. Integrating this binary worldview and being, then, able to balance them in a creative and responsible fashion through life constitutes the differentiation between childhood and adulthood.

To create a new concept within an already old and established school of analysis and therapy is no small undertaking. But, as we have seen, Klein was not inclined to demur from an idea worth pursuing merely because of the challenge or even the professional danger involved. Such is the history of the concept of the object relations theory. In such an august field as psychoanalysis to be known for having developed a theory which deepens and expands that field is what Klein has done. For, though she is known for having greatly expanded and elaborated the field of Freudian psychoanalysis, she is always and firstly remembered for her object relations theory. In psychoanalytic psychotherapy, we understand that social behavior and the unconscious are linked. This we credit Freud for first explicating demonstrably and clinically. And, we further know, thanks to orthodox psychoanalysis, that repeated experiences from within the matrix of infancy and childhood have resulted in internalized images of our parents and significant others and subsequent experiences and behaviors are a manifestation of those images as they have been modified in the unconscious mind over time. This we know from Freud. Object relations theory, however, extends this depth of understanding by suggesting that the infant mind early on engages objects, even minimally comprehends those objects, in terms of their functions and the maturation process fosters an expanding comprehension of the scope of these objects which manifest both good and bad characteristics held in the child's consciousness in a sort of tolerant ambiguity. Initially, this experience of the oscillation of good and bad fosters anxiety and fear within the child but gradually through maturation allows for a more tolerant acceptance of such ambiguity. To the extent that the child develops this tolerance, to that extent the child in adulthood will have avoided mental illness and fostered mental health. Where there is a consistent failure to cultivate a tolerant posture towards these ambiguities of life, neurosis looms.

As we know, Freud proposed a developmental scenario in which the ego developed later than Klein felt it did owing to her clinical studies of early childhood anxiety and fear. She wished to push back to infancy the child's first experience of the tensions arising from the oscillating ambiguities regarding good mother/bad mother. Here, she felt, anger and frustration were experienced within the context of good breast/bad breast complexes while other dynamics in the relationship produced such deep emotional response as dependence on the mother. At this time, this realization that mother is more than breast begins to take form in the child's consciousness. Klein contended that these emotional pulses, oscillating between positive and negative characteristics, could and often did overwhelm the child's developing individuality and the struggle to resolves these conflicting emotions were configured to reflect the parent's own personality. The emotionally troubled child, then, reflects the emotionally troubled parent -- the child is the reflection of the adult caregiver, for good or ill. This was considered at the time an original and profoundly insightful revelation in the etiology of mental illness. Nevertheless and it must be pointed out here before we move on that within the London psychoanalytic community, there was a conflict of loyalties between those who favored Klein's new and expanded view of object relations theory (called by some at the time "id psychology") and that of Anna

Freud and what she preferred to call "ego psychology." Understandably, Anna Freud dominated American psychoanalysis from the 1940s through the 1960s owing to both Sigmund Freud's having come early to America to receive an honorary doctorate from Clark University in Massachusetts and to the quick and enthusiastic embrace of Freud's brand of psychoanalysis by the psychiatric community in New York City particularly.   In London, it was somewhat different with, in the English tradition, a tendency to walk the middle path between Anna Freud and Melanie Klein in what became amusingly called the "Middle School" with, however, such notables involved in it as Wnnicott and Balint. Because the tensions between the two schools were so great in America, it was not until the 1970s that American psychoanalysts would acknowledge the influence of Melanie Klein in their own work.

True to both her independence and her imaginative creativity when it came to theory building and nomenclature, Klein was keen to reflect her own nuancing of Freud's concept of the unconscious and its relationship to instinct particularly as she used the term in child psychotherapy.   Therefore, she began to use the term "phantasy" (not fantasy lest it be confused with that word) to indicate instinct within the context of the unconscious. Phantasy, explained Klein, consists of a psychic life of the child which moves from the inner self towards the outside world. This process constitutes a developmental movement towards an ever increasing complexity of the child's mental life. This unconscious phantasy, suggested Klein, within the infant's own emerging mental life is inevitably adjusted and modified by the social environment of parental interaction.   According to Klein, this process of movement towards the outside world occurs much earlier in the infant's maturation process than was recognized or allowed by Freud. The infant finds himself "testing" the viability, relevance, and practicality of his experience and encounter with the world of reality. Phantasy-testing constitutes the fundamental agenda of the child's maturation process.   The relationship between the child's thought processes and the phantasies which he has developed constitutes the maturing process resulting from this reality-phantasy interactive evaluation. Thought processes within the child are actually based upon the more primordial phantasies and, indeed, actually derive from them. Reality constitutes the corrective for these instinctually-generated phantasies which are, in turn, used to "test" the real world.

Here Klein has made one of her most profound and long-lasting contributions to psychoanalytic theory, namely, the recognition that the role of these unconscious phantasies is essential for the development of cognitive processes within the child. Thinking, simply stated, is based upon unconscious phantasy in the testing process related to the world of reality. Image creation within the child's psyche (Klein's description of the unconscious phantasy world) is both a prerequisite and a precondition for the creation of a thought, a mental image, resulting from the convergence of experience and imagination. Thought, then, is a derivative of this mental convergence of phantasy and experience, the latter serving as a corrective to the former. The real world of experience essentially serves to modify the phantasy world of imagination. The brilliance of this insight into "thought formation" was recognized far and wide as a significant contribution to both cognitive process studies and psycho-linguistics. The convergence of phantasy and reality, of "preconception and realization" constitutes the matrix within which thought occurs. Illustrative of this process is that of the nipple-rooting infant which Klein understood to be the instinctual rooting as the "preconception" and the finding of the nipple (or mother's presenting the nipple) constitutes the realization from the world of experience. Through repeating this process over and over again, preconception and realization coalesce to create the concept. Maturation, then, occurs as these two counter-balancing components of preconception and realization interact thereby producing thought complexes and constellations of packaged experiences. This process, Klein explained, then produced first memories and these external experiences of the real world are meshed into the complex of phantasies such that eventually and ever progressively faster and faster the child's phantasies are able to conjure images as well as experiential sensations such as visual, audible, taste, touch, smells thereby producing an increasingly accurate encounter with the external and real world.

CONCLUDING REMARKS

The brilliance of Melanie Klein's version of psychoanalysis is not open for dispute for her courage in venturing out into unchartered waters as both a novice therapist trained in the psychoanalytic school of Freudian psychotherapy and a woman in a man's world and professor speak for themselves. Her contribution to the study of children, her work within the confines of psychoanalysis in her bold application of that analytical school of therapy in the treatment of children, and her formulation of a play therapy that has stood the test of time and clinical practice all bespeak both a genius of intellect and a monumental personality. Jewish, divorced, alienated from her own daughter, facing the demands of an immigrant's life in a new country, all of these things converged in her life and conspired, even unwittingly, to make her the giant she became in the field of child psychology. Today, too often overlooked and too quickly discounted, Melanie Klein has earned her place among the leading voices in psychoanalytic psychotherapy in the treatment of children even though the general population is unaware of her greatness and the professional community is too easily distracted with their own aspirations for acknowledgment to give to her that which she has so profoundly earned, namely, respect and admiration as a pioneer in her field of study, research, and practice.

BIBLIOGRAPHY

MELANIE KLEIN'S PRIMARY SOURCES (collected in four volumes):

Vol. 1 - *Love, Guilt and Reparation: And Other Works 1921-1945*, London: Hogarth Press.

Vol. 2 - *The Psychoanalysis of Children*, London: Hogarth Press.

Vol. 3 - *Envy and Gratitude*, London: Hogarth Press.

Vol. 4 - *Narrative of a Child Analysis,* London: Hogarth Press.

SECONDARY SOURCES

Alford, C. Fred (1990). *Melanie Klein and Critical Social Theory: An Account of Politics, Art, and Reason Based on Her Psychoanalytic Theory*, New Haven, CT: Yale University Press.

Grosskurth, P. (1987). *Melanie Klein: Her World and Her Work*, NY: Karnac Books.

Hinshelwood, Robert et. al. (1993). *Introducing Melanie Klein*, London: Icon Books.

Hinshelwood, Robert (1989). *A Dictionary of Kleinian Thought*, London: Free Association Books.

Hinshelwood, Robert (1993). *Clinical Klein*, London: Free Association Books.

Jacobus, Mary (2006). *The Poetics of Psychoanalysis: In the Wake of Klein,* Oxford, UK: Oxford University Press.

Kristeva, Julia (2004). *Melanie Klein (European Perspectives: A Series in Social Thought and Cultural Criticism)* tr. Ross Guberman, NY: Columbia University Press.

Likierman, Meira (2002). *Melanie Klein, Her Work in Context*, London: Continuum International, Paperback.

Meltzer, Donald (1998). *The Kleinian Development* (New edition), London: Karnac Books, Reprint edition.

Meltzer, Donald (1993). *Dream-Life: A Re-Examination of the Psycho-Analytical Theory and Technique*, London: Karnac Books.

Rose, Jacqueline (1993). *Why War?-- Psychoanalysis, Politics, and the Return to Melanie Klein*, London: Blackwell Publishers.

Rosenfeld, Herbert A. (1987). *Impasse and Interpretation: Therapeutic and Anti-Therapeutic Factors* in the *Psycho-Analytic*

Treatment of Psychotic, Borderline, and Neurotic Patients, NY: Tavistock Publications.

Segal, Julia (1992). *Melanie Klein*, London: Sage.

CHAPTER ELEVEN
Fritz Perls and the Development of Gestalt Psychotherapy

INTRODUCTION

Some theorists think alone while others work with a colleague or a group of like-minded professionals in the field of interest. When we think of the great thinkers of the 19th or 20th century, we tend to think of them as solitary figures working quietly alone in the secluded privacy of their laboratory or library. Darwin, Freud, Einstein and Hawking come to mind. Of course, spending a little time investigating the biography of these lofty scientists disavows us of these mythic images for, as we know, Darwin had ten children and Freud had six which alters the elevated image of the isolated scholar. Fritz Perls did not work or think alone for it was with his wife Laura, that together they have produced one of the most fascinating all the while controversial schools of psychotherapy in modern times.

Developing and naming their system "Gestalt therapy," the Perls spent their lives developing and elaborating a system of psychotherapy which focuses upon an enhanced awareness of sensation, perception, bodily feelings, emotion, and behavior existentially realized and embraced. The "relationship," with oneself and with others, constituted the core ingredient of their psychotherapeutic analysis and therapy. Whereas *Gestalt psychology* emphasizes the notion that the human brain itself is a self-organizing, holistic unit that is greater than its combined parts, *Gestalt therapy* is concentrated upon the existential reality of the moment and the individual's personal responsibility within each moment.

Both existentialistic as well as humanistic, Gestalt therapy employs cognitive insight to identify and interpret immediate experience, stressing in this process what the Perls called mindfulness. This mindfulness focus, explains Perls, elicits from the client a ready willingness to explore his own creativity in the quest for satisfaction in life in areas which may have been blocked due to life circumstances, situations, and experiences, from infancy into adulthood. The emphasis, explains Perls, is upon the individual's own willingness to bring into focus a personal awareness of his behavior, his emotions and feelings, and his perceptions and sensations in the existential moment of reflectivity.

Relationships, explains Perls, is the operative word in this existential approach to therapy, relationships which include encountering the world, the social environment, and one's own self. Three key components of this approach to Gestalt therapy should be noted here: First, Perls emphasized that the therapist-client relationship is itself a potential healing tool. As with Carl Roger's client-centered therapy, Gestalt therapists do not direct the client to action but rather foster self-confidence through dialogue in search of self-authenticity out of which the client produces a plan of action. Second, there is a balance between behavioral data and subjective experience and rather than choosing one over the other Gestalt therapy seeks to integrate and validate both using a method called "phenomenological awareness." And thirdly, the individual is encouraged to embrace the reality that he is more, neither less nor equal to, than the sum of all of his life experiences. Gestalt therapy, Perls is insistent to point out, views the client as greater than a mere accumulation of experiences, symptoms, anxieties, fears, and frustrations encountered in life. Rather, the individual is perceived to be a composite dynamic organism in perpetual motion of change and development. Existentialism as the philosophical infrastructure of Gestalt therapy emphasizes the reality and relevance of on-going life experiences and the potential for the development of modalities of encounter and assessment of those experiences.

Gestalt therapy as developed by the Perls and elaborated by many professional adherents subsequently is understood to be an existentially oriented experiential form of psychotherapy which focuses its emphasis upon personal responsibility, that is to say, the understanding that the individual's own experiences in the present existential moment occurring with the therapist-client relationship combined with the social contextualization of the individual's personal life and the self-regulating adjustments needed to be made to live in the world of their own situational context constitutes the essence of the theoretical matrix of Gestalt therapy.

Fascinating and creative in his work with his equally innovative wife, Fritz Perls is worthy of a closer look as a founder of one of the most highly acclaimed and promoted schools of psychotherapy to emerge in the 20th century. Because it continues in the 21st century to have a great following of professional practitioners, we will explore both the nuances of his own life's story and then delve into a careful delineation of the key components of Gestalt therapy as he developed and practiced it.

BIOGRAPHY

Growing up on the bohemian side of Berlin at the turn of the last century was not an easy road by anyone's standards and Frederick Salomon Perls, who early on gained the shorthand nickname of "Fritz," found it as difficult for himself as for his Jewish friends and family. Born on July 8, 1893, in a troubled Germany, he would die in a quieter place in America on March 14, 1970. With his friends, he was somewhat early on involved in the Expressionist movement and in Dadaism wherein the shifting of the artistic and literary community towards the radical revolutionary left was the agenda. The advancing militarization of Germany, the impending world war, the inevitable and perinnial rise of anti-Semitism, and the coming of the Holocuast all fall within the matrix of Perls' life experience.

Contrary to the familial expectations of his Uncle Herman Staub, Perls chose not to pursue the study and practice of law but rather turned towards medicine as the arena within which he felt a true calling. The trench war experiences as a member of the German Army during World War I proved sufficient motivation for him to complete his medical studies following his military discharge and happily he became assistant to the highly regarded physician, Dr. Kurt Goldstein, who specialized in soldier's brain injuries. Goldstein's work in Gestalt psychology was a branch of traditional academic psychology combined with existential philosophy which somewhat constituted an alternative to what was then called associationist psychology. Gestalt psychology contended that human beings perceive instinctively configurations as wholes and complex patterns rather than merely building up their perceptions in bits and pieces. This holistic approach to understanding mental processes constituted a key component of this kind of psychology. Perls worked at this time at the Institute for Brain Damaged Soldiers located in Frankfurt. It has been suggested that this early experience precipitated a drift of Perls towards psychoanalysis and psychogenic behavioral disorders. At thirty-four years of age, Perls became a member of the noted medical psychologist Wilhelm Reich's technical seminars in Vienna. During these seminars Reich's early and deeply influential work in character analysis was a major point of attraction for Perls and within a short time, 1930, Reich became Perls' supervising senior analyst in Berlin. Perls had been early on even as a teenager drawn to the work of Sigmund Freud which was at the time highly touted as the coming new approach to behavioral disorders. Perls experiences, therefore, treating brain-injury patients in the military hospital drew him further into the pursuit of Freudian psychoanalysis and its relevance to mental illness. He studied at the Berlin Institute of Psychoanalysis as well as subsequently for a short time in Vienna.

That same year, Perls married Laura Posner, a psychologist who early on in her training had contact with the Gestalt school of experimental psychology, and they had two children, Renate and Stephen. With the looming rise of Nazism and the Third Reich coming to power under the ominous leadership of Adolf Hitler, Fritz, Laura, and Renate determined to leave Germany and did so in 1933 owing to their Jewishness and outspoken antifascist political activities. They fled to Holland and subsequently to South Africa where happily Perls established a psychoanalytic training institute. Alas, in 1936, Perls had a brief but extremely disappointing meeting with Sigmund Freud and that negative experience stayed with Perls for the duration of his life. Joining the South African Army (he had served in the German Army as a soldier) as medical staff in the capacity of psychiatrist with the rank of captain, he served from 1942 to 1946. During his "South African period," as it was sometimes and only slightly tongue-in-cheek referred to, Perls became enamored with the concept of "holism" developed by Jan Smuts. During this time the

Perls became increasingly dissatisfied with traditional Freudian psychoanalysis for their clinical experiences were leading them to believe that Freud's school was too intellectual and, thus, less effective owing to its cerebral complexities and not, in actuality, dealing with the whole person but only with components of the psyche. Failure on Freud's part, they argued, had to do with his lack of recognition of the central importance of oral aggression in human development. Melanie Klein was here addressing some of these same issues at the same time as was Perls.

Perls' phenomenological and existentialist approach to psychotherapy constituted a departure from traditionalist psychoanalysis for Perls believe that individuals suffering from mental illness have a tendency to separate out their experiences of thoughts, sensations, emotions which prove uncomfortable to confront and, therefore, the primary goal of psychotherapy should be to encourage and facilitate the individual's willingness to cluster these experiential matrices into a healthy wholistic view of self and life, what he called Gestalt therapy. The Perls commenced, therefore, to actually "revise" Freudian theory and method and, indeed, even gave a subtitle to their first jointly written book which suggested this new agenda. Borrowing from the scholarly work of the early Gestalt psychologists of whom Laura knew much, realizing that these practitioners were more concerned with laboratory experiments in perception than in psychotherapeutic application *per se*, Perls began to apply these principles of perceptual organization towards and understanding of the actual structure of the human personality as it functions in the real world, that is, the social environment of interpersonal relations. It did not please the orthodox psychoanalysts but nevertheless gained the Perls much attention within the general field of psychotherapy. His first book, *Ego, Hunger, and Aggression: A Revision of Freud's Theory and Method* (1942; 2nd edition 1947) contained two chapters by Laura Perls herself but, to her disappointment and resulting in some professional criticism of Perls himself, the American 1947 edition gave no acknowledgment of Laura's contribution. It was Perls belief, based on clinical experience, that at the time an infant develops teeth and has the capacity to chew, there is an analogy to the infant being able to "break apart experience" itself, to taste, accept, reject or assimilate that experience. Of course, this was contradictory to the Freudian psychoanalytic position that only introjection, rather than reflection and cognition, occurs in early childhood experience. Perls preferred the concept of "assimilation" rather than the Freudian concept of "introjection," arguing in this first book that the primary means by which growth occurs in therapy is through assimilation of life's experiences and the contextualization of those experiences within a matrix of reason and relevance.

Going from Germany to Holland to South Africa, the Perls ended up in New York City where, to his great professional advantage, he was able to somewhat briefly work with the then already highly recognized psychoanalytic social psychotherapist Karen Horney as well as with Wilhelm Reich with whom, throughout Perls professional life, Reich continued to have a role and play a part. Ending up in Manhattan was preceded by a brief stint in Montreal as a cruise ship psychiatrist, but in New York he was able to write his second book with collaborative help from Paul Goodman, a notable New York intellectual and writer in his own right. Always eager to reach out to the artistic and intellectual communities around them, the Perls found themselves immersed in the New York City scene with persons actively involved in philosophy, psychology, medicine, and education as well as in the arts. The result of this intellectual stimulus lead to the formation of their training programs which produced the first generation of Gestalt therapists who themselves assisted in the production of theory, method, and clinical practice of Gestalt therapy leading to the collaborative writing of the big book on the subject.

The second part of the book was theory and though Goodman wrote the first draft, the work was essentially Fritz Perls' own work. Influenced by both Kurt Lewin and the highly recognized and somewhat controversial psychologist Otto Rank assisted by Ralph Hefferline, the book appeared under the title *Gestalt Therapy: Excitement and Growth in Human Personality* in 1951. Hefferline was himself a professor of psychology at Columbia University and the book eventually became known as the "Gestalt Therapy bible" and, indeed, is still today the relevant text in this broad field of theory and practice. The significance of this book is of two kinds, namely, first because it actually presumed to criticize Freudian theory in the practice of psychoanalysis, and second, because it also set out to establish a new system of psychotherapy going beyond the orthodoxy of Freud. This new school was initially called "concentration therapy" owing to its emphasis upon synthesis rather than mere data analysis. It called for a naturalistic and holistic approach to both the human mind and the human body, a revolutionary emphasis at the time it was proposed, and a clarion call for the face-to-face encounter between the therapist and the "client" (Perls preferred this term rather than "patient"). Perls was, in this book, extremely critical of Freud's insistence upon the use of the couch for, argued Perls, this artificial situation merely reinforced the distance of the patient from a real-life experience of personal encounter with another person.

The significance of this book in its profound originality had to do with the practical use it provided the practitioner as a valuable introduction to Gestalt therapy theory and methodology. Seeking intentionally to create a whole new school of psychotherapeutic theory and practice based on a holistic and organismic recognition of the whole person rather than a mechanistic differentiation of the human psyche into merely id, ego, and superego as occurs in Freudian orthodox practice, Perls' focus was upon the physicality of therapy, the concreteness of the human body as relates, for example, to oral and anal problems in personality development in which he suggests "dental aggression" as a concept worthy of employing. This book and the theories they had devised based on clinical experience and training in psychoanalysis led to the establishment of the first Gestalt Institute in New York created by the Perls and hosted in their Manhattan apartment. Traveling, workshops, and training stints were the result of this highly touted book.

With a back story yet to be told, Perls moved in 1960 from Manhattan to Los Angles, leaving Laura behind, and there he established a psychotherapeutic practice with Jim Simkin and, to mark the beginning of a new era in Gestalt therapy, he began offering workshops at the Esalen Institute in Big Sur, California, in 1963. His international fame quickly was established and began to grow with leaps and bounds owing to his rather unorthodox and confrontational style of therapy and training with an emphasis upon "present-centeredness" as well as body awareness and sensory experience, speaking disparagingly of the over-intellectualization used by traditional psychoanalysis and other schools of psychotherapy.

His interests had moved far beyond, but not away from, traditional Freudian psychoanalytic theory and practice and he became increasingly interested in Zen Buddhism, a topic of great popularity among medical practitioners as well as academic philosophers and religionists of the time in California. The Zen concept of *mini-satori,* translated as "a brief awakening" was adapted by his psychotherapeutic practice and integrated into his developing theories in Gestalt therapy. He even traveled to Japan where he resided briefly in a Zen monastery all the while studying the relationship between western and eastern thought and concepts of the psyche.

The Esalen Institute became increasingly the focus of his life and practice and eventually he built a house on the grounds of the Institute. The relationship was early on most enjoyable and productive but later became somewhat turbulent and problematic between Perls own strong ego and the management and leadership of the Institute. In 1969, he left the Esalen Institute and started a Gestalt community of his own at Lake Cowichan on Vancouver Island in Canada. This same year saw him produce both an autobiography titled *In and Out the Garbage Pail* and another book on his developing theories of psychotherapy titled *Gestalt Therapy Verbatim.* Following heart surgery at the Louis A. Weiss Memorial Hospital in Chicago, Perls died of complications on March 14, 1970.

THOUGHT

Rarely, if ever, a completely new school of thought in whatever field comes along. Denying, as we might, that there are no new ideas under the sun, only refurbished and modified ones, we can feel comfortable in suggesting that new ideas and new schools do emerge but not in a vacuum. The relatedness and the connectedness of human thought must always be kept in mind but, that being said, we must forever be prepared to recognize and acknowledge that something new has been thought. Without that acknowledgement, we are doomed to simply continue the repetition of thought and action without further advancement in either. Perls was aware of the originality of his ideas while affirming their relatedness to already well-established schools of thought. Freudian psychoanalysis was entrenched in European and American psychotherapeutic practice, based on his method of free association. Likewise, the behavior therapy mode of analysis and treatment based on the recognition of the role of stimulus-response learning was gaining ground rapidly within both the academy and the professional field of psychiatry. Perls, however, set out to construct a school of theory and practice based on the fundamentals of Gestalt principles.

The Gestaltists, including particularly Wertheimer, had made great strides in establishing the viability and validity of their school of thought as relates to the role of perception and cognitive theory. Yet, reasoned Perls, they had neglected the broader and more challenging areas of the personality, psychopathology, and psychotherapy in their obsession with perception and cognition. Perls saw here both a failure of that school of thought and an opportunity to make a major advance in theory and practice by calling more specific attention to the personality within the context of the entire person – body and mind. Behaviorism, he argued, had reduced personality to merely a composite of additives rather than a wholistic view of personhood. Freudian psychoanalysis with its emphasis upon associative-symbolic manifestations of the human psyche likewise was be-limiting to the whole person.

For Perls, Gestalt therapy as he envisioned it constituted a conceptual and methodological basis upon which the counseling profession can establish its practice by embracing two central ideas, viz., that the single most important focus of psychotherapy should be the experiential moment of the existential here-and-now immediacy of life, and that every individual is caught in a web of interpersonal relationships which establish the contextualization of their self-image and self-consciousness. Perls then argued that it is only within the context of these two realities, the existential immediacy of life and the centrality of relatedness can healing occur. Only within this binary matrix can anyone hope to understand who they are. The development of this binary matrix of theory and practice constitutes the core of Gestalt therapy and theory. The historical impact of this creation has been profound. Within the framework of this construct, there are, Perls explained, four fundamental theoretical formulations essential to the practice of Gestalt therapy and these we will explore.

Perls was quick to emphasize the existential nature of Gestalt therapy for, as he explained it, this approach to psychotherapy places primary emphasis upon the "process of living," namely, what is actually happening at this very moment, over what other forms of psychotherapy such as psychoanalysis do which is to place an emphasis upon therapeutic content or what is just being talked about. The difference is crucial for the former is radically existential and the latter is clearly analytical. Gestalt therapy is an action-filled encounter between therapist and client. The interest is on what is occurring at the time of encounter – done, thought, said, felt – at the phenomenal moment of engagement between therapist and client *vis a vis* the other forms of therapy which draw upon the historical nature of relationships – what was done or said or thought and what might have happened or could have happened or even should have happened.

Gestalt therapy, then, is fundamentally a method of attention to the moment of encountered events, of what has been called an awareness practice or sometimes called "mindfulness." In such situations of therapeutic encounter, what is being perceived, felt and acted upon are considered essential ingredients in interpreting, explaining, and conceptualizing the experiential encounter. These experiential ingredients constitute hermeneutical tools for analysis. This differentiation between what "is happening" and what "did happen" places heavy and immediate emphasis upon direct experiential encounter in therapy rather than the indirect or secondary interpretation which characterizes psychotherapeutic techniques designed to explore the unconscious through dream analysis and free association techniques. With the emphasis upon the immediate and the need to encounter, acknowledge, and embrace this reality this process can lead the client to explore alternative responses to his normative and too often dysfunctional responses to life.

The aim is live action rather than passive reflectivity upon remembered and recounted life experiences. Rather than being the victim of one's own blocking mechanisms which have resulted in the unfinished business of life, Gestalt therapy challenges the individual to grasp the moment and act upon it. The diminishment of personal satisfaction in life, of a sense of fulfillment and growth, are the result of a disinclination to own the moment in which one lives. Living creatively by focusing on the experiential encounter with every moment of life is the challenge and the attraction of Gestalt therapy. With such an emphasis, Gestalt therapy has always considered itself to have a rightful place among the humanistic psychotherapies such as within the Third Force of Maslow and Rogers or that of the logotherapy of Viktor Frankl. The emphasis upon meaning-making and meaning-seeking places it not only with the existentialists such as Heidegger and Sartre in the philosophical school but with Frankl and Erikson as well as Adler and Fromm in the psychotherapeutic school of humanistic and cognitive behavior therapy. With Harry Stack Sullivan and interpersonal psychotherapy, Gestalt therapy finds a broader context of operation and acceptance owing to its emphasis upon the interactional value of the client-therapist relationship, not upon distance and separation but upon existential encounter.

Gestalt theory, as Perls and his followers were quick to point out, is not uniquely distinct from any other school of psychotherapy but rather proposes to offer a particular insight into treatment which may appear scattered throughout the counseling profession but this school of thought has been formalized into a system of analysis and treatment meriting it being considered a school of theory and application in its own right. The complementarity with other fields of theory and practice may most commonly be identified in the emerging neurosciences as well as psychiatric medical practice. However, it is within the general fields of behavioral and social sciences where the greatest instances of complementarity are found, particularly in what is now regularly referred to as ecological psychotherapy, dialogue between gestalt and object relations therapies, attachment theory, and the humanistic schools of psychology called client-centered therapy developed by Abraham Maslow and especially Carl Rogers. Gestalt therapy draws heavily upon the existentialist, phenomenological, and hermeneutical methodologies popularized since Jean-Paul Sartre and company as well as the more developed aspects of Aaron Beck's cognitive therapy. Not least in importance is Perls' gradual leaning towards the East and the Zen Buddhist techniques adopted and adapted from Cognitive Behavioral Therapy. CBT is the most commonly used system of analysis and treatment today in America owing to its quantifiable behavioral results and, therefore, insurability as well as accountability on the part of the practitioner. "Mindfulness" has become the latest and most popular term and concept in the developing school of Gestalt therapy.

Any school of thought proposing to embody both theory and practice must so formalize its organizational self-understanding as to provide a pedagogical posture towards the enquiring professional desiring to both affiliate with and practice a particular school of thought. Perls was fully aware of the need for the organizational component of Gestalt therapy, realizing, as he had observed with Freud, Adler, and Jung, without a "major book" and without an organizational structure of both practitioners, for example, the Berlin Psychoanalytic Society, Freud's school of thought could not be sustained. Early on both Perls were eager to establish "institutes" for theory development and skills training of aspiring practitioners. Within this mindset, Perls insisted upon the four pillars of Gestalt theory and therapy, viz., (1) phenomenological method, (2) dialogical relationship, (3) field-theoretical strategies, and (4) experimental freedom. These four pillars constitute the foundation upon which Gestalt therapy is built.

Initially, these four pillars were somewhat delineated and explicated in both of the Perls' books, *Ego, Hunger and Aggression* (1947) and *Gestalt Therapy: Excitement and Growth in the Human Personality* (1951). The early recitation of these building blocks placed a heavy emphasis upon personal experience and what Perls chose to call "safe emergencies" which essentially meant experiments within the context of experiential episodes in life. Balancing experience and experiments, Perls began to build a theory basis for Gestalt therapy. These early writings were replete with case studies and living examples of how both experience and experiment fit together in their analysis and treatment plan. Later and as his theory and practice developed, there emerged a second major emphasis, namely, the central important of interpersonal relationships which emerge between the self and others and between the client and the therapist. Further development included what the Gestalt therapists began to call a "field theory." Therefore, as Gestalt theory continued its development, the four pillars supporting experience and experiment were reinforced by the emphasis upon interpersonal relationships resulting in a field theory of analysis and practice as a fully developed school of psychotherapy. Since the early 1990s, Gestalt therapy has thrived in America producing multiple training centers and scholarly journals to further explicate the range of theory and practice resulting in such spin-offs of the therapy as organizational development counseling and coaching. Most recently, something called Gestalt Practice has emerged combining orthodox Gestalt theory with a mixture of meditation practices. Unlike the school of psychoanalysis, Gestaltists have no desire to monitor or control such proliferation of their theories and practices.

The first pillar of Gestalt theory is that of the phenomenological method which has as its primary purpose and focus the exploration of personal awareness within the client and within the context of the therapeutic encounter and relationship. This exploration through personal awareness operates within the individual client to systematically reduce the effects of a skewed worldview or personal prejudice through repeated observations of a particular pattern of behavior, an event of particular interest, or an attitude which may be especially debilitating to healthy mental and behavioral function. This method of phenomenological assessment consists of a three step process, viz., (1) the rule of *epoche*, (2) the rule of description, and (3) the rule of horizontalization. *Epoche* is a term in classical philosophical phenomenology which essentially means to bracket or circumscribe a specific entity. The intent is for the client to make a conscious decision to place in restrictive brackets one's initial prejudices or biases towards a particular event, attitude, or experience in order to both hold in abeyance expectations as well as assumptions regarding this event, attitude, or experience. Then, as a procedure method, the client is asked (and assisted where needed) to apply the rule of description which simply means for the client to engage in a systematic delineation of the empirical components of this particular phenomenon being analyzed – event, attitude, or experience – rather than and quite apart from any attempt to explain. Description rather than explanation is the agenda in step two. Then, the client is asked to apply the rule of what is called "horizontalization" to this description such that each identified and delineated component of the phenomenon – event, attitude, or experience – has equal value and significance.

This rule of *epoche* functions in its entirety as a method to dispense with any other theories or analytical processes when the client is engaged with the therapist. Furthermore, the rule of description insists upon the immediacy of specific observations in which the client is admonished to refrain from any interpretations or explanations of the phenomenon being analyzed, particularly refraining from any theories of analysis brought in from outside the client-therapist encounter lest some extraneous interpretation be superimposed upon the counseling session. The attractive feature of the rule of horizontalization is that it precludes the ranking of components within the phenomenon being analyzed thereby maintaining an egalitarian assessment of all of the reported and described data for analysis without prior prejudice of ranking or prioritizing. Though the therapist, as professional practitioner, is at liberty to make a private and non-disclosed assessment of the various components of the troubled phenomenon being analyzed, the therapist's assessment is, of course, kept from the client during the reporting stages of the therapy. Note-taking is a proven valuable aid to the therapist over time for future reference and integration into the therapeutic counseling engagement with the client.

The second pillar of Gestalt therapy, as Perls explains it, is that of the dialogic relationship. This further development of the dialogic relationship between client and therapist is predicated upon the already functioning phenomenological methodology wherein experience and experiment are taken seriously. It is only then that the creation of a "dialogic moment" in the therapeutic encounter can occur. Perls, even more so than Freud, was insistent upon the establishment of the right environment and right attitude of relationship between client and therapist before any serious analysis and treatment could take place. It begins with the therapist, says Perls, that the establishment of the right sense of attending presence on the part of the therapist is a prerequisite for the proper clinical environment to exist. This right emotional environment Perls calls "inclusion" and it constitutes the right atmosphere for the commencing of a dialogic process of interpersonal relationship. The client must feel safe, secure, and affirmed in order for there to be a genuine atmosphere of acceptance rather than, as in orthodox psychoanalysis, one of the therapists being in complete control of the encounter.

Not unlike the environment Carl Rogers speaks of in the client-centered therapy session of "unconditional positive regard," the Gestalt therapist "shows up," as Perls points out, as both an authentic human being and a person of trust and confidentiality. Rather than a *persona* of authority or a role of judication regarding the problem at hand, the therapist is one in whom the client can trust to have the ability to identify the strengths, weaknesses, and values operative within the client's worldview. This created space of interactional integrity is essential in order for both the phenomenological method and the rule of description to actually occur with authenticity and immediacy. Inclusion as the primary practice posture is an indispensable component of the relationship if the client is to feel comfortable with whatever self he wishes to initially present to the therapist, whether that be one of suspicion, distrust, hostility or vulnerability. The practice of inclusion as the presenting character of the therapeutic encounter requires that the therapist support the "presence of the client" regardless of how and in what manner the client chooses to expose or reveal himself, even if resistant for, as Perls is eager to emphasize, it is here, not somewhere else, that the relationship must begin. It is the process itself which is sacrosanct, according to Perls, and the Gestalt therapist must learn both to trust the process and to bring the client along in this discernment process.

The third pillar Perls would have us recognize and embrace is that of the strategic field theory which has two levels of functionality, viz., the ontological dimension and the phenomenological dimension. He speaks of the therapist having a "field" in which he functions as a therapist and though there is some hesitancy on the part of younger Gestalt therapists to employ the term "field theory" owing to its authentic use within modern physics, Perls used it in terms of a broader contextualization of therapeutic environment and practice. The first level of the field theory, called the phenomenological dimension, has to do with the actual physical and environmental context within which we live and interact. This is true of both the therapist and the client for everyone without exception has an arena of living – home, office, school, etc. On the other hand, the ontological dimension consists of the objective reality that supports and nurtures our physical space.

Whereas the phenomenological dimension consists of the physicality of living space and place, the ontological dimension consists of those mental realities which make a person who he thinks of himself as being, one's subjective experience and not merely the physical environment or phenomenal props. These ontological realities include memories, reflections, experiential encounters with others which defines oneself, etc. The use of the data of these "field dynamics" constitutes the tools with which the Gestalt therapist must work and this kind of work Perls thought of as "strategies," so the concept of the field theory strategy was developed. It is within this field theory that the individual's character structure begins to emerge, a structure which is dynamic rather than static and is revealed gradually over time through an inter-play of the information gleaned from the phenomenological dimension and the ontological dimension, that is, the interfacing of one's physicality of space with one's emotionality of the psyche.

The fourth and final pillar of Gestalt therapy is that of experimental freedom. Perls was always insistent that a fundamental characteristic of Gestalt therapy was action rather than the mere talking therapy of orthodox psychoanalysis and, therefore, by all accounts this school of psychotherapy is experientially based. Through the use of experiments (about which more later), the Gestalt therapist encourages the client to explore his direct experience of this newly created environment of affirmation and freedom rather than merely, and too often counter-productively, exploring the possibilities of life. This entire therapeutic process and relationship is characterized as a genuine experiment in relational learning and interpersonal encounter owing to the fact that it is rather a corrective to traditional relational experience for it is established on the firm footing of a "safe environment." There is no script and, therefore, the direction is known only in the traveling of it. It is truly experimental in that personal experience constitutes the map as the map itself is continually drawn and extended into the unknown. Furthermore, this experiment is didactic and pedagogical in that it teaches the client, rather than the therapist being the teacher, how to explore his own psyche through experience and experimentation.

Contrary to the perceived effectiveness of the medical model of health and healing whereby the ill patient is helped by the well physician, Gestalt therapy does not presume that the client is ill and the therapist is well nor that the self of the client must be coached into health by the self of the therapist. The relationship is much more dynamic than that model. The nature of the therapeutic encounter is that of an exploration of the client in the company of the therapist in which the existential nature of the relationship constitutes an opportunity for creative insights to be gained by both parties, not just the one seeking help but the one offering assistance as well. The character of this encounter is existentially unique and *sui generis* to the therapeutic session and not, Perls insisted, transportable outside that face-to-face here-and-now experience.

Problems in the encounter can and do occur when there is either a lack of self-definition on the part of the client which has a tendency to lead to psychotic behavior and emotional chaos, or the rigidity of the self-definition of the client is such that spontaneity in the encounter is precluded. However, when either of these two conditions are present, they are always treatable as dysfunctions rather than as malfunctions. These negative characteristics are at first the cause of a dysfunctional encounter but do not necessitate a malfunctioning result. Whereas Freud was keen to emphasize the central importance of transference and counter-transference in the therapeutic encounter, Perls was also eager to emphasize the central importance of the therapist within the matrix of the therapeutic session. He used the word "co-create" to characterize the venture shared by both client and therapist in their mutual pursuit of self-wholeness. There is no script and the Gestalt therapist does not operate from a pre-set curriculum or agenda but allows the experience and experimentation of the client to lead the way.

This theory of self-defining behavior, then, can however be seen as a neurosis which is predictably fixed into a Gestalt behavioral matrix while the aim is for the therapist to free the client from this predictability of response into a freer and more spontaneous world of self-definition. This existential spontaneity constitutes the aim and goal of the therapist's companioning with the client on this journey of self-discovery. Such a therapeutic posture disallows, even forbids, the therapist from having a pre-set notion of where the client should go but rather encourages the client to experiment for himself the direction in which health and wholeness might be found. Perls was insistent upon the holistic (mind, body, personality, culture) matrix of Gestalt therapy. It was present-centered in the here-and-now as a existentialist therapy with emphasis upon personal responsibility for taking charge of one's own life situation. He early on explored the possibility of actually calling his school the "existential-phenomenological therapy," but thought better of it as Viktor Frankl's logotherapy school of psychotherapy was initially called "existential analysis." The naming of a school of theory and practice is no easy task as Adler and Jung as well as Frankl and Rogers found out. Horney struggled with "psychoanalytic social psychotherapy," as a troubling example. Perls was sympathetic to the philosophical writings of the great and notable Jewish philosopher Martin Buber whose work on the concept of the "I-Thou" relationship between man and God resonated well with Perls emphasis upon the interpersonal relationship of people-to-people encounters. Once he even used the expression to characterize his school of thought the "I and Thou in the Here and Now!"

Though the relationship through the developmental years of Gestalt therapy with Freudian psychoanalysis was problematic and sometimes troubling, Perls was not eager to radically disassociate himself from that pivotal and seminal school of thought and practice. Indeed, he had trained as a neurologist at several major medical institutions in Europe and more significantly as a Freudian psychoanalyst in both Berlin and Vienna, Vienna being the most important international training center for psychoanalysis of the day. Vienna produced three schools of psychotherapy – Freudian psychoanalysis, Adlerian individual psychology, and Franklian logotherapy. Trained and then working as an analyst with the official recognition of the International Psychoanalytic Association, Perls was by all professional standards a recognized and admired clinical practitioner. Thus, the influence of psychoanalytic theory and practice is not inconsequential to the development of Gestalt therapy. From the early Freud of infantile sexuality to the later Freud of ego analysis along with the character analysis of Wilhelm Reich and his notion of non-verbal behavioral therapy, Perls had a repertoire of broad based clinical and theory experience in preparation for launching his own school of psychotherapy. Laura Perls' background in dance and what became known as "movement therapy" informed the somatic emphasis of Gestalt therapy's use of the mind-body matrix for analysis.

Perls was adamant in his opposition to the psychoanalytic practice of the Freudians in proposing to the patient insights and interpretations which the patient was called upon to integrate into his own self-understanding. It was the analyst, then, who did the interpretation of the data divulged by the patient from dreams and free association and it was left to the patient to demonstrate an acceptance of this interpretation. Perls was diametrically opposed to such a superimposition of the therapist over the patient/client. Rather, Perls emphasized, it is left to the client to encounter his own experience and experiment with an interpretation which to himself makes sense and serves to open up a new world of self-understanding. It was the therapist's role to facilitate this inner quest for meaning and understanding but it was the responsibility of the client to make the effort and to make the journey. Discovery on the part of the client was the goal rather than creative interpretation of the therapist which the client was expected to accept. It is at this juncture that Gestalt therapy and psychoanalysis parted company and this approach became increasingly the hallmark of dynamic analysis and treatment by the Gestalt therapist. Gestalt therapy calls upon the client to grow, to deepen his own self-understanding by becoming himself the experiencer and experimenter with his own existential encounter with life. The client is called upon to assimilate the meaning of the experience in a gradual process of natural emergence from repression to that of a freedom of exploration and expression.

Rather than lean upon the therapist in a transference/counter-transference vortex, Gestalt therapy precludes the role of interpreter of experience for the client by the therapist but rather points towards self-discovery.

This is not to say that the Gestalt therapist is not creative or experimental in the therapeutic encounter. On the contrary, it is the responsibility of the therapist to seek out ways and means of provocation for the client, encouraging him through various contrivances to probe deeper, reach more expansively, seek higher levels of self-understanding by analyzing personal experience in search of new possibilities of selfhood. Experiments proposed by the therapist and embraced by the client may be focused upon problem-solving, re-interpretation, dislodging projections and reformulating retro-reflections, for it is the client's selective choice as to what he will employ in this question. Unfinished business is a common phenomenon upon which the therapeutic encounter directs its attention such as unexpressed emotions and stifled and repressed feelings of anger, anxiety, fear, and even love. Whatever the experiments employed by the client and suggested by the therapist, the essence of the therapeutic encounter is experiential rather than interpretative and this constitutes the core distinction between Gestalt therapy and psychoanalysis.

The similarities with other psychotherapeutic schools of thought are, of course, obvious and numerous. The uniqueness of Perls' Gestalt therapy is that the theory grew out of the practice, i.e., existence before essence in an existentialist worldview. Rogers' client-centered counseling has significant points of similarity with Gestalt therapy for each are active phenomenologies seeking to assist the client in self-discover through an exploration of existential reality, viz., the here and now of existence. Perls extends the Rogerian model by placing emphasis upon the whole-body experience rather than merely talking catharsis. Perls, like Rogers, evolved a theory out of a praxis-based therapeutic approach evolving from a systemic understanding of the complex relationship between client and therapist. Rather than the traditionalist view of Freudian transference/counter-transference, Gestalt therapy embraces the dynamics of the encounter through experience and experimentation in the self-discovery process. It is engaging and existential rather than distance-oriented and directive. Not only differing from Freud but also and profoundly differing from Jungian analytical psychology's employment of dream analysis, Gestalt therapy avoids probing into the past except to reinterpret or reconfigure a perception which might have been proving counter-productive to self-discovery. As is evident in this context, Karen Horney and Wilhelm Reich have major points of continuity with Gestalt therapy's heavy emphasis upon the existential efficacy of the here-and-now moment of existence rather than plumbing the unconscious psyche through dream work and free association.

In Gestalt theory, the therapist (sometimes called the "facilitator") is trained to pay close attention to patterns in the holistic configuration of the client's sense of being for it is precisely here in the existential moment that experience is actually embedded. The goal of this therapeutic approach to counseling, thought of as personal growth, is for the client to become increasingly capable of handling his own "self-regulation," which simply and profoundly means taking charge of his own situation and circumstances with confidence in his ability to manage the interpretation of his life's experiences, encounters, frustrations, successes, etc. This capacity, of course, requires, according to Gestalt theory, that the individual manage the full spectrum of his being, viz., the sensory, intuitive, emotional, and cognitive modes of his experience. Developing this managerial capacity is predicated upon the individual's direct and immediate awareness of the total perceptual field of personal experience – the field theory discussed above. This is the fundamental work of Gestalt therapy.

This work, however, requires the development and employment of both practical techniques for heightening one's awareness of the social environment in which one lives as well as becoming more intensely aware of one's defenses, repressions, and the vortex of thought and emotion which stand between the individual and his ability to perceive clearly the situation in which he finds himself. This Gestalt process requires the use of phenomenological assessment of one's circumstances in order to address and redefine the situation which is blocking self-discovery. Dismantling of one's counter-productive self-defenses constitutes the first step in this work. Such blocking experiences include such things as unfinished business from the past, anxiety regarding the future, or painful memories of emotional trauma all may function as deterrents to self-discovery. These experiences function as self-discovery impediments and though they are continually being carried around as emotional baggage they are not being addressed in the here and now. Gestalt therapy proposed to address this unfinished business by confronting them head on, existentially, in the moment of existence. Whereas psychoanalysis will focus on the "why" of these experiences, Gestalt therapy redirects the analytical attention of the individual to the "what" and "how" of their occurrence with an eye towards "re-defining" and "re-configuring" their relevance to further self-discovery.

As noted earlier, the Gestalt therapist does not engage in interpretation of any experience or circumstance of the client. This is a key rule in this school of practice. It is the responsibility (and privilege) of the client to explore interpretations, even various options of interpretations, of debilitatingly negative events which are stifling self-discovery. It is not the place of the therapist, unlike in psychoanalysis, to propose interpretations but rather to facilitate the individual in exploring his experiences by experimenting with interpretations which constitute a re-positivization of a previously negative memory, anxiety, fear, trauma, etc. The Gestaltist will emphasize how valuable this awareness on the part of the client is *vis a vis* any proposal which the therapist himself may make. It must not be forgotten that Perls was thoroughly trained in traditional Freudian psychoanalysis in both Berlin and in Vienna. His emphasis, however, focused increasingly upon the phenomenological and subjective approach to therapy rather than the tendency to objectification of the patient's reported dreams for external analysis by the psychoanalyst. Believing that persons suffering from neurosis have a strong self-defensive tendency to what he called "split off" experiences, thoughts, sensations, and emotions which they have found to be problematic or uncomfortable, Perls believed that this tendency created a fragmentation and decomposition of the individual's personality. His agenda as a Gestalt therapist was to facilitate the individual's re-owning of these split off phenomena for without doing so the individual is destined to live an unfulfilled life of disjointed fragmentation. Creating an environment within which the owning of one's own experiences, the existential proprietorship of one's immediate life, constituted Perls' agenda. Conflict and ambiguity within one's own life constitutes the major deterrent to self-fulfillment.

Perls was pragmatic, being an existentialist, and believed in individuals' ability, when given the proper tools for assessment and analysis, to help themselves. Six factors constituted what Perls thought of as the deterrents to mental health or what he sometimes called "psychological discomfort." Eager to assist the individual in helping himself, Perls labeled and defined these factors without reference to professionally sophisticated nomenclature. (Unlike most other schools of psychotherapy, beginning with Freud all the way to Beck, Perls was determined not to create a rarified glossary of proprietary nomenclature unique only to Gestalt therapy preferring, as he said, that his concepts be labeled with easy to understand and remember terms useable by the general public). First, the individual may suffer from a lack of social contact or contextualization of his experience. Furthermore, there is the possibility that the social environment within which anxiety, fear, anger, and ambiguity occur constitutes a deterrent to the individual's ability to control his situation. Events, in other words, often conspire to stifle personal initiative. There is always the matter of "unfinished business," namely, those lingering unresolved issues, memories, events, thoughts which cannot be resolved and thus, no closure to these enduring deterrents to emotional well-being. The splitting off of these various events and experiences results in the perpetuation of self-fragmentation and the resulting inability to resolve issues related to value/expectation conflicts wherein the individual is always judging himself based on a naïve notion of winners and losers. Finally, Perls is eager to have the individual challenge his simplistic assessment of his life and events surrounding him in terms of things always needing to be right or wrong, black or white, up or down. The fully mature individual who is fostering self-discovery and self-fulfillment comes to the realization that life is mostly a compromise between two extremes. Life is usually gray rather than black or white according to Gestalt therapy.

The existentialistic emphasis upon Gestalt therapeutic practice focuses upon what Perls called the "Now" factor, namely, it is this moment in the here-and-now face-to-face reality of encounter with life which constitutes the most important matrix for self-discovery. Concentrating on the past (as is done in psychoanalysis) or being superficially self-deceived into believing that only looking to the future will provide an outlet from mental illness is both wrong and naïve. Both the past and the future orientation can have a tendency to disempower the individual whereas the challenge to face the moment in the moment can be empowering for it calls upon the individual to act rather than ponder and imagine. The confronting of such feelings as isolation, meaninglessness, confusion, uncertainty, anxiety, fear, and embarrassment constitutes the challenge for living creatively and responsibly and this must be done in the immediacy of the moment. Existentialism, then, is the practice of addressing the conditions of being a human person here and now, not once upon a time or sometime in the future, but here and now for it is in this moment of life that we are presented possibilities and opportunities for self-fulfillment.

CONCLUDING REMARKS

Gestalt therapy, because it is existentialist, is a humanistic psychotherapy addressing what it means to actually be a human person in the world. Individuals have both the capacity to make their own choices and to embrace the responsibility which comes with those choices. And, it is also a phenomenological approach to experience for it calls upon the individual to stand outside the familiar ways of thinking and being in order that distinctions may be made by employing experimentally new ways of interpreting familiar experiences. Rather than conjuring up the past with its own familiar ways of interpreting and responding to memories of events, thoughts, episodes fraught with anxiety, fear, anger, and frustration, the phenomenological perspective calls upon the individual to confront those experiences within the context of the here and now, face to face, without reference to the same old ways of seeing things. To bracket those old methods of interpretation is the challenge of phenomenology and to explore and experiment with new approaches to old experiences, new interpretations to old worn out yet still debilitating notions of what things once meant versus what things might now be seen to mean in the immediacy of this analytical moment, this constitutes the Gestalt agenda.

Happily, there are many centers and organizations which offer high level professional training in Gestalt therapy. These training centers and programs are built upon the fundamentals of Perls' philosophy that every person has the capacity for mental health given the right environment and right motivation. Commitment to such qualities as authenticity, optimism, holism, self-discovery and personal trusting relationships constitute features worthy of the therapist and characteristic of this type of psychotherapeutic practice. The Association for the Advancement of Gestalt Therapy hosts a biennial international conference in various world cities, the first having been held in New Orleans in 1995. Other cities have included San Francisco, Cleveland, New York, Dallas, St. Pete's Beach, Vancouver, and Manchester (UK). Furthermore, the AAGT hosts regional conferences which has developed a network resulting in major events hosted in Holland, England, and Australia as well. The Research Task Force is particularly active in fostering and publishing major projects of research in the broad field of Gestalt theory and therapeutic practice.

Clearly Gestalt therapy, unlike Freudian psychoanalysis and other schools and systems of psychotherapy built around a codified set of rules, theories, concepts, and practices, does not have a set formula for practice. It does, however, focus upon the basic goal for the individual of seeking self-realization and deeper self-awareness. This is the highest level of therapeutic goal. Gestaltists believe that the client has the innate ability to regulate his behavior such that self-fulfillment and self-actualization is within his reach. Due to this deepening sense of who one is in actuality, one's growing realization that fulfillment through personal growth is possible and attainable. Assuming ownership over one's own world of experience and interpretation of that experience constitutes the highest goal in therapy and Gestalt therapy has proven its value in facilitating this growth. With emphasis upon personal responsibility and combined with a positive humanistic orientation towards the meaning of personhood, Gestalt therapy facilitates the individual's personal quest through reinterpretation and reassessment of one's life experiences and encouragement to experiment with new and broader definitions of who the individual is and what his potential might be. Perls was insistent that in the broadest sense of the word, this type of therapy is scientific because it is based on reported and observed facts and data gleaned from the client/therapist encounter and it is a human science because it is designed specifically to investigate the workings of the human mind and human behavior and the convergence of both mind and behavior in one matrix of being human.

BIBLIOGRAPHY

FRITZ PERLS' PRIMARY SOURCES

Perls, F. (1969) *Ego, Hunger, and Aggression: The Beginning of Gestalt Therapy*. New York, NY: Random House. (first published in 1942, and re-published in 1947 under the title *Ego, Hunger, and Aggression: A Revision of Freud's Theory and Method*).

Perls, F. (1969) *Gestalt Therapy Verbatim*. Moab, UT: Real People Press.

Perls, F. (1969) *In and Out the Garbage Pail*. Lafayette, CA: Real People Press.

Perls, F., Hefferline, R., & Goodman, P. (1951) *Gestalt Therapy: Excitement and growth in the human personality*. New York, NY: Julian.

Perls, F. (1973) *The Gestalt Approach & Eye Witness to Therapy*. New York, NY: Bantam Books.

SECONDARY SOURCES

Brownell, P. (2012) *Gestalt Therapy for Addictive and Self-Medicating Behaviors*. New York, NY: Springer Publishing.

Levine, T.B-Y. (2011) *Gestalt Therapy: Advances in Theory and Practice*. New York, NY: Routledge.

Bloom, D. & Brownell, P. (eds)(2011) *Continuity and Change: Gestalt Therapy Now*. Newcastle, UK: Cambridge Scholars Publishing.

Mann, D. (2010) *Gestalt Therapy: 100 Key Points & Techniques*. London & New York: Routledge.

Bocian, B. (2010): "Fritz Perls in Berlin 1893 - 1933. Expressionism - Psychonalysis – Judaism." Bergisch Gladbach: EHP Verlag Andreas Kohlhage.

Brownell, P. (2010) *Gestalt Therapy: A Guide to Contemporary Practice*. New York, NY, US: Springer Publishing.

Truscott, D. (2010) Gestalt therapy. In Derek Truscott, *Becoming An Effective Psychotherapist: Adopting a Theory of Psychotherapy That's Right for You and Your Client*, pp. 83–96. Washington, DC, US: American Psychological Association.

Brownell, P. (2009) Gestalt therapy. In Irmo Marini and Mark Stebnicki (eds) *The Professional Counselor's Desk Reference*, pp. 399–407. New York, NY, US: Springer Publishing Co.

Staemmler, F-M. (2009) *Aggression, Time, and Understanding: Contributions to the Evolution of Gestalt Therapy*. New York, NY, US: Routledge/Taylor & Francis Group; GestaltPress Book.

Brownell, P. (ed.) (2008) *Handbook for Theory, Research, and Practice in Gestalt Therapy*. Newcastle, UK: Cambridge Scholars Publishing.

Polster, E. & Polster, M. (1973) *Gestalt Therapy Integrated: Contours of theory and practice*. New York, NY: Brunner-Mazel.

Shorkey, C. & Uebel, M. (2008). Gestalt Therapy. In Terry Mizrahi and Larry Davis (eds) *Encyclopedia of Social Work*, 20th Edition. New York: Oxford University Press.

Woldt, A. & Toman, S. (2005) "Gestalt Therapy: History, Theory and Practice." Thousand Oaks, CA: Sage Publications.

Zinker, Joseph. (1977). *Creative process in gestalt therapy*. New York, NY: Random House Publishing.

CHAPTER TWELVE
Eric Berne and Transactional Analysis

INTRODUCTION

Transactional Analysis is not just post-Freudian but quite decidedly by design and development non-Freudian. We have seen the neo-Freudian schools of thought represented in Horney and Klein and even, to a certain extent, in the Gestalt therapy of Fritz Perls but when it comes to the newly created school of psychotherapeutic theory and practice developed by Eric Berne, we have actually moved beyond Freudian psychoanalytic theory. Not being able with integrity to deny its psychoanalytic roots, however, Transactional Analysis is admittedly the product of a trained psychoanalytical psychiatrist and, therefore, must be thought of as a dissenting school of thought which has chosen to place its therapeutic investment in the area of transaction versus the psyche, i.e., Transactional Analysis rather than psychoanalysis.

This shifting of emphasis from the focus of Freud upon the internal psychological dynamics of mental illness to the dynamics involved in the relationship of people with each other and the movement away from psychosis and towards special transactions needed to produce mental health became the new orientation. It is not, says Bernes and company, the contents of the unconscious which contributes to mental health but rather, in Transactional Analysis, it is precisely the content of interpersonal relationships which constitutes the basis for both mental illness and mental health. Rather than probing the dark recesses of the unconscious through dream analysis and free association in search of the etiology of mental illness, Transactional Analysis chose to investigate the complexities of interpersonal relationships for the basis of both mental illness, namely neuroses and psychoses, as well as the foundations for mental health. This shift constituted the fundamental basis for the creation of this psychotherapeutic school of thought and practice.

Furthermore, Transactional Analysis also is at variance with Freudian psychoanalysis in that this new school of thought emphasizes the fact that the individual's emotional state is, in the final analysis, the result of deep inner dialogue which occurs between the various regions of the psyche which consists an extremely complex matrix of human self-understanding and behavior. Freudian psychoanalysis, as we well know, proposes that the imagination operative within the psyche, particularly the unconscious regions of the psyche, is the primary determiner of the individual's inner emotional state. Using TA language and concepts, for example, the Transactional Analyst will suggest that depression can be the result of an inner psychic dialogue between the Parent and the Child conversing within the depressed person's psyche. During early childhood the individual's capacity to identify these dialogic encounters are absent owing frequently to parental suppression. If this adult suppression had not occurred most adults would be able to decipher the meaning and significance of the dialogue. However, parentally orchestrated disincentives to understand the dialogue of the psyche between the Parent side of the psyche with the Child side of the psyche have made an understanding of this interior conversation difficult to decipher by most individuals.

Contrary to Perls' radical disinclination to speak of "curing" the client of mental dysfunction, Berne was most eager to speak freely and frequently about the task of the Transactional Analyst to "cure" the patient rather than simply to facilitate the patient's interior capacities for self-help. The up-shot of this radical orientation towards "cure" in the psychotherapeutic relationship is that Transactional Analysis moved to what this school of thought likes to refer to as a "contract" in which there is a reciprocal agreement between the therapist and the patient (rather than client) to pursue specific changes which the patient has himself identified as desirable. The patient sets the agenda based on desired goals and the therapist attempts to facilitate this agenda towards the realization of these goals.

Rather than continuing to employ the orthodox psychocartography of the Freudian psychoanalytic schema of id, ego, and superego, Berne was eager to propose a different schematic based upon Transactional Analysis' concept of the three "ego states," viz., the Parent, Adult, and Child, states (capitalized for emphasis) which are essentially creation of early childhood interpersonal experiences. They are not, for certain, parallels to the Freudian tripartite schema of id, ego, and superego but rather all three ego states as understood and employed by Transactional Analysis are parallel components of Freud's concept of the ego. There is no equivalent to the orthodox notion of the id or of the superego in TA. Berne and Transactional Analysts are quick to point out that the early development in childhood of these ego states may either be healthy or unhealthy, depending on the nature of the interpersonal relationships which occurred during the maturation process. The ego states of the unhealthy child have been developed within the pathology of failed interpersonal relationships between the young child and his parent or caregiver such that the Child and Parent ego states may constitute a fixation on his dysfunction which produces discomforts to the individual which manifest a range of mental illnesses.

Unlike the psychoanalyst who focuses attention upon the unconscious through dream analysis and free association, the Transactional Analyst rather focuses his attention upon the individual's interpersonal relationship with others and, then, assesses how the ego states of Parent, Adult, and Child have an impact upon each of the investigated transactions between the individual and persons within the patient's social matrix. The identification of dysfunctional relationship (psycho-pathological and socio-pathological) characteristics, which are either unproductive or counterproductive to meaningful transactions between individuals, are considered by Transactional Analysis to be signs of what is referred to as "ego state problems." Getting better, according to Berne and company, is based upon the Transactional Analysis of these dysfunctional transactions in the individual's personality developmental history. With Freud, Berne believed everyone has some dysfunctional issues and interpersonal relationship problems evidenced in their ego states which could be addressed and corrected by TA. Like Perls, there was a strong emphasis upon treating the whole person, not just identified interpersonal problems evidenced in the ego states.

Treating the whole person rather than simply a presenting symptom of dysfuctionality is the intent in Transactional Analysis.

One of the most fascinating characteristics of Berne's Transactional Analysis is his willingness to popularize this form of psychotherapy for the general public's consumption in both the development of common-use terms such as "game playing" and the publishing of his works in both a highly professional style of scholarly writing and paralleling that with a highly readable style of popularist writing. He was severely criticized by many professionals in the field of psychotherapy, both academics and practitioners, but the successful launching and perpetuation of Transactional Analysis throughout the U.S. and Europe proved the effectiveness of both his style of presentation and the public popularity of his marketing style. Of special and massive appeal to the field of psychotherapy was his use of the term "games" as related to common counterproductive social dysfunctional interaction appearing as personality disorders and mental illness. Two books by Berne constituted the launching of Transactional Analysis as an international phenomenon, viz., his 1964 *Games People Play* and his much later 1975 *What Do You Say After You Say Hello?* However and ironically, the most popularly known work in the field of Transactional Analysis was written by a close friend and colleague of Berne, namely Thomas Anthony Harris, titled *I'M OK, You're OK* published in 1969.

Many schools of psychotherapy, beginning with Freudian psychoanalysis and going all the way to Aaron Beck's cognitive behavioral therapy, are characterized by the refined and esoteric nomenclature developed by each school to distinguish it from other schools of theory and practice. The linguistic distinctiveness of the various schools of psychotherapy greatly aid in the identification of the particular theoretical orientation of psychotherapists when writing and speaking about their work. Like all professions, psychotherapy is a sophisticated complex of analytical concepts requiring particular language to identify the various levels of assessment, description, and treatment modalities. Furthermore, it enhances the professional profile of the practice in the mind of the general public and serves to align the practitioner with a particular grouping of like-minded professionals. This terminological esotericism Berne did not approve of and chose rather intentionally to label his concepts such that there did not appear to be (though there was) a highly technical meaning to the common-sounding terms of Transactional Analysis.

Technical language, Berne argued, has a tendency to threaten the laity and besot the professional so that the former is intimidated and the latter is superficially empowered by the use of such terms. Today, and somewhat regrettable, owing to the commonality of TA terminology, many practicing psychotherapists who are not trained Transactional Analysts employ TA terminology to convey familiarity and foster comfort-level acceptance by their clients and patients. This Berne's did not mind but rather offered up his terminology to all who could find usefulness in its employment. Not surprisingly, many hard line professionals in psychotherapeutic practice accuse TA practice, especially for those who use the terms without having had the formal training at a recognized TA training center, as being a pseudoscience. It is a philosophy rather than a scientifically based psychotherapy according to these critics. Not surprisingly, given the rapid production of new schools of psychotherapy, Transactional Analysis as a national phenomenon began to decline in its popularity during the late 1980s but still maintains itself in some quarters as a viable, even strongly popular, school of theory and practice. Those who are most serious about the effectiveness of this style and theory of psychotherapeutic practice early in the 1960s created with Berne's participation and assistance a research and professional accrediting body known as the International Transactional Analysis Association (ITAA) which continues to offer training and certification as a Transactional Analyst. Not a few of the classical psychotherapists did the same thing following Freud's lead himself when he first formed the Psychoanalytic Society for training and validation through credentialing and certification. Today, we assume that any formalized training requires validation of some kind usually in the form of certification and so it is with Transactional Analysis.

BIOGRAPHY

Like the other founders of the modern schools of psychotherapy with the exception of Karen Horney, Eric Berne (Eric Lennard Bernstein) was Jewish. Born on May 10, 1910 in Montreal, Canada, Berne was the son of a physician, David Bernstein, and writer, Sara Gordon Bernstein. Eric and his sister Grace were raised by their mother after the early death of their father from tuberculosus. Eric Berne was a graduate of McGill University in Montreal, receiving his bachelor's degree there followed in 1935 with the M.D. for medical practice. A prolific writer even while in university, he frequently wrote for the campus newspaper, but commonly used a pseudonym. A residency in psychiatry at Yale University Medical School provided him an opportunity of studying and working with Paul Federn of Yale fame where he completed his psychiatric training in 1938 and the very next year became an American citizenship.

Four years later in 1943 during the middle of World War II, he changed his name legally to that of Eric Berne but, interestingly enough, he continued to write and use various pseudonyms including such names as Cyprian St. Cyr even in the writing of humorous articles in the fledgling *Transactional Analysis Bulletin*. During the War, his training was temporarily interrupted while he served as a member of the United States Army Medical Corps rising to the rank of Major before the War's end. While in military service, he worked in the Busnell Army Hospital in Ogden, Utah, and completed his military service in 1945. Further study and training in psychiatry after the War found him working under the oversight and direction of Erik Erikson at the San Francisco Psychoanalytic Institute while carrying on his medical practice at Mt. Zion Hospital as staff Assistant Psychiatrist.

Ambitious and well-trained at McGill, Yale, and San Francisco, Berne was actively involved in the publishing of technical papers in the field of psychoanalysis and two years after leaving military service he published a book titled *The Mind in Action* (1947). Self-promotion was his personal style of operating and recognition within the professional community as a real talent and asset to the psychiatric as well as to the psychotherapeutic community of practitioners was the pay-off for him. Berne launched his private career as a group therapist attached to several hospitals in the San Francisco Bay area and it was at this time that he began actively and systematically to develop the "ego-state" model which he had learned from Federn. However, and as one might expect having seen the same trend within the work of such psychotherapists as Horney, Klein, and Perls, Berne's work began to drift away from the orthodox psychoanalytic theory and practice of the traditional Freudians.

Though he was publishing extensively in the exploration of divergent views of theory and practice within the psychoanalytic professional community, he was not met with great enthusiasm by his more established colleagues in the field. His final and formal break with orthodox psychoanalysis came in 1949, two years after the publication of his first book, when he was formally rejected to membership in the San Francisco Psychoanalytic Institute. This was the final step in Berne's leaving classical psychoanalytic practice and he would never look back. It was in his writing and research on the subject of "intuition" that Berne began to flesh out his theories related to the development of a whole school of thought called Transactional Analysis. In the published papers and articles on intuition, he presented the idea in a popular periodical that he had developed a unique ability to guess the civilian occupation of discharged military personnel within a brief conversational encounter. These reflections upon the nature and meaning of this intuitive capability pushed him further and deeper into ideas related to TA.

Rather than attempting to plumb the unconscious through the techniques employed by traditional psychoanalysis, viz., dream analysis and free association, Berne was more focused on the interpersonal relationships in which mental illness and personality disorders actually manifest themselves. Here he developed a psycho-social cartographic schema based on the universal experience of every person which involves having had a parent, once being a child, and now that of being an adult. These three ego-states of Parent, Adult, and Child represent separate states based on personal life experiences which have occurred during the maturation process. When those experiences have been good, positive, and life affirming, the individual has benefited. When those experiences have been negative and counter-productive to self-discovery and self-actualization, then the individual is likely to develop a dysfunctional personality and mental illness. As with Harry Stack Sullivan in the classical schools of psychotherapy, the etiology of mental illness can be traced to failed interpersonal relationship skill development in childhood.

Based on this tripartite configuration of the ego, Berne believed that an assessment and analysis of interpersonal communication between individuals could occur using this schema as a grid. These interpersonal interactions which constitute the data for analysis he chose to call "transactions," and then used the concept of "games" to reference the various patterns of interactional configurations which result in human communication – whether as Parent, Adult, or Child. These ego-states are normative to all individuals and the recognition of them within each interpersonal communication event provides a basis for their assessment and evaluation in terms of being effective, positive, and meaningful or, on the contrary, being ineffective, negative and fraught with dysfunction. The term for this analytical posture, i.e., Transactional Analysis, was an emergent label based on his group therapy work in the 1950s and by 1964 had evolved into a professionally sophisticated organization of professionally certified practitioners of TA called the International Transnational Analysis Association. The fact that the already pervasive psychoanalytic community refused to acknowledge or recognize this newly formed body of post-psychoanalytic psychotherapists made no difference to the ITAA membership and their rapidly growing reputation in the U.S. The publication in the 1960s of his two major books cited above simply added to the popularity of this school of thought both among the laity and increasingly among professionally practicing psychotherapists seeking new methods of analysis and treatment. In 1963 and in anticipation of the creation of the ITAA, he published a full-length professional and scholarly explication of the theory and practice of Transactional Analysis which became the recognized textbook for all professionals practicing in the field. The book was titled *Transactional Analysis in Psychotherapy: Structures and Dynamics of Organizations and Groups*. This book launched TA into the professional world as both a solidly scholarly scientific approach to interpersonal relationship analysis and as a method of treatment.

However, the book that made Berne famous as a household word among the non-professionals was his 1964 book *Games People Play* which, though purportedly written for the professional practitioner, was so popularistic in its writing style and simple in terms of the basic application of TA theory that the average person in the street bought it and talked about it in cocktail parties and in the office and at church! It was a massively successful book both financially and in terms of popularizing Transactional Analysis. The approach of the book was everyday life and the games we all play in that life with each other for purposes of manipulation, deception, control, and influence. We are, as Berne makes it so very clear, caught up in gamesmanship and his naming of these games with catchy glitzy titles made them all the more memorable, such as "Now I've Got you, You Son of a Bitch," "Wooden Leg," "Why Don't You.../Yes, But...," and "Let's You and Him Fight." He called them by their anagrams such as NIGYYSOB, WL, WDYYB, etc. Berne explained that in these transaction games, when the transaction is a zero-sum game which means one must win at the other's expense, the individual winning or benefiting from the transaction wins the game and is referred to as "White," and the victim is referred to as "Black," which, he pointed out, represent the pieces in a chess game. These games became a common point of conversation and communication within the general public such that their very names, like many of Freud's terms, have become part of American culture.

Married three times, Berne's first wife was Elinor McRae with whom he had two children. The divorce was ugly and very public in 1945. Four years later he married Dorothy DeMass Way with whom he had two children before their divorce in 1964. After he had become extremely successful and an international figure, he married a third time to Torre Peterson in 1967, but that marriage ended in divorce in 1970. That year on July 15, he died of a heart attack in Carmel, California, at the age of 60.

THOUGHT

Owing to the broad medical training Berne was fortunate in receiving from McGill and Yale University Medical School and the profoundly important experience of working with such giants in the field as Erikson, it is not surprising that with Berne's creative mind and imagination he would advance the theory and treatment options of psychotherapy beyond the classical schools. His synthetic mind of ideas and their interrelatedness led, of course, to Transactional Analysis being, not a hodgepodge of differing theories and modalities of treatment but rather a tapestry of concepts and theories woven into a systemic approach combining psychology, psychotherapy, and components of traditional psychoanalysis resulting in a cognitive-humanistic school of theory and practice. Transactional Analysis is not just a system of analysis and treatment of personality disorders and mental dysfunction but includes a whole philosophy of life, i.e., a worldview (*weltanschauung*). It is a theory of personality as well as a systematic psychotherapeutic approach to personal growth and self-realization.

Berne was convinced that in order for a psychotherapeutic treatment plan or modality of emotional care to be effective, it must have a philosophically sound footing. Existentialism had proven its indispensable value in the development of many of the classical schools of psychotherapy as well as the modern schools of Horney, Klein, Perls and others who likewise found existentialist thought a basis for their worldview. Berne felt that the philosophy of a psychotherapeutic school of thought must nurture the treatment plan as well. In the philosophy of Transactional Analysis, he argued for several domain assumptions about the human person, a philosophy of being and a psychology of personhood. Because people are fundamentally and by nature "OK," each person's thoughts must have validity, importance, and equality of respect both within himself and from others. What Carl Rogers has called "unconditional positive regard" was a prerequisite for a Transactional Analysis treatment plan. Furthermore, positive reinforcement from others including the therapist increases this innate feeling of being accepted. Since all people have a basic core which is lovable and a desire for positive affirmation and self-development, positive regard constitutes the starting place for therapy. Because everyone has the capacity for cognitive processes, i.e., the ability to think and be self-reflective (with the exception of the severely mentally challenged, possibly), each person has the capacity, whether developed or not depends upon their life situations, to develop each facet of their personality to a higher level of functionality. Individuals are free in the telling of their own story and the embracing of their own destiny and, therefore, given this freedom of choice there is a concomitant capacity for real change of direction and meaning and purpose in an individual's life. Finally, Berne believed that all emotional difficulties, all personality disorders and behavioral dysfunctions with a psychogenic etiology are curable. These are the fundamental ingredients in the philosophy of Transactional Analysis as developed by Eric Berne.

However, the philosophical foundations of TA constitute the basis upon which the theory and practice of this school of psychotherapy can occur and are themselves, rather than the basis for analysis and treatment, the domain assumptions upon which analysis and treatment have been built. Berne was insistent from the beginning that Transactional Analysis was built upon a solid theory of personality development and that TA actually describes phenomenologically the structure of the human psyche. The best known model for this structural analysis is the now well-known concept of the Adult-Parent-Child ego-state (about this construct more later). The function of this analytical model of personality analysis is to identify and delineate the personality functions and processes operative within the matrix of interpersonal relations. The ego-states, Berne explains, determine the nature, character, and level of communication between individuals and frequently these levels are at odds in this interaction such that one person may be operating at the ego-state level of an Adult while the other is employing the ego-state of a Child or even a Parent. This is evident where communication problems occur, for example, with one person's Adult ego trying to communicate with another person's Child ego, etc.

Further explicating this fascinating schematic, Berne suggests that every person operates on the basis of essentially "four life positions." These positions determine the nature of all interpersonal relationships and all personal communications between peoples. He suggests that these positions are operational in all forms of human communication and the explication of the components of these four positions' constitutes the basis of mental health and mental illness, or even of personality disorders and interpersonal dysfunctions. The first position Berne explored consisted of the notion that "I'm OK and you are OK." He contended that this constitutes the healthiest position because it suggests that the individual feels good about himself as well as feeling good about others as well. However, the next position down from this ideal state of self-actualization is the notion that "I'm OK and you are not OK." In this position, whereas I feel good about myself, I do not feel good about others for they are less than they should be or could be and, therefore, less healthy than I am. In descending order, the third level simply states that "I'm not OK and you are OK." Here, the individual does not feel good about himself and, therefore, is the weak and more or less dysfunctional person in a relationship where the other person is perceived to be OK. This position leaves the holder of it vulnerable to abuse, being discounted, and lacking in self-esteem. The final level in this four-stage scenario is "I'm not OK and you are not OK." Naturally, this is the worst position to be in for the individual not only discounts his own worth but the worth of everyone else also. In this position, there is the absence of hope, of desire for improvement, the absence of any confidence that self-actualization is even possible.

The practical effectiveness of this treatment model of interpersonal relationship analysis is its broad-based utility. Not only can it be used in personal, couple, family and group counseling situations but it has proven extremely effective in systems analysis and organizational analysis. It offers a theory for child development by virtue of its clinical description of how interpersonal relationship skills have developed from childhood. Berne used the concept of a "Life Script," or sometimes called a "Childhood Script" based on the insightful notion that adults continue to re-play their childhood strategies well into their adult life even when those strategies no longer work or work in reverse or actually prove counterproductive. A childhood strategy of dealing with others may have been most effective in childhood but to attempt to continue the same behavioral scenario in adulthood often proves detrimental to mature relationship building. In the analysis of this matrix of behavior Transactional Analysis proposed a therapeutic approach to this kind of psychopathology.

The theory of psychopathology developed by Berne and the Transactional Analysis school includes its utility in the diagnosis and treatment of various types of relationship disorders and personality dysfunctions and, therefore, can provide a method of therapy for working with individuals, couples, families, and groups as well as with organizational matrices which Berne began to explore towards the end of his life. Furthermore, outside the therapeutic arena, TA has become increasingly popular among educators demonstrating how this ego-state model of interpersonal relationship analysis can assist the teacher in maintaining his appropriate level of communication with his students lest the teacher, for example, moves down from the Adult ego-state to the Parent or even Child ego-state in dealing with a disciplinary problem with a student. Too often, teachers unwittingly move down the chart and find themselves in a "spat" with a student as two children having an argument rather than as an Adult instructing a Child.

The therapeutic agenda, Berne explains, is to free the individual from a dysfunctional reliance upon old relationship strategies which may have then and certainly will prove in the here and now to be mal-adaptations to relationships requiring adult ego-state responses. The Childhood Script inevitably will prove counterproductive and, too often, can lead to neurotic and even psychotic behavioral responses to otherwise harmless interpersonal relationship conflicts. To be free from these inappropriate, inauthentic and displaced emotional responses scripted from childhood and carried into adult relationships is the TA goal of therapy. Change is possible, Berne suggests, and it is change which must be sought and implemented. Freedom from childhood scripts which are non-productive means that an individual can move towards a greater degree of personal autonomy from the misplaced behavioral matrices of their childhood and draw upon the beneficial strengths of spontaneity, intimacy, problem-solving behavior as opposed to childhood avoidance and passivity. Change means cure, says TA, and the Transactional Analyst believes in the possibility of an individual being actually "cured" from this misplaced dependence upon the Childhood Script.

Sometimes thought of as neo-Freudian, Transactional Analysis is more appropriately characterized as post-Freudian for, though it draws from concepts and personality schematics developed early on by Freud and his colleagues, Berne has so transformed and revolutionized these concepts and schematics as to make them conspicuously at odds with orthodox psychoanalysis. To continue to label all post-Freudian developments in psychotherapeutic theory and method "Freudian" is a disservice not only to the newly developing schools of thought but to Freud himself. Nevertheless and in fairness to the historical development of modern psychotherapeutic theories, Berne did rely upon Freud's schematic of id, ego, and super-ego in the development of his ego-states of Adult, Parent, and Child. Not paralleling them, of course, this tripartite configuration of the ego-states of Transactional Analysis lent itself quite profoundly to the construct of gamesmanship in relationships. But, owing partially (but not exclusively) to the over-popularization of Transactional Analysis notion of games people play within the general population, traditional psychoanalytic practice did not accept nor often even recognize the professional nature of TA as practiced by Berne and associates. Being more user-friendly and an easily accessible modality of treatment proved off-putting to the more refined and esoteric psychoanalytic practices of the Freudians. However, there are other more receptive schools of psychotherapy today which do not overtly distance themselves from the TA community, such as the existentialists, the humanistic schools of Maslow and Rogers, and cognitive behavioral therapists like Aaron Beck.

Berne was, as we have pointed out, a trained psychoanalyst and psychiatrist and was keen to present Transactional Analysis as a phenomenological approach to treatment based on the philosophical foundations of Freudian psychoanalysis with the added feature of observed data. Theory and clinical case studies constitute the matrix for the development of TA. This was Berne's intention. Basing his scientific approach on the work of Wilder Penfield and Rene Spitz in consort with the traditionalist approach to psychoanalysis of Paul

Federn, Edoardo Weiss, and Erik Erikson, he wanted to move away from the attempt to analyze the unconscious through dream analysis and free association. His interest was in interpersonal motivational theory not dissimilar to Harry Stack Sullivan and, to be fair, to the Third Force of the humanistic schools of Maslow and Rogers. He was fully cognizant of the distancing of TA from Freudian psychoanalysis and was willing to pay the price for that dissociation. Dissatisfied with the rarified ethos of the professional practice of psychoanalysis with its radical distinction between the doctor and the patient, Berne strove for a more user-friendly system which would include life-scripts, ego states, transactions, and group therapy.

One of the strikingly attractive features of Transactional Analysis is the design and description of key concepts and ideas without the over-use of technical nomenclature. This Berne was insistent upon and whereas Sullivan was very much against esoteric terminology, he nevertheless spawned a plethora of words requiring eventually a glossary for his psychotherapeutic system. Berne did not. His concepts and terms can easily be categorized into a few terminology pyramids. For example, "Structural analysis" essentially addressed the analysis of the individual psyche; "Transactional analysis proper" consisted of the analysis of interpersonal transactions based upon the structural construct of the individual's psyche involved in interpersonal relations; "Game analysis," for which TA became popularly famous, addressed the behavioral characteristics of repeating transaction sequences which ended in predetermined consequences mutually agreed upon by the persons involved in the interaction; and "Script analysis" which was essentially a life plan which involved long-term behavioral patterns from childhood carried over into adult relationships.

Let's take a closer look at some of these operational concepts beginning with the Ego-State model of Parent, Adult, and Child (called the PAC Model) which is the most distinctive and descriptive of Transactional Analysis. While not a replica of Freud's id, ego, and super-ego, the tripartite nature of the PAC Model lends itself to confusion with Freud's schematic. Unlike Freud, Berne is not interested in plumbing the depths of the client's unconscious mind through dream analysis and free association. Berne prefers rather to take a close look at the interpersonal relationship skills (or lack of them) which a client manifests during treatment. Regarding the Ego-state schema, Berne is eager for us to understand that every person's personality is a complex of experiences and expressions constituting a mix of behaviors, thoughts, and emotions. TA suggests that this complex of behaviors consist of three ego-states reflecting the individual's developmental acquaintance with Parent, Adult, and Child models of response in interpersonal relationships.

Exteropsyche is the term TA uses for the Parent ego-state characterized by a behavioral matrix consisting of how individuals act, feel, and think to situations based on their unconscious reenactment of how their parents (or parental figures) acted in given situations or at least how the child interpreted the actions of their parents. The Parent ego-state in every individual is a composite of these recollected behavioral responses and are, therefore, referred to and drawn upon by the individual in specific situations reminiscent of their parents' behavior.

Neopsyche is the term for the Adult ego-state which is the behavioral matrix most nearly embodying the mature and reasoned responses to interpersonal relationships. The primary goal of Transactional Analysis is to foster this Adult ego-state as the preferred behavioral complex of acceptable responses in interpersonal relationships because it most nearly approximates the world of reality unlike the Parent ego-state which is predicated upon a childhood recollection of a perceived parental response.

Archaeopsyche is the Child ego-state which all people have as a complex of behaviors, feelings and thought patterns based on their own childhood experiences. For the adult plagued with an overly responsive Child ego-state, there is the tendency to resort to that individual's childhood behavioral patterns when dealing with real life encounters, anxieties, fears, and stresses. Naturally, this proves, as with the Parent ego-state response, to be counterproductive to a mature interpersonal relationship.

Lest the patient too easily identify with this schematic of adult, parent, and child, Berne chose to use the capitalized form of each word – Adult, Parent, Child – to make the distinction between the patient's self-identity and the analytical model for therapeutic purposes. And, within each of the three basic ego-states, there are subsets so, for example, the Parental figure can either function as a "nurturing" or as a "criticizing" parent-ego. The nurturing parental figure is represented by being permission-giving or security-giving, thus a positive portrayal of the Parent, whereas the criticizing parental figure may reflect the negative recollections of the individual's own childhood relationship with such a parent, thus in this case a negative portrayal of the Parent. Furthermore, childhood behavior may be portrayed as either "natural" or "adaptive" in relationship to others but in every instance of the subset which characterizes the individual patient's behavioral repertoire of patterned responses to social interaction whether it be related to behavior, feelings, or ways of thinking, there is always the option of the functional nature of the response being either positive and beneficial or negative and both dysfunctional and counterproductive.

Because the intent in Transactional Analysis is to foster and facilitate growth of the individual by providing analytical models for self-discovery, the proposed plan of treatment for what Berne thought of as a cure for dysfunctionality in interpersonal relationships, there emerged four types of diagnostic assessments of the ego states operative within every individual and identifiable specifically in reference to the patient seeking help from the therapist. These four types of diagnoses are (1) behavioral, (2) social, (3) historical, and (4) phenomenological. A thorough-going diagnosis would naturally include all four types. However and as a tribute to the creatively developmental posture of the professional practitioner of Transactional Analysis, there has emerged a fifth type of diagnostic assessment of the patient's behavioral matrix, namely, that of (5) contextual, meaning simply but profoundly that similar behavioral patterns may appear as differently typed according to the presenting context.

As we have been emphasizing, the three ego-states of TA do not, in fact, correspond to Freud's tripartite psychocartographical schematic of Id, Ego, and Superego. There are, however, clearly identifiable parallels and some TA practitioners have suggested the relevance and utility of these parallels, such as Superego/Parent, Ego/Adult, and Id/Child. Berne was insistent that ego-states are consistent within each individual and, therefore, are more obvious to the analyst than the more elusive and frequently repressed Freudian schematic because, unlike psychoanalysis which must use dream analysis and free association to delve into the murky unconscious of the patient, Transactional Analysis contends that the ego-states are self-evident in the actual communication between the therapist and the client in terms of behavior, manner, and expression. What is freeing to the TA professional is the matter-of-factness of these behavioral presentation configurations which make identifying the "problem" easier at the outset and allows for the establishment of a modality of treatment early on in the patient-therapist relationship. TA suggests that it provides a fast-track approach to personality dysfunctions and interpersonal relationship disorders allowing for a speedier resolution of the presenting problem whereas psychoanalysis insists upon an extended and lengthy time for psycho-archeological probing of the unconscious mind of the patient before anything like the resolution of the presenting problem can be produced.

Berne was always insistent that no universal ego-state exists because each Child ego-state is unique to the childhood experiences of each individual. There is no generalized childhood ego-state for the individual experiences of every person during childhood in terms of their mentality, intellect, family dynamic and life situation are uniquely different. That the Child ego-state exists in every individual is unquestionably true as every adult has gone through childhood! Indeed, the same can be said of the Parent ego-state since every child has had a parent (or parenting overseer) regardless of their life situation and, of course, every individual has had encounters with adults from whom the Adult ego-state emerges.

An interesting twist to the three ego-states of Transactional Analysis is the suggestion, developed first by Berne and further elaborated by subsequent TA clinicians, that one ego-state can actually contaminate and affect another ego-state. Examples presented by practitioners of TA include such things as an individual mistaking Parental rules as actually applicable in the here-and-now Adult reality or, say, when an individual feels certain that everyone is "laughing at him" because "they always did," i.e., the individual perceiving the real life situation of the here-and-now adult world is invaded by his childhood experience. In this instance, the childhood experience of humiliation is projected onto the adult world of the here-and-now real-life situational context. These are the matrices to which the Transactional Analyst must address the assessment and treatment plan following the diagnosis of the ego-state contaminations.

The skill involved in labeling concepts is not common and does not come easily. Freud was one of the best and the first to find just the right terminology for what he was proposing to do. The term "psychoanalysis" is second to none in its accuracy and descriptive appeal. "Id, ego, superego" are likewise excellent and elegant in their simplicity. Adler was less successful with his term "individual psychology" for what he was about and so with Jung and his "analytical psychology." Sympathy has been extended to Viktor Frankl for the unfortunate term "logotherapy" for what was essentially existential analysis and one wonders at the wisdom of Karen Horney's "psychoanalytical social psychotherapy" but can be somewhat magnanimous in Melanie Klein's "object relations therapy." Berne joins the ranks of the great with Freud in selecting the term "transaction" as the basis for his psychotherapeutic analytical school of thought for it was the transaction itself which constituted the focus of his enquiry into the etiology of personality disorders and emotional dysfunctionality.

Transactions, explains Berne, are the composites of human communication with particular attention to the unspoken but observable emotional and psychological dynamic of the flow of communication encompassing, nevertheless, both the audible and the observable whether the same or parallel in execution between individuals. As he pointed out, interpersonal relationships are based upon communication, verbal and non-verbal, and often these two characteristics are at odds with one another – the gentle voice of one's mother with severe implications serves as an example. Both surface and non-verbal perception are necessary in order for the full range of communication to occur with maximum effect and import.

Strokes, on the other hand, are comprised of those features of recognition, acknowledgement, attention, and responsiveness which occur between individuals from one to the other in varying proportions of balanced reciprocity. These so-called strokes can carry a positive connotation and benefit, sometimes called "warm fuzzies" or they may convey a decidedly negative quality called by some "cold pickles." Berne was eager to emphasize the human desire for personal recognition and affirmation and people will on occasion seek this kind of attention even if it be from a negative source such as the misbehaving child desirous of father's attention which is seldom given but greatly sought after. The Child ego-state is replete with strategies and techniques for eliciting strokes from parents and significant others. And, as Transactional Analysis points out to us, we often carry these behaviors into adulthood which, when used, often bring disappointment rather than the desired satisfaction. Transactions and strokes are two sides of the same phenomenon, viz., recognition in search of positive affirmation. Berne suggested that there are essentially three kinds of transactions characterizing all forms of human community, viz., (1) reciprocal/complementary (being the simplest form), (2) crossed transactions, and (3) ulterior-Duplex/Angular (being the most complex form).

Reciprocal or *complementary transactions* are basically simple interactional communications which occur when two individuals are communicating using the same ego-state as the other, i.e., a commonality of transactional modalities called complementary transactions when two individuals are operating on the same wave length. The ego-state level within which both are communicating may be that of Adult, Parent, or Child. The key is that both individuals must be operating within the same ego-state, that is, Adult to Adult, Parent to Parent, Child to Child. For TA practitioners, it is a fascinating occupation to imagine a wide range of examples illustrating each of these and students often find it most helpful to construct such creative models.

Crossed transactions, on the other hand, constitute just the nightmare scenario anticipated when transactions fail! Crossed transactions occur when the individuals communicating are doing so from within a different ego-state level and the results can be and often are either disastrous, humorous, or fraught with complications. When one individual is operating, say, on the Adult ego-state level in communicating with another person who, unbeknownst to the first adult, is receiving communication at the Child ego-state, the failure to communicate may become apparent only in the passage of time which may result in embarrassment or anger or simply confusion. Though most crossed transactions tend to be negative and produce ineffective or counter-productive results, occasionally there is a positive benefit say, for example, when the first person addresses the second person from within the Parent ego-state and the second person hears and responds from the Child ego-state. If one or the other senses the confusion and shifts to that of the Adult ego-state, this then might cue the first person to make a comparable shift to mutual satisfaction of both.

The most complicated of these transaction types is that of the *ulterior transaction* owing to the complexity of ego-state over-lappings in which communication between individuals can become so convoluted as to create difficulty in deciphering the intentionality of the initial communication. This occurs when the "explicit" ego-state is at odds with the "implicit" ego-state such that, for example, an individual uses the Adult ego-state as the platform for explicit communication while conveying a different message entirely through the use of say the Child ego-state. Such physiognomic features as "the wink" or "the nudge" or "the grin" give away the Adult ego-state to the Child ego-state.

Another brilliant and ingenious concept developed by Berne and employed in Transactional Analysis is that of the "Life script," or the plan of life which evolves in every individual's life to which he refers in directing his actions and choices. It is, essentially, a life plan though not intentionally thought out but simply the result of an evolutionary process of intermittent self-reflection and futuristic musings about one's life situation. The script, Berne explains, is both decisional and responsive, which is to say that it is a scripted plan of life evolved out of childhood experience in response to the perceived world based on what the child imagines as being necessary to live in and to make sense of existential reality. Furthermore, it is reinforced by parents and significant others and has to do with the encounter with the outside world of contextual living in which the script provides a mechanism for "navigating" through life as an interpretive grid defining reality, i.e., the real world as the child imagines and perceives it.

Berne contended that every child commences the writing of this script (figuratively speaking) at a very young age during the process of trying to make sense out of the world of experiences within which he finds himself immersed and driven by a desire to understand the situation in which he finds himself. This is called the contextualizing of one's life in the here-and-now reality of daily living. The script is constantly being revised and modified based on on-going life experiences, but Berne believed that the core of the script was more or less set by the age of seven. In adulthood, of course, there is no conscious awareness of its function or impact upon self-image, self-esteem, or self-actualization. Nevertheless, it is still there and has an on-going function in adult behavior. One is limited only by one's own imagination in terms of the scenarios which might be created in illustrating how these scripts continue to function in adulthood. Not necessarily all bad, they can even be effectively beneficial to the individual depending on the script he wrote as a child based on the positive or negative experiences during the early maturation years of personality development.

Two more concepts developed by Berne and Transactional Analysts are those of "redefining" and "discounting," the former being a procedure the individual engages in when there is an unconscious desire to distort the world of reality to conform to what the individual would like for the world to be. Redefining one's life situation to conform to a happier childhood script constitutes the basis for the eventual emergence in the individual's emotional state of anxiety, anger, frustration, fear, or disappointment. When the world does not conform to the script one has written for oneself in childhood, one is forced to redefine it in order to survive. Furthermore and in continuity with the redefining of life's situation, Berne called attention to what he called "discounting," meaning simply the tendency motivated by a disconnect with the child's life script of belittling a thing for less than its true value. Such reactions as non-responsive, passive, incapacitation, or even over-adaptation constitute signs of discounting caused by a disconnection between one's life script and the world of reality.

Another feature of Transactional Analysis is the perceived relevance of what are called "injunctions and drivers" operative within the individual. Not unlike the propensity of Erikson and Maslow to list things, Berne and colleagues were eager to create itemized lists of components of any concept or theory which lent themselves to being placed on a roster. Twelve was the number given to the injunctions and six drivers directed towards children as control mechanism. The twelve injunctions can simply be listed without comment as they are fundamental components of the child's life script. They convey and carry power as mandates for behavioral compliance embedded in the life script.

- Don't be (will not exist)
- Don't be who you are (Don't Be You)
- Don't be a child
- Don't grow up
- Don't make it in your life (Don't Succeed)
- Don't do anything!
- Don't be important
- Don't belong
- Don't be close
- Don't be well (don't be sane!)
- Don't think
- Don't feel.

Likewise what are called here "drivers" for the child as they function as mandates for positive behavior in terms of what the child "must do" to please, be successful, be liked, valued, loved, etc. They are:

- Please others!
- Be perfect!
- Be Strong!
- Try Hard!
- Hurry Up!
- Be Careful!

When one hears the term Transactional Analysis, the games people play immediately come to mind for it was Berne and TA which developed the concept and demonstrated the analytical value of the study of games in the treatment of personality disorders and dysfunctional interpersonal relationships. Berne defined the "game" as a series of transactions which are complementary and reciprocal always with an ulterior motive involved. The result is predictable and the result constitutes the rationale for playing the game in the first place. It is the switch in the playing of a game that constitutes the focus of its intention and the game is not played between Adult ego-states but always, explains Berne, between Parent and Child ego-states. Any number can be involved in playing the game and individuals involved in the game can shift roles as well as play multiple roles. Since the playing of the game does not permit awareness on the part of the players, the conscious functioning of the Adult ego-state is disallowed.

Berne was gifted at identifying a plethora of games and, as he pointed out, these games all have a similar structural pattern, direction and intentionality. And, as TA therapists illustrate, each game has a "payoff" for those playing it including such things as the gaining of sympathy from the players, securing satisfaction or even experiencing vindication or a range of other emotions which are pursued for the nurturing and validation of the life script. If the payoff is dislodged, then the game is broken. The three overriding characteristics of the game are flexibility, tenacity, and intensity. Flexibility is crucial because the individual players can change or shift from the use of various kinds of currency (words, money, the body, etc.) without notifying the other players. Furthermore, the tenacity with which the game is played is a reflection of its central importance for winning and losing. Finally, the intensity of the game is measured by either how easy it can be played or how hard it is to play.

As with other kinds of games such as in sports, the degree of acceptable or potential harm must be measured and calculated when being played. Three levels of measurement characterize a game's potential harmfulness to the players, viz., the First Degree Games are generally socially acceptable for all persons in the social group whereas Second Degree Games are played by individuals who would like to hide the fact that they are actually playing a game in which others are being manipulated, and most serious are the Third Degree Games where individuals stand to experience serious emotional harm and injury to members of the gaming group. Games at all three levels of seriousness may be analyzed based on their aim, roles, social and psychological paradigms, dynamics, and advantages to the players in terms of payoffs. In transactional games, unlike rational or mathematical games, the participants are not required to always conduct themselves according to the rules of reason and logic but may conduct themselves more in terms of the way real people behave. Also, and very unlike other kinds of games, the transactional game is usually characterized by ulterior motives on the part of some or all of the players.

A simple listing without detailed explanation may prove of value here. The detailed explanations seem unnecessary as the title of the games themselves are usually sufficient to suggest the nature and motivation for playing them. Here is a simple listing of some of the more popular games described by Berne in his highly successful and popular book titled *Games People Play.*

- WDYYB: Why Don't You, Yes But. Historically, the first game discovered.
- IFWY: If It Weren't For You
- WAHM: Why does this Always Happen to Me? (setting up a self-fulfilling prophecy)
- SWYMD: See What You Made Me Do
- UGMIT: You Got Me Into This
- LHIT: Look How Hard I've Tried
- ITHY: I'm Only Trying to Help You (becoming a neglected martyr)
- LYAHF: Let's You and Him Fight (staging a love triangle)
- NIGYYSOB: Now I've Got You, You Son Of a Bitch (escalating minor disagreements or errors into major interpersonal conflicts)

Berne's uncanny ability to express the ideas of Transactional Analysis in such a fashion that any generally educated individual can make sense of the theory and its practice, particularly as relates to the analysis of the games we all play, constitutes one of the major reasons for the success of this school of psychotherapy. It is not enough to have a good idea. That idea must have the capacity to resonate with a sufficiently large number of people, not just professionals but the general public, such that the school of thought connects and is thereby perpetuated throughout society. His terms and his books, the scholarly ones for the professionals and the popular ones for the educated general public, both converged into a juggernaut of popularity and vitality. The compliment to Berne's work was that of a book written by Berne's friend, Thomas Harris, titled *I'm OK, You're OK.* What the book did was to show how in everyday life and at the most practical level of interpersonal relationships Transactional Analysis had utility.

CONCLUDING REMARK

When Transactional Analysis finally came of age, it swept the country like a breath of fresh air full of enthusiasm and excitement. Finally, there was accessible a psychotherapeutic theory and method which could be understood and explained to the general public to their satisfaction and confidence while at the same time providing a formalized and professionally articulated system of therapeutic training and theory building worthy of the title of professional. Berne's major books had established the scientific and professionally responsible nature of Transactional Analysis and the popular spin-off books such as Harris' simply served to feed the flame of public interest and fascination. The terminology of Transactional Analysis, particularly in the gamesmanship field, became public fair in daily conversations among all kinds of people, professional and otherwise. Berne firmly believed that TA should be so easily explainable in terms of theory and practice that a child should be able to grasp the fundamental concepts of games and transactions.

In turn, it became not only a psychotherapeutic treatment for personality disorders and emotional dysfunctions but became for many the preferred modality of clinical treatment for children and use in the field of education. However and in spite of its popularity, it was the scientific sophistication of clinical practice which established it as a *bona fide* field of psychotherapy. The formalized training and the articulated theory behind the clinical use in therapy lead eventually and inevitably to the establishment of the International Transactional Analysis Association which has developed high standards for qualifications, training, and ethical conduct of practitioners in the field.

At the time of Berne's death in 1971, Transactional Analysis was viewed with great respect and much acclaim and though he did not live long enough to refine the theories and the concepts for assessment and treatment about which he spoke and wrote much, the certainty of its perpetuity was well established. Though experiencing conflict and controversy, like all schools of thought and systems of theory and treatment before it, Transactional Analysis is today an established field of training, teaching, theory, and practice.

BIBLIOGRAPHY

ERIC BERNE'S PRIMARY SOURCES

Berne, E. (1947) *The Mind in Action.* New York: Simon & Schuster.

Berne, E. (1961) *Transactional Analysis in Psychotherapy.* N.Y.: Grove Press.

Berne, E. (1963) *The Structure and Dynamics of Organizations and Groups.* N.Y.: Grove Press.

Berne, E. (1964) *Games People Play.* N.Y.: Grove Press.

Berne, E.(1972) *What do you say after you say Hello?* N.Y.: Grove Press.

Berne, E. (1975) *A Layman's Guide to Psychiatry and Psychoanalysis. NY:* Grove Press.

SECONDARY SOURCES

Steiner, Claude (1990) (Paperback re-issued.) *Scripts People Live: Transactional Analysis of Life Scripts.* New York: Grove Press.

Briggs, Dorothy Corkille (1986) *Celebrate Your Self.* Corkille Briggs, Dorothy. N.Y.: Bantam Doubleday Dell Publishing Group.

Clarke, Susan L. *Clarke's Dictionary of Transactional Analysis* [Paperback 2012].

English, F. (1969) "Episcripts and the Hot Potato Game," *Transactional Analysis Bulletin*, 8(32), 77-82.

English,F. (1977a) "Rackets and Racketeering as the Root of Games," In R. Blakeney (ed.) *Current Issues in Transactional Analysis* (pp.3-28) N.Y. Brunner-Mazel.

English, F. 1977(b) "What Shall I Do Tomorrow? Re-conceptualizing Transactional Analysis," In G. Barnes(Ed), *Transactional Analysis after Eric Berne: Teachings and practices of three TA schools* (pp.287-347). New York: Harper's College Press.

English, F.(1988) "Whither Scripts?" *Transactional Analysis Journal* (18) 294-303.

English, E. (2003) *How are you? And How am I? Ego States and Inner Motivators.* In C. Sills & H. Hargarden(Ed), *Ego States* (pp.55-72). London W9, Worth Publishing, Ltd.

John H. Morgan

James, Muriel and Dorothy Jongeward (1971) *Born to Win: Transactional Analysis with Gestalt Experiments* N.Y.: Addison-Wesley, 1971.

Jorgensen, Elizabeth Watkins; Jorgensen, Henry Irvin (1984), *Eric Berne, Master Gamesman: A Transactional Biography*, New York: Grove Press.

Karpman, S.B. (1968) "Fairy tales and script drama analysis," *Transactional Analysis Bulletin,* 7 (26) 39-43.

Novey, T. (2002) "Measuring the effectiveness of transactional analysis. An International Study," *Transactional Analysis Journal,* (32) 8-24.

Perls, F. (1969) Gestalt therapy verbatim. Lafayette, Ca. Real People Press.

Rosner, Rachael (2005), "Eric Berne,"in Carnes, Mark Christopher; Betz, Paul R., *American National Biography: Supplement*, New York: Oxford University Press.

Steiner, Claude, and JoAnn Dick (illustrator). (1977) *The Original Warm Fuzzy Tale: A Fairytale*. Sacramento: Jalmar Press.

Stewart, Ian (1992), *Eric Berne: Volume 2 of Key Figures in Counselling and Psychotherapy*, London: SAGE.

Stewart, Ian; Jones, Vann (1987), *TA Today: A New Introduction to Transactional Analysis*, Nottingham: Lifespan Publishing.

White, Tony (2011) *Working with Suicidal Individuals by Tony White*. N.Y.: Jessica Kingsley Publishers.

White, Tony (2012) *Working with drug and alcohol Users by Tony White*. N.Y.: Jessica Kingsley Publishers, 2012.

CHAPTER THIRTEEN
Erich Fromm and Social Criticism and Existential Psychoanalysis

INTRODUCTION

Somewhat reminiscent of the later Freud's social commentary and criticism of western culture in Freud's now classic *Civilization and Its Discontents,* we find with Erich Fromm a social philosopher as well as a psychologist interested in and fascinated by society itself, its social values and its worldview. Furthermore, we find for the first time a Jewish psychologist not reluctant to draw from the rich tradition of Judaism for his sources of social commentary. Though considering himself an "atheistic mystic," Fromm's central worldview *(weltanschauung)* was based on his interpretation of both the Talmud and the traditions of Hasidism. While beginning his studies as a young man under the tutelage of Rabbi J. Horowitz and later Rabbi Salman Baruch Rabinkow, who was himself a Chabad Hasid, Fromm took a doctorate in sociology at the University of Heidelberg.

The cornerstone of Fromm's humanistic philosophy centered upon the biblical story of Adam and Eve's exile from the Garden of Eden and, in classic rabbinic style, he drew upon his knowledge of the Talmud to point out that the ability of the human person to distinguish between good and evil, right and wrong, has always been thought of as a fundamental virtue. The "sin" of the first human parents (in mythical terms) was the result of disobeying God's mandate not to eat of the Tree of Knowledge. Fromm, however, chose rather to value the human initiative in taking independent action employing reason to establish morality rather than simply complying with the authoritative mandate from God regarding right behavior. This divergence from the traditionalist perspective on social behavior and moral development reflects the enduring characteristic of Fromm.

Fromm was able to draw from the allegory of Adam and Eve and their encounter with moral dilemma to suggest that human evolution and existential angst both find their place in this old biblical story. Separate from but integral to nature itself, these two mythical persons found themselves experiencing both their "nakedness" and their "shame," nakedness coming as a result of the emergence of consciousness within the evolving human animal and their shame as a result of their realization that their decision to exercise their own freedom of will resulted in their separation from nature itself to which, prior to the "sin" of self will, they had been an integrated part. This sense, according to Fromm, of a "disunited human existence" is the basis for our common sense of guilt and shame. The solution or resolution of this existential dichotomy of the complex experience of guilt and shame is to be found in the development of the individual's own personal capacity for love and reason. The explication of his specific meaning of the term love, distinct from the unreflective notions in the popular mind of what love means, constitutes one of the major contributions of Fromm.

Fromm chose early on in his life to focus his philosophy and psychology upon one of the most fundamental characteristics of the human person, but a characteristic which virtually all previous psychotherapists had opted to by-pass owing, it could be argued, to the complexity of the topic, namely, that of love. He considered love to be an essential ingredient to personhood and as an interpersonal dynamic of creativity *vis a vis* the notion of love being simply a highly valued emotion. Fromm was eager to distance his notion of love as a creative dynamic within the human psyche from what he considered a shallow and diminished notion of love in the popular mind which, he explained, essentially functions as a form of narcissistic neurosis embodying a sado-masochistic inclination frequently thought of as "true love." Love, for Fromm, consisted of care, responsibility, respect, and knowledge of the other person which would, therefore, preclude any simplistic and naïve notion of "falling in love" which, he believed, evidenced a genuine failure of emotional immaturity to grasp the creative dynamic intrinsic to love itself.

As with love, Fromm believed that freedom was a fundamental characteristic of human nature and one had the choice of either embracing it or fleeing from it, depending on the maturity of the individual. Freedom, when embraced whole-heartedly and enthusiastically, brings inner peace and emotional health. The avoidance of freedom (and all that it implies) through the use of escape strategies as articulated, for example, by Transactional Analysis, constitutes the basis for personality disorders, dysfunctional relationships, and emotional conflicts. The three most common escape mechanisms, Fromm explains, include automaton conformity, authoritarianism, and destructiveness. All three constitute the basis for social problems as well as personality developmental problems. The first of these strategies of freedom avoidance, automaton conformity, is indicative of the individual who conforms to the expectations of what he imagines others to believe to be the right personality type. Authoritarianism is the ready willingness to relinquish personal autonomy and personal freedom to someone else or some other entity thereby divesting oneself of responsibility as well as accountability. Destructiveness, Fromm explains, is essentially a mechanism or procedure designed to dispose of or dispense with others and the world around oneself which constitutes a divesture of responsibility and accountability which are characteristics of true personal freedom. The inclination to destroy the world or individuals within it, Fromm suggests, is evidence of a desperate attempt to protect oneself from being destroyed by the world or individuals in it. In other words, destructiveness is an irrational attempt at self-preservation.

It is within this dual matrix of freedom and love that Fromm developed his school of thought, a school which consists not only of a theory of personality but one which includes social criticism. Fromm believed that it is not enough to offer psychotherapeutic assistance to an individual suffering from personality disorder of dysfunctional interpersonal relationships without also and concomitantly addressing the social matrix within which the individual is living. The contextualization of an individual's life situation, the *Sitz im Leben* of the individual, must be fully accounted for if therapy is to have meaning and value. It is a mistake to assume that any individual suffering from emotional problems can have those problems solved without a substantive address to the social context of interpersonal relationships within which these problems have been developed and endure.

BIOGRAPHY

The only child of Orthodox Jewish parents, Erich Seligmann Fromm was born in Frankfurt, Germany, on March 23, 1900. He was raised by his father Naphtali, a wine merchant and his mother, Rosa Krause Fromm, in Frankfurt. He was educated in the traditional Jewish style by parents whom he described as "highly neurotic" and himself, to be fair, as "probably rather an unbearable, neurotic child." He was immersed in a world of Jewish scholarship with a somewhat substantially infused rabbinic presence including, among other distinguished teachers of the time, Hermann Cohen, a neo-Kantian, rabbi Nehemia Nobel, a celebrated Talmudic authority who was happily also well versed in psychoanalytic thought, and most importantly Rabbi Salman Baruch Rabinkow who was a student of Jewish, especially Hasidic, mysticism as well as being an outspoken adherent to socialist thought of the day. This, Fromm would later say in adulthood, constituted the environment within which he was encouraged to be outspokenly opinionated and aggressively enthusiastic about human freedom of expression. Naturally and quite expectedly, he was intent upon pursuing the rabbinate as a vocation.

In early childhood, as was the tradition, Fromm began the formal study of the Talmud under Rabbi J. Horowitz's oversight and subsequently continued that study under Rabbi Rabinkow who was a Chabad Hasid and highly respected. Fromm was eventually to study for the doctorate in sociology at the University of Heidelberg. Fromm's studies under Rabbi Shneur Zalman, the founder of Chabad from whom he also studied the Tanya. Subsequently he studied under Nehemia Nobel and Ludwig Krause when earlier studying at the university in Frankfurt. Fromm's grandfather and two of his great grandfathers on his father's side had been rabbis as well as a great uncle on his mother's side who was himself a noted Talmudic scholar. Eventually and owing to an emotional trauma in dealing with the issues of the First World War, Fromm turned from Orthodox Judaism and became an adherent to a secular interpretation of the biblical and Talmudic idealism. He had become, he explains in an autobiographical statement, "obsessed by the question of how war was possible," and his quest became a desire to understand the irrationality of mass behavior which produces such things as wars and riots and, conversely, he was driven towards peace and international understanding among all peoples. He turned from ideologies, both religious and secular, and became suspicious of all attempts to control human behavior, individually and collectively.

First studying for two semesters in jurisprudence at the University of Frankfurt, Fromm helped Martin Buber and Franz Rosenzweig establish in 1920 the Freies Judisches Lehrhaus. At the University of Heidelberg where he studied during the summer semester having switched from the study of law to sociology under Alfred Weber (Max Weber's brother), he took the doctorate in sociology in 1922. Postdoctoral studies in psychoanalysis Fromm commenced in 1924 at both Frankfurt and then at the Berlin Institute of Psychoanalysis. It was during this time that he began to drift away from religious practices and eventually gave them up completely. Frieda Reichman, whom he met and trained under in her own psychoanalytic sanatorium, became his wife in 1926 but the marriage was to be of short duration. Fromm had two other analysts before he moved to Berlin, where in 1927 he was analyzed by the Viennese Hanns Sachs. Frieda was ten years older than Fromm and had served as his psychoanalyst during his training period, a combination ready-made for disaster. Four years into the marriage, they divorced while still remaining friends and professional colleagues. Frieda is still recognized for her work in psychoanalysis particularly as it relates to the treatment of schizophrenia.

Fromm became a recognized member of what was known as the "Frankfurt School" as a result of his assisting in founding the Frankfurt Psychoanalytic Institute which led to his being invited to become a member of what formally was named the Frankfurt Institute for Social Research. During the period 1929 to 1932, he lectured at the Psychoanalytic Institute in Frankfurt as well as at the University of Frankfurt in psychoanalysis. At the time, he was working on a study of the authoritarian character of the German worker prior to the rise of Hitler and the Third Reich and though insightful and acclaimed by colleagues did not actually reach publication until 1984. The uniqueness and brilliance of this young academic centered around his interest in combining the insights of psychoanalysis upon the nature of social structure which was, common at the time, greatly influenced by the work of Karl Marx. Fromm was the first serious scholar to attempt an interfacing of Freud and Marx for, as he explained it, he wanted to both understand the laws governing individual behavior as well as social behavior. "I tried to arrive at a synthesis" he once wrote about this early effort. During the 1930s and for about ten years, Fromm practiced and taught as an orthodox traditional Freudian but thereafter became concerned about the moral and philosophical foundations of psychoanalytic theory because, as a Marxist, Fromm was quick to identify those middle-class liberal domain assumptions which Freud took without questioning. Fromm's significant theoretical contributions to psychoanalytic theory have to do with his ability to understand the social forces which are used to either stabilize or undermine the political establishment. This Marxist sensibility would greatly inform his subsequent writings.

The unfortunate dispelling of the Frankfurt Institute by the Third Reich in consort with the rise of Nazism led to the happy occurrence, in 1934, of the Institute's relocation to Columbia University in New York City. The Chicago Psychoanalytical Institute arranged for his visit to the U.S. in 1933 and the following year he decided to leave his homeland permanently and become a U.S. citizen. Suffering from tuberculosis, Fromm was forced to delay his relocation to the United States for a short time but was eventually invited to teach at the New School of Social Research in New York from 1934 to 1939 followed by teaching stints at Columbia University (1940-1941), Yale University (1949-1950), and Bennington College (1941-1950). During these early years in the United States, Fromm began to publish highly critical articles of Freud and the philosophical underpinnings of psychoanalysis. The unfortunate result of this enthusiasm for critical essays on Freud and company meant that he became somewhat alienated from members of the Frankfurt School and other professionals within the New York establishment. Shifting his focus from merely Freudian criticism related to the traditional psychoanalytic treatment of unconscious motivations, he directed his attention now towards an emphasis upon the social nature of being human and the inscription of that nature upon the society and culture within which each individual lives. This essentially constituted a major shift of research and writing on his part.

Escape From Freedom was published by Fromm in 1941 and it became an instant success and one of the most influential books of the decade of World War II. The argument was clear, namely, freedom from the traditional bonds of medieval society produced both a sense of new and vital independence while concurrently fostering loneliness and isolation. Doubt and anxiety was greatly evidenced in daily life within modern society and unwittingly fostered a new and troubling sense of submissiveness to authority. This new and strange sense of loneliness and isolation from place and community with the resulting experience of uncertainty about the future and the confidence in social stability and progress all converged to foster a desire for security even at the price of lost personal and social freedoms. Authoritarianism and fascism within the social order became imaginable and was courted by many societies in Europe and America. The subsequent McCarthy era was predicted by Fromm's analysis of the modern quest for security and stability in a rapidly changing world even if the cost of such was the relinquishing of personal and social freedoms. Better safe than free became the troubling mantra of society. Fromm's criticism of Freud and psychoanalysis was so severe as to precipitate his dismissal from the New York Psychoanalytic Institute in 1944. This move happily resulted in the formation of the Alanson White Institute with the enthusiastic collaboration of such distinguished psychotherapists of the time as Clara Thompson, Harry Stack Sullivan, and Frieda Fromm-Reichman. The distinguished psychoanalyst Karen Horney became purportedly infatuated with Fromm and this attraction was covered in one of her most important books in the field titled *Self Analysis*. Happily, he also became friends and a working professional colleague with such notables in New York as Margaret Mead of the Natural History Museum, and the two distinguished Columbia University anthropologists Ruth Benedict and Ralph Linton.

1944 was a benchmark year for Fromm because in addition to be expelled from the New York Psychoanalytic Institute and participating in the founding of the Alanson White Institute, for the second time he got married and this time to Henny Gurland. He also became that year an American citizen. Six years later, he and his wife moved to Mexico where he assumed a faculty post at the National Autonomous University in Mexico City and taught until 1965 as well as at the Mexican Society of Psychoanalysis until 1974. Henny had taken ill and the medical advice which they heeded suggested that a milder climate would be to her benefit and Mexico became a viable solution. Regrettably, she died just two years after the move to Mexico but Fromm continued his psychotherapeutic practice long after her death as well as being actively involved in the founding of the Mexican Institute of Psychoanalysis which he directed until 1976 when he retired from the post at age 76.

Fromm was a prolific writing and a major sequel to *Escape From Freedom* (1941) was his 1947 *Man For Himself* followed in 1956 with *The Sane Society* and during the time from 1958 to 1962 he taught psychology at Michigan State University. Owing to the popularity and soundness of this last book, Fromm became involved in the creating of the National Committee for a Sane Nuclear Policy in 1957. A common theme in his work was that of "escape from freedom" which seemed more and more to characterize western culture. The escape to which he continued to refer had to do with the alienation, loneliness, and emotional isolation individuals were experiencing in modern society. The political underpinnings of Fromm's work was not overlooked by his professional colleagues even though the general public, though fascinated with his popular writing style and the poignancy of his criticism of western society, seemed not to have noticed the heavy Marxist and socialist orientation of Fromm's social criticism. The amazing thing about the popularity of Fromm's work was the fact that at the same time his writings were sweeping the United States, the U.S. was experiencing some of its greatest radical political conservatism where the climate was dangerous for politicians and public figures who dared to entertain radical socialist positions.

Annis Freeman became Fromm's third wife in 1953 as he pressed on with a very demanding life style and professional engagements as well as research and writing. For fourteen more years after his marriage at age 53 he continued to teach three months of the year in the U.S., becoming a Professor of Psychology at the New School for Social Research in 1961. He continued his work, of course, in Mexico and his political activities were substantial including such hot topics as the civil rights movement, the campaign for nuclear disarmament, the anti-Vietnam War and the ecology movement. Though his books continued to enjoy massive sales among the reading public, he did not maintain a high level of acknowledgement or respect from the psychoanalytic community in the U.S. and of a particular point of issue with that professional establishment centered around his two very popular books at the time, viz., *The Art of Loving* (1957) and *Sigmund Freud's Mission* (1959).

Love, of course, had remained a primary topic of his concern and writing but during the 1960s he broadened his topical interest to that of western societies' fascination, even obsession, with the topics of death and with object culture, namely, the things which we make, buy, possess, and cherish. The material cultural artifacts which characterize western culture's apparent fixation on the making and having and buying and selling of "things" occupied his time during the 1960s. The subject of death constituted the focus of two subsequent books titled *The Heart of Man* (1964) and *the Anatomy of Human Destructiveness* (1973). This "driving force" as he called it centering around western society's obsession with death and dying was the manifestation of the decline in a sense of authentic being and selfhood and constituted a substitute for self-fulfilling life. *To Have or To Be* (1976) was his last major work and many considered it his most poignant critique of western culture and society.

There are essentially two ways of existing in the world, he suggested in this book, and these two ways are competing for dominance of the *zeitgeist*, the spirit of the age, namely, that of either "having" or "being." The former has to do with possessiveness and material culture and is established upon aggression and greed whereas the later, that of "being," is founded upon love and focuses its drive towards shared experience and productivity and creative action. That the modern world is teetering on the edge of global disaster, ecological, social, and psychological, is precipitated by the dominant drive to "have" (a point he graphically illustrated in his *The Anatomy of Human Destructiveness*). Replacing the having mode with the being mode is the only thing that will save western society from psychological and financial disaster. He retired in 1976 and chose to live his last years in Switzerland where he died of a heart attack on March 18, 1980, just five days before his 80th birthday. His wife Annis Freeman Fromm died in September of 1985.

THOUGHT

Erich Fromm is unique among the modern theorists of psychotherapy in that he was as distinguished and acclaimed as a social theorist and critic as he was as a psychotherapist. His passion, growing from his early religious upbringing and its tradition of sensitivity to issues of social justice and personal responsibility, was always directed towards both the individual and society. He also had a real gift for writing at the highest levels of thought for the average person so that his psychological theories combined with his social criticism to make for a convincing evaluation of social problems and their possible solutions. His criticism of both Freud and Marx, from both of whom he had gleaned a great deal of insight regarding both the individual and society gave him a breadth of credibility in his role as public commentator and critic of western culture's preoccupation with materialism and selfish motivation. Today, Fromm is no longer looked to as a major voice in either psychotherapy or public commentary on social issues. Nevertheless, there endures a deep admiration among academics and public intellectuals for the contributions he has made to our current thinking about our future as a culture and our need to redirect our drives from self-interest to broad global concerns for social justice and human rights. The themes of his life's work – freedom, alienation, love and being – continue today to be those concerns about which much is written and about which all of the classical schools of psychotherapy as well as the modern schools have given much attention for these are ingredients which make up our social consciousness out of which our individual self-awareness has grown.

Fromm is credited with having created the word and concept of "biophilia" as early as 1963 and in his 1964 book *The Heart of Man: Its Genius for Good and Evil,* he suggests that the term is best used to describe the "state of being" of the individual and society. It is a productive psychological orientation which, when employed in our dealings with each other and the world, can lead to a profoundly creative and energetic world experience. According to Fromm, there are essentially three productive orientations and they are (1) biophilia, (2) love for humanity and nature, and (3) independence and freedom. Biophilia was originally used by Fromm as an alternative to "necrophilia" or love of death and dying. Often times the term "biophobia" was used to indicate a dislike of life and love, a destructive inclination in western culture about which Fromm had much to say in several of his books but particularly his 1973 book titled *The Anatomy of Human Destructiveness.*

Beyond biophilia or love of life, Fromm was keen to emphasize the nature and meaning of the basic needs operative within the human spirit believing that there are needs which are far more significant than just the physiological ones about which Freud as well as the behaviorists have had much to say. These basic needs unique to the individual Fromm has chosen to call "human needs" as in distinction from merely "animal needs" of which we are also dependent, though not completely. Fromm believed that these needs can be summarized in a simple but profoundly insightful statement about being human and that statement is simply that human beings need to find an answer to our existence. Rabbi Abraham Joshua Heschel once said, "Tell man he is an end in himself, and his answer will be despair." Fromm had left the formal practice of his Jewish faith but the relevance of the rabbinic teachings about the meaning and value of life carried through all of his work and his study of basic human needs constitutes one of the most illustrative points of his rabbinic education.

The fundamental feature of human culture, Fromm suggests, is to provide us with tools for the answering of this question, viz., "What is the meaning of our existence?" He suggests that cultures are like religions in that they both attempt to assist the human individual and society in answering this question with an answer which is meaningful, valuable, and has utility when confronted with events in life which call out for explanation when none seems apparent, such as great natural disasters, injustices, meaningless destruction, etc. Religion and culture both attempt to provide a workable answer to questions regarding the meaning of life. The negative side of this function of religion and culture is that of providing answers in an effort to stave off insanity for, explains Fromm, neurosis itself is essentially an effort to answer the questions of the meaning of life which are no longer effective. Every neurosis, he explains, is a kind of personal and private religion to which an individual turns when culture fails to provide a viable answer to the meaning of life. Thus, the irrationality of religion is just that which justifies its on-going existence for it attempts to provide answers based on magic and superstition in the absence of any answers based on reason and logic. Essentially, religion is the sickness of which it claims to be the cure.

There are, Fromm suggests, five basic human needs of every individual and every society. Here we will list and briefly consider them. They are (1) relatedness, (2) creativity, (3) rootedness, (4) a sense of identity, and (5) a frame of orientation or reference. As a basic human need, relatedness becomes evident to us in our experience of separateness from each other and it is this relatedness in the face of personal isolation which Fromm calls "love" in its broadly applied sense. Love, he explains, is a kind of union between people and with other things outside ourselves without losing our own sense of personal independence. This personal independence is what nurtures a genuine sense of relatedness to other beings and other things. We are able to experience personal transcendence without self-destruction. This is such a strong basic human need that we are willing to satisfy this need even at our own expense such as submission to another person in an unhealthy, self-effacing and self-demeaning manner, or to a group, or to a conception of God. The converse is also true that some individuals seek to satisfy this basic human need through dominance of others thereby creating a false sense of dependence and relatedness. An alternative to satisfying this basic human need of relatedness is by denying it and this Fromm has chosen to call narcissism. Love of self, i.e., narcissism, is nature in infancy but in adulthood it becomes a major source of pathology. It is not unlike schizophrenia in that the narcissist recognizes only one true reality and that is that the world and all things in it – thoughts, feelings, needs – are relevant only to himself. The narcissist creates the world in which he wishes to live and all things in it circle around him thereby and inevitably causing him to lose touch with the real world.

Fromm was eager to emphasize creativity, or at least the potential for creativity, which characterizes human nature at its best. This is the second basic need of the individual. There is a drive or a sense within each individual which desires to rise above indolence, indifference, and destructiveness and that drive is the drive to create, to make, to build, and to develop within ourselves a greater sense of who we are destined to become. Not everyone will, of course, be innovative in the same manner for there is a multiplicity of creative expressions within the repertoire of the human person. Fromm goes on to suggest that the very act of creation is an expression of love. However, he suggests, where there is the absence of creativity, when the individual is unable to discover a way to be creative, frustration, anxiety, even anger at the world sets in, resulting in counter-productive behavior, indeed, even destructive behavior. Stifle or preclude the opportunity to be creative, Fromm suggests, and the alternative becomes the mode of operation, namely, destructiveness. The alternative to positive creativity is the exercise of destructive power over others and over the environment. Little wonder, says Fromm, that social environments such as the ghetto or prison where there is the absence, even intentional absence, of opportunities for creative expression that destructive behavior becomes the norm.

Another basic need of the human person and society itself is what Fromm calls a sense of "rootedness," a feeling of being at home in the world even in the face of natural disasters and environmental deterrents such as disease. The most primordial and fundamental expression of this rootedness is found in our attachment to our mothers, since every human being has one (or a mother surrogate). But this is not sufficient for personal growth and development. Every person needs to reach out to a broader sense of connectedness, attachment, involvement, and integration into the wider world where "brotherhood and sisterhood" is to be found and nurtured. To stay attached only to mother's love, Fromm observes, is to engage in what he chose to call a "psychological incest" and it will prove in the long run counterproductive to maturity. The pathological expressions of this basic drive include the schizophrenic retreat into interiority, the neurotic fear of leaving home, and the fanatic attachment to religion or country as the only good *vis a vis* the rest of the world.

Another basic need of the human person is that of a sense of identity for, as he suggests, we are the only animal which can say "I" and the drive for a personal identity, of individuality, of a sense of myself is crucial to our humanity. Though the drive is healthy, even indispensable for a growth into personal maturity, this drive is so very strong for a sense of identity that we will sometimes go to great lengths, even dangerous lengths, to secure designations of our status, our rank, our position within the social matrix of our humanity.

The fifth and related basic need of the individual is that of a frame of reference or what Fromm calls a frame of "orientation," namely, the need to understand the world and our place within it. Religious institutions, for example, function in this capacity by providing a ready-made worldview, a *weltanschauung,* wherein all questions of the meaning of life are supposedly answered. Karl Mannheim has suggested that ideologies provide the same service to society as political and philosophical ideologies do such as Marxism, capitalism, socialism, existentialism, and behaviorism. The intent is to provide the individual with a ready-made system of answers for all of the questions and troubles encountered in life. Problems, however, occur when these ready-made systems of comprehensive worldviews fail in their attempts to answer all the questions of life, then the individual finds himself adrift in a world fraught with uncertainty, ambiguity, and even danger. Fromm wrote extensively on this basic need in his 1947 book *Man for Himself* in which he suggests that there are actually two ways people relate to the world around them. The first way is by acquisition and assimilation (getting things and arranging things in some sort of logical order), and the second is by socialization (interacting with people which then contextualizes one's own life).

These two ways of relating to the world Fromm believed served in the place of our animal instincts which, Freud notwithstanding, we have divested ourselves of since becoming self-reflective rational beings.

Fromm was eager to relate his assessment and characterization of the orientations of individuals based on their family relations and in doing so he specifically identified two poignantly dysfunctional family types which have contributed to social problems in western society. These two are the symbiotic family type and the withdrawing family type. These he calls "unproductive" for they provided two specific mechanisms for the "escape from freedom" which have been assimilated by the child during his personality developmental years in the family circle. Though we have mentioned these two family types briefly in the above discussion, let us explore these two family types a bit more thoroughly here before moving to an analysis of Fromm's major works.

The *symbiotic family* is based on the concept of symbiosis which simply indicates the interdependence of two organisms and their inability to survive in the absence of the other. In this type of family, Fromm points out, some of the members are what he calls "swallowed up" by other members such that there is a stifling of personality development. In these extreme circumstances, the child's personality simply becomes a copy of the dominant parent's personality and such instances often occur, explains Fromm, in traditional societies and in poor family situations dominated by an over-powering parental figure, whether mother or father. Girls, explains Fromm, seem to be disproportionately affected by this negative environment. The converse can happen, though less frequently, where a parent is "swallowed up" by the dominance of a child where manipulation becomes the *modus operandi* of the powerful child over the weak parent.

The *withdrawing family*, on the other hand explains Fromm, is primarily characterized by the "cool indifference" if not outright cold hatefulness of the parent-child relationship. Fromm believes that the rise of this somewhat later style of family life to that of the symbiotic family is the product of the bourgeoisie or the merchant class. In this context, parents have a tendency to be very demanding of the child with expectations that they are to live up to the high standards set by the family given its position in the merchant class as representatives of the elite in society. Either very formalized physical punishment for non-compliance or a more refined style of punishment in which guilt plays a major part or even the use of the withdrawal of affection constitute mechanisms of serious punishment. The whole driving force of the withdrawing family ethos is success and conforming to the cultural norms and expectations of the privileged classes.

The *productive family*, according to Fromm, that is, the family which creates the living environment of nurture and freedom, does so by virtue of fostering responsibility and accountability within the context of reason and love. This, he says, will produce good, healthy and productive families for it is in the acknowledging of personal freedom and individual responsibility that love can thrive and in this love-freedom-responsibility matrix, both the individual and society as a whole benefit and prosper.

Within the context of this discussion, Fromm was eager to point out five "malignant" character types which he had identified in his clinical practice. These he believed helped to inform his notion of the frame of reference of orientation within which we all must live. These five types are (1) receptive, (2) exploitative, (3) hoarding, (4) marketing, and (5) necrophilous, being true to his optimistic nature, there is a positive type he calls "productive." Believing as he did, Fromm suggested that in order to understand our "social unconscious," we must examine closely the economic systems of the world which govern human behavior. Here we see the early influence of Marx on his psychotherapeutic thought. If one will notice, the five negative character types and the one positive type all reflect an economic model of description. Let us explore these a bit more closely.

The character types in Fromm's schema are related to the "orientation" of individuals or, as we have been saying, the "frame of reference" of individuals. The receptive orientation character is a person who has every expectation of getting what he wants when he needs it. These needs and services expected by this receptive character are external to the individual and, therefore, must come from outside themselves. The receptivity of these individuals is this characteristically dominant trait. These individuals are most commonly found within peasant societies, societies with an over-abundance of natural goods and resources, and, not surprisingly, also individuals at the bottom of any society such as slaves, serfs, welfare families, and migrant workers, all of whom are dependent upon their social environment and are necessarily receptive to whatever is provided them. Not dissimilar to Freud's notion of the orally passive, Adler's concept of the leaning-getting, and Horney's compliant personality, these individuals are most commonly found in what Fromm called the "symbiotic family" where the child is figuratively "swallowed up" by parents including the masochistic (passive) form of authoritarianism. On their better side, they are optimistic and creative.

The exploitative personality character is an individual who anticipates the necessary taking of what he needs rather than receiving what he needs. This character orientation is descriptive of an individual who places a rising sense of value upon those things taken from others in relationship to the difficulty in securing them – the harder they are to take from others, the greater value they have. Wealth, ideas, even love is greater in value when taken with difficulty. Fromm suggests that these types are found among the aristocracy of history and the upper classes and landed gentry of colonial empires. This type, like the reception type, are associated with the symbiotic family (swallowing up, masochistic, authoritarian). Fromm points out that they are Freud's oral aggressive personality, Adler's ruling-dominant individual, and Horney's aggressive type person. They can be aggressive, conceited, and seducing while on the positive side assertive, proud, and captivating.

The third character orientation is that of the person who hoards, who is intent upon keeping the things of the world because the world is an environment of objects to be possessed. Fromm suggested that even relationships are possessions to this character type including loved ones for they are possessions as well. Fromm reminds us that Marx identified this type of individual within the bourgeoisie including the merchant middle class and associated it with the Protestant work ethic of "God helps those who help themselves." The family type most characterized by the hoarding mentality is that of the "withdrawing family" and with the destructive personality type. Perfectionism is related to this personality type to which Freud related the anal retentive personality, Adler the avoiding type, and Horney the withdrawing type. Personality traits such as stubbornness, stinginess, and being rather unimaginative are common features of this orientation. Less negative features such as steadfastness, economical, and practical are found in this character orientation.

Owing to Fromm's early interest in Marx and socialism as a youngster and university student, he was never far from a discussion of economics as relates to human growth and development. The fourth character orientation he delineated was called "marketing" for it is the person who expects to be involved in the selling of one's self, i.e., the creative presentation of the self constitutes the social agenda in interpersonal relationships with this character type. The correct displaying of cognates of the individual – family, school, work, appearance, car, etc. – all constitute the advertising and marketing of oneself. And, a common theme with Fromm, even love and marriage are thought of as components of this advertising and marketing agenda. Fromm believed that this character orientation, more so than the others, was essentially the orientation of western industrial society. This is who we are he suggested, for good or ill. This modern industrial type of character is the product of the "cool withdrawing family," and embraces a sort of regimented conformity in *lieu* of a real sense of personal freedom. This type of person may be opportunistic, childish, and even boorish but may also embody such traits as being purposeful and sociable.

The most negative of the character orientations according Fromm is that of necrophilous type because this person is intent upon destroying things rather than attempting in any way to integrate himself into society. Death, war and fighting are the obsessions of this character type for though not necessary these are desirable activities. For this type of individual, there is no concern here for the isolation, alienation, and separateness of people for it is this situation in which destruction is most prevalent. Procedural, technical, and mechanistic are the descriptive terms for this individual's personality as this person is inclined to conservatism which maintains the status quo and defends against the wider, outside, alien world of others such as strangers and foreigners.

True to his nature, Fromm is eager to identify one character orientation which is positive and he labels this one the "productive orientation." This healthy personality is without a mask, says Fromm, for this individual embraces his social and biological nature all the while seeking after freedom, responsibility, and accountability to the social world around him. This individual's family environment is one of love while fostering freedom rather than conformity and reason rather than rules for living in the world. We do not yet have such a society which readily and enthusiastically fosters the productive character type, what he calls "humanistic communitarian socialism." Taking a strong existentialist bent to his philosophy of living in the world, Fromm emphasizes in this productive orientation living without a mask, being true to oneself and to others, being involved in making the world livable, lovable, and nurturing.

Within the context of character orientation, it seems relevant to explore just briefly Fromm's primary criticism of Freud and psychoanalysis, especially since he was trained in this traditionalist school of psychotherapy and was for more than ten years a practicing orthodox psychoanalyst himself. Not just a practicing psychiatrist, Fromm was a scholar and teacher and spent a great deal of time working through the literary corpus of Freud's massive clinical studies. He was among the first to dare mention the "early" Freud as well as the "later" Freud, suggesting, to the horror of many of Freud's adherents, that Freud's thought and clinical practice experienced an evolution of developing ideas and concepts. Just one instance will illustrate Fromm's point. Prior to World War I, Freud suggested that human drives were essentially the manifestation of a tension between desire and repression, but following the War Freud shifted to a position which suggested that human drives consisted of a struggle between the fundamentally biological instincts of life and death (Eros and Thanatos). This, Fromm was convinced, constituted a significant contradiction in the meaning and function of human drives but was never acknowledged by the psychoanalytic school or by Freud.

Furthermore, and not making friends by doing so, Fromm suggested that Freud suffered from unwitting dualism (rather than the commonly touted monism of the world of science) by pointing out that Freud's description of human consciousness consisted of a struggle between two poles, i.e., life and death. Nevertheless and in fairness to Fromm, Fromm was keen to emphasize the great contribution Freud had made to modern man's self-understanding, calling Freud one of the "architects of the modern age" alongside Einstein and Marx. Fromm never lost his interest in economic oppression of the working class growing out of his youthful fascination with Marxism and the socialist critique of western capitalism. So, in the early 1960s, he published two books specifically dealing with Marx and socialism with the major one being titled, *Marx's Concept of Man* and *Beyond the Chains of Illusion: My Encounter with Marx and Freud.* He also published a series of articles in book form titled *Socialist Humanism: An International Symposium* for which, in 1966, he was named by the American Humanist Association the Humanist Man of the Year.

While being a prolific writer with over twenty books to his credit, Fromm's most celebrated works include three major studies of the human psyche and social criticism spanning over a thirty-five year period. These three major books were *Escape from Freedom* (1941), *the Art of Loving* (1956), and *To Have or to Be?* (1976). Let us summarize the key points in each of these three books before concluding our discussion of Fromm's contribution to social theory and its relevance to psychotherapy.

Fromm's 1941 book, *Escape from Freedom,* was published in the United Kingdom and received international distribution and acclaim under the title *The Fear of Freedom.* This first major book of Fromm set the stage for his entire career. It explored the complex and ever-changing relationship of modern society to the concept of freedom with special attention to the personal consequences of its failure to be present and function in society. This, as he explains, constituted the environment within which the Third Reich and all forms of fascism rise and prosper. For Fromm, there are two types of freedom, viz., "freedom from" being the negative form and "freedom to" being the positive. Whereas the former is an emancipation from culturally and socially restrictive behavioral conventions very much suggesting, says Fromm, the existentialism of Sartre and leads too often to destructive intrusion into the social fabric, the latter freedom is towards spontaneity and creativity, to the exercise of one's being liberated for the purpose of exploring new realms of being and doing and thinking. This freedom to do and be and create constitutes the context within which personality grows and not merely and only a freedom from restrictions and oppressions.

Fromm wished us to understand that being "free from" a thing is only the first step towards being "free to" a thing and when the first freedom comes there is often a feeling of hopelessness, of a lack of direction or purpose and meaning to life. This can only be reconciled by embracing the second freedom, namely, free to explore, to create, to engage, and to develop. In true Hegelian terms (or we might suggest Marxian terms), Fromm saw the dialect between the first freedom "from" to the second freedom "to" as providing the matrix of true freedom. An interesting feature of this book and of Fromm's interest in it has to do with his treatment of the emergence of Protestantism especially as reflected in the theologies of Calvin (the father of Presbyterianism) and Luther (the father of Lutheranism). The maintenance of the moral authority of God following the Protestant Reformation in which the authority of the Catholic Church was called into question posed a major cultural shift in consciousness on the part of the general populace. As Luther explained it, the individual had a personal and private relationship with God outside the jurisdiction of the institutional Church while Calvin promoted the notion of predestination in which people could not actually work their way to heaven but rather have been chosen by God himself for salvation. Both notions, Fromm suggested, were the result of a new sense of a freer economic context for modern society. Whereas Luther gives individuals more freedom to seek righteousness in the world, on their own, without the complicity of the Church ecclesiastical authorities intervening, Calvin provided a formalized method for individuals to actually "work out their own salvation with fear and trembling," as the Apostle Paul had said in Scripture. Changing one's destiny was not possible for God had chosen them one by one rather than they having chosen God. However, every individual could work towards their salvation by committing themselves to hard work and frugality which were virtues greatly valued by the Protestant ethic. This makes people work harder to "prove" their selection by God for salvation in his Kingdom, i.e., "God helps those who help themselves."

In this classic test, *Escape from Freedom*, Fromm is quick to emphasize that the "freedom from" is used by many people to provide some form of security in an uncertain world. These forms of security, though never really working over-time but momentarily satisfying the need to feel secure in an insecure world, include authoritarianism, destructiveness, and conformity. Fromm was greatly applauded by the liberal social science community for this schematic owing to the poignancy of its critique of western social values. Authoritarianism, for example Fromm points out, characterizes the personality of an individual who embodies a sadistic trait and a masochist trait, an individual who seeks to exercise control over other people in an effort to impose his own worldview upon them despite their protests to the contrary. These individuals are particularly susceptible to submission to what they think of as a superior force operative within the world, such as religion or a political ideology. On the other hand, the destructive personality, though carrying with it traits of the sadistic features of authoritarianism, rather than exercise control over others prefers rather to destroy others, their way of life, their ideology, their goal and mission in life, anything that it cannot on its own bring under control. It is conformity wherein individuals unwittingly embody the normative beliefs and worldview of the society and embrace them as their very own whether they truly feel allegiance to them or not. This embracing of the normative worldview and ethos exempts these individuals from having to engage in original and genuinely free thinking which might naturally produce anxiety and ambivalence and uncertainty.

In his *Escape from Freedom*, Fromm offers a carefully constructed assessment of both democracy and freedom. The freedom produced and enjoyed by modern democracies in the industrialized nations of the world constitutes both a model for praise and a point of caution by Fromm. However, the kind of freedom enjoyed by these societies can only have meaningful and lasting value within the context of personal inner freedom of each individual. Being free from authoritarianism and totalitarian regimes does not mean that we are free from the domination of experts in the field of advertising and marketing! The path to personal and individual freedom, according to Fromm, is to be spontaneously committed to personal self-expression in quest of self-actualization. The existential mandate which says "there is only one meaning of life: the act of living it" was the mantra of Fromm and his followers. The only way to be truly in touch with our own personal humanity, Fromm argues, is to be truly and completely in touch with the needs of those with whom we share the world!

Fifteen years after his great and first major blockbuster, *Escape from Freedom* and with several other monographs which followed such as *Man for Himself* (1947), Fromm addressed one of his enduring themes in his life's work, titling the book *The Art of Loving* (1956). In this now classic text, Fromm focused his attention upon a theme struck in his earlier works but here he centered all of his psychotherapeutic as well as his social commentary analysis to it, namely, that of the central importance of love and loving as the cement of social cohesion and individual self-fulfillment. Love, Fromm emphasizes, does not just happen, it is not something that drops from the sky or simply wells up within an individual's behavioral repertoire as a naturally instinctive response to others and to the world. It can and must be taught, there must be effort expended for its true development. It is not magical and mysterious eluding critical analysis and assessment, criticism and evaluation. Helplessness as a characteristic of love such as perpetuated by popular literature and the theatre is a false portrayal and even wrong-headed understanding of the nature and meaning of love. It is not something that one falls into and out of depending on the situation of the moment. Owing to the alienation and loneliness which western industrial society has created for itself in its eager rush for things, for an uncritical enthusiasm for consumption, we turned to a shallow and false notion of "romantic love" as the solution to this isolation from each other. However, Fromm is eager to point out, love is not and must not be thought of as a sentimental state of helpless abandonment in the arms of an equally lonely person. Real love, rather than sentimental drivel, comes from the development of one's whole personality.

Only with the cultivation of this sense of one's own self-realization through a truly humble, courageous, faithful, and disciplined concern for others can one genuinely experience the love which lasts. It is rare, to be sure says Fromm, because the inclination towards a self-actualizing love is short-circuited by the sentimentality of a shallow romantic love perpetrated understandably but unfortunately by popular fiction and the movies. This real and true love, rare as it is but sought by all in a loneliness and isolation which has been fostered through capitalism and consumerism and the drive for personal success, is characterized by four essential elements, explains Fromm. They are care, responsibility, respect, and knowledge. In other words, he continues, love is really hard work requiring vigilance and an undivided commitment but, if one persists, it is the most rewarding of all human efforts. Care, responsibility, respect, and knowledge all are relevant to the three types of love explored by Fromm. These types are what he calls self-love which, rather than conceit and self-centeredness, means caring about oneself genuinely as a person with responsibilities, respecting oneself and reaching a sense of self-knowledge including being realistic and honest about one's strengths and weaknesses. Furthermore, there is brotherly love including care, responsibility, respect, and knowledge of the other person, and there is naturally erotic love which involves these same four characteristics directed toward the person with whom one wishes to establish and maintain a physical a well as emotional intimacy. When the book was released, it was heralded as one of the most provocative and insightful addresses ever proposed to the concept of love in western society. It continues to this day to maintain that high level of respect.

Twenty years later and at the age of 76, Fromm addressed himself to an enduring concern which had loomed large but in the background throughout his career, namely, the pervasive materialism and egocentrism which so blatantly characterizes western society. Fromm had these concerns early in his young life as a Jewish student raised in a rabbinic home environment in which religious values of service and love of God dominated the terrain of his intellectual interests. When he drifted away from these religious moorings towards Marxism and socialism, these feelings of concern for the well-being of society actually deepened. He began in his own professional work as a psychotherapist (as well as social critic) to differentiate between the human desire to "have" and the human need to "be." This distinction became serviceable to him in both roles as therapist and social critic. This western industrial notion of unlimited happiness, unrestrained possessiveness, and domination of the physical environment was a plague upon the individual's quest for personal meaning and self-actualization, Fromm believed. With the naïve promise of unlimited production and, thus, unlimited consumption, the western individual could unleash a personal ambition without restraints. Everything is possible in terms of possessions and power over the world. No limits, no restraints, no check to ambition. It was a deception self-perpetuated by industrialization and capitalism. Unlimited pleasure and self-assertion in the environment was the promise. Hedonism and egoism were elevated to a sacrament of devotion by industrial societies the world over. Within the matrix of selfishness for the individual and for society, an economic system based not upon what is good for the individual and society but what will feed the industrialization process itself became the normative governance for all human activity. This, Fromm believed, was a prescription for disaster, both for the individual who would encounter a deepening sense of isolation and loneliness without the balancing satisfaction of self-fulfillment as well as society itself having lost a sense of responsibility and accountability to each other. It is the "being" in the world which constitutes the full description of who we are, not the possessions we hold nor the dominance of the environment which we cherish. Not "having" things but "being" a human person constitutes the highest ideals and agenda for the individual and for society. This is the beck and call of our higher selves as individuals and as a society of love and compassion.

More so than with the previously discussed modern psychotherapists, Fromm was as well-known and respected as a social critic as he was as a psychotherapist, being admired for his social and political commentary on western society equal to the admiration he received for his philosophical and psychological insights into the profession of counseling. His work constituted the foundations for what is today called "political psychology," and the combination of his *Escape from Freedom* with his *Man for Himself: An Inquiry into the Psychology of Ethics,* established the foundations upon which Fromm's understanding of human nature and the potentiality of the human spirit were well received by the general public as well as by his professional colleagues. Unlike the work of Perls and Berne who lost favor with their professional community owing to their drifting into popularist writing, Fromm was never abandoned by his profession. Fromm's notion of being "free from" as well as being "free to" constituted a bipartite foundation upon which to counsel the individual in search of meaning in life. He complimented this schematic with his distinction between "having" and "being," and with these two concepts regarding freedom and personhood, Fromm became the voice of reason during the troubling years of social unrest in America during the 1960s and 1970s.

CONCLUDING REMARKS

Both an existentialist and an outspoken humanist (calling himself once an "atheistic mystic," Fromm's concern for and insights into the heart of western industrialized society and the impact consumerism and egoism has had upon the personhood of western society is even today considered profound. Human potential, though latent with promise, is, according to Fromm, greatly stifled and impeded by both consumerism (everything is mine) and egoism (I can be everything I wish to be). We are desperately in need of a sense of being who "we have the potential to be" rather than simply having "all that we have the capacity to have." We are, in a word according to Fromm, more than what we possess or of what we dominate or of what we have power and control over. We have the potential to self-fulfillment through self-actualization and this requires a mature understanding of the meaning and nature of love in our lives and in the world. Concerned over the destructive tendencies within modern society, Fromm was nevertheless a long-term optimist about our future even if he appeared to be a short-term pessimist about our present situation.

What is missing today is the absence of a serious critic of western society's passion for the production and consumption of goods. Our consumerism is destroying our sense of responsibility to the world and for each other. Our desire for more and more things with unlimited ambition on the part of the individual and the wider society has driven us into a state of complete dependence upon our egoism and consumerism without any regard for the need for self-actualization, for a sense of being rather than just having. Freud and Marx were quite decidedly the two most important influences in the formative years of Fromm's intellectual development. He acknowledged this himself, affirming that his training in psychoanalysis and the Freudian school of psychology was of enduring value to him in his psychotherapeutic work as a practicing clinician. Though he came to disassociate himself from much of Freudian orthodoxy, joining the neo-Freudians and even the post-Freudians including such notable figures as Jung, Horney, and Sullivan, he held on to what he thought was of great value in the traditionalist camp of psychoanalysis and much of his social criticism was informed by Freud's own *Civilization and Its Discontents*.

But with Marx, there was no caveat or disclaimer of his importance in the intellectual life and work of Erich Fromm. Fromm was all admiration for Marx's brilliant insight into industrial western society and Marx's deep humanistic concern for the emergence of individual isolation and loneliness perpetrated, albeit unwittingly, by the industrialization of manufacturing and its inevitable diminishment of the value of the human person. Marx's criticism of middle-class society and its devaluation of the working class was accepted without restraint by Fromm. What was missing from the Marxist critique, explained Fromm, was a thorough-going critical psychology of the individual and a social psychology addressing the emotional ills of modern society itself. Fromm's agenda, then, proved to be an all-out commitment to the interfacing and merging of psychoanalysis with Marxist social thought. Fromm believed that a sound psychological theory would be able to demonstrate that the economic foundations of western society produce the social character of its people and, in turn, this social character then produces an ideology designed to foster this self-concept. Therefore, to critique the economic principles of a society provides the matrix within which an address to the emotional and psychological ills of that society may likewise occur. Doing good economic theory sets the stage then for doing good psychological assessment and criticism.

The determinism and pessimism of psychoanalysis and the nihilism of Marxist ideology were countered by the optimism of Fromm's humanistic, existentialist, psychological, and social theory. Fromm was called the "voice of conscience" for he maintained that love and freedom were the basis upon which a society can fulfill its potential for good and the basis for the self-actualization of individuals. With little room for doubt, Fromm is today thought of as one of the most important voices of reason within the psychotherapeutic community. His contributions to humanistic psychology along with the work of Abraham Maslow and Carl Rogers are profoundly important and universally recognized and valued.

BIBLIOGRAPHY

ERICH FROMM'S PRIMARY SOURCES

(1941) *Escape from Freedom.* New York: Holt, Rinehart, and Winston.

(1947) *Man for Himself.* Greenwich, CT: Fawcett Premier Books.

(1950) *Psychoanalysis and Religion.* New Haven: Yale University Press.

(1951) *The Forgotten Language: An Introduction to the Understanding of Dreams, Fairy Tales, and Myths.* New York: Rinehart.

(1955) *The Sane Society.* Greenwich, CT: Fawcett Premier Books.

(1956) *The Art of Loving.* New York: Harper.

(1958) *Sigmund Freud's Mission. An Analysis of His Personality and Influence,* N.Y.: Peter Smith's Publishing.

(1959) *Sigmund Freud's Mission: An Analysis of his Personality and Influence*. New York: Harper.

(1961) *Marx's Concept of Man*, New York: Frederick Ungar.

(1966) *You Shall Be Gods*, New York: Holt, Rinehart and Winston.

(1970) *The Crisis of Psychoanalysis. Essays on Freud, Marx, and Social Psychology,* New York: Holt, Rinehart and Winston.

(1973) *The Anatomy of Human Destructiveness*. New York: Holt, Rinehart, and Winston.

(1976) *To Have or to Be?* New York: Harper and Row.

(1984) *The Working Class in Weimar Germany. A Psychological and Sociological Study*, London: Berg Publishers.

SECONDARY SOURCES

Burston, D. (1991) *The Legacy of Erich Fromm*. Cambridge, MA: Harvard University Press.

Engler, Barbara (2008) *Personality Theories.* Boston: Houghton Mifflin Harcourt Publishing Company.

Funk, Rainer (2003) *Erich Fromm: His Life and Ideas*. Translators Ian Portman, Manuela Kunkel. New York: Continuum International Publishing Group.

Mills, C. W. (1959) *The Sociological Imagination*. New York: Oxford University Press.

CHAPTER FOURTEEN
Albert Ellis and Rational Emotive Behavior Therapy

INTRODUCTION

Any serious treatment of the history and development of the many schools of psychotherapy must, of course, begin with Freud and psychoanalysis.   Whatever subsequent schools emerged, and there are several enduring ones today, they all rose up within the context of Freudian theory of the unconscious and his school of psychoanalysis. Now, there are neo-Freudians, post-Freudians, non-Freudians, crypto-Freudians and even pseudo-Freudians but no school worth mentioning has appeared outside the context of Freud's work.   And yet, several schools have appeared which have so distanced themselves from Freud that one is hard pressed to easily identify points of continuity even though those points exist. Albert Ellis is just such a psychotherapist who began as a Freudian psychoanalyst but by the early stages of his development of Rational Emotional Behavior Therapy there was no real point of continuity with Freud left. Over thirty years ago, in 1982, there was a professional survey done among American and Canadian psychologists in which they were asked to rank the most influential psychotherapists in history and the first three listed were in this order, Carl Rogers, Albert Ellis, and Sigmund Freud.

Albert Ellis was a recognized leader in the creation of the cognitive revolutionary paradigm shift within psychotherapy away from depth psychology of the unconscious as in psychoanalysis and towards a more pragmatic and existentialist approach to the relationship between behavior and cognition. Though Ellis early experienced severe criticism from the traditionalist professionals in psychotherapy, whether psychoanalysts or not, during the 1950s and 1960s, he began to gain recognition and respect as he persisted in his quest for a more viably and practical therapy based on his clinical experience and research in the field of cognition and behavior analysis called Cognitive Behavioral Therapy (CBT). As we will explore in much detail later in this book, Aaron T. Beck was the recognized founder of CBT which became one of the most important alternative schools of psychotherapeutic practice to Freud's psychoanalysis and it was CBT which grew out of this early work of Ellis. Ellis's work constituted the development of a therapeutic approach to cognition and behavior resulting in the creation both of a research and treatment institution of his own as well as the launching of a professional journal to further his work and recognition. It was "The Living School" for children created in the 1970s by Ellis which was responsible for the development of a curriculum that embodied what he was by this time labelling REBT or Rational Emotive Behavior Therapy. In the early 1980s, the professional survey conducted by the psychology community mentioned above which found Ellis to be number two in popularity following Carl Rogers and preceding Sigmund Freud, that same study indicated that Ellis was the most cited psychologist in the scholarly literature after 1957. This led to his recognition by the American Psychological Association in 1985 in which they presented Ellis with its most prestigious award for "distinguished professional contributions."

Ellis' Rational Emotive Behavioral Therapy (REBT), historians of behavioral science point out, preceded the Cognitive Behavioral Therapy (CBT) of Aaron T. Beck. Rather than focus upon early childhood experiences as done in psychoanalysis with its dream work and free association analysis or even the child's family relationships which many neo-Freudian schools were doing such as family systems therapists particularly as evidenced in the work of Klein, Ellis preferred to concentrate his analytical skills and clinical practice upon the actual belief systems operative within a child's mind which lead to self-defeating behaviors. This was pragmatic, existential, and in some ways akin to Perls' Gestalt therapy in its emphasis upon the here-and-now experience of the troubled child. Clearly, Ellis's work had been influenced by Adler, Horney, and Fromm, and he proceeded to challenge the viability and utility of psychoanalysis in the persistent failure of that school of thought to produce empirical evidence of its effectiveness in the treatment particularly of children.

Based on his own extensive clinical experience and judged within the context of the history of clinical studies put forth by the psychotherapeutic community dealing with measurable effectiveness of the various schools of analysis and treatment including particularly psychoanalysis, Ellis chose to end his relationship with and practice of psychoanalysis in his clinical work with the aim of developing a new and measurably effective approach to psychotherapy. Initially calling his new approach simply Rational Therapy, he later refined both the theory and practice to be called Rational Emotive Behavioral Therapy (REBT). Universally recognized as the precursor to the now extremely popular school of thought called Cognitive Behavioral Therapy (CBT), REBT has as its therapeutic agenda the behaviors and belief systems of the client, both child and adult. This interfacing of behavior (action) and belief systems (ideology) constituted a major development. Though slow to gain recognition and respect even after the founding in 1959 of the Institute for Rational Living, it is now quite decidedly one of the major dominant schools of psychotherapeutic practice in America and Europe.

BIOGRAPHY

As were most of the previous modern psychotherapists considered in this study, Albert Ellis was born into a Jewish family. He was born in Pittsburgh, Pennsylvania, on September 27, 1913, the eldest of three children. Ellis' father was a businessman who was seldom at home and not given to parental expressions of warmth and caring whereas his mother, as explained by Ellis, suffered from a bipolar disorder which made her self-absorbed. While being what he called a "chatterbox," the children were fully aware that she never listened to them but was quick to make strongly opinionated statements about everything whether she knew of what she spoke or not. As with her husband, she was emotionally uninvolved in the lives of her children's development, expressing little regard for their education – she would be in bed when they left for school and would usually be gone when they returned. Rather than rebellious and resentful, Ellis took on the role of the parent seeing to it that his younger siblings got up for school, ate breakfast, and got themselves dressed. Though a sickly youngster, experiencing eight hospitalizations between the ages of five and seven, Ellis, like his siblings, worked during the years of the Great Depression to help out the family's meager financial situation. Illness plagued him throughout his long life and during these early years, once spending nearly an entire year in hospital, he learned to cope with the indifference of his parents, who hardly ever actually visited him during these confinements, by training himself not to expect their love and care and, thus, avoided disappointment when they were not forthcoming.

Realizing that the only way he was going to be able to overcome his extreme shyness around women, at the age of nineteen he gave a series of talks at the Bronx Botanical Gardens before a large gathering of women and through this process "desensitized" himself from this inordinate fear of female rejection. Earning a Bachelor of Arts degree in business from the City College of New York in 1934, he briefly tried a career in business and then as a writer, neither of which he enjoyed nor at which he was successful. Though not good at fiction, he discovered that he was quite good at research and non-fiction writing and was particularly gifted in writing about sexuality which led him to pursue a new career in clinical psychology. In 1942 at the age of 31, he enrolled in a Ph.D. program in clinical psychology at Teachers College, Columbia University, where psychoanalysis was the primary focus of the department. Completing the Master of Arts in clinical psychology the following year, he commenced a part-time private counseling practice while continuing to work for his Ph.D. as licensing of psychologists in New York did not occur this early in the development of the profession. A rigorous researcher and prolific writer, he began being published in the scholarly journals well before completing his doctoral studies. His 1946 in-depth study of a wide range of personality tests then being used throughout the country led him to contend that only the Minnesota Multiphasic Personality Inventory met anything like scientific standards for research methodology.

The following year, 1947, Ellis earned the Ph.D. in clinical psychology from Columbia University, and he believed, understandably given the Freudian orientation of the degree-granting department, that psychoanalysis was the most effective form of psychotherapy then available to practitioners in the field of counseling. Postdoctoral training in more advanced psychoanalysis was his next pursuit but interestingly enough and somewhat prophetic of the end results, Ellis sought additional and alternative training in the field of Jungian analysis from Richard Hulbeck whose teacher had been Hermann Rorschach who himself had been trained at the Karen Horney Institute and who had created the Rorschach inkblot test. This experience in further postdoctoral training in another school of thought constituted the initial inklings that Ellis was decreasingly passionate about psychoanalysis as a therapy. After receiving his Ph.D. in clinical psychology Ellis taught both at New York University and Rutgers University in New Jersey. While conducting his part-time practice in New York, Ellis worked full-time as a psychologist for the State of New Jersey and became chief psychologist of the State in 1950. However, by 1952 he had left his position and expanded his private practice to full time.

Early in Ellis' professional life as he launched his private practice and began to financially support himself such that marriage was possible and realistic, he married. That marriage ended in a speedy annulment and soon thereafter he married again but that one ended, somewhat amicably, three years later in a divorce as well. Though he engaged in many sexual relationships throughout his life, he never had children. However and somewhat ironically, it has been suggested by his colleagues and fellow psychotherapy practitioners that the many love relationships he had over the years actually provided him with a substantial background of experience which served well his research and writing in the field of human sexuality. In his fifties, he developed a relationship with Janet Wolfe, an intern at the Albert Ellis Institute eventually becoming its Executive Director, and this relationship was one of the longest in his life. Later, however, in the early 2000's, he established the final relationship in his life with Debbie Joffe, an Australian psychologist, who had actually come to New York to study with him at his Institute. They eventually married in 2004 and it lasted until his death in 2007 at the age of 94.

As a young aspiring clinical psychologist with a fledging practice in New York City, Ellis was surprisingly one of the few in the field who was able to make a full living through his private practice. This was due, however, to his growing reputation as a sex therapist, one of the very few in the City of New York at the time. Continuing to modify and tweak his theory and technique in this specialized field, he was still essentially practicing traditional psychoanalysis on his clients. Part of his dissatisfaction with traditional psychoanalysis was its non-interventionist and passive posture relative to the client. His temperament drove him to explore a more actively involved participation in the therapeutic process with his clients. What stimulated his interest most was the realization that clients suffering from neurosis were most often inclined to justify their irrational behavior with irrational ideas and beliefs. Irrational behavior, Ellis came to understand, was the result of irrational ideas! Drawing from his reading of a 1950 book by Dollard and Miller titled *Personality and Psychotherapy,* Ellis took into consideration their position that the neurotic person's situation is the result of the repression of thoughts or behaviors which produce anxiety. Therefore, he reasoned, a generally intelligent person will behave in ways which are self-defeating and foolish if they suffer from neurosis which has been produced by irrational and illogical thoughts and beliefs. Most people, Ellis suggested, will hold on to these irrational beliefs even when it is made clear to them that they are, indeed, irrational leading to counter-productive behavior patterns which produces neurosis (1961). Neurosis appears as a result of the way an individual "sees the world," not how the world really is. Therefore, therapy is effective when these irrational beliefs and ideologies are confronted and dispelled thereby providing the neurotic person a way out of counter-productive behavior by replacing irrational ideas with reasonable ones which, then, produce reasonable behavior patterns.

Of course and inevitably, Ellis broke with the society of psychoanalysts in New York and commenced to more actively promote his interventionist and pro-active style of psychotherapy. By 1955, he had labeled his approach Rational Emotive Therapy and this new approach placed the responsibility on the therapist to engage the client in an investigation into the worldview held by the client wherein irrational ideas and beliefs might be found. The intent in this therapeutic approach was to assist the client in identifying this counter-productive complex of ideas and beliefs which foster counter-productive behavior leading to emotional pain and suffering. The goal was to change the client's self-defeating beliefs with positive behavior.

No one thinks alone and there are no completely new ideas Martin Heidegger has reminded us and Ellis was quick to identify the influences in his intellectual growth and the development of his cognitive therapy. Adler, Horney, Fromm, and Harry Stack Sullivan are cited as major influences in Ellis' life and he especially credited Alfred Korzybski, the author of *Science and Sanity,* as having a great influence on him particularly as relates to the philosophical foundations for the development of rational therapy. This book combined with the earlier psychologists and his own clinical experience gained during his private practice all conspired for the making of his own school of psychology, what would become known as Rational Emotive Behavioral therapy (REBT). This new idea of the relationship between action and thought, between behavior and ideology, began to take shape during the late 1940s and marked the decisive break with traditional psychoanalysis when Ellis began to refer to himself as a "rational therapist."

At this juncture, Ellis began to promote his newly discovered ideas regarding a more active and directive type of psychotherapy. In 1954, Ellis began formally discussing this new approach and the next year he advanced the label "Rational Therapy" (RT) to this perspective. In Rational Therapy, Ellis explained, the therapist attempts to facilitate the client's own self-understanding which contains ideas or beliefs contrary to his health and are factors contributing to the client's stress and anxiety. But, explained Ellis, not only must the client understanding the nature and function of these ideas and beliefs as negative factors in the client's emotional well-being, the client in turn must also act upon this new understanding which has been facilitated by the rational therapist. Unlike Freud's psychoanalysis and Rogers' non-directive counseling, rational therapy stressed the importance of the therapist working with the client to understand his self-defeating ideas and beliefs and the resulting behavioral matrix by showing the client how these ideas and beliefs, owing to their irrationality, are self-destructive. "Rational analysis" and "cognitive reconstruction," Ellis believed, would foster a client's understanding of his life situation, i.e., contextualization of ideas and beliefs, such that these ideas and beliefs might either be discarded or "reconstructed" so as to offer rational and viable explanations about the world and the individual's place in it.

By 1957, Ellis had developed his system of thought in terms of both analytical sophistication and therapeutic application such that he could formally set forth his RT school as a professional posture to take within psychotherapy. The therapist in this system of analysis and treatment, explained Ellis, was expected and empowered to help the client modify, alter, and adjust their ideas and beliefs and the behaviors resulting from them for the resolution of emotional problems and distresses. In 1959, Ellis published his first book on the subject titled *How to Live with a Neurotic* in which the modality of treatment in RT was delineated. The following year and based on his new book, he presented a paper delineating this new method and theory of analysis before the American Psychological Association annual meeting held in Chicago of that year. Friendly but not particularly enthusiastic was the general reception to this new thought system for the dominant school of thought at this time was that of experimental psychology's new darling, behaviorism. The psychotherapeutic schools of Freud, Jung, Adler, and Perls were the ruling names in clinical psychology.

Due to the strongly promoted cognitive emphasis within Rational Therapy and in spite of the relevance of emotive and behavioral methods in this system of thought, he was greatly ostracized by the prevailing psychotherapeutic schools of Freud and Jung though the Adlerians did not participate in this censorship. Though ignored or banned from national conferences of psychologists and psychotherapists frequently, he pressed on with his newly developing system of analysis and treatment of mental illness and personality disorders by holding seminars during which time he would actually demonstrate the method and effectiveness of Rational Therapy by bringing a client up on stage for a practical and on-the-spot therapeutic demonstration. The slow growth of interest in his approach led to his decision to establish his own institute for research, training, and clinical practice. In 1959, therefore, he established the Institute for Rational Living (subsequently known as the Albert Ellis Institute) as a non-profit organization in the State of New York.

By 1968 it was chartered by the New York State Board of Regents as a training institute and psychological clinic. This was no trivial feat as New York State had a Mental Hygiene Act which mandated psychiatric management of mental health clinics. Its purpose was to further promote, by teaching and clinical practice, the development of Rational Emotive Behavior Therapy as a comprehensive theory of psychotherapeutic practice. Educational training in REBT was offered to professional practitioners as well as paraprofessionals and the general public. Beginning by offering everything through his own private practice as a psychologist, in 1964 he purchased a six story townhouse in Manhattan which had previously been the Woodrow Wilson Institute. By donating all of the earnings from his books (many being bestsellers), the purchase of the building and funding the operation costs of the Institute, Ellis made certain of the financial security of the Institute he founded. He practiced psychotherapy, marriage and family counseling, and sex therapy for over sixty years in the Institute's Psychological Center in New York City.

Dating from his early work as an undergraduate student at the City College and then further on in his graduate work at Teachers College/Columbia University, Ellis was recognized along with several other psychologists as one of the important figures in the American sexual revolution. Known for his early work as a sexologist with strong liberal humanistic and sometimes controversial opinions on the subject of human sexuality, Ellis worked closely with the noted zoologist and sex researcher Alfred Kinsey writing several books and many articles on the topic of human sexuality and love. Preceding his book on Rational Therapy, Ellis published in 1958 what was destined to become his classic work on sexuality titled *Sex Without Guilt*. It was a major scholarly treatment of the topic with strongly liberal positions taken against the Puritanical *zeitgeist* of the day. He followed this book and this topic with numerous articles, both for the popular press as well as for the scholarly journals.

It was natural and inevitable that the subject of religion would have to be addressed owing to the title of his book on sex and guilt. In this book, he rather boldly expressed the opinion and demonstrated its correctness with clinical cases that religious restrictions on such things as sexual expression often precipitated mental illness, being harmful to emotional growth and development especially among children and juveniles. He argued that too often there is psychiatric fall out from religious ideologies. Ellis was an outspoken nontheistic humanist and in 1971 was honored by the American Humanist Association as the Humanist of the Year and as late as 2003 he was a signer of the Humanist Manifesto. Once describing himself as an "atheistic mystic" and on another occasion as a "probabilistic atheist" (by which he meant that though he could not prove that God does not exist there is little probability that he does exist!). Ellis would have done himself a real service if he had simply called himself an agnostic rather than attempting to create labels for which he spent far too much time trying to define and defend!

However, in spite of his personal atheism and strong humanistic emphasis, his attitude towards the meaning and value of religion in society and in the individual's life changed over time. Early in his career he was outspoken in his conviction that religious beliefs and practices were harmful to mental health. In 1980, he wrote a small pamphlet titled *The Case Against Religiosity* in which he defined religious practice as any devout, dogmatic or demanding belief but made a subtle distinction between religious codes of behavior and religiosity, the former often being the oppression of genuine human emotions and feelings while the latter reflect more of a pattern of behavior not unlike what is found in politics and even among fanatics of differing ideologies including atheism. Eager to disassociate his own personal atheism from REBT, he contended that there is nothing in rational therapy which religious professionals and the clergy cannot use in their own counseling practice. Late in life Ellis had a tendency to tone down his outspoken atheism considerably, all the while arguing that his thoughtful form of atheism was most likely the healthiest position to hold in life though acknowledging that some studies have shown that a belief in God (whether he exists or not is irrelevant) can be psychologically nurturing and comforting. Eventually, he would publish two books in which he demonstrated the effective interplay between REBT and the religious establishment as a way of moving forward with therapeutic treatment of the religious person by the religious professional. These two books were *The Road to Tolerance* and *Counseling and Psychotherapy with Religious Persons: A Rational Emotive Behavior Therapy Approach.*

Ellis finally in the 1960s and onward became the darling of American psychotherapy schools and practices and as a result began to glean honors and recognitions for his writings and his clinical work. The American Psychological Association put him in charge of the Division of Consulting Psychology and the Society for the Scientific Study of Sexuality placed him in a leadership role within that professional body. Other organizations followed by honoring him and calling upon his leadership including the American Association of Marital and Family Therapy, the American Academy of Psychotherapists, and the American Association of Sex Educators, Counsellors, and Therapists. Scholarly journals pressed him into service on their editorial boards as well. By the mid-1990s, he had so refined his theory and methodology as to move it more solidly into a category distinctive to his own personal school of thought which he named the Rational Emotive Behavior Therapy (REBT). This REBT refinement, he contended, illustrated by the name itself precisely the scope of the theory and the practice. The aim, he explained, was to emphasize the relatedness of cognition, emotion, and behavior in both theory and therapeutic practice. The 1994 revision of his 1962 classic, *Reason and Emotion in Psychotherapy,* further illustrated this refinement. Throughout the remainder of his life, he continued to emphasize that any psychotherapy designed to foster behavioral change must focus upon the integration and relatedness of cognition, emotion, and behavior.

The passion with which he continued his life's work into his 90s was indicative of his commitment to both the theory and practice of psychotherapy. In 1992, he fell ill at the age of 92 but until that time his common practice was to work 16 hour days including writing his books and articles, seeing his clients, and teaching. Messages of congratulations on his 90th birthday in 2003 were received from such notable figures as President George W. Bush, New York senators Charles Schumer and Hillary Clinton, former President Bill Clinton, New York City Mayor Michael Bloomberg, and the Dalai Lama. His continued demanding work schedule was greatly facilitated by his wife, the Australian psychologist Debbie Joffe Ellis. He died on July 24, 2007, while living in his apartment on the top floor of the Albert Ellis Institute in New York. The author of 80 books and 1,200 scholarly and popular articles, he died at the age of 93. Arguably the highest honor ever awarded Ellis came posthumously by the American Psychological Association in 2013 for "Outstanding Lifetime Contributions to Psychology." Though most of his 80 books included autobiographical elements owing to their use of clinical case studies, two of his last books were more explicitly autobiographical in nature. These two books titled *Rational-Emotive Behavior therapy: It Works for Me – It Can Work for You* (2004) and *All Out!: An Autobiography* (2009) were published by Prometheus Books and the first one focused upon his early life and struggles as a beginning professional psychotherapist and the latter one was a more traditional recitation of his life and work. He once said at 90 years of age: "I'll retire when I'm dead, while I'm alive, I want to keep doing what I want to do. See people. Give workshops. Write and preach the gospel according to St. Albert."

THOUGHT

The mindset of Ellis could not have been more different from Freud in terms of the posture the therapist must take in relationship to the client. Traditional Freudian psychoanalysis was based upon the distance to be maintained between the therapist and the patient even though there was the inevitable "collapse of distance" in the transference/counter-transference phenomenon of which Freud had much to say. Nevertheless, the simple physical positioning of the therapist vis-à-vis the patient – patient reclining on the couch and the therapist sitting in an easy chair at the head and behind the patient – in psychoanalysis is not only classic but indicative of the relationship between the two persons in the counseling session. Subsequent neo-Freudians and post-Freudians would modify or radically alter this posture but at the time Ellis was training and practicing in psychoanalysis this was the standard. Ellis was not pleased with this as he aspired to a more engaging interaction between therapist and client (not patient). Whereas Freud wished to assist the "patient" in embracing their own existential situation through dream analysis and free association, Ellis wanted to help the "client" gain insight into their own worldview in which the agenda was to identify the self-defeating beliefs and ideas which lead to dysfunctional behavior. By correcting or altering these irrational beliefs and ideas, the client may foster more productive and self-affirming behaviors.

Karen Horney and Alfred Adler were two major forces in the development of Ellis's ideas as they informed his delving into behavioral therapies of the time. An "action-oriented" approach to psychotherapy was the goal for Ellis for it fit his experience and his personality. Helping clients manage their own emotions, cognitions, and behaviors constituted the agenda upon which he built his theory and practice. It is not the real world which bothers neurotic people but the way they see the world. The truth of experience is not relevant, explains Ellis, but the perception of truth, that is what affects the way people think and act. In his newly developed school of thought called Rational Emotive Behavioral Therapy, Ellis emphasized that the feelings of people about their situation has everything to do with the way they think about those situations. Irrational beliefs and ideas about the world result in problems affecting behavior. Emotional problems and mental stress can be over-come, Ellis believed based on his own clinical experience, by assisting the client to change the beliefs and negative thought patterns which produce problematic behavior. This way of theory building was the first type of cognitive therapy and constituted the precursor to Aaron T. Beck's now famous Cognitive Behavior Therapy (CBT). The final naming of Ellis's system came in 1992 after having gone through several names to become finally Rational Emotive Behavior Therapy.

Ellis was the consummate teacher and everything he did in the development of the theory and practice of REBT grew out of his desire to be able to teach and train other practitioners in this newly created school of psychotherapy. For example, individuals too often assume that their unhappiness is caused by external situations or events – the bad spouse, the poor job, the mean parent, the ugly environment, etc. Ellis proposed, to the contrary, that it is the individual's "interpretation" of their situation and events which constitutes the true basis for anxiety, mental anguish, emotional stress, and unhappiness. It is how an individual perceives the world, not the way the world is objectively, which determines their assessment of their situation within it. Ellis, therefore as a teacher, developed the ABC model of analysis in which "A" stands for the activating event as in the case of something happening in the environment around the individual; "B" stands for beliefs which characterize the individual belief about what has happened around them; and "C" stands for consequences which essentially represents the individual response to that belief about the external happening.

Having set up the operational grid of the ABC model, Ellis then proceeds to explain how REBT goes about the task of implementation. The basic steps in the REBT are three: First, there must be the identification of the underlying irrational thought patterns and beliefs which had produced emotional distress in the individual. Frequently, these irrational beliefs and ideas are characterized by absolutes such as "I must," "I should," or "I cannot." Common to this sort of irrational belief or idea are such things as the individual being particularly distressed at other people's shortcomings, mistakes, and misbehaviors, or the individual believing that he or she must be completely and thoroughly perfect or competent in everything undertaken of value and worth, or the naïve notion that avoiding difficult and challenging situations will bring happiness, or even that the feeling that the individual has no control over their own happiness because all happiness in a satisfied life depends completely upon external situations and events. For individuals to hold on tightly to these irrational views of the world and their life situation within it makes it impossible for them to respond to these situations in a mature, reasonable, and psychologically healthy manner. These counter-productive ideas and beliefs create an impossible situation where disappointment, recrimination, regret, and anxiety are the only possible result.

However, the second basic step in Ellis's Model is that of challenging these irrational beliefs and ideas about the world and one's situation within it. Ellis was keen to emphasize that simply identifying these irrational beliefs and ideas is not sufficient for mental health. Rather, this is simply the first step for once they have been identified and acknowledged by the individual suffering from mental distress of whatever kind and in whatever form, such as personality disorder or depression or even emotional distress, the next step in this three step process is to confront, challenge, question, engage, debate, argue with them. This is the point at which the therapist must, along with the client if the client is so inclined, to become confrontational in this method of analysis. Here, Ellis and REBT radically depart from traditional psychoanalytic practice. Shocking to some practitioners and disconcerting to others if not down-right off-putting was his insistence that the therapist must at this crucial juncture, once the troublesome beliefs and ideas and thinking patterns have been duly identified, become aggressively confrontational with the client, even blunt and cold blooded in calling these impediments to rational thought what they are, viz., irrational and counter-productive. Change is the goal and change will not come without the client "giving up" some deeply cherished beliefs and ideas and thoughts upon which they may have been relying for years and that to their own detriment.

The third step in this process is that of gaining recognition of and insight into the irrational thought patterns which have been so destructive or counter-productive in the life of the client. There is no question but that this therapeutic methodology is uncomfortable, challenging, even disturbing to the client for it is hard work giving up one's cherished beliefs even when they have finally been seen for what they are, namely, destructive and disempowering. To be called upon to divest one's self of beliefs, ideas, and thoughts which have previously been thought to be not only true and real but nurturing and meaningful in one's life is not easy. Furthermore, to be willing to acknowledge and accept the fact that these same beliefs, ideas, and thoughts are not only wrong but have been the cause of one's own dysfunctional behavior is even more problematic. If the identification of these counter-productive beliefs, ideas, and thought has been difficult, disassociating one's self from them is an even greater and more demanding challenge.

Ellis is quick to point out that his years of clinical experience had taught him that the goal of psychotherapy and, therefore, the goal of the therapist should be to help the client in minimizing their anxiety and hostility to a world which they are not able to control or even sometimes understand clearly. There are tools for fostering these therapeutic goals and he has delineated them in clear and easy to understand terms. There are, he says, at least nine of these goals (and individual therapists may come up with more) which he is committed to nurturing within the client-therapist relationship. He sometimes calls these "personality traits" as equivalent to personal goals for the client as set by the therapist. First is self-interest which insists that the healthy individual has the responsibility first and foremost to be true, honest, and candid to himself and not, as is the tendency of the neurotic person, to masochistically sacrifice himself to others. Treatment of others, kindness and consideration, must be a derivative from within the individual who realizes that freedom from pain and repression can only come by virtue of his willingness to help others realize the same goal. Second, self-direction requires that the individual be responsible for his own life, solving his own problems, assuming accountability for his own decisions, at the same time desiring the collaborative relationship with others without his personal sense of fulfillment being in any way dependent upon that collaboration.

Tolerance, Ellis explains, is a crucial personality trait which requires that the individual must be willing to allow others to be wrong while avoiding the counter-productive danger of judging their behavior to be unacceptable even when their beliefs, ideas, and thoughts are abhorrent to the individual. Acceptance of the fallibility of every person is a step in the right direction of a tolerance which, while not lending even tacit assent to that which is unacceptable, permits there to be an agreement to disagree without being disagreeable. Furthermore, the acceptance of uncertainty in life is a prerequisite for a healthy mental state for life is fraught with uncertainty. It is unrealistic to seek for or to believe in the possibility of certainty in life and that very quest itself bespeaks a neurosis dangerous to mental health. A fifth personality trait needed for mental health is that of flexibility of ideas, situations, thoughts, and circumstances for with change, which is inevitable, flexibility is necessary to maintain a healthy balanced life.

The healthy person must be ready and willing to embrace an objective, rational and scientific view of the world and compliance with the laws of logic and nature as explicated by scientific method. This constitutes the basis for a reasonable view of the world. Commitment, says Ellis, indicates a capacity to concentrate and focus upon what is perceived by the individual as something important, whether it be to a person or to an idea. Often, he explains, this is expressed in creative endeavors whether that be of artistic expression, idea development, or public service. The taking of risks is not the sign of an unstable person but the personal trait of risk-taking often bespeaks a ready willingness to venture into the unknown, to question the unquestionable, to dare go where no one has gone before with ideas and deeds. Finally, Ellis explains, the personality trait of self-acceptance is a key to the balanced healthy person, one who is fully aware of the inequities, the injustices, the fortuitous events in life but one who is willing to "role with the punches," to acknowledge the limits of his own power of interpretation and control over the unwitting events of life. These personality traits, Ellis suggests, are those which the therapist should embody and those to which the therapist drives his client to embrace.

Within the context of his clinical practice and over an extended period of time, Ellis came up with what he considered "five major ideas" which he believed functioned as irrational notions with virtually every seriously disturbed person. One of the persistent characteristics he noticed through his many years of practice was the connection between these notions and religious beliefs. Noted for his strong feelings against religious beliefs and ideologies, Ellis was not disinclined to demonstrate the relationship between mental illness and religious behavior. Let us briefly explore these five irrational notions or ideas which constitute the context for mental illness. The first irrational idea is the belief by the mentally disturbed person that every person must be loved and approved by all significant persons in his life. Ellis believed that this idea is reinforced by the religious notion that if one cannot get this kind of love and approval from his social environment, God is always there to fall back on for this all pervasive love. The very idea that it is possible to live a healthy and meaningful life in the absence of this all-pervading love from one's social relations is, explains Ellis, "foreign to both emotionally disturbed people and religionists."

A second irrational idea which characterizes the mentally ill person is the notion that he must be completely competent and achievement-oriented in all activities. The alternative to this thorough obsession for perfection is a feeling of worthlessness. On the other hand, the religious person argues that one is at liberty to be inadequate just so long as God loves you and you are a member of a church in good standing. The irony here is that the religious person, while not perfect, must put forth effort to be acceptable within the religious community and in the eyes of God! A further irrational notion common to an individual suffering from mental illness is the simplistic idea that some people are wicked and that they should be blamed and punished for their evil behavior. This notion is, of course, specifically endemic to religious faith. A fourth irrational idea is that it is awful and catastrophic when things are not going the way an individual thinks they should be going and, therefore, the only panacea for this frustration is belief in a God who is in control and can make everything right, keeping the frustrated person safe from harm.

The final irrational idea, explains Ellis, in the minds of the mentally ill person is that human unhappiness is caused by outside factors and that people have little or no control over those factors causing the unhappiness or sadness in one's life. Therefore, only by trusting in God and relying upon one's influencing God through prayer (sometimes prayer groups are actually called "prayer Warriors"!) can an individual be able to bear the sorrows and unhappiness which come through living in a sinful world. Ellis believed, then, that there is a close connection between mental illness and religion based on these five irrational ideas or notions he experienced in the lives of his clients through clinical practice. In making his case, he suggested (to the horror of some of his professional colleagues) that neurosis is quite frequently and simply an elevated name for childishness and debilitating dependency on someone or something outside the individual's own capacity to cope. With Freud, he was content with concluding that at the end of the day religion is simply neurosis however sophisticated it might be portrayed through the traditions of its practitioners. This connectedness of religion and neurosis is evidenced in the irrational beliefs and ideas of its adherents. Both religion and neurosis keep the individual susceptible to such notions by being both dependent as well as griped by anxiety and fear. Here, Ellis is eager to distance himself from the likes of Jungian analysts as well as the client-centered and existentialist therapists who are unwilling to dislodge the neurotic person from his irrational ideas. On the contrary, Ellis argues that it is precisely the therapists responsibility to assist the client in identifying the irrational nature of such notions and then to alter one's behavior in relationship to those notions. Assisting an individual to live comfortably with their irrational beliefs, explains Ellis, is tantamount to irresponsible psychotherapeutic practice.

The Albert Ellis Study

Comparing his rational psychotherapy to the psychoanalytic psychotherapy of such practitioners as Karen Horney and Melanie Klein in an empirical study he conducted in 1957, Ellis was able to demonstrate to his clients that strong negative feelings such as anger, depression, anxiety, or guilt are not cured by merely exploring deeply the inner workings of the unconscious through dream analysis and free association as done by the psychoanalysts. On the contrary, these feelings of distress are themselves the product of situational contextualization of the individual's irrational beliefs and notions about those situations. Whereas psychoanalysis proposes that negative emotions and counter-productive behavior arise from conflicts deep within the psyche spawned by childhood experiences and fantasies requiring a kind of psychological archaeology of the unconscious mind to divulge the source and cause of mental distress, the truth of the matter is the assessment of the individual's perceptions of his life situation constitutes the basis for potential mental health. Mental health is the result of a careful reconfiguration of the individual's perception and assessment of these irrational notions and ideas.

Change the perception and mental health is close at hand, explains Ellis.

Ellis was keen to demonstrate that the results of his newly created therapeutic approach to mental illness were scientifically constructed and, therefore, empirical evidence could be gleaned from his findings. Not that every practicing psychotherapist then or now is concerned about the strict "scientific" character of their practice or the capability of measuring the results, but Ellis was, like Freud, obsessed with the conviction that quantifiable data could be gathered to confirm his REBT's effectiveness in the counseling arena. He used his own client base as the pool from which data was gleaned. Three groupings of two primary clusters of clients constituted the total composite and each one contained seventy-eight clients closely matched as to the diagnosis of their disorder in terms of age, sex, and education. Thirty-five sessions were given to each client and they were sorted into those who were to receive psychoanalytic psychotherapy and those who were treated with rational psychotherapy. A third group consisted of sixteen clients who were treated in ninety-three sessions with classical orthodox psychoanalysis. What made Ellis's study strongly convincing was the fact that he was a trained psychoanalyst in the traditional sense well before establishing his own rationalist school of psychotherapy. Therefore, he could hardly be criticized for "not knowing his stuff!"

All of the treatment for all three groupings was provided by Ellis himself and in that way he was certain of the consistency of treatment using each of the three distinct psychotherapeutic methods being tested. Each client in each group was ranked according to whether or not there was (a) little or no progress, (b) some measurable improvement, or (c) considerable improvement. Not surprising either to himself or those who both embraced his rationalist approach and those who did not was the fact that he concluded that the therapeutic results of this massive quantitative study confirmed the effectiveness of rational analysis over that of the other psychoanalytically oriented therapies. The actual measurement in terms of percentages of improvement were 90% for rational psychotherapy, 63% for psychoanalytically oriented psychotherapy, and 50% for orthodox psychoanalysis. And this, he emphasized, was based on psychoanalytic therapy being administered three times more frequently than that of the rationalist therapy. Though many were not pleased with his study or with his findings, few would argue persuasively that the methodology was not scientifically sound and the findings empirically verified and verifiable. Ellis was applauded by the psychological community throughout the profession for this first of its kind data base study of results from psychotherapeutic treatment. Evidence-based studies are now normative but at this time his was a first.

CONCLUDING REMARKS

Albert Ellis was considered by most professionals during his long life to be the most important and most celebrated psychologist in the U.S. His innovative and creatively constructed Rational Emotive Behavior Therapy brought about a paradigm shift in the way counseling was to occur in the psychotherapeutic setting. The grandfather, if you will, of all of the subsequently generated cognitive behavioral therapies, Ellis is given credit even by Aaron Beck for prodding himself towards the development of Beck's Cognitive Behavior Therapy which today is the most utilized and professionally validated system of counseling in the U.S. Ellis shifted away from Freud's fascination with the unconscious and away from B. F. Skinner's obsession with measurable behavioral response towards what Ellis believed to be the tripartite matrix of mental health – cognition, emotion, and behavior. To interface "action and idea" was a shift in the concept of therapy and Ellis was at the forefront of this shift. For Ellis, the therapist's responsibility is to assist the client in changing his self-defeating beliefs and ideas about the world he perceives to be fraught with distress, anxiety, and danger, and towards a reconstituted world of ideas, thoughts, and action based on a self-affirming view of the world. Divesting oneself of such self-defeating beliefs as "I must be perfect" and "I must be loved by everyone" constitutes the beginning of the road to mental health. The client, Ellis says, must analyze his own beliefs and notions about the world, identify and acknowledge the irrational ones, and then construct a more rational configuration of these ideas and beliefs designed to remove fear and anxiety and to foster self-actualization.

The Albert Ellis Institute in New York City became a monument to his genius, and the American Psychological Association recognized that genius in 1985 by recognizing his "distinguished professional contributions" to the field of psychology, the highest award the APA can present to a member of the Association. The founder of Cognitive Behavior Therapy, Aaron T. Beck, said of Ellis: "I believe he's a major icon of the twentieth century and that he did help to open up a whole new era of psychotherapy." Acclaimed the second most important psychotherapist in North America after Carl Rogers and immediately preceding Sigmund Freud himself who ranked third, Albert Ellis is still today recognized as the creator of a school of psychotherapy which is responsible for having moved the profession beyond both behaviorism and psychoanalysis, beyond B. F. Skinner and Sigmund Freud. After Ellis' death, Robert O'Connell, Executive Director of Albert Ellis Institute, noted: "We all owe a great debt to Dr. Ellis. His students and clients will remember him for his tremendous insight and dedication as a psychotherapist. His innovations in the field will continue to influence the practice of psychotherapy for decades to come, and the institute he founded will continue to provide outstanding professional education programs and treatment based on the principles of REBT which he originated."

BIBLIOGRAPHY

ALBERT ELLIS' PRIMARY SOURCES

The Folklore of Sex, Oxford, England: Charles Boni, 1951.

Sex Beliefs and Customs, London: Peter Nevill, 1952.

The Homosexual in America: A Subjective Approach (introduction). NY: Greenberg, 1951.

The American Sexual Tragedy. NY: Twayne, 1954.

Sex Life of the American woman and the Kinsey Report. Oxford, England: Greenberg, 1954.

The Psychology of Sex Offenders. Springfield, IL: Thomas, 1956.

How To Live with a Neurotic. Oxford, England: Crown Publishers, 1957.

Sex Without Guilt. NY: Hillman, 1958.

The Art and Science of Love. NY: Lyle Stuart, 1960.

A Guide to Successful Marriage, with Robert A. Harper. North Hollywood, CA: Wilshire Book, 1961.

Creative Marriage, with Robert A. Harper. NY: Lyle Stuart, 1961.

The Encyclopedia of Sexual Behavior, edited with Albert Abarbanel. NY: Hawthorn, 1961.

The American Sexual Tragedy, 2nd Ed. rev. NY: Lyle Stuart, 1962.

Reason and Emotion in Psychotherapy. NY: Lyle Stuart, 1962.

Sex and the Single Man. NY: Lyle Stuart, 1963.

If This Be Sexual Heresy. NY: Lyle Stuart, 1963.

Nymphomania: A Study of the Oversexed Woman, with Edward Sagarin. NY: Gilbert Press, 1964.

Homosexuality: Its causes and Cures. NY: Lyle Stuart, 1965.

The Art of Erotic Seduction, with Roger Conway. NY: Lyle Stuart, 1967.

Is Objectivism a Religion?. NY: Lyle Stuart, 1968.

Murder and Assassination, with John M. Gullo. NY: Lyle Stuart, 1971.

A Guide to Rational Living. Englewood Cliffs, N.J., Prentice-Hall, 1961.

Humanistic Psychotherapy, NY McGraw, 1974 Sagarin ed.

A New Guide to Rational Living. Wilshire Book Company, 1975.

Anger: How to Live With and Without It. Secaucus, NJ: Citadel Press, 1977.

Handbook of Rational-Emotive Therapy, with Russell Greiger & contributors. NY: Springer Publishing, 1977.

Overcoming Procrastination: Or How to Think and Act Rationally in Spite of Life's Inevitable Hassles, with William J. Knaus. Institute for Rational Living, 1977.

How to Live With a Neurotic. Wilshire Book Company, 1979.

Overcoming Resistance: Rational-Emotive Therapy With Difficult Clients. NY: Springer Publishing, 1985.

When AA Doesn't Work For You: Rational Steps to Quitting Alcohol, with Emmett Velten. Barricade Books, 1992.

The Art and Science of Rational Eating, with Mike Abrams and Lidia Abrams. Barricade Books, 1992.

How to Cope with a Fatal Illness, with Mike Abrams. Barricade Books, 1994. *Reason and Emotion in Psychotherapy, Revised and Updated*. Secaucus, NJ: Carol Publishing Group, 1994.

How to Keep People from Pushing Your Buttons, with Arthur Lange. Citadel Press, 1995.

Alcohol: How to Give It Up and Be Glad You Did, with Philip Tate Ph.D. See Sharp Press, 1996.

How to Control Your Anger Before It Controls You, with Raymond Chip Tafrate. Citadel Press, 1998.

Optimal Aging: Get Over Getting Older, with Emmett Velten. Chicago, Open Court Press, 1998.

How to Stubbornly Refuse to Make Yourself Miserable About Anything: Yes, Anything", Lyle Stuart, 2000,

Making Intimate Connections: Seven Guidelines for Great Relationships and Better Communication, with Ted Crawford. Impact Publishers, 2000.

The Secret of Overcoming Verbal Abuse: Getting Off the Emotional Roller Coaster and Regaining Control of Your Life, with Marcia Grad Powers. Wilshire Book Company, 2000.

Counseling and Psychotherapy With Religious Persons: A Rational Emotive Behavior Therapy Approach, with Stevan Lars Nielsen and W. Brad Johnson. Mahwah, NJ: Lawrence Erlbaum Associates, 2001.

Overcoming Destructive Beliefs, Feelings, and Behaviors: New Directions for Rational Emotive Behavior Therapy. Prometheus Books, 2001.

Feeling Better, Getting Better, Staying Better: Profound Self-Help Therapy For Your Emotions. Impact Publishers, 2001.

Case Studies in Rational Emotive Behavior Therapy With Children and Adolescents, with Jerry Wilde. Upper Saddle River, NJ: Merrill/Prentice Hall, 2002.

Overcoming Resistance: A Rational Emotive Behavior Therapy Integrated Approach, 2nd ed. NY: Springer Publishing, 2002.

Ask Albert Ellis: Straight Answers and Sound Advice from America's Best-Known Psychologist. Impact Publishers, 2003.

Sex Without Guilt in the 21st Century. Barricade Books, 2003.

Dating, Mating, and Relating. How to Build a Healthy Relationship, with Robert A. Harper. Citadel Press Books, 2003.

Rational Emotive Behavior Therapy: It Works For Me—It Can Work For You. Prometheus Books, 2004.

The Road to Tolerance: The Philosophy of Rational Emotive Behavior Therapy. Prometheus Books, 2004.

The Myth of Self-Esteem. Prometheus Books, 2005.

Rational Emotive Behavior Therapy: A Therapist's Guide (2nd Edition), with Catharine MacLaren. Impact Publishers, 2005.

How to Make Yourself Happy and Remarkably Less Disturbable. Impact Publishers, 1999.

Rational Emotive Behavioral Approaches to Childhood Disorders • Theory, Practice and Research 2nd Edition. With Michael E. Bernard (Eds.). Springer SBM, 2006.

Growth Through Reason: Verbatim Cases in Rational-Emotive Therapy Science and Behavior Books. Palo Alto, California. 1971.

All Out!. Prometheus Books, 2009.

Rational Emotive Behavior Therapy, American Psychological Association.

How to Master Your Fear of Flying. Institute Rational Emotive Therapy, 1977.

How to Control you Anxiety before it Controls you. Citadel Press, 2000.

Are Capitalism, Objectivism, And Libertarianism Religions? Yes!: Greenspan And Ayn Rand Debunked. CreateSpace Independent Publishing Platform, 2007.

Theories of Personality: Critical Perspectives, with Mike Abrams, PhD, and Lidia Abrams, PhD. New York: Sage Press, 7/2008 (This was his final work, published posthumously).

SECONDARY SOURCES

Emmett Velten. *Under the Influence: Reflections of Albert Ellis in the Work of Others*. See Sharp Press, 2007.

Emmett Velten. *Albert Ellis: American Revolutionary*. See Sharp Press, 2009.

Joseph Yankura and Windy Dryden. *Albert Ellis (Key Figures in Counselling and Psychotherapy series)*. Sage Publications, 1994.

CHAPTER FIFTEEN
Thomas Szasz and the Social Critique of Psychiatric Practice

INTRODUCTION

In some ways it is ironic that in a book on the modern schools of psychotherapy that there would be the inclusion of a research medical scholar who has spent his entire professional life challenging and questioning the viability, the authenticity, the actual integrity of the practice of both psychiatry and psychotherapy. The only justification for taking time to consider the life and work of Thomas Szasz is that in all honesty to not be willing to hear and consider the criticism of a respected critic of this field of mental health would be less than professionally responsible. Whether one decides to accept some or all of Szasz's criticisms of this branch of health care or not, to be unwilling to hear the delineation of the criticisms would indicate a bias and prejudice unworthy of those who have gone before, the classicists, and those whose systems of thought and practice, the moderns, are still very much in use. Let us consider Szasz and his criticism of psychiatric practice.

The fundamental starting point in Szasz's work is that the mental illnesses delineated by the psychiatric and psychotherapeutic communities are not really illnesses at all in the same way such things as pneumonia or cancer are real. His position is that there are no verifiable texts or analytical mechanisms to identify and label mental illnesses which are psychogenic in nature, those listed for example in the *Diagnostic Statistical Manual* (DSM) of the American Psychiatric Association. Those very few biogenically verifiable diseases of the brain such as Alzheimer's disease constitute the exception to this general claim. Szasz has been a respected professor of psychiatry at the State University of New York Upstate Medical University in Syracuse for many years with a distinguished medical, clinical, and publishing career well established. His criticism of the moral and scientific basis for the profession of psychiatry has caused him to be an international figure and of his many books, *The Myth of Mental Illness* (1961) and *The Manufacture of Madness* (1970) constitute major contributions to the on-going discussion and debate about the legitimacy of both psychiatry and psychotherapy as practiced in the U.S.

Szasz's scathing criticism of the misuses of psychiatric incarceration, for example, has won him a great deal of attention and in my liberal circles much respect for his outspoken defense of the rights of individuals who have been, rightly or wrongly, diagnosed with mental illness which has precipitated their seclusion and forced treatment for so-called mental disorders. He believes, and has written many books defending his position as a psychiatrist and respected member of the medical community, that every individual has the natural right to what he calls "self-ownership" and that right includes freedom from violence in medical practice. Such things as suicide, the practice of medicine, the use and sale of drugs and sexual relations all should be private, contractual, and legal. These stands on the social issues affecting the lives of many if not most Americans earned him the 1973 American Humanist Association designation as Humanist of the Year and in 1979 he was honored with an honorary doctorate in behavioral science at the Francisco Marroquín University, a private, secular university in Guatemala City, Guatemala.

BIOGRAPHY

Thomas Szasz was born April 15, 1920, in Budapest, Hungary, into a comfortably well-off secular Jewish family, the younger of two sons with a brother named George. His father, Gyula, was a successful attorney practicing law in Budapest and the family passion, encouraged by his mother Lily Wellisch, was education and science. George, according to Thomas Szasz, was a "wunderkind" and became in adulthood a successful organic chemist who made his home in Zurich. As a youngster, Thomas studied at the local gymnasium in Budapest and distinguished himself at tennis. Even as a young student, he was concerned that jails and psychiatric institutions were two places in which people went but never came out. Owing to the rising anti-Semitism in Europe and with the encouragement of friends and family, the Szasz's moved to the United States in 1938 where fortunately Thomas was able to attend the University of Cincinnati from which he earned his Bachelor of Science followed by the Doctor of Medicine in 1944. After completing his residency at Cincinnati General Hospital, he then worked from 1951 to 1956 at the Chicago Institute for Psychoanalysis followed by five more years as a member of staff (with two years off for military duty in the U.S. Naval Reserve). Joining the State University of New York in 1956, he was tenured there in 1962. In 1990 he was named Professor Emeritus of Psychiatry at the State University of New York Health Science Center in Syracuse, New York.

As early as 1958, Szasz began his criticism of the field of psychiatry, challenging what is referred to as "mental illness." In the *Columbia Law Review* issue that year he contended that mental illness was simply as irrelevant and meaningless as a suspect's guilt of devil possession. Never veering from the exaggerated metaphor, Szasz in 1961 testified before the U.S. Senate Committee on mental health practices that the use of mental hospitals for the purpose of incarceration of the diagnosed patient suffering from a mental disorder was a blatant violation of the patient-doctor relationship and as a result reduced the physician to that of a prison warden. Szasz was called before this influential committee owing already to his national reputation as a critic of psychiatry and owing to the tremendous popularity of his 1960 book titled *The Myth of Mental Illness*. His wife Rosine died in 1971 with whom he had two daughters, Margot and Suzy, the one becoming a physician and the other a journalist.

Critical of what he called "the Therapeutic State," Szasz went on the offensive in his fight against what he thought of as the misuse of medical practice as relates to those who have been by the medical community diagnosed and labelled as mentally ill. He was particularly eager to launch an attack upon the misuse of medical science in applying its influence to such things as addiction, suicide and homosexuality as constituting a misuse and even abuse of the power and influence of the medical community in America. He argued that by allowing the medical community to label, arbitrarily it seemed to him, certain behavior as mental illness or indications of mental instability, that very step empowered the medical community to dictate morality to the general public. Szasz's attack on psychiatry's invention of homosexuality as a disease was congruent with the rise of gay activism in the 1970s leading to the removal of homosexuality from the DSM III in 1974, i.e., the *Diagnostic and Statistical Manual* published by the American Psychiatric Association.

Szasz's 1960 book on the myth of mental illness came at a particularly vulnerable time for psychiatry for Freudian psychoanalysis was beginning to drift to the sidelines as other psychotherapies began to gain attention and respect. These new schools of psychotherapy were aspiring to be more "medical" and, therefore, to employ more empirically based methodologies thereby validating their so-called findings, according to Szasz. Psychiatry, he believed, was a dubious medical field akin to alchemy and astrology and he did not refrain from saying so in very high and lofty circles through his publications and extensive lecturing circuit. This first major book of his, of which he subsequently wrote over twenty-five more, became a sort of resource for the disenchanted public consumers of psychiatric medicine.

Szasz fought against all forms of coercive treatments including involuntary confinement which was particularly anathema in his criticism. Furthermore, he railed against the use of psychiatric diagnoses in the courts of the land considering such a practice to be both unscientific as well as unethical. His reputation found him associated with such international figures of medical criticism as the Canadian sociologist Erving Goffman (who seriously challenged the "labeling" of what was unfortunately called within the academy "abnormal behavior") as well as with Michel Foucault, the French philosopher. Szasz's outspoken reputation earned him the characterization as "the biggest of the antipsychiatry intellectuals." Never satisfied with the international attention he was getting, he pressed on with his attacks and eventually he wrote hundreds of articles and more than 30 books, including *Ideology and Insanity: Essays on the Psychiatric Dehumanization of Man* (1970) and *Psychiatric Slavery: When Confinement and Coercion Masquerade as* Cure (1977), two of his three books to become best sellers.

Of course, everything did not always run smoothly nor in his favor as the psychiatric community specifically and the medical community generally were both aggravated at his persistence and troubled by the criticism. In the 1960s, for example, he was barred from teaching at a state training hospital in New York in spite of his protests to this stifling of his criticism of the profession of which he was one of the most nationally recognized members. Many professionals felt conflicted about Szasz's work for, as Dr. E. Fuller Torrey, founder of the Treatment Advocacy Center in Arlington, VA, once pointed out, he was too extreme in his public denunciation of much of the mental health community's treatment but his criticism did call attention to abuses and misuses of psychiatry both inside and outside the medical institutions of the country. Szasz was honored with over fifty prestigious awards including the Award for Greatest Public Service Benefiting the Disadvantaged, an award given out annually by the Jefferson Awards (1974); the *Martin Buber Award* (1974); the *Humanist Laureate Award* (1995); the Great Lake Association of Clinical Medicine *Patients' Rights Advocate Award* (1995); and the American Psychological Association *Rollo May Award* (1998). At the age of 92, he died from a fall in his home in New York, on September 8, 2012.

THOUGHT

Thomas Szasz was the first major member of the psychiatric profession to challenge the abuses and misuses of psychiatry and he did so with persistence, tenacity, and with aggressive assaults upon the very core of that branch of medical practice. He was convinced of the "metaphorical character" of mental illness and what troubled him, and he did not bother keeping it a secret, was the personal injuries emotionally done to patients through psychiatric treatments as well as the blatant immorality of coercions employed by psychiatric incarcerations. The delegitimization of those private, state, and federal agencies which wielded authority over individuals diagnosed as mentally ill or mentally unstable or even mentally insane was his driving agenda. The misuse of the great power vested in the mental health laws of the land as well as rulings by the civil courts in cases related to individuals diagnosed by psychiatry as mentally ill troubled him greatly. He was no novice having studied psychiatry and practiced psychiatry in extremely respected institutions. He was a veteran and many in the medical community supported his concerns while others fled from his heavy-handed methods.

He was more than a psychiatrist. He was a social critic, even a social philosopher and sociologist. He was greatly troubled by the inordinate influence the medical community was gleaning to itself over secular society, calling the practice of modern medicine the secular alternative to religion. Secular society, he complained, had become obsessed with eternal life and expected the medical community to provide the means for such. He challenged the intrusiveness of medical practice into the private lives of individuals employing medical images and metaphors and esoteric nomenclature to shore up the medical practitioner's reputation, particularly in the field of mental illness. The labeling of certain forms of behavior became the agenda of the psychiatric community and by labeling a particular behavioral matrix as "abnormal" or "deviant" or even "dysfunctional," power accrued to the practitioner who could diagnose and prescribe treatment for these labeled behaviors. His attack upon the politicization of mental health treatment and the resulting influence gleaned from the general public for their own professional uses made medicine a perpetrator of a kind of religious faith in science, particularly medical science. On one occasion he compared "pharmacracy," or the rule of medicine, with democracy (the rule of the people) and theocracy (the rule of God).

Szasz was a word smith or a master at creating nomenclature to highlight or emphasize his concerns, such as the creation of the word "pharmacracy" to make his point about the dominance of medicine over society. For example, he suggested that the use of the expression "mental illness" is a metaphorical term describing behavior which is offensive, or disturbing, shocking, or troublesome in terms of conduct or a pattern of behavior, such as schizophrenia, and thus is labeled a "mental illness" not unlike the labeling of a disease such as small pox. Humorously, Szasz suggests, by way of illustration, "If you talk to God, you are praying; if God talks to you, you have schizophrenia." The foundation of Szasz's criticism of psychiatric treatment of a set of behaviors has to do with the distinction he makes between having a disease and engaging in a variant behavioral matrix. A disease is something someone actually "has" where as a behavior is something someone actually "does." The difference between having and doing is profoundly important in this debate about whether or not mental illness is real and can be diagnosed and treated.

Whereas medical science has taught us that a disease is characterized as a malfunction of the human body such as the heart or liver or kidney or even the brain, there is, however, no behavior as such, whether functional or dysfunctional, which can fairly and scientifically be characterized as a disease. The danger of permitting psychiatry to traffic in the language of diseases is the empowerment of a medical practice which is permitted to resend individual rights by denying the patient the responsibility of self-expression and freedom of movement. Forced incarceration of an individual who has been diagnosed by the psychiatric community as suffering from mental illness results in ease of constraint and management by the attending medical personnel but at the expense of individual rights of expression and movement on the part of the labeled individual. This, Szasz says, is all predicated upon a behavioral matrix being inappropriately defined as a disease.

What troubles Szasz about the diagnostics of psychiatric practice has to do with the arbitrariness of the labeling for whereas a legitimately identified biogenically induced disease can be diagnosed using scientifically validated and approved procedures, diagnosing "mental illness" or even worse a "mental disorder" (what Szasz enjoys calling a "weasel term" for mental illness) is at best a professional "judgment" employed by the psychiatric community in consort with, if not professionally complicit with, the labeling function of the American Psychiatric Association's guidebook called the *Diagnostic and Statistical Manual*. The greatest offender in the "disease" category of mental illness is that of schizophrenia because, as Szasz is quick to point out, it constitutes the "sacred symbol of psychiatry" in that it has provided, and continues to do so, professional justification for the perpetuation of a plethora of psychiatric theories, treatments, abuses, and reforms! Szasz is so exercised by what he considers in this specific instance as gross incompetence and blatant professional neglect that he suggested that the image of a psychotic or schizophrenic person (so labelled by the profession) is somewhat analogous to the heretic or blasphemer to theologians of the Church.

Eager to demonstrate how scientific method itself is responsible for the indictment of psychiatry as a pseudo-science, Szasz gives the prescription for what a disease is in medical terms, viz., to truly be a disease, he explains, the thing being observed must have the capacity of being approached, measured, or tested in scientific fashion as well as then being able to demonstrate a pathology at the cellular or molecular level. Short of that, there is no disease even if there is an aberrant matrix of behavior or biological function. Most certainly evidence of a truly verifiable disease must be found on the autopsy table meeting a pathological definition rather than only being found in the living person and receiving a vote by members of the American Psychiatric Association. A consensus vote does not constitute good medical diagnosis whereas an autopsy does without question. At his most visceral, Szasz has claimed that "psychiatry is a pseudo-science that parodies medicine by using medical sounding words invented over the last 100 years." To confuse a heart break with a heart attack or spring fever with typhoid fever constitutes a categorical error in classification and treating one for the other is essentially the practice of voodoo. Psychiatrists, concludes Szasz, are essentially the last vestiges of the "soul doctors" of traditional societies who have historically dealt with spiritual conundrums, dilemmas, and vexations brought on by life itself. They are not really medical practitioners. Psychiatry, thanks to various state and federal sponsorships through funded medical legislation, has become in his term "a modern secular state religion" operating illegitimately under the flag of legitimate medical practice by having labeled its "treatment" with "medical terminology."

It is somewhat surprising to see a distinguished psychiatrist such as Thomas Szasz manifest such suspicions of the mentally ill diagnosis, so called. Mental illness, as we have been seeing throughout this discussion, is a topic about which Szasz has strong opinions and his readiness to discount claims of mental illness by the patient and claims of treating mental illness by the psychiatric community are well known. Szasz has gone so far as to suggest that much of what goes under the heading of mental illness is not much more than an individual's "malingering," the so-called patient having something in his life which is bothering him or causing some problem in living becomes in the modern day with psychiatric encouragement a health malady called mental illness. These "feelings" of whatever short, be they depression, anxiety, fear, or anger, have all been appropriately allocated medical descriptions in the DSM guidebook so that the individual sufferer, the physician, the psychiatrist, and the insurance company are all able to label the malady and treat it as an illness, a real illness with all of the appropriate accolades of description. Much of this, argues Szasz, constitutes a sham conspiracy against the individual, the medical profession, and the insurance companies!

The whole argument of Szasz is that a scenario of labeling, diagnosing, and treating behaviors which have been arbitrarily labeled mental illness have empowered both the medical community and the government, state and federal, to intervene in the care and treatment of individuals by prescribing the parameters within which the individual as patient may be treated, going so far as to limit access to medication and the prescribing of detention if deemed relevant or necessary. Believing mental illness as a medically validated label implying the need for medical intervention to be only a "euphemism for behaviors that are disapproved of," says Szasz, then the state and federal government should have no right to interfere in the patient-doctor relation nor should it have the right, which it presently does, of dictating treatment for such individuals including their incarceration in a mental detention facility "for their own good." In these circumstances, it seems that government has the right to dictate medical procedures as well as limitations on medications, types and dosages of medications, and restrictions on usage. The "medicalization of government," explains Szasz, leads inevitably to the Therapeutic State, implying that the government essentially has the right to determine who is to be judged "insane" or "an addict."

In 1973 Szasz published a book titled *Ceremonial Chemistry* which caused a great debate within the psychiatric community and in the general public as well. Here he argued that the methods of persecution employed over the centuries against Jews, witches, Gypsies, and even homosexuals are the same methods now being employed against drug addicts and so-called insane people. These persecutions, he contended, were the continuation of religious ideologies into the medical community, using medicine to punish what religion once did but is no longer validated by the government to do. Medicine has then become the arm of the Church as well as the government to enforce its own ideas of morality and "right behavior." Szasz was particularly keen to bring this argument to a discussion of suicide for, using the analogy of birth control, he argued that individuals should be able to determine when and how they are to die without interference from either the medical community or the government just like the decision of an individual to conceive is exempt from both the doctor and the law. Suicide, Szasz contended, was one of the most fundamental rights of an individual living in a free society and he went so far as to argue that the government should have no say in this very personal decision, not even legally sanctioning it. As with conception, so with suicide, both the medical community and the government should not be considered a legitimate component of the decision-making process.

Pressing his argument for independence from Church and government as well as from the prying eyes and interventionist practice of medicine, Szasz believed that addictions of whatever sort should not be classified as a "disease" to be cured through legal drugs but rather should be assessed as a "social habit." He proposed a free-market approach to drugs, calling the war on drugs essentially a victimless crime and suggesting that the prohibition on free-access to drugs of choice by the consumer constituted the real crime. We learned nothing from Prohibition, he argues, since prohibiting behavior merely makes that behavior more expensive and does not lead to its disappearance from society. People will drink. To make it illegal simply creates the opportunity for organized crime to take over, jack up the price of the prohibited product, and generate crimes such as theft for the securing of the funds to purchase the over-priced product which, were it not illegal, would be easily affordable by the average citizen who wishes to exercise his freedom of purchase. Szasz favored essentially the repeal of all drug prohibitions, leaving the decision to individuals exercising their democratic right of personal choice. If, then, a crime is committed, punish the crime, not the choice made freely by the individual. Crime is perpetrated by the government by having placed restrictions on certain products which, were those restrictions non-existent, the crime would not occur. Let the free citizen decide what he will do with his life and if he commits a crime because of a bad choice, punish the crime, not the exercise of free choice. This was Szasz's argument put succinctly.

As early as 1963, Szasz was using the term "Therapeutic State" to characterize the present situation in America where there appears to be a linkage between psychiatric practice and government legislation. This collaboration, he contends, leads to this Therapeutic State in which certain behaviors and emotions are "cured" through proper medical intervention or what Szasz has chosen to call "pseudo-medical intervention." The Therapeutic State has now determined that such behaviors as suicide, unconventional religious beliefs and practices, racial bigotry, unhappiness, anxiety, shyness, sexual promiscuity, shoplifting, gambling, overeating, smoking, and illegal drug use are all illnesses which are in desperate need of being cured, explains Szasz. Therefore, the medical community, having defined these as illnesses, is now ready with treatment to address these illnesses with psychiatrically-validated labels, diagnostics, and treatment plans. Once, Szasz observes, the theological state assumed comprehensive responsibility and jurisdiction for all forms of human behavior with its God-given right to punish and reward according to its own understanding of Divine Will. These days, the Therapeutic State has assumed that role on behalf of health and medicine, using the medical practitioner as the priest in charge of enforcement. Since nothing falls outside the domain of God, nothing, then, in an earlier time could fall outside the domain of the theological judicatories. These days, that same proprietorial posture towards the individual and society is assumed by the medical community. Alas, everything then falls into the categories of health and illness, determined by the priests of medicine and their governmental enforcers, the makers of laws. Just as the U.S. constitution has placed a brick wall between the

Church and State, Szasz believes that a similarly strong and power wall must be built between psychiatry and the State.

Szasz's 1961 classic, *The Myth of Mental Illness,* gained him international recognition and earned him the admiration of many and the disdain of his professional colleagues in psychiatric practice. His initial interest in writing on this topic began as early as 1950 when, after being licensed in the practice of psychiatry, he became increasingly convinced, based on his own clinical practice and his work in psychiatric hospitals, that the concept of "mental illness" was ambiguous, non-scientific, and fraught with potential misuse. Beginning to write the book in 1954, upon being called to active duty in the military thereby freeing him of the pressures and demands of his private medical practice, he found after completing the draft of the book that finding a publisher willing to take on such a topic was not going to be easy. Finally, in 1961, the book was released by Harper and Brothers in New York and it soon became a best seller. For the first but far from the last time, Szasz benefited financially from his medical writings.

In the book, Szasz challenged the practice of the psychiatric community of labeling individuals as mentally ill merely on the basis of their being "disabled by living." Psychological problems are not diseases or illnesses, he argued, and that by calling them mental illness constitutes a breakdown in logic and leads to a conceptual as well as a perceptual error, both on the part of the general public which easily accepts medical labeling as a given as well as the medical and particularly the psychiatric community which eagerly employs medical terminology. The use of the terms mental illness to apply to psychological problems constitutes an inappropriate metaphor for, in his view, there are no diseases of the mind (though there may be brain damages from injury or biogenic dysfunctions). Szasz was not a politician and he chose not ever to develop politically-correct methods of communicating his message. He questioned openly and outspokenly the legitimacy of the field of psychiatry using such descriptive terms as alchemy and astrology as analogies to psychiatry. He discounted the meaning and value of the concept of "mental illness," calling it harmful because it is misleading. Rather than treating instances of ethical or legal deviations from the acceptable norm as illnesses needing curing, by using for example tranquilizers and psychotropic drugs, psychotherapy, on the other hand, is regarded by Szasz as useful in helping people learn about themselves and how to live in the world.

The distinction made by Szasz between psychiatry, the pseudo-medical practice of treating unacceptable behaviors as mental illness, and psychotherapy, the counseling practice of assisting people in understanding themselves and their relationship to their social environment, constituted a major contribution which, alas, was too easily overlooked by the general public (Are not, then, psychiatry and psychotherapy the same thing? they may ask.) and intentionally disregarded by the psychiatric community for its own survival. The psychotherapeutic communities all chose to distance themselves entirely from the controversy about the legitimacy of medicine in the treatment of what psychiatry choses to call "mental illness." Shortly after Harper and Brothers published the book in 1961, the Commissioner of the New York State Department of Mental Hygiene demanded that Szasz be dismissed from his university position. The University refused and Szasz stayed on to retirement in 1990, being made emeritus professor as well. Wrongly accused of being a member and spokesperson for the anti-psychiatry movement of the 1960s and 1970s, Szasz is not opposed to the practice of psychiatry for he himself is a psychiatrist and a practitioner of that medical specialty. Psychiatry, he contends, should constitute a contractual agreement between consenting adults and the medical practitioners without governmental intervention or involvement. He did, however, believe and said so in 2006 in a documentary film titled *Psychiatry: An Industry of Death* that involuntary mental hospitalization is a crime against humanity.

Before we take a look at Szasz's arguments against the misuse of psychiatry as articulated by the psychiatric community itself, let us give a brief summary of his two major points of criticism. They consist of (1)the myth of mental illness, and (2) the separation of psychiatry and the government. These are the two fundamental ingredients in his long-standing criticism of the profession of psychiatry. As we have been saying, mental illness is a ludicrous concept according to Szasz because it functions merely as a metaphor for aberrant behavior matrices such as anxiety, depression, fear, and loss of self-esteem all of which are behavioral characteristics of an individual. They are not a disease or an illness for they are not biogenic but psychogenic (excepting in rare cases of biogenic imbalances in the body or due to physical injury). Szasz accuses psychiatry of actively obscuring the distinction between misbehavior (or aberrant behavior to be more generous) and disease. By calling a person mentally ill, as does psychiatry, the responsibility and accountability of the individual is divested from that individual and invested in a medical treatment plan. In psychotherapy, on the other hand, the responsibility and accountability of the individual's behavior rests with the individual.

This medical labeling of an individual's behavior also creates an environment within which the government becomes involved as a collaborator with the psychiatric community in stripping the diagnosed patient labelled mentally ill of his personal rights and freedoms. Szasz argues, for example, that drug addiction is not a "disease" to be cured by the use of legal drugs (sometimes equally addictive) but constitutes what he calls a "social habit." He believes in a drug free-market, allowing the consumer to decide for himself what and when, if at all, he wishes to use drugs of his own choice. Szasz would make all drug access an over-the-counter relationship between the individual and the pharmacy. Just as with alcohol or with tobacco, if the individual user is involved in committing a crime while using the product (drug/alcohol/tobacco), then prosecute the criminal and the crime, not the product. Drug-related crime, he explains, occurs almost exclusively because of the cost of the addictive product, not the product itself. Make the addictive product cheap and legal with easy access and the drug-related crime goes away! Szasz once said: "Because we have a free market in food, we can buy all the bacon, eggs, and ice cream we want and can afford. If we had a free market in drugs, we could similarly buy all the barbiturates, chloral hydrate, and morphine we want and could afford." Prisons are full of convicted drug users because the government passed laws making drug use illegal. If drug use was not illegal, prisons would be virtually empty.

Of course, as we have been saying, not everyone agreed with Szasz, particularly within the psychiatric profession itself. The reasons for the criticism of his work are several and, from the point of view of the profession, well founded. First, it should be kept in mind today that much of his criticism of the practice of psychiatry was based upon the early-mid 20th century form of psychoanalytic psychiatry in the tradition of the Freudians, neo-Freudians, and post-Freudians rather than the contemporary practice of psychiatry based on a biologically-oriented model which relies heavily upon psychopharmacology. It has even been suggested that contemporary psychiatry is really the practice of psychopharmacology given the fact that much if not most of the psychiatrist-patient relationship centers around medication monitoring without any attempt at psychotherapeutic counseling. A second criticism is the fact that Szasz fails to recognize that some so-called mental illnesses may have a neurological basis, but he defends himself by arguing that in such cases these should be classified as brain diseases rather than mental illnesses. However, contemporary biological psychiatry makes precisely that argument, namely, that so-called mental illnesses are actually brain diseases and modern psychiatry, therefore, has essentially dispensed with the idea of mental illness entirely, concluding that the notion that psychiatric disease is mainly psychogenic is not a part of biological psychiatry. In such cases, we still have psychiatry fundamentally functioning as a practitioner's branch of psychopharmacology. Thirdly, there is some evidence to suggest that psychiatric illness does, indeed, have a biological basis and there is a litany of examples of such cases and here we can cite Hypothalamic-pituitary-adrenal axis (HPA) dysregulation, a positive dexamethasone suppression test result, and shortened rapid eye movement sleep latency in those with melancholic depression as examples of this evidence. These are merely examples of the clinical validation for the psychopharmacological psychiatry being practiced today which Szasz's criticisms were not based upon but rather a somewhat now outdated notion of psychoanalytic psychiatry of a by-gone era.

CONCLUDING REMARKS

The fact that such professional bodies as the American Medical Association, the American Psychiatric Association, and the National Institute of Mental Health all soundly disagree with Szasz's assessment of the state of mental health treatment in this country that the professions which purport to be involved in the treatment of aberrant behavior have failed. Rather, the response to Szasz by these professional bodies is that the state of mental health in this country and the professionalization of those branches of medical practice which have primary responsibility and accountability in the treatment of mental illness are doing a good job of it. Their recorded position is that mental illnesses "are now regularly approached, measured, or tested in scientific fashion." Furthermore and quite substantially important is the medical community's response to his criticism of the use of medication in the treatment of so-called mental illnesses. The pharmacological industry and the practitioners of psychopharmacology have joined ranks with the biologically-oriented psychiatrists in their defense of the use of increasingly sophisticated medications in the treatment of specific behavioral disorders such as depression and anxiety as well as biogenic schizophrenia.

One outspoken and highly respected defender of contemporary psychiatric practice is that of Donald F. Klein, M.D., who has pointed out that "it is that elementary fact, that the antidepressants do little to normal, and are tremendously effective in the clinically depressed person, that shows us that this is an illness." Furthermore, it should be noted that the *New England Journal of Medicine* reported on January 17, 2008, in a published trial, about 60% of people taking the drugs report significant relief from depression, compared with roughly 40% of those on placebo pills. However, and not to detract from Dr. Klein's case, when the less positive, unpublished trials are included in the report the advantage shrinks, the drugs outperform placebos, but perhaps only by a modest margin and for a brief period of time. During this debate, Frederick K. Goodwin, M.D., asserted that "the concept of disease in medicine really means a cluster of symptoms that people can agree about, and in the case of depression we agree 80% of the time. It is a cluster of symptoms that predicts something." That the psychotropic medications work is not questioned but studies are showing increasingly that their long-term effect is minimal and some studies have suggested that psychotherapy, over the long haul, seems to be consistently more meaningful in showing results in the treatment of depression.

Judging by his years of service and his prolific output of major books and articles in the field of psychiatry and its professional criticism, there can be no doubt of the relevance or significance of Szasz's contribution to the on-going discussion of the practice of psychiatry in American society. That he is a recognized critic of an earlier form of psychoanalytic psychiatry with a lessoned value to his criticism today of biologically-oriented psychiatry cannot be the basis for a dismissal of his general concern for the individual and his right to freedom and privacy in the securing of medical attention. That mental illness has too easily been classified as a treatable and curable illness by the medical community when a strong case can be made that much if not most of what goes under the classification of mental illness is more correctly classified as aberrant or dysfunctional or counter-productive behavior must be noted. And, in those cases where such symptoms merit classification as a behavioral matrix rather than illness, Szasz has made a convincing case for the ineffectiveness of psychopharmacologically-oriented psychiatry and a strong case for counseling-based psychotherapy.

BIBLIOGRAPHY

THOMAS SZASZ'S PRIMARY SOURCES

(1974) *The Second Sin*. N.Y.: Doubleday.

(1973) *The Age of Madness: A History of Involuntary Mental Hospitalization Presented in Selected Texts (editor)*. London: Routledge & Kegan Paul Ltd.

(1977; 1974; 1967; 1961) *The Myth of Mental Illness: Foundations of a Theory of Personal Conduct*. Harper & Row.

(1976) *Heresies*. N.Y.: Doubleday Anchor.

(1975; 1984) *The Therapeutic State: Psychiatry in the Mirror of Current Events*. Buffalo NY: Prometheus Books.

(1974; 2003) *Ceremonial Chemistry: The Ritual Persecution of Drugs, Addicts, and Pushers*. Syracuse, New York: Syracuse University Press.

(1963; 1965; 1968; 1972; 1989) *Law, Liberty, and Psychiatry: An Inquiry into the Social Uses of Mental Health Practices*. Syracuse, New York: Syracuse University Press.

(1965; 1971; 1988) *Psychiatric Justice*. Syracuse, New York: Syracuse University Press.

(1965; 1974; 1988) *The Ethics of Psychoanalysis: The Theory and Method of Autonomous Psychotherapy*. Syracuse, New York: Syracuse University Press.

(1957; 1977; 1988) *Pain and Pleasure: A Study of Bodily Feelings*. Syracuse, New York: Syracuse University Press.

(1976; 1988) *Schizophrenia: The Sacred Symbol of Psychiatry*. Syracuse, New York: Syracuse University Press.

(1977; 1988) *The Theology of Medicine: The Political-Philosophical Foundations of Medical Ethics*. Syracuse, New York: Syracuse University Press.

(1978; 1988) *The Myth of Psychotherapy: Mental Healing as Religion, Rhetoric, and Repression*. Syracuse, New York: Syracuse University Press.

(1980; 1990) *Sex by Prescription: The Startling Truth about Today's Sex Therapy*. Syracuse, New York: Syracuse University Press.

(1990) *The Untamed Tongue: A Dissenting Dictionary*. Lasalle IL: Open Court. 1990.

(1976; 1990) *Anti-Freud: Karl Kraus and His Criticism of Psychoanalysis and Psychiatry.* Syracuse, New York: Syracuse University Press. 1990 (1976). ISBN 0-8156-0247-2. (First published in 1976 under the name: Karl Kraus and the Soul-Doctors: A Pioneer Critic and His Criticism of Psychiatry and Psychoanalysis. – Louisiana State University Press, 1976.)

(1970; 1991) *Ideology and Insanity: Essays on the Psychiatric Dehumanization of Man.* Syracuse, New York: Syracuse University Press.

(1993; 2003) *A Lexicon of Lunacy: Metaphoric Malady, Moral Responsibility, and Psychiatry.* New Brunswick, New Jersey: Transaction Publishers.

(1992; 1996) *Our Right to Drugs: The Case for a Free Market.* Syracuse, New York: Syracuse University Press.

(1994; 1998) *Cruel Compassion: Psychiatric Control of Society's Unwanted.* Syracuse, New York: Syracuse University Press.

The Meaning of Mind: Language, Morality, and Neuroscience. Westport CT: Praeger Publishers. 1996. ISBN 0-275-95603-2.

(1987; 1997) *Insanity: The Idea and Its Consequences.* Syracuse, New York: Syracuse University Press.

(1977) *Psychiatric Slavery.* Syracuse, New York: Syracuse University Press. 1977.

(1970; 1997) *The Manufacture of Madness: A Comparative Study of the Inquisition and the Mental Health Movement.* Syracuse, New York: Syracuse University Press.

(1999) *Fatal Freedom: The Ethics and Politics of Suicide.* Westport CT: Praeger Publishers.

(2001) *Pharmacracy: Medicine and Politics in America.* Westport CT: Praeger Publishers.

(2002) *Liberation by Oppression: A Comparative Study of Slavery and Psychiatry.* New Brunswick, New Jersey: Transaction Publishers.

(2004) *Words to the Wise: A Medical-Philosophical Dictionary.* New Brunswick, New Jersey: Transaction Publishers.

(2004) *Faith in Freedom: Libertarian Principles and Psychiatric Practices.* New Brunswick, New Jersey: Transaction Publishers.

(2006) *My Madness Saved Me: The Madness and Marriage of Virginia Woolf.* New Brunswick, New Jersey: Transaction Publishers.

(2007) *The Medicalization of Everyday Life: Selected Essays.* Syracuse, New York: Syracuse University Press.

(2007) *Coercion as Cure: A Critical History of Psychiatry.* New Brunswick, New Jersey: Transaction Publishers.

(2008) *Psychiatry: The Science of Lies.* Syracuse, New York: Syracuse University Press. 2008. ISBN 978-0-8156-0910-0.

(2009) *Antipsychiatry: Quackery Squared.* Syracuse, New York: Syracuse University Press.

(2011) *Suicide Prohibition: The Shame of Medicine.* Syracuse, New York: Syracuse University Press.

SECONDARY SOURCES

Barker, P; Barker, P (February 2009). "The Convenient Myth of Thomas Szasz". *Journal of Psychiatric and Mental Health Nursing* 16 (1): 87–95.

Bracken, Pat; Thomas, Philip (September 2010)." *Philosophy, Psychiatry, & Psychology* 17 (3): 219–228.

Evans, Rod E. (2008). "Szasz, Thomas". In Hamowy, Ronald. *The Encyclopedia of Libertarianism*. Thousand Oaks, CA: SAGE; Cato Institute. pp. 497–8.

Powell, Jim, (2000). *The Triumph of Liberty: A 2,000 Year History Told Through the Lives of Freedom's Greatest Champions*. Free Press.

Vatz, R. E. (2006). "Rhetoric and Psychiatry: A Szaszian Perspective on a Political Case Study," *Current Psychology,* 25: 173.

Schaler, Jeffrey A., Editor. (2004). *Szasz Under Fire: The Psychiatric Abolitionist Faces His Critics*. Chicago: Open Court Publishers.

Vatz, R. E., and Weinberg, L. S., eds., (1983). *Thomas Szasz: Primary Values and Major Contentions*. Prometheus Books.

Vatz, R. E. (1973). The myth of the rhetorical situation. *Philosophy and Rhetoric, 6*, 154_161.

CHAPTER SIXTEEN
Aaron T. Beck and Advances in Cognitive Behavior Therapy

INTRODUCTION

We have already seen the profound influence cognitive therapy has had on the American psychotherapy professional seen in the life's work of Albert Ellis who refined his Rational Emotive Behavior Therapy (REBT) and, as we noted earlier, it was out of this movement that a variety of cognitive therapies developed. Nevertheless, it is the American psychiatrist Aaron T. Beck who is credited with creating what is today in virtually all professional circles (outside the psychoanalytic schools) who is seen as the perpetrator of the most advanced form of Cognitive Behavioral Therapy (CBT) first proposed and developed since the 1960s. Cognitive therapy is based essentially upon the model proposing that thoughts, feelings, and behaviors are interconnected and that any improvement in the emotional life of a troubled individual can only occur when the client is able to overcome his difficulties by acknowledging, identifying, and addressing dysfunctional ideas and thoughts as well as counter-productive behaviors and distressing emotional responses to life's situations.

The ethos of cognitive therapy involves a pro-active engagement of the therapist with the client such that the client is empowered to collaborate with the therapist in developing strategies for altering, changing, or modifying these counter-productive ideas, emotions, and behaviors to foster, nurture, and solicit self-affirmation and self-fulfilling ideas, emotions, and behaviors. Change is the agenda and it is an actively engaging collaboration between therapist and client which makes this kind of treatment work towards being "cured." There is something called the "tailored cognitive case conceptualization" which consists of a pattern of strategized behavioral matrices designed to foster the change needed in the distressed client's life.

A key approach in Cognitive Behavior Therapy is the challenging of basic operational assumptions within the mind of the client with regard to his life's situation and the realization that these assumptions must be altered or substituted with new perspectives, new insights, new re-defined information relative to the outside world which could then lead to a reconfiguration or restructuring of the world as seen by the client. This altered vision of the world will, then, produce different responses built upon a more positive and self-affirming view of the world. Of course, as we can see, change itself constitutes the therapy side of cognitive therapy and cognition has to do with the ideas and beliefs of the client which cause this misconception or misperception of the world in which he lives. Change the perceptions based on his beliefs and ideas about the world and mental health is on the way.

As can easily be anticipated in this therapeutic model, it was depression which Beck and other cognitive therapists first focused their attention upon and this effort led to a listing of "errors" in thinking on the part of the client which Beck believes constituted both the etiology and perpetuation of the debilitating depression, such errors as arbitrary inference, selective abstraction, over-generalizations, and magnification of the negative and the minimization of the positive. We will explore these more carefully later.

The attractiveness of cognitive therapy for both the client as well as the therapist has to do with the practical application of the process of therapeutic insight into the client's life situation, an insight which the client himself can quite easily see and understand when explained by the therapist. This is a far cry from psychoanalysis in which there is less emphasis upon explaining the process to the patient by the attending analyst and more emphasis upon the analyst's interpretation of the data gleaned through dream analysis and free association from the patient. In cognitive therapy, the client is called upon to be pro-active in working with the therapist in exploring alternative ways of thinking about situations and imagining alternative ways of responding to those situations.

The client is admonished to question everything – his perception of those stress-causing situations, his explanation of them, his interpretation of them, and his response to them. The aim is to reconfigure and reconstitute the situation, a kind of phenomenological rendition, in such a fashion as to place a positive assessment upon it rather than a negative one which then leads to a more acceptable response. The relationship between idea or belief and behavior is the crucial characteristic of cognitive behavior -- relating ideas to action! Building analytical skills in assessing one's life situation – perception, reconstruction, innovation – all facilitate the client becoming "his own therapist" in the process.

The precipitation of this movement towards cognitive therapy on Beck's part came as a result of his growing dissatisfaction with the lengthy nature of psychodynamic and psychoanalytic approaches to mentally distressed individuals. In addition to the frustration with the length of time these psychotherapies took in making any progress towards behavioral resolutions, sometimes years and certainly months, there was the problematic of delving into the unconscious emotions and drives of the client which necessitated in-depth exploration through a kind of archeological psychology probing the inner repressed recesses of the client's past. Once upon a time, lengthy heart-rending therapies by psychoanalysts were the thing and Freud and the next generation particularly in New York and along the East coast found themselves busy and successful. However, the impatience with delayed improvement and the rising cost of such an extended treatment plan paved the way for another way of approaching the patient who now preferred to be the client in a therapeutic relationship with an engaging therapist rather than with a distant analyst in a patient-therapist relationship.

In this *zeitgeist*, Beck began to realize that the best way to get at the client's problem was to focus, not upon the unconscious rubbish of repression but upon what the client himself perceives, interprets, and attributes meaning to in his daily life, called "cognition." Beck believed this would be the arena within which help could be found for the dysfunctional and distressed individual. It should be remembered that at the time Beck was moving in this direction, Albert Ellis was developing his now famous Rational Emotive Behavior Therapy (REBT). Beck's approach was first formalized in his 1967 book titled *Depression: Causes and Treatment,* later expanding his focus to include anxiety disorders in his 1976 book titled *Cognitive Therapy and the Emotional Disorders.* His conceptualization of cognitive therapy led to his creation of what he called the underlying "schema" or the ways in which individuals process information about themselves, the world, and their future in it.

The behaviorist school at the time was dominating the counseling scene with its emphasis upon the tried and true behaviorist agenda of assessing stimulus-response behavioral matrices. However, the cognitive revolution was being launched and gaining much recognition. Behavior modification techniques and cognitive therapy techniques were finding themselves in a collaborative relationship resulting in the formation of what would quickly become recognized as Cognitive Behavioral Therapy. Beck, however, was keen to advance his own particular interpretation of this merger by placing emphasis, a unique character of his school of thought as he imagined it, upon the "cognitive shift" within the Cognitive Behavioral Therapy movement as the key component of the change his therapy was designed to facilitate. The eventual outcome of this effort was to formalize and professionalize the theory and training of cognitive therapists. The Academy of Cognitive Therapy was created as a credentialing body of cognitive therapists for the purpose of fostering research and professional education for practitioners and for the purpose of popularizing this school of thought to the general public. Beck was the prime mover in this initiative and Cognitive Behavior Therapy has been the profound beneficiary of his gifts, talents, and initiative in this regard.

BIOGAPHY

Of Russian Jewish parentage, Aaron Temkin Beck was born July 18, 1921, in Providence, Rhode Island, the youngest of four children. A 1942 *magna cum laude* graduate of Brown University, Beck distinguished himself during his university years by being elected a member of the Phi Beta Kappa Honor Society. He became the associate editor of the student campus newspaper, *The Brown Daily Herald,* and was the recipient of the prestigious Francis Wayland Scholarship as well as winning the William

Gaston Prize for Excellence in Oratory. The Philo Sherman Bennet Essay Award was also won by Beck who later attended Yale University Medical School, graduating with a M.D. in 1946. Beck was married four years later to Phyllis W. Beck who became the first woman judge on the appellate court of the Commonwealth of Pennsylvania. They now have four children and eight grandchildren. Judith S. Beck, their older daughter, holds a Ph.D. and is a recognized educator and clinician in the field of Cognitive Behavior Therapy and presently serves as President of the Beck Institute, a non-profit educational and training center in New York.

During Bech's two-year fellowship in training psychiatry at the Austin Riggs Center in Massachusetts, he had the happy experience of being supervised by Erik Erikson himself, a leading psychoanalyst at the time but one who, amazingly, had no academic credentials whatsoever, not even a bachelor's degree but was himself recognized as a senior professional in the training of psychiatrists. Beck was board certified in psychiatry in 1953 and after completing his analytic training at the Philadelphia Psychoanalytic Institute he took up his post on the faculty at the University of Pennsylvania becoming, in 1959, assistant professor of psychiatry there. Prior to becoming a member of the University of Pennsylvania faculty, he had served as the assistant chief of neuropsychiatry at Valley Forge Army Hospital as a member of the United States armed forces. The irony of Beck's enthusiastic commitment to traditional psychoanalysis was the very thing that led him away from it because in his early researches on depression using psychoanalytic theories he discovered, to his amazement, that the traditionalist's interpretation and explanation for the meaning and function of dreams failed miserably in his therapeutic encounters with soldiers. Rather, he began to realize that the etiology of the depression was traced to the individual's holding a distorted view of themselves and the world in which they lived. Working with these depressed military patients, Beck began to realize that they regularly and persistently experienced a stream of negative thoughts which he chose to label "automatic thoughts," and went on to discover that the content of such negative thoughts fell into three categories, viz., negative ideas about themselves, about the world, and about the future. The validity of these thoughts for the patient was directly related to the amount of time they spent thinking of them. Clinical experience rather than textbook theory predominated in his study of depression and, it can be said, resulted in his shifted allegiances from orthodox psychoanalysis to experimentally based Cognitive Behavior Therapy.

Before his retirement as emeritus professor at the University of Pennsylvania in 1992, he had served as a visiting scientist at Oxford University in 1986 as well as being an adjunct professor at both Temple University and the University of Medicine and Dentistry of New Jersey. Beck has been honored by receiving honorary degrees from several outstanding institutions including Yale University, University of Pennsylvania, Brown University, Assumption College, and the Philadelphia College of Osteopathic Medicine.

Not unlike several other founders of the various modern schools of psychotherapy, Beck is a prolific writer and researcher having published over 600 scholarly and professional articles as well as having authored or co-authored 25 books. In 1989, *the American Psychologist* named him as one of the "Americans in history who shaped the face of American Psychiatry and one of the five most influential psychotherapists of all time." The continuing Honorary President of the Academy of Cognitive Therapy (of his own creating), this is an organization of more than 500 professional members who are cognitive therapists engaged in the support of research and education in this field as well as providing clinical training to aspiring professionals in psychotherapy. The 2006 Albert Lasker Clinical Medical Research Award was presented to Beck in recognition of his development of cognitive therapy which, according to the wording of the Award, "fundamentally changed the way that psychopathology is viewed and its treatment is conducted." In 2007, he was elected a Fellow of the American Academy of Arts and Sciences. In 2013, Beck became the first recipient of the Kennedy Community Health Award which marked the 50th anniversary of the Community Mental Health Act signed by President John F. Kennedy.

As the founding father of what has become universally known as cognitive therapy, Beck went on to establish a treatment scenario for clinical depression within the context of his commitment to scientific research methods used in both the study of depression as well as anxiety and eventually a range of personality disorders producing dysfunctional self-images on the part of the distressed client. The Beck Depression Inventory (BDI) was a self-reporting measurement of depression and anxiety which became very popular owing to its ease of use and analysis as well as something called the Beck Hopelessness Scale, the Beck Scale for Suicidal Ideation, the Beck Anxiety Inventory, and the Beck Youth Inventories. The Beck Hopelessness Scale consists of twenty statements with which a person can either agree or disagree and the scale functions to measure feelings about the future and is sometimes used to evaluate suicide risk. The Beck Depression Inventory is commonly used in conjunction with the Hopelessness Scale and consists of 21 multiple-choice questions used to measure depression and it continues to be one of the most widely used diagnostic tests in the field because it functionally measures both affective states such as depressed moods as well as somatic states such as loss of appetite or headaches.

The BDI is still the most popularly used measurement for studying depression severity. He distinguished himself with his researches in the various components and applications of theories in psychotherapy, psychopathology, the study of suicide, and in the growing field of psychometrics. Working with Maria Kovacs, Ph.D., they developed the Children's Depression Inventory, using the BDI model of schematic presentation. Beck's influence even energized the famous University of Pennsylvania psychologist Martin Seligman to further extend the development and use of his cognitive techniques particularly as relates to "learned helplessness." Eventually, Beck became the Honorary President of the Academy of Cognitive Therapy which offers training and certification in cognitive therapy.

What proved most insightful to Beck and greatly facilitated his development of cognitive therapy had to do with his experience of helping patients identify and assess the value of these thought patterns – about themselves, the world, and their future in it – and he thereby discovered that by doing so, these patients who were suffering from debilitating depression were actually able to think more realistically and rationally. This identification and value assessment of such thoughts by the individual himself, measuring them against rationality and reality, led them to actually feel better about themselves emotionally and in terms of their behavioral patterns. His deepest insights into Cognitive Behavior Therapy led him to understand that different emotional disorders were associated with different types of "distorted thinking," a misperception of the social environment within which the individual lives. Thought and behavior, going hand in hand, led Beck to realize that distorted ideas produce distorted behavior. He was able to explain how a successful intervention constitutes essentially an educational activity for the depressed person who needs to understand and become fully reflective and cognizant of their self-defeating thoughts and the resulting behaviors from such thoughts. By challenging the thought pattern, the patient would inevitably change the behavioral response, explained Beck. He believed that these "negative automatic thought" patterns are an indication of the fundamental core beliefs of an individual suffering from depression and that these core beliefs have been a long time in the making, from childhood, and constitutes what the individual perceives and emotionally feels to be the truth about everything. To divest the patient of these misguided core beliefs constitutes the agenda of CBT. Today, Beck and his colleagues have demonstrated empirically and clinically the effectiveness of this cognitive approach to therapy in the treatment of a wide range of personality disorders and dysfunctional emotional disorders beyond debilitating depression. Evidence-based treatment has been applied to such disorders as bipolar disorders, borderline personality disorder, suicide and self-harm personality types, eating disorders, drug abuse, anxiety, and numerous psychogenic disorders not least of which is schizophrenia.

Beck is eager for the client to understand that knowledge of the origin of particular thoughts and behaviors is not important but rather the key to cognitive therapy is the recognition and understanding of the thought pattern and the value of stopping that automatic processing behavior. Change the way one thinks about a thing – himself, the world, the future – and change in behavior is inevitable. The mental health of everyone, says Beck, is related to their "core beliefs" about themselves, the world, and the future.

"Automatic thoughts," for example, such as "I'll fail at that" or "This will go poorly" are indicators of negative core beliefs held by an individual whose behavioral response is often self-defeating and self-denying. By developing "alternative" thought patterns, having identified and acknowledged the negative ones, and experimenting with strategies designed specifically to stifle the negative ones and foster the positive ones, the individual will find that the behavioral change which results will prove constructive as well.

Beck often spoke of the speed with which he moved from the practice of traditional psychoanalysis to the use of cognitive behavior as his method of analysis and treatment in clinical cases. It took less than two years, he once said, to make the complete shift to cognitive therapy. In the actual "creation" of cognitive therapy, Beck indicates the four stages of development of the theory and practice, viz., first must be the observation of the patient and methods for measuring these observations; second, producing an operationally viable theory to explain these observations; third, creating interventions designed to address them; and fourth, developing research to confirm or discredit the whole enterprise. Beck was insistent upon this empirically based research methodology for, he contended, if the therapy is not scientifically validated, then it is completely open to criticism and challenge. This mentality, of course, led to the plethora of research measurement instruments we have listed above and their continued use speaks for their validation within the profession of psychotherapy. Of course as we know, Beck was not thinking alone about alternative models and methods in psychotherapy for many who had been initially taken with psychoanalysis as well as Skinnerian behaviorism were looking to improve, alter, and substitute ways of treatment and the development of theories underlying these new methods. It was a very experimental time in the field of mental health. A prolific writer and drawing from his research, Beck published two articles in 1963 and 1964 in the journal *Archives of General Psychiatry*, exploring his notions about cognitive therapy in which there were several articles dealing with the biological basis of depression. What made his contributions to the discussion unique was his heavy emphasis upon "cognition," in which he emphasized the need to elucidate the patient's thoughts and feelings rather than attempting to extricate the subconscious motivations accessible only through psychoanalytic techniques such as dream analysis and free association. Whereas other adventurous psychiatrists and psychotherapists were turning from phenomenology to biological and pharmacological treatments, Beck was emphasizing cognition!

THOUGHT

Both the attraction and the criticism of cognitive therapy have been its easy application to a variety of behavioral health issues including such widely diverse topics as academic achievement, addiction, anxiety disorders, bipolar disorder, phobias, schizophrenia, substance abuse, suicidal ideation, and even weight loss. However, and somewhat problematic to the lay person is the fact that there are several self-acclaimed "cognitive therapies" falling under the general title of cognitive therapy. Cognitive therapy is based on the cognitive model which suggests that thoughts, feelings, and behavior constitute a tripartite inter-dependence, each affecting the other in both positive and negative ways. Re-directing cognition, or how an individual thinks about himself, the world, and the future, constitutes the primary mechanism by means of which long-term emotional, behavioral, and self-affirming changes can take place. The relationship between the therapist and the client is one of aggressive interaction involving a collaborative reliance upon the development of a re-configuration and re-conceptualization of the client's worldview and strategized behavioral response to it. Rational Emotive Therapy (RET) is based on the conviction that most problems confronted by the distressed individual actually originate in irrational thoughts and ideas about oneself, the world, and the future.

The etiology of dysfunctional behavior and counter-productive reactions to life situations is essentially linked to the misperceptions and false conceptualizations of what is happening to the individual and his misguided reaction to it. These cognitive distortions which lead the individual to misdirected and misguided responses can be corrected through a process of recognition of these cognitive mis-readings and the experimentation with response mechanisms based on a corrected reading of life's situations. Cognitive Behavioral Therapy (CBT) is a system of approaches to the distressed individual based on both the cognitive and the behavioral systems of psychotherapy. Unlike psychodynamic approaches such as traditional psychoanalysis, CBT requires the client to become an active partner in the exploration of his dysfunctional behavioral matrix with the therapist. The purpose is a collaborative effort to create a strategy of reconfiguring the client's misguided responses to a misreading of life's events. The successful CBT client often becomes something of a lay practitioner of CBT himself based on the effectiveness of the collaboration with his therapist. Beck thought that one of the aims should be to foster a sense within the client that he can be his own therapist, providing answers for himself once the analytical methodology is learned.

The earliest and still one of the most convincing fields of CBT effectiveness is that of the treatment of depression. Beck believed that the etiology of depression, its origin within the individual, occurs by virtue of the depressed individual having developed a negative perception of himself, the world, and the future during childhood and early adolescence. It is developed early and Beck believes it to be fairly set in motion by the age of seven (though other professionals wish to push it a bit further into early adolescence). There is no one cause of this early experience precipitating depression for it could be the loss of a parent, the rejection by one's siblings or peers, an experience of bullying, criticism from teachers, parents, and significant others, or the exposure to a depressed parent or significant other person within the social *milieu* of the young child. Beck explains that the cognitive nature of experience is reliant upon thought patterns including ideas and beliefs about oneself and the world. When an adult person encounters situations reminiscent of their childhood of a negative sort, the negative response is quite often the result. These we have seen called by Beck "automatic thoughts." The response to a given situation conjures up recollections of similar experiences from the past and if those experiences were negative then the new response is more likely to be negative, following the predictable pattern. Depressed individuals, Beck explains, mobilize negative feelings based on early negative experiences related to one's own self-image, or a view of the world, or an attitude towards the future. This "negative triad," as Beck called it, constitutes the environment within which the negative behavioral response derives. There are a range of "cognitive distortions" according to Beck and they can include such things as arbitrary inference, selective abstraction, overgeneralization, magnification and minimization.

Though not correctly credited with creating cognitive therapy approaches to the study and treatment of depression and other personality disorders, Beck is clearly and justifiably credited with the refinement of that approach which he calls Cognitive Behavior Therapy (CBT). It is now one of the most commonly used methods in psychotherapy. Once the effective validation of psychotherapy was on the basis of reported case studies but since the coming of Beck and his propensity to empirical studies using a quantitative data-base, things have changed. Beck, as we have said, created several research instruments for analyzing results from the use of CBT on patients and this has elevated the profile of counseling therapy to a higher level than it has ever experienced before. It is now not enough to say that psychotherapy produces results and then drag out a few case studies indicating as much. Now, the profession has research instruments used to validate the results through the use of empirically demonstrative data-based studies with the specific scientific capacity of replication. Evidence-based studies are now the norm.

Furthermore and to the credit of Beck and his colleagues who are more focused on psychogenic rather than biogenic etiologies of such disorders as depression and anxiety, their studies have consistently shown that CBT is effective in the absence of pharmacological intervention. Therapy without medication is the flag under which CBT operates and the results have proven consistently to be outstandingly successful. Disenchantment with psychoanalysis and the methods used in probing the unconscious mind – dream analysis and free association – led Beck to a discovery of a whole new way, pragmatic and practical way, of assisting individuals in understanding what they do and why they do it. Redirection from the unconscious, which requires the skilled labor of a trained psychoanalyst, to a focus upon the individual's thoughts and the patterns of those thoughts as relates to their own negative self-image and misreading of their social environment has led to the Beck's discovery of the profound relationship between ideas and action, between thoughts and beliefs and the behaviors which result. Change the negative self-image, the self-destructive ideas and the dysfunctionality of certain beliefs and direct the individual away from that negativity to a reconfigured positive complex of beliefs and ideas about themselves, the world, and their future in it and the individual is on the way to recovery and healthy living.

We could not do better than spend a little more time explicating the nature and function of Cognitive Behavioral Therapy (CBT). It is Beck who has taken on the responsibility of creating a formalized complex of theories and treatment modalities. CBT is an action-oriented type of psychosocial therapy which takes for granted, based on clinical experience, that dysfunctional and counter-productive thinking patterns related to beliefs and ideas constitute the cause of dysfunctional and counter-productive behavior as well as equally dysfunctional and counter-productive emotions. Beck uses the word "maladaptive behavior" to describe counter-productive behavior which disrupts everyday life. When ideas about the individual, the world, and the future are negative as a result, often, of a misperception of the social environment, then both the resulting emotions precipitated by this negativity in the individual's worldview also generates negative emotions as well. Change the ideation and the behavior and emotions change as well. Alter the misdirected or misguided or falsely construed views of the individual and his social environment and the behaviors and emotions will also change. This is the point of CBT therapy, viz., to bring about change in behavior by changing the view of the world. Change in emotions follow in tandem as well.

Cognitive Behavioral Therapy, Beck is keen to point out, could be used in minor as well as major cases where change in the individual's behavior is required as a result of depression or anxiety. The scope of this treatment approach is expansive and always open to experimentation. The rule is, if there is a behavioral matrix producing depression or anxiety which requires change, CBT can help. CBT, however, is not for everyone as Beck is quick to point out. Individuals simply seeking to deepen their own self-understanding through probing of their past through the use of psychoanalysis or other psychodynamic psychotherapies will not directly benefit from CBT because it calls upon the patient to be willing to take a very active role in the treatment process. It is certainly not applicable in biogenic disorders or in extreme cases of psychosis or traumatic brain injury.

However, CBT is particularly relevant in the treatment of clinical depression and other anxiety-related distress maladies because, as Beck has demonstrated, CBT constitutes a convergence of both cognitive therapy and behavioral therapy into a joint effort to understand how a patient "thinks" and the resulting "behavior" from that cognitive matrix. Cognitive therapy addresses itself to the individual's need to become aware of his distorted thinking patterns or what is called "cognitive distortions," and once the individual has been able to consciously acknowledge the presence of these negative ideas and thoughts to then actively engage in re-scripting his response to his social environment towards a more healthy positive assessment of himself and this environment, what Beck has chosen to call "cognitive restructuring." On the other hand, behavioral therapy, sometimes called "behavior modification," has as its agenda the retraining of the individual under stress to substitute these distorted perceptions with a reconfiguration of the social environment designed to foster a healthy worldview and self-image.

Radically dissimilar to psychodynamic therapies including specifically psychoanalysis, CBT avoids focusing upon unconscious contents discoverable, if at all, through analytical probing using dream work and free association. CBT prefers, rather, to assist the individual in identifying for himself those distorted and dysfunctional ideas and beliefs which he himself can expend self-reflective energy redirecting. The issue for CBT is not the "why" of a behavior but the "cause" of that undesirable behavior and then to focus upon changing it based on having identified the cause. CBT has distinguished itself in its creative convergence of cognitive and behavioral therapies by demonstrating how the integration of the "cognitive restricting approach" of cognitive therapy with the "behavioral modification techniques" of behavioral therapy can produce the desired results of altered behavior by altering the worldview. CBT has demonstrated that stress, anxiety, and depression are caused by "wrong ideas" (also called "irrational cognitions") or misconstrued understandings of the individual's social environment – his self-image, his view of the world, and his ideas about the future – and by altering these wrong ideas, emotions adjust themselves accordingly and behavior is changed.

The attractiveness of CBT for both the professional practitioner and the lay person alike is the commonsense and pragmatic approach to dysfunctional behavior employed by this therapeutic approach to psychotherapy. A number of techniques have been developed over the years by both Beck and his many colleagues to be used in CBT treatment of individuals suffering from depression as well as a range of personality disorders. Seven of these techniques are most common and worthy of our delineation and discussion. They include *behavioral homework assignments, cognitive rehearsal, journaling, modeling, conditioning, systematic desensitization* and *validity testing.*

Behavioral homework assignments are based on the conviction by CBT therapists that the patient will become actively engaged in his own therapeutic treatment and recovery based on his willingness to record his behaviors between sessions including particularly his willingness to "try out new responses" to pre-set circumstances encountered regularly in his normal daily routine. Keeping a record of these new responses constitutes what CBT therapists like to call "homework," something that virtually everyone understands.

Furthermore, *cognitive rehearsal* is predicated upon the patient's capacity to imagine specifically difficult life situations which are shared with the therapist who, in turn, works with the individual who is scripting a step-by-step process of both acknowledging these situations and re-scripting a response to them which is positive, creative, and self-affirming in character. The idea is for the patient to "practice" and "rehearse" his pre-scripted responses to these otherwise and previously debilitating situations with the aim of turning a "bad" experience (ideas/beliefs/emotions/behavior matrix) into a "good" experience.

It's up to the individual to assume the responsibility of rehearsing based on his shared belief with the therapist that the script is reasonable and doable.

Journaling and modeling are two techniques which have proven extremely valuable in this therapeutic approach. The patient is asked to maintain a daily diary of thoughts, ideas, beliefs, and feelings as relates to a behavioral pattern in response to them. Every situation is based upon a "perspective" or "view of the situation" by the individual and then there is inevitably a response, a behavioral pattern, which results. The journal constitutes the individual's own record of his distorted thoughts or counter-productive ideas and beliefs about specific situations as well as a log of not just "what I thought" but "what I did in response." To learn to see the relationship between an idea and its resulting behavior is considered to be "consequential learning," so that the pattern of negative or counter-productive behavior can be related to distorted ideas. Also, and very importantly, in cases where the outcome has been positive, the individual is able to see the positive side of the right kind of response. One cannot control what happens to oneself, but one must control his response to it. This is the CBT mandate. Modeling is used as a mechanism for role-playing in which the therapist demonstrates to the patient how appropriate responses can produce positive benefits. The use of journal episodes can constitute the content of the role-playing exercise.

Beck and his CBT colleagues believe that patients must go through a *conditioning exercise* in order to become self-confident in their own ability to define and alter situations which they have found counter-productive in their daily lives. Conditioning is simply the use of reinforcements to foster positive responses to negative situations. The offering of rewards, however defined by the individual or his therapist, constitutes the nature of the conditioning. So, for example, when the individual handles a particularly negative life situation responsibly and creatively based on his therapeutic training, he should reward himself for the successful encounter. On the contrary, when a situation was handled poorly and the patient resorted to negative emotional responses to self-negating experiences, the patient is encouraged to deprive himself of something desirable. This is called by CBT the conditioning of the patient for eventual self-monitoring.

Every individual in therapy has a repertoire of life situations which produce fear or anxiety or emotional distress which they wish to avoid, knowing that when they experience these negative encounters they will respond badly. It is the role of the therapist to mobilize techniques designed to assist the individual to face these situations through the use of coping mechanisms to foster a more relaxed, less tense, less apprehensive attitude towards the coming situation. This is called *systematic desensitization* by which is simply meant that the patient is shown ways of de-valuing the encounter, discharging its emotive power over the individual, and redirecting the individual's anticipatory response towards the positive rather than the negative emotional reaction. The shift from anxiety-producing response to relaxation-producing assessment is the goal of CBT therapy in this situation.

Finally, the seventh technique used by CBT in the treatment of depression and similar affective disorders is called *validity testing* in which the patient is asked to test the validity of his "automatic thought" patterns against the pre-scripted plan of response based on what has been learned in the therapy sessions. When the patient's "plan of response" is tested and proven valid in producing positive results, then the plan of response is authentic. When it fails scrutiny by the patient and the therapist, more work is required in developing a plan of response which stands up under scrutiny and produces a positive result.

Quite different from traditional psychotherapeutic sessions, the first meeting with a CBT therapist is essentially spent educating the client as to the nature and function of Cognitive Behavioral Therapy. Unlike other psychotherapies, particularly psychoanalysis where the analyst is the expert and the patient simply provides information for therapeutic analysis, CBT requires and is built upon a collaborative relationship between therapist and client with the intent of working towards a positive realignment of the client's worldview. Rather than being the dependent member of the dyad, both the therapist and the client are co-partners in the quest for wholeness. The process is designed to empower the client by virtue of instilling within him a sense of his responsibility in an active role in the function of therapy. There is a stifling of any tendency for transference and counter-transference, so crucial in psychoanalytic treatment, for an over-dependence by the client upon the therapist will prove counterproductive to the CBT agenda of client empowerment.

Using both individual and group sessions on an outpatient basis, the therapist employing CBT is usually a psychologist, clinical social worker, counselor, psychiatrist, or psychotherapist. Many clergy trained in clinical pastoral psychotherapy and clinical pastoral education also employ CBT methods of analysis and treatment. Though some professionals practice with only a master's degree (M.P.C., M.S.W., M.Div., M.A.), the most common practice is for the therapist to hold a doctoral degree (Psy.D., M.D., or Ph.D.). Unlike psychoanalysis which is designed to take years for completion, CBT is designed for a relatively short period of consultation not normally taking more than 16 weeks to reach the desired and specified goal set out in the first session.

There are many versions and varieties of cognitive therapy as well as behavior therapy. Beck has merged them into a self-contained system of Cognitive Behavior Therapy which is built upon the belief that an individual's past experiences are relevant in the development of their belief system and consequential thinking patterns. Individuals create for themselves illogical, irrational thinking scenarios which in turn become the basis for both their negative emotions and the resulting counter-productive behaviors thereby producing even further irrational and dysfunctional ideas and beliefs. These negative ideas producing emotions resulting in negative behaviors constitute essentially a downward spiral of dysfunction and demeaning self-confidence. Cognitive Behavioral Therapy addresses itself to assisting the client in identifying and acknowledging these irrational beliefs and ideas responsible for counter-productive emotional responses and behaviors with the aim of replacing them with rational beliefs and thoughts leading to responsible emotions based on a fair assessment of their life situation.

CONCLUDING REMARKS

Cognitive Behavior Therapy (CBT) is the latest developing school of psychotherapy and its professional profile justifies it being the last system of analysis and treatment to be considered in this study of the modern schools of psychotherapy. From traditional psychoanalysis to Cognitive Behavior Therapy is no small leap and the radical development of a system of analysis and treatment in psychotherapy not based on the study of the unconscious through dream analysis and word association accounts for an exciting and adventurous travel through psychological models of therapy. Beck began, as we have mentioned as did many of the other founders of the modern schools of psychotherapy, as a traditional psychoanalyst well trained in Freudian psychology and was himself a practitioner of psychoanalysis for several years before his clinical experience began to raise concerns about effectiveness and verifiable results. The awareness of the relationship between ideology and action, between beliefs and ideas as relates to emotion and feeling as reflected in resulting behavioral matrices, led him to question psychoanalytic theory. This questioning caused a professional turmoil resulting in his departure from traditional Freudian therapy and the development of a variety of measurements used to establish empirically demonstrative effectiveness verification. Cognitive Behavior Therapy was the eventual results and it today continues to be the reigning school of thought and practice within the professional world, particularly government agencies and insurance companies which require some sort of empirical evidence of desired success.

BIBLIOGRAPHY

AARON BECK'S PRIMARY SOURCES

Beck, A.T. (1967). *The Diagnosis and Management of Depression*. Philadelphia, PA: University of Pennsylvania Press.

Beck, A.T. (1972). *Depression: Causes and Treatment*. Philadelphia, PA: University of Pennsylvania Press.

Beck, A.T. (1975). *Cognitive Therapy and the Emotional Disorders*. Madison, CT: International Universities Press, Inc.

Beck, A.T., Rush, A.J., Shaw, B.F., & Emery, G. (1979). *Cognitive Therapy of Depression*. New York, NY: Guilford Press.

Beck, A.T. (1989). *Love is Never Enough: How Couples Can Overcome Misunderstandings, Resolve Conflicts, and Solve Relationship Problems Through Cognitive Therapy*. New York, NY: Harper Paperbacks.

Scott, J., Williams, J.M., & Beck, A.T. (1989). *Cognitive Therapy in Clinical Practice: An Illustrative Casebook*. New York, NY & London, England: Routledge.

Alford, B.A., & Beck, A.T. (1998). *The integrative power of cognitive therapy*. New York, NY: Guilford Press.

Beck, A.T. (1999). *Prisoners of Hate: The Cognitive Basis of Anger, Hostility, and Violence*. New York, NY: HarperCollins Publishers.

Clark, D.A., & Beck, A.T. (1999). *Scientific Foundations of Cognitive Theory and Therapy of Depression*. New York, NY: Wiley.

Beck, A.T., Freeman, A., & Davis, D.D. (2003). *Cognitive Therapy of Personality Disorders*. New York, NY: Guilford Press.

Wright, J.H., Thase, M.E., Beck, A.T., & Ludgate, J.W. (2003). *Cognitive Therapy with Inpatients: Developing a Cognitive Milieu*. New York, NY: Guilford Press.

Winterowd, C., Beck, A.T., & Gruener, D. (2003). *Cognitive Therapy with Chronic Pain Patients*. New York, NY: Springer Publishing Company.

Beck, A.T., Emery, G., & Greenberg, R.L. (2005). *Anxiety Disorders and Phobias: A Cognitive Perspective*. New York, NY: Basic Books.

Beck, A.T., Rector, N.A., Stolar, N., & Grant, P. (2008). *Schizophrenia: Cognitive Theory, Research, and Therapy*. New York, NY: Guilford Press.

Clark, D.A., & Beck, A.T. (2010). *Cognitive Therapy of Anxiety Disorders: Science and Practice*. New York, NY: Guilford Press.

SECONDARY SOURCES

Abela, J. R. Z., & D'Allesandro, D. U. (2002). "Beck's Cognitive Theory of Depression: The Diathesis-Stress and Causal Mediation Components." *British Journal of Clinical Psychology, 41,* 111-128.

Boury, M., Treadwell, T., & Kumar, V. K. (2001). "Integrating Psychodrama Cognitive Therapy: An exploratory Study." *International Journal of Action Methods, 54,* 13-28.

Brown, G. P., Hammen, C. L., Craske, M. G., & Wickens, T. D. (1995). "Dimensions of Dysfunctional Attitudes as Vulnerabilities to Depressive Symptoms." *Journal of Abnormal Psychology, 104,* 431-435.

Clark, D. A., Beck, A. T., & Brown, G. (1989). "Cognitive Mediation in General Psychiatric Outpatients: A Test of the Content-Specificity Hypothesis." *Journal of Personality and Social Psychology, 56,* 958-964.

Epkins, C. C. (2000). "Cognitive Specificity in Internalizing and Externalizing Problems in Community and Clinic-Referred Children." *Journal of Clinical Child Psychology, 29,* 199-208.

Gonca, S., & Savasir, I. (2001). "The Relationship between Interpersonal Schemas and Depressive Symptomatology." *Journal of Counseling Psychology, 48,* 359-364.

Lewinsohn, P. M., Joiner, T. E., Jr., & Rohde, P. (2001). "Evaluation of Cognitive Diathesis-Stress Models in Predicting Major Depressive Disorder in Adolescents." *Journal of Abnormal Psychology, 110,* 203-215.

McGinn, L. K. (2000). "Cognitive Behavioral Therapy of Depression: Theory, Treatment, and Empirical Status." *American Journal of Psychotherapy, 54,* 254-260.

McIntosh, C. N., & Fischer, D. G. (2000). "Beck's Cognitive Triad: One Versus Three Factors." *Canadian Journal of Behavioral Science, 32,* 153-157.

Moilanen, D. L. (1993). "Depressive Information Processing Among Non-Clinic, Non-Referred College Students. *Journal of Counseling Psychology, 40,* 340-347.

Moilanen, D. L. (1995). Validity of Beck's Cognitive Theory of Depression with Non-Referred Adolescents." *Journal of Counseling & Development, 73,* 438-442.

Reed, M. (1994). "Social Skills Training to Reduce Depression in Adolescents." *Adolescence, 29,* 293-304.

Salmela-Aro, K., Nurmi, J., Saisto, T., & Halmesmaki, E. (2001). "Goal Reconstruction and Depressive Symptoms During the Transition to Motherhood: Evidence from Two Cross-Lagged Longitudal Studies." *Journal of Personality and Social Psychology, 81,* 1144-1159.

Sato, T., & McCann, D. (2000). "Sociotropy-Autonomy and the Beck Depression Inventory." *European Journal of Psychological Assessment, 16,* 66-76.

Sherry, S. B., Hewitt, P. L., Flett, G. L., & Harvey, M. (2003). "Perfectionism Dimensions, Perfectionistic Attitudes, Dependent Attitudes, and Depression in Psychiatric Patients and University Students." *Journal of Counseling Psychology, 50,* 373-386.

Weinstein, N. (1983). "Unrealistic Optimism about Future Life Events." *Journal of Personality and Social Psychology, 39,* 441-460.

CONCLUSION

From Freud to Beck is not only a monumental leap in time but a quantitative leap in personality theory and psychotherapeutic theories of practice. From the birth of Freud in 1856 to the present day work of Beck, the world of psychology and the practice of both psychiatry and psychotherapy have undergone a development comparable to that in biology and physics in the last hundred years. From Freud's fascination with the possibilities of exploring the "unconscious" of a patient through the use of dream interpretation, word associations, and hypnosis to Beck's clinically demonstrated insight into the fundamental nature of interpersonal relationships skills as the determiner of mental health, one can argue that the discipline of psychology has remade itself. From deterministic behaviorism to the Third Force is no easy leap and with the initial and somewhat overpowering influence of the "depth" psychologists, Freud and Jung, the gradual emergence of the humanistic school of psychotherapy under the leadership of such clinical practitioners as Maslow, Frankl, and Rogers, and the monumental advances in cognitive behavioral therapy and its plethora of cognates is nothing short of profound.

Interpersonal psychotherapy arrived upon the scene just when it seemed that "depth" psychology of the psychoanalytic type was waning in terms of both interest in and viability for those in counseling. The arrival of "the will to meaning" followed by the Third Force movement has reinvigorated counseling psychology like no previous theoretical development in the history of the field. With Franklian psychology more and more taking the field with power and influence, Rogerian client-centered therapy and Sullivan's interpersonal psychotherapy have likewise shared in this resurgence of professional interest in counseling psychology. It is my hope that this journey through the lives and literature of the great thinkers over the past one hundred years has brought a sense of historical continuity and a genuine sense of existential validation to the practice of counseling psychology and clinical psychotherapy.

GENERAL RESOURCE BIBLIOGRAPHY

Amada, Gerald. *A Guide to Psychotherapy* (NY: Madison Books, 1985).

Chan, Henry A. *the Mediator as Human Being: From a Study of Major Concepts of Sigmund Freud, Carl Jung, Erik Erikson, and Abraham Maslow* (Lima, OH: Wyndham Hall Press, 2005).

Feist, Jess. *Theories of Personality* (NY: Holt, Rinehart and Winston, 1985.

Graber, Ann V. *Viktor Frankl's Logotherapy: Method of Choice in Ecumenical Pastoral Psychology, 2nd edition* (Lima, OH: Wyndham Hall Press, 2004).

Hall, Calvin S. and Gardner Lindzey. *Theories of Personality* (NY: John Wiley & Sons, 1957).

Hjelle, Larry A. and Daniel J. Ziegler, *Personality Theories: Basic Assumptions, Research, and Applications* (NY: McGraw-Hill Book Company, 1976).

Jones, Ernst. *The Life and Work of Sigmund Feud* (3 volumes) (NY: Basic Books, 1957).

Kendler, Howard H. *Historical Foundations of Modern Psychology* (Chicago, IL: The Dorsey Press, 1987.

Lundin, Robert W. *Theories and Systems of Psychology*, Third Edition (Lexington, MA: D. C. Heath and Co., 1985).

Millon, Theodore. *Theories of Personality and Psychopathology*, Third Edition (NY: Holt, Rinehart and Winston, 1983).

Monte, Christopher F. *Beneath the Mask: An Introduction to Theories of Personality* (NY: Holt, Rinehart and Winton, 1987).

Morgan, John H. *Being Human: Perspectives on Meaning and Interpretation (Essays in Religion, Culture and Personality) 2nd Edition.* (South Bend, IN: Cloverdale Books, 2006).

Morgan, John H. *Beyond Divine Intervention: The Biology of Right and Wrong* (Lima, OH: Wyndham Hall Press, 2009).

Morgan, John H. *Clinical Pastoral Psychotherapy: A Practitioner's Handbook for Ministry Professionals* (Mishawaka, IN: GTF Books, 2010).

Morgan, John H. *From Freud to Frankl: Our Modern Search for Personal Meaning* (Lima, OH: Wyndham Hall Press, 1987).

Morgan, John H. *Geriatric Psychotherapy: Essays in Clinical Practice and Counseling Psychology* (Mishawaka, IN: GTF Books, 2017).

Reber, Arthur S. *The Penguin Dictionary of Psychology* (NY: Penguin Books, 1985).

Zeig, Jeffrey K., Edtior. *The Evolution of Psychotherapy* (NY: Brunner/Mazel, Publishers, 1987).

ABOUT THE AUTHOR

John H. Morgan, Ph.D.(Hartford), D.Sc.(London), Psy.D. (Foundation House/Oxford) is the Karl Mannheim Professor of the History and Philosophy of the Social Sciences at the Graduate Theological Foundation in Indiana and Director of Doctoral Programs in Clinical Psychotherapy. Until his retirement, he was Senior Fellow in Behavioral Sciences of Foundation House/Oxford (1995-2015) in the United Kingdom. He has taught a doctoral-level seminar and served as a member of the Board of Studies for twenty years in Oxford University's international summer programs' division of the Department for Continuing Education. The author of over thirty books, he has held postdoctoral appointments to Harvard (1998, 2011, 2015), Yale (1973, 1974), and Princeton (1978) and is a former National Science Foundation Science Faculty Fellow at the University of Notre Dame (1980). In 2010, he was a Visiting Scholar at New York University and in 2015 was appointed Visiting Scholar at Harvard University for the third time in his academic career. His latest book (2nd Edition, 2017), *Understanding Ourselves: Essays in the History and Philosophy of the Social Sciences* is an expanded treatment of his earlier book (2005), *Naturally Good: A Behavioral History of Moral Development (from Charles Darwin to E. O. Wilson)*.

www.ingramcontent.com/pod-product-compliance
Lightning Source LLC
Chambersburg PA
CBHW050329270326
41926CB00016B/3379